THE CAPABLE EXECUTIVE

The Capable Executive

Effective Performance in Senior Management

Paul H. Dainty

and

Moreen Anderson

First published 1996 by
MACMILLAN PRESS LTD
Houndmills, Basingstoke, Hampshire RG21 6XS
and London
Companies and representatives
throughout the world

ISBN 0–333–63086–6

A catalogue record for this book is available
from the British Library.

10   9   8   7   6   5   4   3   2   1
05   04   03   02   01   00   99   98   97   96

Copy-edited and typeset by Povey–Edmondson
Okehampton and Rochdale, England

Printed in Great Britain by
Antony Rowe Ltd
Chippenham, Wiltshire

To Jennifer

Contents

List of Figures   ix

List of Tables   xi

Preface   xiii

Acknowledgements   xvii

1   The Capable Executive:
    What the Executive Role Involves and What it Takes to
    Succeed   1

PART I   THE PERSONAL CAPABILITIES:
**   SELF-UNDERSTANDING AND**
**   DEVELOPMENT**   **31**

2   The Executive Mind:
    Managing One's Thoughts and Emotions at Senior
    Levels   33

3   The Development Capability:
    Building and Maintaining Senior Managers' Capacity to
    Learn   67

PART II   THE INTERPERSONAL CAPABILITIES:
**   UNDERSTANDING AND MANAGING**
**   OTHERS**   **93**

4   The Influence Capability:
    Influence, Power and Politics in Senior Management   95

5   The Leadership Capability:
    The Essentials of Leadership for Senior Executives   126

6   The Integration Capability:
    The Design and Development of Senior Teams   158

**PART III   THE DIRECTIONAL CAPABILITIES:
            UNDERSTANDING AND MANAGING THE
            JOB**   **189**

.7   The External Capability:
     Understanding and Managing the External Environment   191

8   The Organisational Capability – Design:
     Designing Corporate Systems and Structures   229

9   The Organisational Capability – Change:
     Managing Organisational and Personal Change   262

10   The Actioning/Structuring and Expertise Capabilities:
     Energy, Purpose and Focus in the Senior Executive Role   290

11   Strategic Leadership   315

Appendix: Senior Executive Capabilities Research   337

Bibliography   344

Index of Authors   357

Index of Subjects   361

List of Figures

1.1	Stages in an executive's career	4
1.2	The senior role – key elements	11
1.3	The Capabilities and how they relate	23
1.4	Senior executive framework	25
1.5	Customising the Capabilities	26
2.1	Decision making and problem solving	36
2.2	The executive mind	38
2.3	Myers-Briggs type indicator	48
2.4	Organisational cause map 1987	59
2.5	Executive mindset	61
3.1	Kolb's learning cycle	70
3.2	Executive learning and development	71
3.3	Executive development	72
3.4	What has to be developed – critical areas	75
3.5	Progressing executive development	91
4.1	Informal influence processes	97
4.2	Political processes	115
4.3	Strategic influence mapping	119
4.4	Strategic influence mapping	122
4.5	Strategic influence mapping	122
4.6	Strategic influence mapping	123
5.1	The four faces of strategic leadership	130
5.2	Situational leadership	148
5.3	Senior executive leadership model	150
6.1	Top teams	161
6.2	Team development wheel	170
6.3	Executive team model	180
7.1	External understanding	193
7.2	Competitive forces model	199
7.3	Boston matrix	210
7.4	Business strength – market attractiveness matrix	213
7.5	Market attractiveness/SBU strength matrix	213
7.6	Competitive strategies	215
7.7	Strategy matrix	218
7.8	Directions for development	221
8.1	Functional structure	238

8.2	Divisional structure	239
8.3	Matrix structure	240
8.4	Integrated structure	242
8.5	Organisational structures	243
8.6	Flow of customer–management organisation	249
8.7	Variables in organisational structure	254
9.1	The Dunphy-Stace change matrix	279
9.2	Transitions curve	282
10.1	Managing the environment	298
10.2	Managing the environment	299
10.3	Managing the environment	299
10.4	Managing the environment	300
10.5	Managing within the area of response	302
11.1	Strategic leadership in context	317
11.2	Strategic leadership model	321

List of Tables

1.1	Managerial work	6
1.2	The senior executive role	7
1.3	Senior executive Capabilities	17
1.4	Senior executive Capabilities	18
3.1	Constraints on improving self-awareness	81
4.1	Currencies frequently valued in organisations	110
5.1	Stages in charismatic leadership	133
6.1	Senior teams – performance factors	165
6.2	Characteristics of an effective team	172
6.3	Developing senior teams	183
7.1	Bases of market segmentation	208
7.2	Indicators of market attractiveness	211
7.3	Aspects of business strength	212
8.1	Corporate focus	244
8.2	Responsibility matrix	252
9.1	Options for dealing with resistance to change	273
9.2	Thirteen major 'families' of OD interventions	278
11.1	Business scenarios and associated management characteristics	329
11.2	Capabilities and different strategic scenarios	331
12.1	Significant factors	341
12.2	Regression analysis	343

Preface

Senior executives play a critical role in all organisations. Despite their importance, however, it is only relatively recently that researchers and writers have begun to focus on this group. Typically the general assumption has been that if an individual is in a senior management position then, 'they must be good'. Consequently, how executives operate, what qualities they need and how these might be developed, are issues that have been relatively underexplored.

However, the consequences of underperformance at senior levels have enormous implications for the individual executive and for the organisation as a whole. Mistakes at a senior level are often harder to rectify and are exploited more quickly in the highly competitive and globally connected industrial environment of today.

In recent years, a growing number of writers have acknowledged that the specific context in which senior executives operate, and the responsibilities of the job, demand a very different set of skills and abilities if an executive is to operate effectively at this level. Other research has shown that promotion to a senior position with multifunctional responsibility is a quantum leap for many executives and a critical point to manage in their careers. They need to make sense of a complex and changing external environment; they have to learn not to get swamped by short-term operational issues and neglect the longer-term goals and direction of the organisation. They need to understand their power base and how to use and develop this to bring people on side. They must judge when and how to build teams at senior levels. They must also be able to design organisational structures which will enable others to produce results. In short, they must bring a range of qualities to the executive role which extends far beyond the technical or specialist skills that may have influenced their career success to date.

This book sets out to describe the skills, knowledge and behaviours needed to produce effective performance at senior levels in an organisation, be this in the public or private sector. It brings together the research and writings of authors who have explored this key management group, to provide a comprehensive picture of the qualities required at this level. This material has been organised and structured around our own research which identified 11 different areas of 'Capability' as being important for effective performance at senior levels. By drawing on examples from organisations in the UK, the US and in the Asia Pacific region, we show there is a degree of commonality as to the issues and problems senior executives face and the qualities they need to respond to these challenges.

Throughout, our focus has been to provide conceptual frameworks and reference points which executives can use as preparation for a top job. Consequently, the book will appeal to senior executives who wish to review and reflect on their performance, executives aspiring to more senior positions in their organisation and human resource professionals responsible for the development of senior personnel.

The book is best read selectively depending on the reader's needs. Although each chapter is self-contained, it is useful to review Chapter 1 at the outset as this describes the principal requirements of the executive role and outlines the Capabilities on which this book is based.

After introducing the Capabilities in Chapter 1, the book is organised into three parts. The first part focuses on the 'Personal Capabilities' of senior executives. These are concerned with self-understanding and development. In Chapter 2, the Capabilities concerned with the executive's intellectual and emotional capacities are explored. It examines the critical mental skills required at a senior level and describes factors which affect the problem solving and decision making process, such as mindset, intuition, values and creativity. Chapter 3 looks at the particular hurdles senior executives have to overcome in order to learn and develop. It also examines different approaches to development at this level.

The second part of the book describes the 'Interpersonal Capabilities'; that is, those Capabilities which help the executive understand and manage others. The Influence Capability, described in Chapter 4, examines the particular skills needed to influence a range of stakeholders both internal and external to the firm. It describes the sources of power open to senior executives and how these can be built and retained. It also offers frameworks to help the executive gain insight into the political behaviour of others. The Leadership Capability is described in Chapter 5. It identifies the leadership factors which are particularly salient to senior level managers. It explores leadership as a change process, the creation and communication of a vision and the motivation of others to achieve corporate goals. The Integration Capability (Chapter 6) is concerned with the capacity to build teams and work with larger groups within the organisation. Here, we look in particular at the challenges of developing top teams and examine the latest thinking with regard to team design and process issues.

The third part of the book explores the 'Directional Capabilities' which help executives understand, shape and direct their environment in order to achieve short and long-term goals. The External Capability (Chapter 7) describes the qualities which are important in scanning and interpreting changes in the organisation's competitive environment. This chapter reviews some of the frameworks and tools senior executives can use to devise an overall strategic direction for an organisation. However, it also highlights how the individual's outlook and mindset can influence their capacity to make sense of the external environment. Chapters 8 and 9 describe the knowledge and skills executives must have to design and change organisations to respond competitively. Chapter 10 offers frameworks and advice to help executives maintain their personal motivation, provide structure for themselves and others and balance short and longer-term priorities. The final chapter, concerned with Strategic Leadership, explores how the Capabilities identified in our research contribute to the executive's capacity to think and act strategically.

We view the Capabilities as a starting point for describing the kind of qualities which contribute to superior performance. They are not an end in themselves but rather a vehicle to help executives review how they operate and develop. Our hope is that the book will give executives and other practitioners involved in the selection and development of senior personnel, a fresh perspective on how to define, describe and develop the behaviours which our own and others' research have shown to be desirable at this level.

Many people have influenced our thinking and have directly, or indirectly, over the years contributed to our overall understanding of top management. Paul Dainty wishes to thank Andrew Kakabadse for his encouragement and the opportunities to investigate this area during his time at Cranfield School of Management. In addition, many practising senior executives and human resource specialists took the time to talk candidly about the challenges associated with top management positions and participated in the survey process which underpinned our research. Additional feedback on many of the frameworks contained in this book was also gained from participants attending our 'Executive Capabilities Program'– an intensive executive development course which we have designed to complement this book.

We extend our particular thanks to our colleagues at Melbourne Business School for their support throughout this project. John Rose, Director of Melbourne Business School, was the first to give support to help us develop our ideas. Leon Mann deserves particular mention for his practical advice, insights and suggestions. We also thank those individuals who critiqued earlier drafts of this manuscript, including Kevan Scholes, Karen Newman, Richard Speed, Rod Chadwick and Tinka Costeo. In addition, Chris Flegg, Jeanette Kieruj, Teresa Garcia and Mary Trudzik gave invaluable research support throughout. Finally, we are particularly indebted to our secretary, Chris Rust for her unflagging support and help.

PAUL DAINTY
MOREEN ANDERSON

Acknowledgements

The authors and publishers acknowledge with thanks permission from the following to reproduce copyright material:

Jossey-Bass, for Table 5.1, adapted from J. Conger and R. Kanungo, 'Behavioural Dimensions of Charismatic Leadership', in J. A. Conger, R. N. Kanungo and Associates, *Charismatic Leadership: The Elusive Factor in Organizational Effectiveness*. © 1988 by Jossey-Bass, Inc. For Table 6.2, from G. M. Parker, 'What Makes a Team Effective or Ineffective', in G. M. Parker, *Team Players and Teamwork: The New Competitive Business Strategy*. © 1990 by Jossey-Bass, Inc. And for Figure 8.7, adapted from D. Limerick and B. Cunnington, *Managing the New Organization: A Blueprint for Networks and Strategic Alliances*. © 1993 by Jossey-Bass, Inc.

Business and Professional Publishing, for Figure 8.7, from Limerick and Cunnington, *Managing the New Organization*. Adapted with permission. © 1993 by Business and Professional Publishing.

McGraw-Hill, for Figure 9.1, from D. Dunphy and D. Stace, *Under New Management: Australian Organizations in Transition*. © 1992 by McGraw-Hill. And for Figure 7.8, adapted from I. H. Ansoff, *Corporate Strategy: An Analytical Approach to Business Policy for Growth and Expansion*. © 1965 by McGraw-Hill, Inc.

Gower, for Figure 2.3, from A. Kakabadse, R. Ludlow and S. Vinnicombe, *Working in Organisations*. © 1987 by Gower Publishing Ltd.

John Wiley, for Figure 5.1, from W. E. Rothschild, *Risktaker, Caretaker, Surgeon, Undertaker: The Four Faces of Strategic Leadership*. © 1993 by John Wiley & Sons, Inc. For Table 4.1, from A. R. Cohen and D. L. Bradford, *Influence Without Authority*. © 1990 by John Wiley & Sons, Inc. For Figure 8.6 and Table 8.2, from D. Ulrich and D. Lake, *Organizational Capability*. © 1990 by John Wiley & Sons, Inc. For Figure 2.4, from M. L. Mazneviski, J. C. Rush and R. E. White, 'Drawing Meaning from Vision', in J. Hendry, G.

Johnson and J. Newton (eds), *Strategic Thinking, Leadership and the Management of Change.* © 1993 by John Wiley & Sons, Inc.

Mahler Publishing, for Figure 1.1, based on W. R. Mahler and S. J. Drotter, *The Succession Planning Handbook for the CEO.* © 1986 by Mahler Publishing.

Prentice-Hall, for Figure 3.1, from D. A. Kolb, *Experiential Learning: Experience as the Source of Learning and Development.* © 1984 by Prentice-Hall, Inc. For Figure 7.4 and Table 7.3, reproduced from G. J. Pearson, *Strategic Thinking.* © 1990 by Prentice-Hall, Inc. For Figure 5.2, from P. Hersey and K. H. Blanchard, *Management of Organizational Behaviour: Utilising Human Resources.* © 1982 by Prentice-Hall, Hemel Hempstead Inc. For Table 7.2 and Figure 7.5, from G. Johnson and K. Scholes, *Exploring Corporate Strategy: Texts and Cases.* © 1993 by Prentice-Hall, Inc.

Free Press, for Figure 7.2, adapted from M. E. Porter, *Competitive Strategy: Techniques for Analyzing Industries and Competitors.* © 1980 by The Free Press, Inc.; and for Figure 7.6, from M. E. Porter, *Competitive Advantage.* © 1985 by The Free Press, Inc.

HarperCollins, for Table 1.1, 'Managerial Work', from H. Mintzberg, *The Nature of Managerial Work.* © 1973 by Henry Mintzberg. Reprinted by permission of HarperCollins Publishers, Inc.

Prentice-Hall, for Table 9.2, from W. French and C. Bell, *Organization Development: Behavioral Science Interventions for Organization Improvement.* © 1983 by Prentice-Hall, Inc., New Jersey.

Harvard Business Review, for Table 9.1, an exhibit from J. P. Kotter and L. A. Schlesinger, 'Choosing Strategies for Change', vol. 52, no. 2 March/April 1979. © 1979 by the President and Fellows of Harvard College; all rights reserved, and for material from John P. Kotter, *Sir John Harvey-Jones*, case 490–013, Boston: Harvard Business School, 1989, p. 9. © 1989.

Kogan Page, for Figure 7.7, based on C. Bowman, 'Charting Competitive Strategy', in D. Faulkner and G. Johnson (eds), *The Challenge of Strategic Management.* © 1992 by Kogan Page Ltd.

Irwin, for Table 5.1 adapted from J. A. Conger and R. N. Kanungo, 'Behavioral Dimensions of Charismatic Leadership' in J. A. Conger, R. N. Kanungo and Associates (eds) *Charismatic Leadership*, San Francisco: Jossey-Bass, 1988, 27, as found in J. L. Gibson, L. M. Ivancevich and J. H. Donnelly, *Organizations: Behaviour, Structure, Process.* © 1994 by Irwin, Inc.

McGraw-Hill, for Table 11.1 from R. Boam and P. Sparrow, *Designing and Achieving Competency: A Company-Based Approach to Developing People and Organizations.* © 1992 by McGraw-Hill, Inc.

A. Campbell, for his article 'The Point is to Raise the Game', *Financial Times*, 14 September 1994, 10.

Financial Times, for material from the editions of 31 July, 8 August, 26 August, 20 September, 28 September, 3 October, 21 October, 17 November, 16 November and 25 November, 1994.

Fortune, for Brian Dumaine © 1993 & 1994 Time Inc., Alex Taylor III © 1992 & 1994 Time Inc., John Huey © 1991 Time Inc., Stratford Sherman © 1992, 1993 & 1994, Time Inc., Douglas Ready © 1992 Time Inc., Thomas Stewart © 1989 Time Inc., Louis Richman © 1994 Time Inc., Kennith Labich © 1993 Time Inc., Wilton Woods © 1993 Time Inc., Shawn Tully © 1994 Time Inc., Myron Magnet © 1992 Time Inc., David Kirkpatrick © 1993, Time Inc., Gary Hamel and C. K. Pralahad © 1994 Time Inc., and Alan Deutschman © 1992 Time Inc.

1 The Capable Executive: What the Executive Role Involves and What it Takes to Succeed

INTRODUCTION

Senior managers play a very important role in organisations. The strength of their performance can mean the difference between company success or failure. Yet, as David Kearns, the former head of Xerox notes, 'All too many executives believe that management at the upper reaches of a company is mysterious and defies any sort of worthwhile analysis'. As a result, activities like recruitment, succession planning and development are often approached in a haphazard way.

Indeed, Kearns and Nadler (1992) point out that many organisations fail to have systematic processes for selecting and promoting their executives. Instead, managers are often promoted on the 'Right Stuff' theory.

> At some point in a manager's career, he gets identified as being imbued with the Right Stuff. Exactly what that stuff is is rarely delineated. It usually boils down to fairly superficial characteristics. The person makes good presentations. He looks attractive. He carries himself with a certain aplomb. And unless he loses it, that person has the Right Stuff forever and gets moved up the ladder. It's wrong, and an often insidious approach.[1]

Finding something better than the Right Stuff theory, however, is not easy. Despite the importance – and cost – of senior personnel, our understanding of what it takes to succeed at this level is still limited. For example, it is difficult to:

- *Define what is meant by the term 'senior executive'.* Definitions and responsibilities of senior executives differ tremendously. However, unless one is clear about what the term 'senior execu-

1

tive' encompasses, one cannot address the issues that are unique
to that group.

- *Fully comprehend the senior executive role.* We have a good idea of
  the pressurised and chaotic nature of the executive role from
  researchers like Mintzberg (1973) and Kotter (1982). However, we
  need a more complete picture of what the role entails if executives
  are to be selected and developed to perform successfully within it.

- *Identify the qualities needed for effective performance.* Establishing
  which qualities are most associated with, or conducive to, executive effectiveness and under what circumstances is also open to
  conjecture. Nevertheless, executives require some kind of picture
  of the qualities needed to perform well at this level.

- *Help executives develop these qualities.* A greater challenge,
  perhaps, is to help executives develop qualities found to be crucial
  for executive performance. We need to improve the ways in which
  we train and develop high potential managers for senior executive
  positions.

Despite these potential difficulties, however, some organisations
are making progress. Companies like AT&T, Xerox, BP and British
Airways have established succession-planning processes, set standards of performance for senior level executives and are giving
considerable thought to development at senior levels. These practices
are, unfortunately, not widespread but they do highlight that
progress in the area of senior executive development is both possible
and necessary.

In this chapter, we bring together ideas, knowledge and approaches
which may be useful to those engaged in such initiatives. We begin by
exploring who senior executives are, what they do and the particular
constraints and challenges they face. We then go on to describe the
range of capabilities required to cope effectively in this very
demanding role. (In Chapter 3 we deal with how the executive might
develop these qualities.)

WHAT DO WE MEAN BY THE TERM 'SENIOR EXECUTIVE'?

The difficulties associated with identifying exactly who belongs to the
category 'senior executive', or merits this title, are well documented.[2]

Whilst there is general agreement that senior executives are located in the upper management levels of the organisation, they can perform a vastly different range of functions and activities. Often, labels such as Vice President, Group Executive or Director offer little insight into what senior level managers actually do. Moreover, accurate comparisons across industries and between individual companies are very difficult. For example, when Kotter (1982) conducted his in-depth study of general managers, he observed that over the years, as businesses grew more diverse and complex, different kinds of general manager had emerged. When he scrutinised the daily schedules of the 15 senior level managers taking part in his research, he noted considerable diversity amongst these depending on the size of business they represented and the complexity of their environment. In all, Kotter identified seven different types of GM.

Some writers have tried to determine at what level of the organisation senior management positions begin. Jacobs and Jaques (1987) and Bentz (1987) point out that as the executive moves higher up the organisation there is a major change in the complexity of the critical tasks to be performed – an increase in what Bentz calls both the scope and scale of the job. This leap in complexity occurs at general management level; that is, the stratum or position where individuals take on multifunctional responsibility. Managers at this level are responsible for the integration and coordination of different functions within a business unit and have overall responsibility for the unit and its profitability. Rod Chadwick, MD of South Pacific Tyres, in applying the work of Mahler and Drotter (1986), describes this and other career changes as a series of 'crossroads' – critical points in the individual's career where real changes occur in how the manager operates (Figure 1.1).

While this portrays the major points at which changes in scope and scale occur, it is important to acknowledge that some managers will not fit neatly into this schema, but can nevertheless be classified as senior executives. For example, finance managers may not have multifunctional responsibility but can be very powerful, occupy senior positions in the organisation and head up sizeable departments. We therefore use the term 'senior executive' to apply not only to those who have multifunctional responsibility, but also to executives with multidepartmental responsibility – incorporating several departments within the same function.

Fig. 1.1 *Stages in an executive's career*

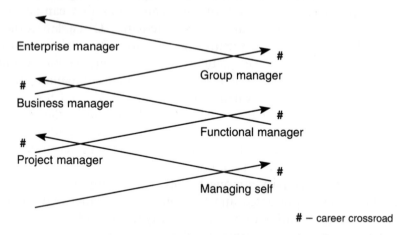

– career crossroad

Source: Based on the work of Mahler and Drotter (1986)

Differences between senior and lower management levels

An alternative way of defining the senior executive role is to compare it with others lower down in the organisation. This approach also gives us a better idea of the issues executives face in their work. There is strong evidence to suggest that senior executives experience different demands, responsibilities and expectations from those in more junior positions.

Some of the factors which distinguish the senior executive role from those lower down the organisation include a capacity to:[3]

- Integrate/coordinate complex functions
- Deal with complex reporting relationships
- Manage more complex/abstract and interrelated tasks
- Deal with longer-term strategic issues
- Have a greater degree of discretion over how work is carried out
- Be held directly accountable for results
- Develop and control agendas of importance to the whole organisation
- Create a greater range of power bases
- Deal with ambiguity and change
- Network with a range of stakeholders within and external to the firm

- Deal with intensified political behaviour at senior levels
- Make decisions which often affect a large number of people
- Undergo a greater degree of employee and public scrutiny

The trend towards flatter organisational structures and management styles emphasising empowerment may mean that lower-level managers will also face some of these challenges. Overall, however, it is the senior executive who will have to deal with most of the demands listed above.

WHAT A SENIOR EXECUTIVE DOES – THE NATURE OF THE ROLE

How do executives respond and cope with these demands in their day-to-day activities? For many years, it was assumed that managerial work consisted of determining objectives, planning, organising, forecasting, directing, coordinating, communicating, commanding and controlling. Although some of the terminology seems out of place today, such descriptions continue to influence the way managerial work is perceived.[4]

Over the past 20 years, Mintzberg (1973) has been especially influential in providing a different perspective. Rather than the orderly world of management portrayed by writers like Fayol, Mintzberg argues that the senior executive's world is characterised by a disconnected web of brief contacts and fleeting interactions. The senior executive reacts rather than initiates, responds rather than plans and deals with fragmented, rather than complete, tasks. According to Mintzberg, the senior executive tends towards taking action rather than sitting back and reflecting. Contact is made mainly in oral form through the telephone and formal and informal meetings. It is a world where the focus is on immediate, concrete and specific problems with constant changes in both the issues and the people with whom the executive deals.

For Mintzberg, the executive's job consists of a number of different, interrelated roles. These centre around the need to make decisions, to gather information and have strong interpersonal contacts (see Table 1.1). One weakness in Mintzberg's portrayal of the senior executive is the lack of emphasis on the need to plan and reflect. Managers often do a lot of mental activity which is unobservable.[5] Isenberg (1984), for instance, notes that managerial

Table 1.1 Managerial work

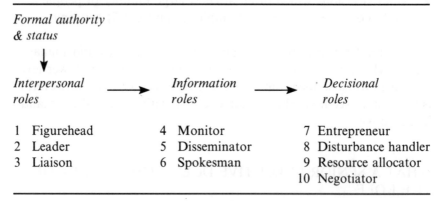

Formal authority & status		
↓		
Interpersonal roles →	Information roles →	Decisional roles
1 Figurehead	4 Monitor	7 Entrepreneur
2 Leader	5 Disseminator	8 Disturbance handler
3 Liaison	6 Spokesman	9 Resource allocator
		10 Negotiator

Source: Adapted from Mintzberg (1973)

work is partly mental work. Moreover, several writers have found that the time spent on planning increases the higher one goes in the organisation, and that goal-setting/planning are related to managerial success and firm profitability.[6]

Thus, what these writers show are the contrasts and some complexities of the executive role. Kotter (1982) brought these strands together to show that while the role is outwardly chaotic, it also requires planning. He suggests that this is achieved by developing loosely connected goals and plans, or 'agenda setting'. He also acknowledges the mental as well as the action-oriented nature of the role. He found that managers were not successful because of any one characteristic, such as interpersonal skill or business knowledge, but as a result of becoming a specialist and a team player with detailed knowledge of the industry, technology, product, market and competitors.

Key activities and processes

There are several similarities in the way writers have portrayed the requirements of the senior executive role. We have organised these ideas into three different areas which we call Establishing, Enabling and Enacting (see Table 1.2).

Table 1.2 The Senior executive role

Key aspects of the role...	What this means...	What this typically involves...
1 **Establishing**	Establishing one's current position and that of the organisation Thinking through options, directions and identifying ways forward	Reviewing... the context in which one is operating; the demands and constraints of the job; understanding self and the organisation Setting Direction... including such aspects as planning, coordinating, pathfinding
2 **Enabling**	Enabling you and the organisation to progress — Deciding what help/resources are needed — Developing frameworks, activities and programmes to pursue chosen goals	Personal... building networks, establishing contacts, exchanging information Organisational... allocating resources to enable organisational plans to be met, developing structure and culture
3 **Enacting**	Taking action to maintain the current momentum of the business and progress it towards longer-term goals	Maintaining satisfactory operations, procedures, staffing levels Acting on critical issues to help progress and move the organisation forward

Establishing

In order to cope with a broad range of demands, executives have to discover what is needed in the job and what outcomes are necessary. The process is about orienting oneself and setting direction at critical points in time – for instance, when first appointed to a new position or when changing the strategic thrust of the organisation.

Reviewing organisational strengths and weaknesses is an important part of Establishing. The executive must determine what external challenges the organisation faces, learn how the organisation works and come to terms with what Stewart (1982) calls the 'demands and constraints' of the job. Nevertheless, these aspects can easily be neglected. One of the prime reasons organisations go off-course is because senior executives sometimes fail to understand the fundamentals of their business. They neglect to ask central questions like 'What is the company's core expertise, what are reasonable short and long term goals, what are the key drivers of profitability. . .?'[7] In addition, personal strengths and weaknesses also need to be reviewed so that the executive can establish what support (for instance staff or additional skills) is needed to operate effectively.

Clearly, Establishing activities are particularly important when moving into a new role. Gabarro (1988) argues that acquiring relevant knowledge and a grasp of the technical issues facing the organisation are critical to a manager's success in 'taking charge'. Such evaluation, learning, assessment and diagnostic work can take up a great deal of the first six months of the executive's job and could still be a preoccupation after 18 months.

The executive must also set a direction – another important part of the Establishing process. Several writers emphasise aspects which come under this label. Kotter, in particular, emphasises the need to set agendas and goals. Leavitt (1986) describes 'pathfinding' which is the vision creation process and is concerned with mission, purpose and asking the right questions, rather than generating the right answers.

The Establishing process is therefore critical, even for the most seasoned manager. In the words of Sir John Harvey-Jones (1989):

> The start of everything is to locate, as honestly as one can, the position of one's company and where the current trends will take one. . . A considerable amount of scanning of the outside world, both the competitors in an individual business sense and the external environment in a broader business sense, is then necessary.

Then the development of broad scale corporate dreams can be carried out by the Board. These have to be married with the individual dreams of each business. . . It is far more important to be moving forward in broadly the right direction than to be stuck still without the businesses going anywhere.[8]

Enabling

The second major area for executives is to develop frameworks and programmes which help themselves and others pursue the organisational goals highlighted in the Establishing process. 'Enabling' occurs at both a personal and organisational level.

At a personal level, network building is a key activity. Networks must be built and maintained in order that information can be gathered and agendas implemented. Other individual enabling processes are highlighted by Gabarro (1988), who emphasises the need to develop a power base when taking charge in a new role. In the short-term, executives also need to have successful work relationships. Gabarro found that executives who failed to make the transition to senior management had a significantly greater number of ineffective relationships with key subordinates, peers and superiors at the end of their first year than did those who succeeded.

At an organisational level, executives will be concerned with ensuring that the organisation has the capacity, design and capability to meet its strategic goals. They have to create infrastructures that will enable everyone else to operate effectively. This will involve making decisions about such things as the allocation and development of resources, reward systems and maintaining and creating appropriate work processes and systems.

Enabling activities are largely concerned with shaping the context in which decisions are made.[9] While senior executives may not have a direct influence on the daily minutiae of marketing, sales and so forth, they can influence activities indirectly, particularly through whom they appoint to critical roles. For example, the executive can:

- Select key executives
- Build a cohesive management team
- Restructure the organisation to influence lower-level decision making
- Influence organisational reward systems, particularly for key executives

- Control the allocation of scarce resources
- Develop a shared set of expectations among all staff members
- Influence the scale and size of resources attracted from outside

Many of these activities were used to drive the restructuring and cost-cutting programme initiated by Mike Walsh, CEO of the Houston based conglomerate Tenneco in the early 1990s.[10] The company's principal divisions were all operating in mature markets. Tenneco's debt stood at US$6 billion. Having established the key issues facing the organisation, Walsh adopted a strategy of being a low-cost producer which required getting operating costs under control. In order to do this, he had to set in place a framework which would enable others to achieve these objectives. One of Walsh's first moves was to make some key appointments. He brought in a colleague from outside the firm to manage a troubled acquisition and boosted the ranks of the senior operating team. He introduced a (TQM) Total Quality Management initiative to help bring operating costs under control. Cross-functional quality teams were formed with cost-cutting goals set for every person in the organisation. Training programmes taught by senior executives and then cascaded down through the organisation helped reinforce the importance of the quality initiative. Through such means, Walsh was able to set up basic systems and processes to enable himself and others to operate more effectively. Tenneco reached its financial cost-cutting targets a year ahead of schedule. Over $1.6 billion was saved and used to pay off debts and reinvest in the business.

Enacting

Enacting is the third area of attention for the executive. It is concerned with the day-to-day decisions and actions that executives take to either maintain current operations or move the business forward.

Kotter (1982) identifies many of the core activities needed to enact. Executives must identify and solve problems, influence their bosses and key stakeholders as well as motivate and control their staff. To do this well, they need to operate *through* the systems, networks and structures that they have established as part of the Enabling process.

However, this is not an easy process given the many demands on senior executives' time. A recent study of 48 top executives in the US found that their working days were full of interruptions with almost

80 per cent of their time spent in conversation with others. Often, it appeared that 'they responded to whatever comes next'.[11]

Despite these pressures, it is important that executives are selective about the activities they choose to get involved in and focus on those which are critical to their own and others performance. This discipline is even more important given that executives face the dual task of not only maintaining the organisation, but also progressing it. As Kanungo and Misra (1992) point out, managing an organisation involves making adaptive responses to both the stable and the changing features of the environment. However, the danger is that the executive gets involved in maintaining the status quo to the detriment of taking action aimed at securing more fundamental changes. A concentration on the wrong, or less important, activities can leave executives and their organisation vulnerable. (In Chapter 10, we consider these issues in more detail.)

In all, these three areas of Establishing, Enabling and Enacting illustrate the principal requirements of the senior executive role. Every executive needs to establish where they are, and where they and the organisation are going. They must enable themselves and others to operate effectively through systems and structures and by providing adequate resources. They must then move the organisation forward through a process of action or enactment.

Clearly, there will be differences between executives, both in terms of what they do and the process and sequencing of how they do it. As Leavitt (1986) argues, senior executive work is an iterative process. Consequently, the three categories will interact and overlap as shown in Figure 1.2.

Fig. 1.2 *The senior role – key elements*

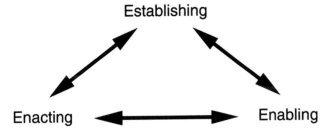

THE QUALITIES REQUIRED AT A SENIOR LEVEL

The discussion so far has concentrated on the nature of the senior executive role. Below, we explore the range of skills and abilities required to manage effectively at this level. Before we do so, however, we examine some of the reasons why this is such a difficult issue to tackle.

Applying a competency-based approach to senior executives

One of the major areas where new attempts have been made to understand the qualities required of senior executives is that of 'work competencies'. The work competency approach is concerned with reviewing the kind of abilities, skills and knowledge needed for work positions.

Over the past decade the study of work competencies has become increasingly popular. However, to date, competency approaches have tended to concentrate on supervisory and middle management levels. At the executive level, development has been slower and the task far from easy. As one commentator remarked, 'Basic skills can be taught. But the ability to codify competence reduces dramatically up the managerial scale.'[12] Despite the problems, human resource managers and consultants are attempting to apply competency-based approaches to senior level managers.[13] In a critique of where executive development is heading, Douglas Ready argues, 'Even though companies are shying away from a definitive list of competency requirements for the recipes of leadership effectiveness, they are sharpening their focus on . . . competency themes.'[14]

Increasingly, executives are being asked to perform against standards which are either company specific or which follow a generic competency model.[15] While individual organisations may feel comfortable with what they have developed, others who are new to the area may be interested in knowing about the various shortcomings of competency-based approaches:

- *Rigid and inflexible.* Generic competency models have been criticised for being too rigid in approach.[16] This is particularly true where competencies have been associated with minimum standards. Baker (1991), for instance, criticises an approach which 'promotes reductionism and sanitising of managerial roles and performance to fit neatly into a preferred classificatory system.'

- *Too vague.* Generic models have also been criticised for being too vague and unsubstantiated to be applicable.[17] There is a danger that as one moves away from immediately observable behaviour, the competencies which emerge become too abstract and remote to be useful for assessment and development.

- *Too applicable.* Ironically, the drive towards applicability has also been criticised. Wilson and Page (1993) argue that there is a bias towards elements which are assessable, trainable and capable of development. Models which exclude more inherent and less easily observable characteristics may be limited.

- *Not comprehensive.* Some models have been criticised for not including important variables such as the 'softer' competencies like sensitivity, creativity and intuition.[18] Boyatzis (1982) focused on personality characteristics to the neglect of knowledge about such factors as information, financial and legal systems. Also, frequently, writers outside the competency area will emphasise one or two variables – such as intellect or 'leadership' – to the neglect of others.

- *Not applicable to changing environments.* Several writers argue that competency models are too static and are based on past successes rather than future needs. Indeed, some argue that the changing nature of the senior executive role means that it is fruitless to pursue competencies which are 'end states' because these can never be achieved.[19]

- *Limited research base.* The empirical foundations on which many models have been built have been limited by a concentration on self-report data, or selective and inconsistent interview data, or no consistent data at all. This is true of both generic and some firm-specific models which are sometimes a product of executives 'throwing it around the table and several of us chewing it over.' Moreover, often no attempt is made to relate the competencies to measures of effectiveness.

- *Theoretical inadequacies.* Some approaches also fail to distinguish between traits, skill or knowledge and hence which aspects can be developed.[20] Others have been criticised for not developing any synergy or theoretical harmonisation.[21] There has also been a tendency to view competencies as dichotomous variables – when in reality a range in performance is far more common.

- *Restricted context.* Competency models also tend to assume management is homogeneous. However, as Kotter (1982) notes, sound theories must account for the fact that the context in which some managers work can vary significantly. Consequently, environmental factors impact on the mix and relative importance of the characteristics needed to succeed in a role.

Where the experts agree

Despite the limitations noted above, there is greater agreement between the various competency proposals than critics sometimes acknowledge. Limerick (1990), for instance, has identified the following competencies as being important at a senior level:

- Empathy
- Transformational leadership
- Proactivity
- Intuitive/creative thinking
- Political/networking
- Personal maturity (self-understanding and value commitment)

Often, these aspects are highlighted in other models. Cox and Cooper (1988) noted how important the interpersonal qualities of the executive are in order to progress in the role. In addition, the well known AT&T studies documented the importance of interpersonal skills for overall managerial effectiveness.[22] Many other writers outside the competency area have also seen the leadership and interpersonal side of the executive as important, such as Bennis and Nanus (1985), Kouzes and Posner (1987) and Kotter (1990).

The cognitive and intellectual processes of executives are another area of significance. Again, the AT&T studies documented the importance of decision making for overall managerial effectiveness. Carroll and Gillen (1987) link planning aspects with interpersonal skills. In carrying out their agendas, managers engage in both mental activities (such as thinking, feeling and planning) and more overt behaviours (such as communicating, signing documents and attending meetings).

Another aspect on which there is some agreement, involves understanding the broader organisational context in which one is working. Kotter (1982) has portrayed this in terms of knowledge of the industry, job and business environment. More recently McCall *et al.* (1994) have highlighted the need to 'know the business' which is concerned with having a strong technical base and understanding how the business works and the 'parts fit' together.

In summary, the broad areas of interpersonal skill, analytical techniques and business or organisational understanding have been identified as being important for some time. More recently, there has been an increasing emphasis on the processes of learning and coping with complexity and change.[23]

Interestingly, there are also similarities between competency models which are developed for specific organisations. For instance, Boyatzis' work has been used by McBer consultants to profile the core competencies required by senior managers at many institutions. Schroder's work has been used to identify senior manager competencies in the National Westminster Bank. Safeway in the UK has blended the competencies developed by the Management Charter Initiative with organisation-specific knowledge and skills.[24] Indeed, Dulewicz (1989) estimates that of the competencies developed by companies, 70 per cent are generic and only 30 per cent are organisation specific.

It is therefore possible to find agreement between the various competency models which have been put forward. Moreover, given the interest in developing senior level managers (through competency-based or alternative approaches), it is clear that such models and frameworks are necessary to help executives become more aware of the range of qualities needed to perform effectively at senior levels.

The goal therefore must be to build frameworks that are flexible, comprehensive, theoretically robust, have a consistent research base and allow for customisation so that different qualities can be applied in different contexts. At the very least, as Kotter (1982) has noted, sound theories of managerial behaviour must include the following variables – individual, contextual, behavioural and some measure of performance.

THE EXECUTIVE CAPABILITIES FRAMEWORK

The Executive Capabilities Framework has been developed by the authors to describe the qualities which contribute to superior executive performance. 'Capabilities' refer to the particular behavioural skills, areas of knowledge, cognitive processes and the emotional makeup of the executive which help the individual perform effectively in a senior management role.

The framework is the result of a research programme conducted over eight years involving over 200 senior executives. (See the appendix for a detailed description of our approach.) A range of research techniques was employed including repertory grid technique, in-depth interviewing, survey questionnaires and exploration of the data through factor and regression analysis. A key element has been to use a 360-degree assessment process; that is, gathering data on the effectiveness of an executive by obtaining evaluations from the individual's boss, peers and subordinates.

Our research identified 11 factors that were associated with senior executive effectiveness. These factors are the basis for the Capabilities. The term 'Capability' reminds us that at a senior level the executive is not concerned with minimum standards but with above average performance. Similarly, it reminds us that the qualities needed to operate at this level are not easily segmented and defined but are more fluid and interrelated.

The Capabilities Framework attempts to take into account some of the criticisms identified earlier. The Framework is empirically based and comparison with other generic (and company-specific) models shows it is also comprehensive. Additionally, we have worked with organisations to use the Capabilities to shape recruitment, succession and development planning processes. The framework is therefore a good starting point for those interested in developing effective senior executives.

We have grouped the 11 Capabilities identified in our research into three areas which relate to the conceptual, interpersonal and business skills of the executive. We have labelled these categories Personal, Interpersonal and Directional (see Table 1.3).

(A) *Personal Capabilities.* These are concerned with self-understanding and development. The following Capabilities come under this heading:

1. Cognitive – analytical and creative processes
2. Maturity – management of emotion and mental resilience
3. Development – the ability to learn and develop.

(B) *Interpersonal Capabilities.* These are concerned with understanding and managing others. They include the following Capabilities;

4. Influence – getting others to act in your interests
5. Leadership – helping others achieve a common goal
6. Integration – building teams and bringing groups together
7. Insight – an awareness of others' needs and agendas.

(C) *Directional Capabilities.* These are concerned with understanding and managing the job.

8. Expertise – functional knowledge needed to fulfil one's role
9. External – understanding the relevance of changes in the environment
10. Organisational – understanding the critical elements of the organisation
11. Actioning/Structuring – taking action and facilitating the achievement of long and short-term goals.

Table 1.3   Senior executive Capabilities

Personal Capabilities	*Interpersonal Capabilities*	*Directional Capabilities*
Self-understanding & development	*Understanding & management of others*	*Understanding & management of the job*
Cognitive	Influence	Expertise
Maturity	Leadership	External
Development	Integration	Organisational
	Insight	Action/Structuring

Brief definitions of each Capability are given in Table 1.4 and described in more detail below.

Personal Capabilities

These are centred around the individual and influence how the executive perceives and approaches the senior executive role. The Cognitive and Maturity Capabilities are concerned with the fundamental analytical, creative and emotional qualities of the executive. The Development Capability is concerned with the executive's capacity to develop both their Cognitive and Maturity Capabilities and the Interpersonal and Directional Capabilities described below.

Table 1.4 Senior executive Capabilities

Capability profile

Cognitive:	Capacity to make decisions, think through issues and analyse and assimilate large amounts of data
Maturity:	Capacity to understand one's emotions and values and handle emotional upset, ambiguity and loneliness
Development:	Capacity to understand one's limitations, take feedback on board, accept new challenges and learn and develop
Influence:	Capacity to get others to accept your point of view, have them act in your interests and prevent them implementing agendas which are contrary to your own
Leadership:	Capacity to help others overcome hurdles to achieve a common goal
Integration:	Capacity to build senior level teams and ensure larger organisational units work together effectively
Insight:	Capacity to understand what motivates others, their mental view of the world and their possible actions and agendas
Expertise:	Having the functional skills needed to fulfil one's role, and ability to see outside one's particular area of professionalism
External:	Capacity to understand and recognise the relevance of changes in the external environment for one's business
Organisational:	Capacity to understand the essential components of the organisation and how these can be managed to achieve corporate goals
Actioning/ Structuring:	Capacity to take action and establish and work within structures which facilitate the achievement of critical short and long-term goals

Cognitive Capability

This relates to the executive's ability to assimilate large amounts of data and think through issues. Increasingly, more writers on senior executives[25] are emphasising the importance of having an intellectual capacity which can cope with the complexity of the executive environment. This involves both taking in large amounts of data, but also being able to sort out from this information what is critical. For example, Lou Gerstner, CEO of IBM, is described as a 'sharp, even brilliant, energetic man who thrives on overhauling corporate cultures'. One of the reasons he was hired as CEO of IBM in 1993, was his 'talent for quickly distilling core problems in complex organisations'.[26]

Maturity Capability

Maturity is the capacity to understand one's emotions and values and handle emotional upset, ambiguity and loneliness. There are considerable pressures in senior jobs, and executives have to understand how to use their emotions effectively to manage themselves and others. Several writers such as Kouzes and Posner (1987) and Quick *et al.* (1990) have emphasised the need for mental resilience at the top.

Development Capability

This is concerned with the capacity to understand one's limitations, take feedback on board, take on new challenges and learn and develop. The need to learn is increasingly being recognised as vital for the improvement of organisations as well as individuals. McCall *et al.* (1994) rank this as the most important attribute of high performing, international executives.

Interpersonal Capabilities

These are concerned with an executive's overall ability to build and develop relationships at different levels within an organisation. The Interpersonal Capabilities place particular emphasis on behavioural skills.

Influence Capability

This Capability is concerned with getting others to take on board one's views, to act in one's interests and prevent contrary agendas being implemented. This capacity to influence is possibly one of the most important, yet most neglected, areas at a senior level. Pfeffer

(1992) is one writer who has explored this area in some depth, as has Kotter (1986). Quinn (1988) also included 'building power bases' within his competency model. However, the nature of influence at senior levels is still relatively underexplored and, indeed, often seen as an aberration or dysfunctional element of behaviour in organisations. Our research highlights the importance to the executive of influencing techniques as well as the need to understand political behaviour.

Leadership Capability

The emphasis on leadership in recent years (and the lack of precision as to its definition) has been such that nearly every executive quality is subsumed under this heading. Our research suggests that leadership is a distinct and vital interpersonal process which entails helping others to overcome hurdles to achieve a common goal. In order to do this, the executive needs vision and the capacity to empower staff.

Integration Capability

This capability is the capacity to build senior teams and bring together large, diverse groups within the organisation. While building and managing an effective senior team is critical, so is the capacity to look more broadly and integrate what are often extremely large and complex parts of the business. More recently, writers such as Kanter and those analysing top management teams have highlighted how important integrating activities are at senior levels. During his tenure at ICI, Sir John Harvey-Jones restructured his board so that it moved from concentrating on turf issues to working as a team. He also integrated several parts of the organisation, such as the Petrochemicals and Plastics divisions to consolidate and focus the business.

Insight Capability

This is the capacity to understand what motivates others and how they see the world. Effective executives use insight to gauge others' likely agendas and the actions they may take. This Capability underlies the executive's capacity to influence, lead and integrate others within the organisation. Again, although this aspect is often assumed or neglected, several writers, including Isenberg (1984) and Limerick (1990), have demonstrated that it is an important capacity at senior levels. Senior executive work is not only about grasping functional and technical issues, but the more ambiguous and subtle world of human issues, agendas and actions. As Kouzes and Posner (1987) note, 'Managers who focus on themselves and are insensitive to others fail. They fail because there is a limit to what they can do by themselves.'

Directional Capabilities

These are concerned with understanding, shaping and directing the executive's environment in order to achieve short and long-term goals. This requires the ability to bring perspective, focus and clarity both to external market issues and internal organisational issues, and to design structures and processes to manage these. This necessity to cope with both the external and internal environments was highlighted in a study of outstanding senior managers by Klemp and McClelland (1986).

Expertise Capability

Over the years, many writers have indicated in various ways how the knowledge base of managers influences their ability to operate efficiently.[27] The Expertise Capability is concerned not only with having the functional knowledge needed for the executive role but, more importantly, the ability to see outside the boundaries of any one particular functional area.

External Capability

This involves the capacity to understand the relevance of events and changes in the environment external to one's business. This capacity is also highlighted by others – particularly in the strategy field – as important. However, it is an aspect which is all too easily overlooked. Often, it is the interpersonal aspects of leadership and the intellectual and analytical capacity of the executive which are emphasised as being important. Yet an External Capability is vital. It is claimed that many of the problems of the American auto industry are a consequence of ignoring the advances of foreign competitors, particularly the Japanese. As one Chrysler executive remarked about his organisation's performance in the 1980s, 'by the time we woke up to the fact that they were really chewing us, they had 20% of the market. From that point on they just chipped away'.[28]

Organisational Capability

The Organisational Capability describes the knowledge needed to design and build organisations which function effectively. Executives must understand the essential components of the organisation and modify and change them when required. Given the pace and scale of corporate restructuring, few doubt the importance of this particular Capability. Indeed, Nadler *et al.* (1992) argue that at a senior level, '. . . the tool with the largest potential leverage is the design of the organization, including the systems, the structures and the processes by which work gets done'.

Actioning/Structuring Capability

This capability is the executive's capacity to get things done, sustain high work loads and be persistent in pursuing important issues. It also involves knowing how to establish and work within a structure which facilitates the achievement of critical short and long-term goals. Executives with this capacity are less likely to do what IBM CEO, Lou Gerstner calls, 'confusing activity with producing results'.[29]

Figure 1.3 brings the Capabilities together and suggests how they might interrelate. The mind of the executive and his or her perception of the world, is most fundamentally effected by their Cognitive and Maturity Capabilities. The Development Capability is then seen as a central link between the core mental processes of the executive and the rest of the Capabilities: it is the capacity to learn which makes improvement possible elsewhere (discussed in Chapter 3).

Developing executive effectiveness is similar to a journey – in Peter's and Waterman's term – 'a search for excellence' rather than a final destination. The Capabilities presented here are best seen as a vehicle for that journey. They are designed to give the senior executive (and those aspiring to a senior management position) some benchmarks, suggestions and guidelines for operating at a senior executive level.

The Capabilities are not 'end states', but rather a means of conceptualising the broad areas in which the seasoned executive will have to demonstrate effective performance. Although our research indicates that all of the Capabilities are important at senior levels, the emphasis on each changes according to the demands of the job. For example, one executive we interviewed had moved from being general manager to take responsibility for investor relations in a company with turnover of $7 billion. He also acted as a sounding board on

Fig. 1.3 *The Capabilities and how they relate*

Directional Capabilities

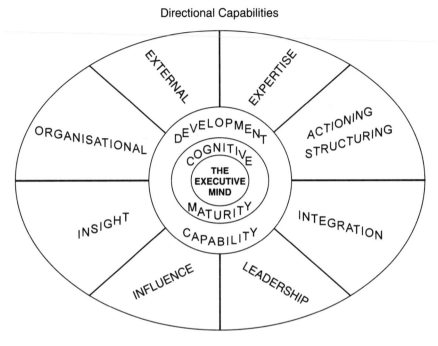

Interpersonal Capabilities

strategy matters for the CEO. In his new position, the External and Influence Capabilities assumed a much greater prominence in his day-to-day activities than they had previously. He needed to be on top of key trends affecting the firm and relied on his influencing skills to network amongst key stakeholders both inside and outside the company.

The emphasis given to each Capability may also change over time, even within the same job. For example, few senior personnel in IBM in the late 1980s believed they would be laying off 15 000 staff worldwide within three years: yet they did. The qualities needed by senior personnel when IBM was turning in seemingly limitless profits in the 1980s were very different to those required in the early 1990s – when IBM was posting massive losses. (The different qualities required under different strategic scenarios are explored further in the final chapter.)

In addition, different Capabilities will be required to different degrees depending on whether the executive is concentrating on the key processes of Establishing, Enabling and Enacting. In Figure 1.4 we bring these together to show that some Capabilities will be more prominent depending on which aspect of the job the executive is tackling. For example, those Capabilities which are more knowledge based and concerned with understanding, will be more evident when the executive takes steps to assess the environment, establish priorities and ways forward. Clearly, the behaviourally based Capabilities concerned more with application, will be of greater significance when the executive enacts his or her plans – others will need to be persuaded, influenced and lead if the organisation is to progress.

Our framework is a starting point which executives can use to develop and apply the Capabilities to their own role requirements (see Figure 1.5). For instance, all senior jobs require leadership – yet what form that takes will depend on the particular challenges the executive faces. Applying the Capabilities involves a detailed assessment process which takes into account present and future job requirements as well as current (and potential) performance of the executive. (A Capabilities instrument has been developed by the authors for this purpose.)

In particular, when applying the Capabilities to the executive's specific work circumstances, the following points need to be addressed:

- Specify what is required within each Capability area. These can be in terms of behaviours, or tasks to be accomplished, or both.
- Identify the minimum level of capability required for each executive. The Capabilities are not 'either/or' states, but need to be thought of in terms of the specific requirements of the role.
- Consider the emphasis between the various Capabilities required at present and identify how this might change in future.
- Assess the strength of the executive's Development Capability as this will indicate whether the executive can grow with the job.

Clearly, this is not a straightforward process.[30] However, rather than reach out for the assessment manuals, our intention is for readers to use this book to explore the key aspects senior executives need to develop. In the chapters which follow, we explore each of the Capabilities identified in our research in more depth. In so doing, we draw on the work of a broad range of academics and practitioners. Each chapter follows a similar style. At the outset, we identify why

Fig. 1.4 *Senior executive framework*

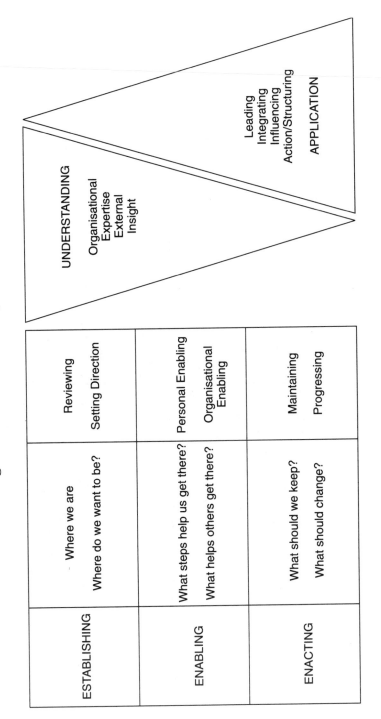

UNDERSTANDING

Organisational
Expertise
External
Insight

Leading
Integrating
Influencing
Action/Structuring

APPLICATION

ESTABLISHING	Where we are	Reviewing
	Where do we want to be?	Setting Direction
ENABLING	What steps help us get there?	Personal Enabling
	What helps others get there?	Organisational Enabling
ENACTING	What should we keep?	Maintaining
	What should change?	Progressing

Fig. 1.5 *Customising the Capabilities*

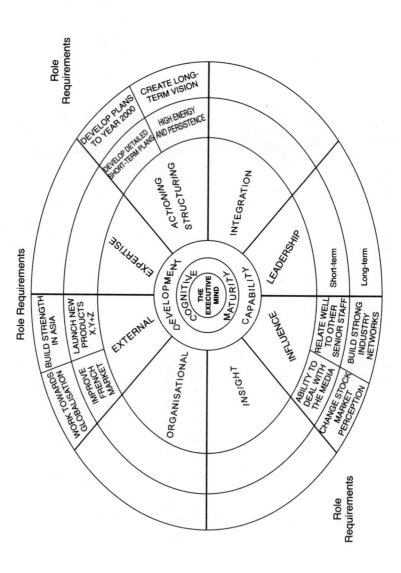

each Capability is important at senior levels. We then go on to review the major issues executives experience when trying to apply or develop such a Capability. As stated in the preface, our intention is for the reader to 'dip' into each chapter and focus on those which are most relevant at any particular point in time.

SUMMARY

Senior executives play a critical role in organisations, yet relatively little is known about their work and the pressures they face. As a result, it is difficult to identify the particular qualities executives require to perform effectively at this level. Development at senior levels is therefore a considerable challenge.

Nevertheless, from the studies that have been done on senior executives several points have emerged. The move into a senior executive position is a critical cross-road in a manager's career. In comparison to more junior management positions, the executive will experience an increase in 'the scope and scale' of the job. For example, they may be responsible for integrating and coordinating complex functions, have to cope with complex reporting relationships and deal with considerable ambiguity and change. Moreover, they make decisions which often affect a large number of people and are held directly accountable for results.

The requirements made of executives can be grouped into three principal areas. Executives need to *establish* what is needed in their job and the outcomes that are required. They must develop systems, structures and processes which will *enable* themselves and others to pursue organisational goals. They must also *enact*; that is, make decisions and take actions which will both maintain and progress the organisation.

Whilst there is considerable diversity of opinion as to the specific qualities needed at senior levels, the broad areas of interpersonal skill, analytical techniques and organisational understanding have long been identified as being important. These aspects are further expanded upon and refined in the Executive Capabilities Framework put forward by the authors. A Capability refers to the behavioural skills, areas of knowledge, cognitive processes and the emotional makeup of the executive needed for effective performance. The Capabilities form the basis of a generic framework which executives can use to determine their own development priorities. In all, 11

Capabilities have been introduced and described, and these are discussed further in the ensuing chapters.

NOTES

1. See Kearns and Nadler (1992, 225).
2. See Pettigrew (1992).
3. These are largely drawn from Ancona and Nadler (1989).
4. Based largely on the work of Fayol. His work was originally produced in 1916, but is now referenced as Fayol, H. (1949) *General and Industrial Management*, London: Pitman.
5. See Caroll and Gillen (1987).
6. Both Mahoney, Jerdee and Carroll (1963) and Hughes and Singler (1985) found that directing, controlling and organising are consistent at all levels of management, but planning increased and staffing decreased as one goes from lower to top management. Also Stagner (1969) found that the time CEOs spent in organisational planning was related to the firm's profitability. Boyatzis (1982) found goal setting/planning related to managerial effectiveness and the AT&T study (Bray *et al.*, 1974) showed planning/decision making as one of the strongest predictors of managerial success.
7. See Kenneth Labich, 'Why Companies Fail', *Fortune*, vol. 130, no. 10, 14 November 1994, 22–32.
8. *Sir John Harvey-Jones*, Case 9-490-013, Harvard Business School, 1989, p. 7.
9. See Gupta (1988).
10. See Laurie Morse's article, 'Sharp Knives at Tenneco', *Financial Times*, 28 November 1994.
11. Study of 48 top executives by S. Wilson cited in Alan Deutschman's article, 'The CEO's Secret of Managing Time,' *Fortune*, vol. 125, no. 13, 1992, 79–84.
12. Professor Leo Murray, Director of Cranfield School of Management, UK.
13. For examples and a discussion of the difficulties associated with applying a competency-based approach at senior levels, see Boam and Sparrow (1992) chapters 9 and 10.
14. See Douglas Ready's article, 'Executive Education: Is it Making the Grade?', *Fortune* Magazine Supplement, 14 December 1992, 39–48.
15. For example, AT&T, British Airways, BP, National Mutual, General Motors and the National Health Service are organisations which are experimenting with this approach.
16. Canning (1990); Sinclair and Collins (1991); Torrington, Waite and Weightman (1992).
17. Furnham (1990); Thorpe (1990).
18. See Jacobs (1989).
19. See, for instance, McCall, Spreitzer and Mahoney (1994).
20. See Sashkin (1992).

21. See Wilson and Page (1993).
22. See Bray *et al.* (1974).
23. See, for example, Cox and Cooper (1988); Morgan (1988); Kotter (1990).
24. See Crabb (1991).
25. These include Jacobs and Jaques (1987) and Kotter (1990).
26. Patricia Sellers and David Kirkpatrick, 'Can this Man Save IBM?', *Fortune*, 19 April 1993, 37–9.
27. See, for example, Ouchi (1981); Pascale and Athos (1981); Peters and Waterman (1982); Kotter (1982a and 1982b); Gabarro (1988).
28. Alex Taylor III, 'U.S. Cars Come back', *Fortune*, vol. 126, no. 11, 16 November 1992, 24–53.
29. As we noted earlier, the literature has long identified the importance of goal setting/planning for executive effectiveness. Other writers, such as Kanungo and Misra (1992) have identified an 'action oriented competence' which highlights similar factors: attention to detail, persistence of pursuit and concern for time frames.
30. The authors have developed several methods which help in this process including a validated questionnaire. There are also several researchers such as Iles (1992) and McCall *et al.* (1994) and several consultancies and companies which have looked at these processes in some detail.

PART I

THE PERSONAL CAPABILITIES: SELF-UNDERSTANDING AND DEVELOPMENT

2 The Executive Mind: Managing One's Thoughts and Emotions at Senior Levels

INTRODUCTION

For some business people, like Clive Thompson, CEO of Rentokil, commerce is essentially an intellectual exercise. Described as a total rationalist, Thompson is 'a man with a logical answer to everything' and someone who believes that every problem can be solved by the application of cool reason. Under his tenure, Rentokil has been transformed into one of the UK's top performing companies with a market capitalisation of about 2.2 billion sterling.[1]

When it came to choosing a strategy for the firm in the early 1980s, however, it was Thompson's beliefs and experience which influenced his decision to turn down the more logical diversification options open to him at that time. This rational executive also admits to a strong emotional attachment to the firm, its culture and people whom he has helped build and develop.

Given the success of Rentokil, Thompson is one executive who can be justifiably proud of his decision making record. At senior levels, Mintzberg (1973) has argued the decision making role is critical to the work of the general manager. Bass (1983) goes further when he argues that the quality of managerial decisions is the yardstick of a manager's effectiveness. Today, as organisations struggle to make sense of the changes in their own industries and the trend towards globalisation, senior executives face a particular challenge and responsibility to provide effective solutions to problems. As our example shows, however, the decision making process can be influenced by things other than logic.

Yet, more often than not, it is the rational, logical thought processes in executives which are most often discussed. In this chapter we explore what form these processes take at senior levels. Whilst acknowledging their importance, however, we also suggest that

33

executives will not be fully effective unless they understand how they think and feel about the problems they face (that is, the Cognitive and Maturity Capabilities). In what follows, therefore, we explore the critical mental skills required at a senior level and also consider those factors which affect the problem solving and decision making process – such as the executive's mindset, values and creativity.

PROBLEMS AND ISSUES AT SENIOR LEVELS

The senior executive deals with issues which are generally much more demanding and difficult than those less senior staff typically manage. They tend to exhibit one or more of the following features:

- *A degree of importance.* The problems faced by senior managers will often have significant implications. Their decisions frequently result in radical change in the organisation, can have serious consequences if something goes wrong and affect many stake-holders, especially employees.[2] Their decisions may also be more difficult to reverse.

- *Unique qualities.* Senior executives often have to cope with problems which are novel and unstructured. For example, no established procedures may exist for handling the development of breakthrough products, or entering new markets like Russia or China. These are what Simon (1977) calls 'non-programmed' decisions.

- *A high degree of uncertainty and limited information.* New investment opportunities, divestitures or amalgamations involve taking decisions on the basis of fewer guidelines, fewer precedents and less certainty about potential outcomes. Rarely in these circumstances will critical information be available, and that which is will be limited and sometimes ambiguous. Nevertheless, the responsibility to 'get it right' is high.

- *Broad scope.* Unlike middle managers, senior executives make decisions which cut across the organisation. Furthermore, most strategic decisions involve a range of technical and functional considerations that have both short and long-term consequences.

- *Interrelatedness.* The problems executives deal with often impact on several interrelated areas. This demands a greater degree of integration than would be necessary at lower managerial levels. For instance, the decision to invest in one technological area can have massive implications for others. As Senge (1990b) notes, at senior levels decisions should not be taken in reaction to isolated events, but seen more as part of a wider process of interconnected aspects.

Thus, senior managers face a complex environment with problems which are important, unique, uncertain, often broadly based and interrelated. Dealing with this complexity demands sophisticated conceptual skills which Jaques and Clement (1991) believe is the most important requirement for effective leadership. Similarly, in Cox and Cooper's (1988) study of CEOs, one of the most consistently mentioned attributes necessary for the CEO's role was 'analytical and decision making skills'.

Traditional responses

Despite the considerable amount written on decision making, few writers have tackled the way senior executives cope with complex problems. The dominant perspective is still the traditional problem solving model (see Figure 2.1). This suggests that problem solving is concerned with:

- Establishing goals and objectives
- Identifying and diagnosing whether a problem exists and its importance
- Looking at alternative possible solutions
- Choosing among alternative solutions and selecting the best option
- Implementing a chosen solution
- Ensuring the solution is maintained and its effect monitored

Models such as these emphasise the need to act rationally. Organ and Bateman (1986) argue that managers should do everything they can to make sure their decisions are as rational as possible. To be a rational manager is to be objective, fair and above reproach. In a similar vein, Janis and Mann (1977) argue that decisions should be judged by the procedures used in making them. If all relevant aspects of the problem are analysed, available and pertinent information is

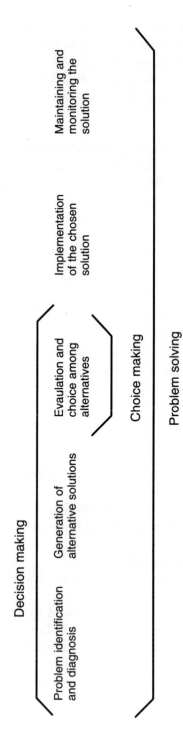

Fig. 2.1 *Decision making and problem solving*

acquired and considered in an unbiased way, alternative courses of action are creatively derived and realistically evaluated, then the decision making process can be judged a good one.

The traditional model has both strengths and weaknesses. Most writers would accept that each of the above elements are important in the problem solving process. Without clear goals there is no direction, no certainty about results and no way of measuring those results. For example, when Xerox embarked on its drive for total quality in the 1980s, staff were taught a step-by-step problem solving process to improve work processes within the organisation. At training sessions, staff were shown how to take a problem, work back and find causes and then come up with a solution. It impressed the CEO at that time, David Kearns. 'From my standpoint, this was the most vocational part of the training. I really learned from it. I don't have the most disciplined mind and I found the systematic process amazingly helpful.'[3]

However, in ambiguous environments, identifying the real problem, considering all alternatives and making the 'right' decision in a limited time scale is fraught with difficulty. Clearly, the traditional problem solving model is valuable for programmed decisions at lower levels and for more routine or operational issues at a senior level. However, it may be less useful for non-programmed decisions. Indeed, Isenberg (1984) found that senior managers seldom think in ways which one might view simplistically as 'rational'.

Consequently, many writers accept that the traditional model is not a reliable description of how executives actually make decisions. Nevertheless, it can provide a useful tool for thinking about how the decision making process is structured.

EXECUTIVE THOUGHT PROCESSES

In order to better understand how problem solving processes might be improved, we have identified a number of factors which influence what information executives receive and how this is processed (see Figure 2.2). Each of these are summarised below and then explored in more detail in what follows. In addition, we highlight a particular capacity effective executives need which we call 'Breadth and Focus'. This is part of the Cognitive Capability and is, we believe, critical to cultivate at senior levels.

Fig. 2.2 *The executive mind*

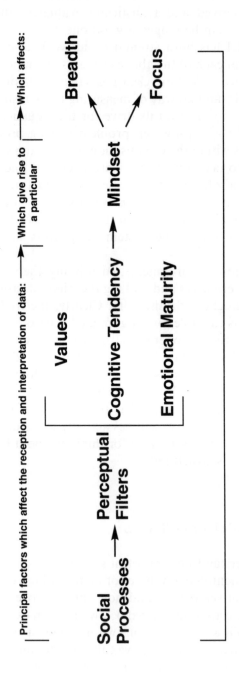

- *Breadth and focus.* The senior executive role demands the ability to both take in a broad range of data and also distil that data and focus on the critical elements. This capacity is not only about analysis but also interpretation and direction.[4]

- *Social processes.* Decisions at a senior level are rarely taken in isolation. A range of external influences (including stakeholder expectations and peer opinion) affect both the data the executive receives and the decisions that are made with them. Indeed, Dunford (1992) argues that decision making is likely to be as much about persuasion and influence as it is a mechanistic process of gathering and assessing 'facts'.

- *Information processing and perceptual problems.* While social processes affect the quality of data we receive, so do our own mental abilities. Our 'frames of reference' influence how we perceive and filter information and how we make sense of it. Decision making depends, as Janis and Mann (1977) note, on how effective we are at this sense-making process.

- *Values.* Underlying our perceptual processes are our values and beliefs which colour what we see and how we interpret events. Understanding these better may help explain why we choose some solutions over others.

- *Cognitive tendency.* Our tendency or predisposition for either left-brain (analytical) or right-brain (creative) thinking also greatly influences what we see and how we manage data. Understanding our cognitive strengths and weaknesses can help identify our biases and where we need complimentary inputs from others.

- *Emotional maturity.* Also important are the emotional responses executives have to the problems they face. Tied in with this is one's propensity to take risks and ability to handle stress. Understanding what affects mental resilience, helps highlight when decision making may be less efficient.

- *Better thinking.* Few senior executives get to the top without a well developed decision making capacity. Nevertheless, it is easy to fall into fixed patterns of thinking which, at times, can be difficult for oneself and others to change. Faced with new challenges and novel situations the executive needs to review the mindset they bring to problems. There are various techniques which help in tackling problems and thinking through issues.

Let us deal with each of these aspects in turn.

Breadth and focus

How well executives diagnose problems, find solutions and take action, depends on their ability to both see the broad picture as well as focus on the critical issues.

The need for breadth is highlighted by Mintzberg (1976) who observed that effective managers have to 'see the big picture'; that is, be capable of thinking through decisions which affect major parts of the organisation and which are important either in the short or longer-term. More recently, Lewis and Jacobs (1992) have argued that senior managers should have 'constructive capacities': namely, the capacity for integration, abstraction, independent thought and the use of broad and complex frames of reference.

In addition, the executive must be able to bring focus to the problems they face. They have to reduce complex situations to the essentials, identify the opportunities and propose a well-founded course of action. Isenberg (1984) found that, in addition to thinking about broader processes, senior managers also think about how to deal with one or two overriding concerns, or very general goals. Similarly, Kotter (1982) found that formulating an 'agenda' for senior managers is crucial. Ford (1977) argues that elite decision makers have the ability to 'lock in on the important, crucial and relevant'. In our terms, they not only have Breadth but also Focus.

Although these two qualities appear contradictory, several writers have highlighted the need for a similar combination. Senge (1990b) talks of the need to have both a broad scope as well as the capacity to focus one's actions through 'leverage'. Both qualities were needed by ex-Motorola chief, George Fisher when he was hired in late 1993 to help lift Kodak from its bureaucratic ways. Essentially an outsider, Fisher had to quickly reduce the major strategic issues facing what is the world's biggest photographic company without getting buried in the detail. Fisher argues that the trick is to learn a few shortcuts, 'Within a matter of days, you can understand a lot of key issues'.[5] Six months later, he and his senior managers had completed an assessment of Kodak's complex environment. They moved swiftly to sell off some of Kodak's non-photographic businesses, announced a major initiative to re-engineer the organisation from top to bottom and formed a new digital-imaging group to spearhead new business development.[6]

Executives like Fisher exhibit the capacity to understand a complex environment and then focus their attention on five or six of the most crucial issues. As each of these is tackled, they then distil the next handful of critical issues to keep both themselves and their staff clearly focused.

While ideas on Breadth and Focus differ between writers, they are, nevertheless, discernible themes running throughout the literature on senior executive decision making. How one develops the ability to both think broadly and yet with some degree of focus is less clear. There are many factors which can prevent the executive seeing interrelationships or focusing on the core issues. Let us explore what some of these might be.

Social processes

Information is fundamental to successful problem solving. Much of the information that senior executives receive is acquired through social processes and interpersonal contact.[7] There are several factors which affect the kind of information the executive receives:

- *Ease of access to information.* Often, information is received from those people executives have easy access to, and who they get on with. Ease of acquisition is sometimes a more important factor or determinant than quality of information. As a consequence, decision makers may use sources that provide lower quality information, but which are readily accessible.

- *Good news versus bad news.* There is a general bias or preference towards receiving positive as against negative information. According to O'Reilly (1983), information is more likely to be used by decision makers if it is supportive of outcomes already favoured, and if it avoids conflict and cannot be challenged. Many subordinates tell their bosses what they want to hear, withholding an opposing personal opinion or neglecting to report all the uncomfortable facts. Superiors will often take 'good news' at face value, failing to consider that the information may be less than perfectly valid.

- *Filling in the gaps.* There is a tendency to provide 'complete' information, that is, people will 'construct' or make up 'facts' so as to create a coherent picture. Organ and Bateman (1986) argue that organisation members who do this are typically uncomfortable with ambiguity and therefore often provide structure, or fill in the gaps that may exist in available information. March (1982) goes further and argues that decision making is influenced by 'the logic of obligation, duty and rules'.

- *Organisational politics.* Political processes may affect the reliability of the information. Lindblom (1959) sees decision making as a process of muddling through – assessing what is possible by taking account of the political reality of the situation. Hickson *et al.* (1986) take the view that an organisation is sustained by a dominant coalition of powerful stakeholders. Decision making is then 'a hubbub of pressure and contention' where common objectives are the result of negotiation and bargaining. Under these circumstances the information the executive receives will be less than 'objective'.

At least some of these factors influenced executives at General Motors who tried to launch a new model to replace GM's range of midsize cars in the 1980s. The GM-10 program, as it came to be known, fell foul of various reorganisations, cutbacks and changes so that by the time the cars came to market (in 1990) the market had moved. (By contrast, Ford had foreseen the change from coupes to sedans and chose never to develop a two-door Taurus.) The GM-10 was costly to promote and sell. It used less than 50 per cent of GM's manufacturing capacity and, to make matters worse, none of GM's factories were sufficiently flexible to manufacture anything else. In the 1990s the model was described as 'the biggest catastrophe in American industrial history.'

> The mess exposed a crucial defect in GM's management by committee. As decisions were passed up through various committees for approval, they developed a momentum of their own. By the time they reached the top, they had an inevitability about them, even if they no longer made sense. GM's top committees were notorious for ratifying not deliberating.[8]

How can executives guard against such distortions? For some, the answer lies in the creation of well developed networks and relying on as many information sources as possible.[9] Moreover, these sources should provide a range of contrasting views and positions. While executives may not be able to remove biased and incomplete information entirely, they can certainly increase the likelihood of receiving more timely and accurate information.

Information processing and perceptual problems

Information sources are only the starting point, however. The other side of the coin is how the executive receives that information. What information is noticed, how it is interpreted and how it is then acted on are subject to a range of internal distortions. At a senior level, executives often have an overwhelming range of information to choose from. As we noted earlier, not all of this information will be helpful, but even when critical information is available, it is not always utilised.

For example, at Xerox in the early 1980s when the organisation was at a point where it could no longer fund its own future and grow without borrowing, it was hard to get managers to face up to the stark reality of the company's true competitive position. The Japanese had established a position in the low-volume end of the copier market and were starting to become a real threat. Despite this, says Kearns, Xerox CEO at that time, managers 'kept drafting overly optimistic predictions and saying things would level off. There was a lot of denial'.[10]

Not surprisingly, this phenomenon is increasingly being written about. When looking at the area of executive decision making, Shrivastava and Mitroff (1984) argue that it is important to discuss the assumptions and constraints that managers have when viewing the world. Executives, like everyone else, have a frame of reference which is a product of their past experiences, assumptions, values and beliefs. These influence the way in which information about problems is gathered, distilled and what conclusions are made. Helping executives make better decisions depends to some extent on helping them understand these 'frames of reference'.

Frames of reference and the perceptual process

Frames of reference are ways of viewing the world. They are part of the perceptual filtering process which enables executives to deal with the complexity of their environment. Like everyone else, executives interpret information quite instinctively. Recently, the filtering processes they use have come under closer examination from management researchers. A variety of terms have emerged which generally refer to the same phenomena. These include 'mindset', 'mental framing', 'perceptual schemas', 'cognitive maps', 'recipes' and 'paradigms'.[11] There are differences between some of these concepts, but in general they refer to the ways the individual organises knowledge. An individual's 'perceptual schemas', for instance, affect how they interact with the environment, what they notice, how they interpret data and how they retain information.[12]

Filtering processes affect both what an executive notices and how this is interpreted. Important influences on what is noticed are what some writers call 'foregrounds' and 'backgrounds'. Foregrounds tend to be at the forefront of our thinking and can cause an executive to overlook, or ignore important background events, thus limiting an executive's Breadth. This can make an individual or company vulnerable. For instance, IBM, which dominated the mainframe computer business, virtually ignored the initial developments of minicomputers, microcomputers and supercomputers to the company's detriment. In the 1980s, these were obviously foreground events for Apple, Digital and Cray.

Success can affect what we notice. Repeated success sometimes creates over confidence which can lead to the creation of buffers which insulate executives from a range of new, potentially adverse events and exclude background stimuli from consideration. For senior executives concerned with complex and changing problems this can be dangerous. The success of NASA, for instance, in overcoming insurmountable technological problems gave rise to confidence. It also gave rise to complacency – one of the contributing causes of the Challenger disaster.

We also have a propensity to see what we want to see. In interpreting data, our perceptual frameworks lead us to categorise and hide data, assign likelihoods and also fill in missing links. These affect the executive's capacity to Focus. Zahra and Chaples (1993) show how such tendencies affect executives' capacity to analyse the competition. They cite research which shows that executives develop simple classifications to help them think about their competitive environments. In doing so, they have a tendency to focus on existing and known competitors and as a result may miss newer entrants to the market. Also, executives 'may discount data that is different from their beliefs or that challenges their values'. Similarly, organisations that are well established tend to analyse the environment less rigorously and fall into the trap of believing that the factors which have contributed to their success to date will continue to be important.

Several writers suggest that improving strategic decision making is a matter of developing new perceptual frameworks that portray problematic situations differently.[13] For example, Zahra and Chaples (1993) encourage executives to see themselves and their industry from their competitors' viewpoint. They argue that executives should encourage the expression of divergent views in order to strengthen their overall understanding of their true competitive position.

Thus, the executive mind consists of thought patterns which are highly stable and resistant to radical thinking, as well as ones which are more amenable to development. Changing perceptual frameworks is therefore easier said than done. In order to understand how this might occur and how decision making might be improved, we need to look in more detail at the executive's personal make-up.

Values

Values are the principles and guidelines a person uses to make choices and judgements. Values, like truth, honesty, integrity and wealth creation, colour our view of the world. They also have a very strong influence on how executives discharge their managerial responsibilities.

For example, the development and direction of Anita Roddick's cosmetics business, The Body Shop, is determined in large part by her very strong values about how businesses should be managed and the contribution industry should make to society. By the early 1990s, the Body Shop had become a global business with more than 600 shops trading in 18 different languages in 37 countries around the world. Roddick argues, 'It is a business unlike any other: we have no marketing department and no advertising department. We operate according to criteria which place more emphasis on human values than on strictly commercial considerations.'[14]

The subject of values has recently gained greater currency in the leadership literature. In one study of 45 senior executives, the investigators found that, with one exception, each of the executives spoke with genuine interest and enthusiasm about shared values. Most said values were a very significant issue and that they spent a lot of time thinking about and discussing them. One executive in a multibusiness corporation referred to values as 'the only glue we have'.[15] Indeed, Peters and Waterman (1982) advocated a management revolution based on shared values in the workplace. 'Every excellent company takes the process of value shaping seriously; either buy into the company's values or get out.'

Personal values influence a manager's perception of the situation and problems he/she faces. They also influence a manager's decisions and solutions to problems. The impact of values is more pronounced in decisions where there is ambiguity and consequently a greater degree of subjectivity.[16]

For example, under the direction of Chairman and CEO Robert D. Haas, senior executives at Levi Strauss have embraced a values-based strategy which they use to guide their decision making. Their guiding precepts highlight the company's position with regard to the treatment of minorities, ethical standards and work practices. When the company embarked on a $500 million project to remake its product – development and distribution systems in 1994, these values came into play. They provided a common framework which guided management on how decision making should be conducted – with extensive consultation and involvement of the workforce and a direct link to senior management for groups representing blacks, Asians, Hispanics, gays and women.[17]

An adherence to traditional or outmoded values can, however, result in a loss of flexibility and slow down the response of the organisation to market changes. At Levi Strass, the decision to re-engineer work processes took much longer to work through because of the need to involve all levels in the organisation. The introduction of teamwork, together with an incentive system based on team results, improved productivity but also led to friction between team members and those colleagues who didn't pull their weight. Many more hours of training were needed to help Levi's workforce get used to teamwork and other empowering work practices. Similarly, Levi's corporate values were also behind the company's decision to withdraw $40 million of its operations from the potentially lucrative Chinese market.

Some suggest that the values and beliefs of the senior executive have more impact on the direction and purpose of the organisation than any other single influence. It is important, therefore, to have a sense of the values one holds and to recognise where they may be both helping and constraining problem solving. Certainly, good decisions are more difficult to make if executives do not know what their guiding values are.[18]

Cognitive tendency

In addition to values, executives have cognitive abilities which will impact on how they gather and interpret data and make decisions. These are classified in different ways by different theorists. A popular categorisation in the management field is the Myers-Briggs Type Indicator (MBTI).[19] This is concerned with several aspects of personality including an individual's preference for gathering information and making decisions. The MBTI highlights how an individual can gather data through their senses in a factual, data driven way, or through intuitive processes. It also highlights the extent to which we make decisions either through logical, rational processes or based on feelings and principles (see Figure 2.3).

It is unlikely that one person will be proficient in all aspects of the decision making process. The MBTI highlights individuals' cognitive preferences and where their focuses lie. This starting point may help identify areas of potential improvement. Although radical changes are unlikely, some change seems possible. More usually, knowing one's decision making preferences helps indicate where one's ability might be supplemented by individuals who have complimentary skills. In addition, it can help prevent an executive stifling the cognitive preferences of others – particularly when they do not fit neatly with their own.

Right and left-brain thinking

An aspect of cognitive style which is implicitly incorporated in the MBTI (but worth emphasising separately) is the distinction between right and left-brain thinking. Although this classification is sometimes overstated, for some years it has been used to distinguish between two different clusters of cognitive activity. In a nutshell, the distinction is between an analytical capacity and an intuitive one. The left side of the brain is concerned with analytical processes and specialises in verbal and mathematical functions. The right side 'intuits' information from a variety of inputs and is concerned with visual imagery, creative synthesis, intuition, fantasy and associative processes.

Depending on which hemisphere of the brain is dominant, people differ in the way they process information. Historically, managers have been encouraged to use rational or left-brain thinking processes. The logical, analytical approach to problem solving is often seen as

48

Fig. 2.3 *Myers-Briggs type indicator*

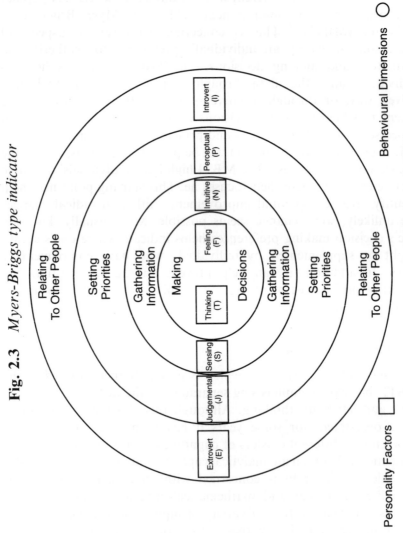

Source: Adapted from Kakabadse *et al.* (1987)

Personality Factors ☐   Behavioural Dimensions ◯

the 'correct' one. Nevertheless, this emphasis has its limitations. Indeed, Peters and Waterman blamed rational thought processes as a major reason for the problems US firms encountered when competing with foreign companies in the 1970s and 1980s.[20]

The right-side – creativity and intuition

Instead, right-brain activities are increasingly being promoted as the kind of thought processes needed at a senior level.[21] Mintzberg (1976) is one of the most influential proponents of this idea. He argues that practising managers rely less on analytical inputs (such as reports and hard statistical data) and more on soft speculative impressions and judgements.

More generally, he has argued against the notion that strategic management is a rational exercise. In *The Rise and Fall of Strategic Planning*, Mintzberg (1994) argues that right-hemisphere activities should be used to think through strategic management problems. 'Strategy should be crafted around insights and discoveries using experiments and learning processes, not planning documents and formal presentations.'[22] For Mintzberg, therefore, strategic management is a craft skill which is concerned with helping strategy to emerge in response to shifting environmental pressures.

Isenberg (1984) has focused on one aspect of right-brain thinking; that is, the way senior managers use intuition. He argues they use it to:

- Sense when a problem exists
- Perform well-learned behaviour patterns rapidly
- Synthesise isolated bits of data and experience
- Check results of more rational analysis
- Bypass in-depth analysis to come up with a plausible solution

Another study of top management by Agor (1986a) found that managers with highly developed intuition can see new possibilities in any given situation. They have a sense or vision of the future and thus are better equipped to move their organisation in response to it. These managers are particularly adept at generating new ideas and providing ingenious new solutions to old problems; usually they function best in rapidly changing environments or crisis settings.

Indeed, Agor (1986a) identifies a number of circumstances where creative capacities can be of use. Namely:

- When a high level of uncertainty exists

- When little previous precedent exists
- When variables are less scientifically predictable
- When 'facts' are limited
- When 'facts' don't clearly point the way to go
- When several plausible alternative solutions exist, with good arguments for each
- When time is limited and there is pressure to produce the right decision

To what extent these capacities can be developed is controversial.[23] Typical creative problem solving techniques are brainstorming, lateral thinking and synectics. Most techniques follow a similar sequence starting with some kind of problem exploration phase, followed by an idea generation phase and ending with some form of evaluation and action planning. Central to these techniques is the goal of producing large numbers of ideas as well as variety – and by so doing to surface a range of fundamentally different possibilities.

Clearly, some executives will be more creative than others. Executives, therefore, not only have to work at their own levels of creativity but also at developing an environment which is supportive of this quality in others. Indeed, this may be more important than any inherent ability the executive may have. In practice, however, the evidence seems to suggest that creative problem solving cultures are not the norm. In part, this may be due to a lingering reticence on behalf of many executives. In his study of top executive decision making, Agor (1986a) reports that over half the managers involved tended to keep their use of intuition a secret because they felt others would not see this as a reliable basis on which to make decisions.

The left-side – rational processes

Does this concern for improving creativity mean that executives should neglect the development of their analytical processes? Certainly not. No executive can survive without clear-headed logic, and it is important that senior executives exploit their cognitive abilities to the full.

Again, however, this is not straightforward and there is a danger that complacency may creep in. Argyris (1983) argues that while executives have great analytical skill, most are usually unaware of the reasoning processes they use. As is true of most skilled behaviour, executives rarely focus on these unless they make an error. When errors do occur, these are usually rectified or played down by others (for example, subordinates) leaving the executive unaware of the mistake. Moreover, executives rarely test their own thinking as they believe it to be so obviously correct.

In order to improve, the executive needs to be prepared to review issues with a trusted colleague and subordinates when errors occur. This is easier said than done. As Senge (1990a) notes, for most of us, exposing our thinking is threatening precisely because we are afraid that people will find errors in it. As a result, Argyris (1983) argues, executives develop defensive routines or entrenched habits to protect them from the embarrassment and threat that come from exposing their reasoning and thinking to colleagues.

When reflecting on his time as CEO of Xerox, David Kearns recognised this pattern of behaviour in himself and others:

> When they are confronted with a problem, American managers typically want it fixed fast – by yesterday. And this can be a deadly disease. I was very much the epitome of that school of thought. I felt I was decisive and impatient, and so I wanted problems solved as quickly as possible. But I didn't think enough about root causes. Rarely would I ask, 'What is the reason we are having this problem?' Now I think a lot about causes.[24]

The executive builds many different kinds of walls which prevent the exposure of thinking processes. One is the belief that 'managers must know what's going on'. Managers who take on the burden of having to know the answers become highly skilled in defensive routines that preserve their aura as capable decision makers by not revealing the thinking behind their decisions.

Another protective ploy is to use intimidation. Senge (1990b) illustrates this by citing the example of a CEO who lamented the fact his staff did not present their views forcefully to him. However, it was his own overbearing nature which prevented others from putting forward their views. As a result, the CEO protected his own views from being challenged.

Another defence is entrapment. Even in a situation where a product is failing there are forces which encourage executives to keep the project going.[25] They may want to justify the rationality of their earlier decision. Initially, no one wants to be perceived as being wrong or, worse, as being indecisive, waffling or erratic. Indeed, quite often the forces for staying with an earlier decision outweigh the forces for change. Most major companies have either a current or past example of a 'dead horse', wasting millions, but being kept alive because some executive or other is reluctant to admit their initial analysis might have been wrong. Thus, Argyris (1983) argues, the first challenge is to recognise defensive routines, then to inquire into their operation. Those who are best at revealing and diffusing these, he says, typically operate with a high degree of self-disclosure regarding their own defensiveness.

In order to get to that stage of learning and self-disclosure, some additional help may be needed. Indeed, as more organisations recognise the importance of having executives who can continue to learn and adapt, the capacity to reflect and be introspective is now being actively encouraged. Increasingly, MBA and other types of executive development programmes include exercises which help encourage this behaviour, in addition to fostering analytical and rational problem solving skills. Several US mainstream corporations (such as AT&T, PepsiCo and Aetna) are also investing in similar programmes.[26]

Emotional maturity

As we have just seen, therefore, executive thought processes are affected not only by things like cognitive style and values but also by ego defensive and emotional responses to situations.

Gimpl and Dakin (1984) argue that much management decision making is better understood as 'anxiety-relieving superstitious behaviour', than as a rational and effective insight into the future. While this is an extreme view, most agree that an executive's problem solving capacities are influenced by their emotional make-up. For example, Agor (1986) studied the problems CEOs experience when they make critical decisions under time pressure, when they are not relaxed or when they are not confident. Typical statements include: 'My wrong decisions come when physical or emotional stress are present': 'Most things go wrong when I don't listen to myself'.

Consequently, coping with the emotional pressures of the senior role is important, not only because of possible impairment to executives' decision making capacity, but also for the sake of their overall health. Several factors play a part in the executive's ability to cope, including their personality, life-style and the support they get from others. Here, we concentrate on executives' mental attitude and their resilience to the problems they face.

Positive attitudes and mental resilience

Ford (1977) found that elite executive decision makers were 'positive thinkers' in contrast with subordinate executives who tended to think more negatively. He also highlighted self-confidence and tough-mindedness as characteristics of these elite senior decision makers. Similar mental approaches have been found by other researchers of managerial work.

Kobasa (1982, 1988) found that managers who remained healthy during the stressful deregulation of AT&T, had an 'optimistic cognitive appraisal'. This included the view that change, good or bad, is an opportunity for growth and an inevitable part of life's experience. Rather than feeling threatened, these executives maintained a sense of control and an appreciation of change. Although they could not always control the changes which occurred they could, and did, control their responses to change.

Executives with these attitudes had 'hardy personalities'. They demonstrated some common themes, namely:

- *Commitment.* The ability to believe in the truth, importance and value of who one is and what one is doing – and therefore the tendency to be involved in many aspects of life.

- *Control.* The tendency to believe and act as if one can influence the course of events, with an emphasis on personal responsibility rather than looking to others' actions or fate.

- *Challenge.* The belief that change, rather than stability, is the normative mode of life. People with challenge seek out change and new experiences and approach them with cognitive flexibility and tolerance for ambiguity.

In addition, several writers also highlight the need to be able to focus under pressure. Focus is not only important in the decision making process itself, but may have a spin-off effect in keeping the executive emotionally able to cope with the difficulties they face. For instance, Quick *et al.* (1990) found the CEOs they interviewed employed a number of different strategies to help them through the difficult times. These involved:

(1) Focusing on the future through planning and goal setting
(2) Focusing on areas where constructive action is possible
(3) Recognising the optimum time to make decisions and then acting

(4)　Not making major decisions alone during a period of extremely high stress and uncertainty
(5)　Maintaining an active and regular schedule during difficult periods.

Looking to the future through planning and goal setting allows executives to focus energy, eliminate surprises and therefore preventatively manage emotional pressure. Quick *et al.* (1990, 53) quote one oil company executive:

> It [planning] minimizes or eliminates surprises, the unknowns. When you [can] do that you have less to worry about . . . down the road. . . I have a list of goals for the company I keep in mind constantly in my daily working environment. As [CEO] the goals and plans for the corporation are foremost and my personal plans must coincide with those to achieve the most success.

Another CEO employed a focused analytic perspective towards his work, that is, during periods of stress he maintained his effectiveness by focusing on areas in which constructive action was possible and by maintaining objectivity.

Risk-taking

Few studies have been done on the senior executive's propensity to take risks. We do know, however, that risk is important and that the fear of unknown risks can exert undue influence on the decision-maker's behaviour.[27]

Also, it would seem that success and measured risk-taking go together at a senior level. MacCrimmon and Wehrung (1990) found that the most successful executives were the biggest risk-takers, while the most mature executives were the most risk-averse. Ford (1977) found that the most profound characteristic which distinguished elite decision makers from other executives was their propensity for making higher-risk decisions. A decision maker with a low aversion to risk, established different objectives, evaluated alternatives differently and selected different solutions from someone in the same situation with a high aversion to risk. Thus, some executives will choose an incremental solution in which the problem is 'nipped at' as opposed to those who adopt 'solution totality' in which the problem is totally attacked.

Ford links risk-taking to the positive or negative mental attitude of the executive. Those with a negative orientation tend to perceive new ideas primarily in terms of potential problems and risks. Positively oriented executives perceive ideas primarily in terms of their profit potential and 'opportunity impact'. Ford argues this distinction is crucial as it establishes two different trains of thought: one is constructive to opportunity, the other destructive. For example, negative thinking executives were more likely to abort new ideas when first introduced and when considering implementation issues. Typical reactions would be, 'It'll never work', 'It's not for us', 'We've tried that before.'

Overall, a positive mental attitude and confidence are related to risk-taking, and the evidence suggests that senior executives are more prone to take risks. Clearly, however, other factors such as the threats facing the organisation and whether the culture of the organisation supports risk-taking will have a bearing on this. However, given the challenges that most senior executives face in a changing world, some degree of risk-taking would seem to be important in moving an organisation forward.

Better thinking

So far, we have argued that executives face particular challenges when trying to tackle problems at a senior level. They need to be able to both see the broad picture and identify from this critical issues and priorities. They need to be aware of the organisational factors which influence the information they receive and how their own perceptual filters, values and overall mental approach affect how this information is interpreted.

In order to gain better insight into these areas, there are three aspects in particular which may be of help. Below, we discuss the notion of balanced thinking, how to challenge mental models, and review an increasingly popular technique senior executives use called cognitive mapping.

Balanced thinking

Mintzberg (1976) gives a flavour of what balanced thinking involves when he argues that effective decision making at the policy level requires the solid analytical input of planners and management scientists – but that 'soft' information and intuitive hunches are crucial as well. In short, 'organisational effectiveness does not lie in the narrow minded concept called 'rationality'; it lies in a blend of clear-headed logic and powerful intuition'. Isenberg (1984) reinforces this notion in his finding that when senior managers 'use analysis for a prolonged period of time, it is always in conjunction with intuition'.

Agor (1986a) also sees the necessity for a balance between analytical and intuitive approaches at the top. In his study, many top executives stressed that good intuitive decisions were, in part, based on input from facts and experiences gained over the years, combined and integrated with a well-honed sensitivity or openness to other, more conscious processes.

Latting (1985) outlines principles which may help achieve balanced thinking:

(1) Temper rational thought with intuitive preference
(2) Use 'opening-up' techniques to bring sublimated data about a situation into awareness
(3) Avoid censorship of ideas during their generation
(4) View divergent, even contradictory, ideas with respect rather than with scepticism or defensiveness
(5) Never ignore internal warnings that something is wrong
(6) Check any rational problem solving method to see whether it feels intuitively good in process and in the final decision
(7) Remain constantly self-aware

Challenging mental models

It is perhaps this latter point (concerning self-awareness) which tends to be emphasised when writers examine senior executive decision making. Most recently, Senge (1990a) has highlighted the need to acknowledge and challenge mental models. He believes many of the best ideas in organisations never get put into practice. One reason is that new insights and initiatives often conflict with established mental models. Thus, the task is to challenge assumptions without invoking defensiveness. Consequently, he recommends that when advocating a view, the individual should:

- Explain the reasoning and data that led to their view
- Encourage others to test their view by asking, 'Do you see gaps in my reasoning? Do you disagree with the data upon which my view is based?'
- Encourage others to provide different views (for example, Do you have different data, different conclusions or both?')

When inquiring into others' views executives need to:

- Actively seek to understand the others' view, rather than simply restating their own view and how it differs from theirs
- Make their attributions about the other and the other's view explicit (for example, 'Based on your statement that. . .', 'I am assuming that you believe. . .', 'Am I representing your views fairly?')

Cognitive mapping

The importance of revealing one's assumptions and views of the world is also reflected in the growing area of cognitive mapping. Cognitive mapping is a process used to investigate and depict the frames of reference or mental models people adopt. Such mapping processes help describe the ways in which managers distil and interpret the significance of events around them and also highlight the assumptions they make when doing so. It also helps managers to see the interrelatedness of the problems they face.[28]

Fiol and Huff (1992) note that cognitive mapping tools are of increasing importance to managers. They have the advantage of:

- Using graphic imagery to help managers make sense of complexity
- Helping simplify ideas and facilitate their transmission to others
- Being neutral ways of putting forward ideas and allowing them to be more easily debated and modified

Several different types of cognitive map have been tested with managers. For instance, work has been carried out to see how mapping can help executives understand how different strategic alternatives in their organisation are perceived by the top team[29] and how managers assess their competitive position.[30]

In Citibank, a mapping process was used frequently by one particular senior executive in charge of the bank's financial institutions business in Europe. Ian Cormack spent a significant proportion of his time thinking through and then producing visual maps or representations of the complex financial markets in which the various business divisions under his supervision operated. In particular, they were used to identify who the main players in any one market were and focus attention on what drove the competitive forces in a market. He would discuss and refine these maps with various members of his senior team to help them gain a shared understanding of these markets and then prioritise the ways in which each division could increase its competitiveness. Over time these were updated, revised and developed. In the process, they helped people within the organisation keep abreast of the major (and frequently diverse) factors which impinged on the business.

Mazneviski *et al.* (1993) describe a mapping process which helped identify several inadequacies in the way one senior team viewed their business. They looked at the management group of a small life insurance company and collected data to build organisational cause maps: that is, maps showing assumptions between cause and effect relationships between key variables such as company success and quality of products.[31] In 1987, using a set of SWOT analyses they compiled a consensual map (see Figure 2.4) displaying seven themes: product quality, service quality, employee quality, internal operations technology and broker/distributor relations. In the map, the size of the concept's circle is proportional to the number of statements related to it. Weak causal relationships are shown with broken arrows, and strong relationships are shown with full arrows.

Several points are important about this study. As a group, the managers perceived no causal connection between internal operations, such as accounting efficiency measures and company success, either through a direct or indirect route. Additionally, while every manager identified the relationship between product quality and the success of the company, few managers noted the importance of service quality and company success. Several new executives who joined the company after this map had been produced found a great lack of service infrastructure, such as policy manuals and systems for updating customers' policies.

In 1990 these results were presented to a new group of executives. They described the 1987 causal map as a 'recipe for suicide in this industry'. They were shocked at the lack of emphasis on service. They declared that any organisation that operated under the 1987 assumptions would either have to change or fail. Armed with the insights gained from the 1987 map, the executives produced a second map in 1990 which enabled them to engage in a dialogue about concerns such as, 'How can we change our attitude towards people? Why aren't there more financial indicators in here? There is nothing here about understanding competitors – why not?' The process helped not only with understanding company issues, but also with helping the executives understand how their own behaviour either perpetuated or helped solve these issues.

Fig. 2.4 *Organisational cause map 1987*

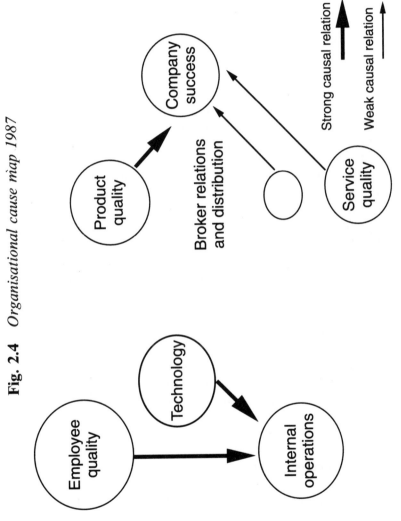

Source: Maznieviski *et al.* (1993)

BREADTH AND FOCUS – THE CAPABLE MIND

In this chapter we have emphasised the importance of Breadth and Focus for the senior executive. Challenging mental models and cognitive mapping techniques are largely aimed at improving one's breadth of outlook.

As we have also seen, Breadth is more appropriate in some circumstances and Focus in others. Brunnson (1985), for instance, argues we may benefit from using multiple sense-making frameworks to appraise events; but we are more likely to act forcefully and effectively if we see things simply. Thus, Breadth is most appropriate when one is trying to understand the environment, identify problems, seek alternatives and find solutions. It is needed when one needs to think outside one's current paradigm, see new possibilities and identify linkages.

Focus, on the other hand, is more appropriate when selecting alternatives, choosing solutions and implementing them. When focusing, there may be a greater reliance on analysis and on a narrower frame of reference to help distil critical elements and prioritise them.

However, Breadth and Focus alone do not give an entire understanding of the executive's overall mindset. As we stated earlier, we also need to consider the emotional maturity of the executive and whether their disposition is positive or negative. An executive not only responds in terms of their Focus or Breadth of outlook, but also in terms of their confidence and positive approach, or lack of it.

To illustrate these points, we have combined Breadth and Focus, and Positive and Negative mental dispositions to produce an overall model of the senior executive mindset which is described below.

An executive mindset model

Figure 2.5 displays four executive mindsets: the Despondent, Conservative, Bounded and Flexible Mindsets. These are not permanent states, and individuals may change from one to another. Indeed, the Capable Executive should be able to move between a Bounded and Flexible set. However, there are consequences of having each one.

Fig. 2.5 *Executive mindset*

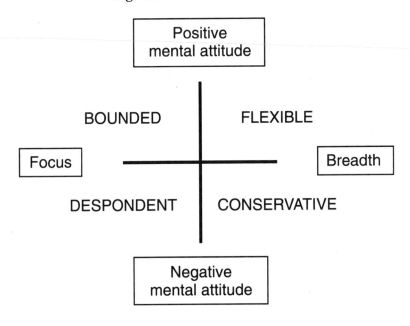

The despondent mindset

Executives have a negative attitude and narrow outlook. Says Ohmae (1982), 'Their attitude almost always turns out to be some variation on: "The way things are, there's not much we can do"'. Often, executives who are operating in general management positions but are overly reliant on their technical expertise exhibit such a mindset. Executives whose predominant mindset is despondent and narrow in focus, typically do not produce optimum results in senior level positions.

The conservative mindset

The individual may have Breadth, see interlinkages and accommodate a wide range of information, but their attitudinal response is to emphasise why things cannot be done, or the hurdles against achieving particular goals. The executive here is typically risk-averse.

A Conservative mindset has its advantages. It can prevent ill-considered judgements being made, and is important in keeping people's feet on the ground. An executive with this mindset may, however, also miss opportunities. For it exemplifies the critic rather than the creator. Their preferred response of 'can't do' rather than 'can do', limits not only themselves but their judgement of what others are capable of achieving. Here, it is not a lack of analysis, but a lack of confidence which is the major problem.

This mindset is illustrated by the case of GM, and Swatch the watch manufacturers. For years these two companies discussed a plan to produce an electric car. In 1991 Swatch announced a joint venture with Volkswagon. The slowness of GM caused by excessive analysis of competitive trends frustrated Swatch enough to move on.[32] The major problem with this mindset is that in a dynamic and quickly changing world, by the time executives are prepared to act, events may have passed them by.

The bounded mindset

This displays confidence and a positive mental attitude, but takes a narrow focus. This mindset is best adopted in situations where there is a clear direction and the executive does not need to worry about scanning the environment or questioning the path being taken. Indeed, in some circumstances (particularly in extremely difficult times when the executive has to drive through difficult change) it may be impossible to succeed without such a mindset. A manager from Isenberg's (1984) research who turned around a subsidiary in 100 days illustrates this: '. . . I dropped all outside activities. Now I have a feeling of just having emerged, like a chap who's been taken by a surf wave and rolled . . . It has been like a single minded rage or madness. At the end of the 100 days, somehow I have awakened. It was overwhelming'.

This mindset can also be a liability. Having confidence, but too narrow a focus at the wrong time, or wrong stage of the decision-making process, can lead to complacency or arrogance. In a survey of top level executives by the Vandermerwes (1991), complacency and a low sense of urgency were cited as the second most important obstacles to making strategic change happen. They described complacency as a kind of 'passive resistance' which happens when things are going too well.

The flexible mindset

This combines a broad outlook with a positive mental attitude. Here, one is positive but also willing to accept a broad range of data, to recognise interrelationships between issues and operate both in the short and long-term. With this mindset, one seeks alternative ways forward based on the underlying assumption that somewhere, there is a solution.

Executives can only develop new directions for their organisations if they have mental resilience, mental flexibility and creative approaches to problem solving. The Flexible mindset is critical during changing times. However, if executives constantly review their position and look for data once a direction has been set, this may be debilitating and create uncertainty for others. As Mintzberg and Waters (1985) point out, when convergent and not divergent thinking is required, a Flexible mindset can lead to unnecessary change and review.

Thus, different mindsets may be more appropriate depending on the circumstances. Capable executives can think more broadly but also focus themselves (and others) when necessary. They also avoid staying in one mindset for too long. Complacency has brought many executives to the brink of personal (and organisational) disaster, but overflexibility may inhibit executives from driving forward quickly.

SUMMARY

Senior executives deal with issues which are complex, interrelated and difficult to solve. They do so under conditions of uncertainty, pressure and ambiguity. If handled badly, the decisions taken by senior executives can have serious consequences for a range of stakeholders in the organisation.

Several factors influence the executive's problem solving and decision making capacity. Executives need to be able to 'see the big picture' as well as bring focus to the problems they face. They must be aware of the social and political processes in organisations which can distort the data senior people receive. In addition, they need to be aware of how their own internal frames of reference or ways of viewing the world can filter and interpret data. For example, the values and beliefs an executive holds can have a very strong influence on how a situation or problem is perceived.

Executives must also be aware of the cognitive processes which affect how they analyse and act on data. Historically, executives have been encouraged to use rational thinking processes. Increasingly, other more intuitive and creative capacities are being emphasised. In order to develop such capacities, the executive must guard against complacency, entrenched habits and defensive behaviour which can serve to protect traditional ways of thinking about and viewing problems.

The emotional responses of executives to the problems, pressures and difficulties they face can also impact on their decision making ability. In particular, positive thinking, openness to change and the capacity to take measured risks all influence the quality of executive decision making.

A number of different techniques exist to help executives question and challenge the assumptions they make and the mindsets they adopt. Cognitive mapping is being used at senior levels in some organisations to help executives understand how different strategic options are perceived and how managers assess their competitive position. With regard to mindset, a model has been put forward which describes four particular mindsets executives may adopt and the consequences of each. It demonstrates how decision making can be influenced both by one's analytical perspective and emotional outlook.

The executive's mental capacity and emotional makeup (the Cognitive and Maturity Capabilities) underscore the rest of the Capabilities in this book. For Jacobs and Jaques (1987), however, cognitive capacity is the most critical element in leadership. Whilst important, the authors also see other Capabilities playing a part. Executives need Capabilities which both help them understand the critical elements of their environment, and direct and shape those elements to best advantage. In the proceeding chapters we explore these elements in detail.

NOTES

1. M. Lynn's Profile of Clive Thompson in *Management Today*, November, 1993, 68–70.
2. See Hickson *et al.* (1986).
3. See Kearns and Nadler (1992, 210).
4. Schroder *et al.* (1967) also talk about something similar with their notion of 'integrative complexity'. They see two components of information processing:

   (1) Differentiation – perception of many dimensions when evaluating an event
   (2) Integration – combining and connecting those dimensions.

5. See Brian Dumaine's article, 'What's So Hot About Outsiders?', *Fortune*, vol. 128, no. 14, 29 November 1993, 40–3.
6. 'Picture Imperfect', *The Economist*, 28 May 1994, 59–60.
7. Mintzberg (1973).
8. Alex Taylor III, 'U.S. Cars Come Back', *Fortune*, vol. 126, no. 11, 16 November 1992, 24–53.
9. Mintzberg (1973) and Kotter (1982) note the importance of networks. See also Chapter 4.
10. Kearns and Nadler (1992, 113).
11. Within the social sciences, terms like 'paradigm' have multiple meanings. Kuhn (1962) is perhaps the most well known user of the term. Possibly the most influential paradigm framework in organisation studies is that of Burrell and Morgan (1979). In management circles a paradigm is seen more simply. In his article, 'Nothing Is Impossible' (*Fortune*, 23 September 1991, 79–84), John Huey describes it as being the 'conventional wisdom about how things have always been done and must continue to be done'.
12. See Mazneviski *et al.* (1993).
13. See Watzlawick *et al.* (1974). They propose four basic strategies for reframing such problematic situations. Namely:

    (1) Redefine undesirable elements to make them appear more desirable, or vice versa
    (2) Re-label elements so they acquire new meanings
    (3) Ignore elements that you cannot change
    (4) Try overtly to achieve the opposite of what you want.

14. See Anita Roddick's (1992) book, *Body and Soul*, London: Vermilion, 1992, p. 23.
15. Stratford Sherman, 'How Will We Live With The Tumult?', *Fortune*, vol. 128, no. 15, 13 December 1993, 59–61.
16. Organ and Bateman (1986).
17. Russell Mitchell and Michael Oneal, 'Managing By Values: Is Levi Strauss' Approach Visionary – or Flaky?', *Business Week*, 12 September 1994, 38–43.
18. See 'Decisions at the Top: Do's and Don'ts', from the Rohrer, Hibler and Replogle Newsletter, *For CEOs Only*, reprinted in *Drake Business Review*, vol. 6, no. 1, 1992.
19. Nutt (1990) has used the MBTI with senior executives to understand their decision-making processes. He argues that despite a wide number of instruments developed to measure decision style only the MBTI has both conceptual and empirical support as a decision-style measure.
20. Cited in Behling and Neckel (1991).
21. See Kelly (1993).
22. Andrew Campbell, 'The Point is to Raise the Game', *Financial Times*, 14 September 1994, 10.
23. Although not completely polarised, there are, nevertheless, two fairly distinct contrasting views on this issue. One position is that highly intuitive

and creative executives are likely to have been born with a preference for intuitive decision making or have acquired it in early childhood. Thus, selection rather than development may be the preferred route.The alternative position is that creativity and intuition are not innate and can be developed in some way or other.

24. Kearns and Nadler (1992, 210).
25. See Staw (1981).
26. Stratford Sherman, 'Leaders Learn to Heed the Voice Within', *Fortune*, vol. 130, no. 4, 22 August 1994, 72–8.
27. Janis and Mann (1977).
28. Mapping processes come in various forms. Tony Buzan, author of *The Mind Map Book* (1993) has developed the process over many years. See also Anderson (1993).
29. See Cliff Bowman and Gerry Johnson, 'Surfacing Managerial Patterns of Competitive Strategy; Interventions in Strategy Debates'. Paper presented at the American Academy of Management Conference, Miami, Florida, 1991.
30. Porac *et al.* (1987).
31. Mazneviski *et al.* (1993) looked at organisational schemas rather than individual ones (although individual schemas form the basis of their research). An organisational schema is a set of knowledge, assumptions and norms which guide thinking and behaviour for organisational members. In some companies it is strong and explicit, in others it is weak and implicit. An organisational schema is the result of interaction among the group of managers who determine the direction of the organisation, usually the top management team. Organisational schemas have been pursued much less intensively than individual schemas.
32. See Zahra and Chaples (1993).

3 The Development Capability: Building and Maintaining Senior Managers' Capacity to Learn

INTRODUCTION

Changes in the global economic and technical environment are so radical and far reaching that many practitioners and commentators now claim that the capacity to learn is the only true source of sustainable competitive advantage.[1] Those at the top of the organisation have a particular responsibility to exemplify this kind of behaviour. Not only do they themselves need to change and adapt, they also act as powerful role models for others in the organisation.

Whether all executives are up to this task is an open question. Clearly, without some ability to learn, few would ever reach the top and the linkage between learning and success as an executive seems clearly established by research both in the US and the UK.[2] However, the ability to learn is not a quality all executives are blessed with at all times. Harper (1992) discovered that while many CEOs have found it tough at the top due to factors such as intense foreign competition, the high cost of capital and changing government regulations – quite a few of the difficulties were a result of an inability or unwillingness to keep pace with changing times. In a major survey of corporate directors, Mumford (1988b) found the ability to learn was not a particular characteristic of those he interviewed. Indeed, Argyris (1991, 99) comments:

> Those members of the organisation that many assume to be the best at learning are, in fact, not very good at it. I am talking about the well educated, high-powered, high-commitment professionals who occupy key leadership positions in the modern corporation. Most don't even know a problem exists.

There have been considerable changes in the past few years both in terms of attitudes to executive development and the seriousness and professionalism with which some organisations have tackled this area. Some companies have been at the forefront of executive development such as GE, GTE, Xerox, Motorola, Lockheed and Hewlett-Packard.[3]

However, these organisations appear to be the exception and other, more fundamental, problems remain. For instance, there is very limited research on how senior executives learn and develop. In part, this is due to a strong resistance amongst many senior executives and companies to the idea that senior people need any special developmental help. As one senior HR manager we interviewed said, 'If they don't know what they're doing then they shouldn't be in the job.' Furthermore, there is criticism of the programmes provided for senior executives by external training institutions.

Ironically, if there is one area where massive strides could and should be made it must be in the development of senior level executives. It is this very group which is faced with new and constantly changing realities; they need to be able to prepare their firms to play by very different rules against increasingly tough competitors. In practice, however, senior level managers are often seen as the ones who need least assistance. The consequences of this are profound. If, as Schein argues, 'organisational learning depends on individual learning'[4] then the chance of building adaptive, flexible and learning organisations is much more circumscribed if those in senior positions are unable to learn and develop themselves.

In this chapter we distinguish between learning and development, and describe in outline what these involve. We examine the ways in which the various Capabilities (described in Chapter 1) may be developed. We also look at the particular hurdles senior executives have to overcome in order to learn and develop in the executive role. Finally, we outline the type of opportunities open to executives interested in pursuing their own development.

Definitions of learning and development

There are no agreed definitions of, or distinctions between, learning and development. Indeed, both encompass a range of different meanings and the concepts are often used interchangeably. Mumford (1988b) notes that there are only a small number of definitions of learning as applied to managers. One of the few is Kolb's (1984) description as, '. . . the process whereby knowledge is created through the transformation of experience'. Honey and Mumford (1986) take the concept beyond Kolb's emphasis on the creation or acquisition of knowledge, arguing that learning has occurred if managers know or can do something they could not before.

This view emphasises learning as the acquisition of knowledge and behaviour. Development is usually seen as something more. Pedler and Boydell (1985) argue that development does not simply involve an increase in knowledge or an improvement in one's skill base but '. . .is a different state of being or functioning'. Mumford (1988b) believes that most authors view learning in relation to issues of definable and immediate concern and in terms of the incremental acquisition of knowledge, skills and abilities. Development is more concerned with a qualitative transformation which Hodgson (1988) has described as a breakthrough to a new level of potential.

The distinction between learning and development is important. We define development as the capacity to acknowledge, confront and change deeply held patterns of thinking and behaving. This is a much more profound process than learning, which is the modification or acquisition of knowledge or new behaviours and a mechanism through which development occurs. While executives learn a whole range of different things, many on a daily basis, most of these do not lead to development. While learning is important, the pace of industrial and technological change in today's organisations demands a more fundamental shift in top managers' thinking and behaviour. Hence the importance of the Development Capability.

HOW MANAGERS LEARN AND DEVELOP

This distinction can be highlighted further by looking at some of the general principles associated with these two processes. (Although, unfortunately, authors do not often use clear labels to distinguish between learning and development in the way noted above.) Two descriptions are particularly relevant to senior executives. The first, by Argyris (1991), distinguishes between 'single loop' and 'double loop' learning. Single loop learning involves dealing with problems as they are currently defined. Double loop learning occurs when individuals or organisations challenge the definition and the circumstances through which the issues requiring learning occur. In this sense double loop learning is more akin to a developmental process. Single loop learning is appropriate for routine and

Fig. 3.1 *Kolb's learning cycle*

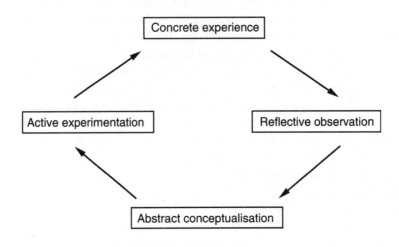

Source: Kolb (1984)

programmed issues: double loop learning addresses underlying individual and organisational values and assumptions.

Double loop learning involves observation, reflection and testing. Although presented differently, these factors are also evident in Kolb's (1984) model (see Figure 3.1). His model emphasises learning as a process which is derived from concrete experience involving reflection and experimentation. Reflection and experimentation are important to both learning and development, but it is important to emphasise that the intended outcomes are different. Using the definition we put forward earlier, learning is more about pattern modification; that is, learning about new IT applications or developing one's negotiation skills. Development, which involves radically reframing behaviours or patterns of thinking, is a much more difficult process (see Figure 3.2).

Whether pattern modification or pattern reframing is necessary, depends on several factors which we pursue throughout this chapter. In principle, however, development can be seen to revolve around three major issues (Figure 3.3).

(1) *Where the executive wants to be.* This is concerned with understanding what aspects the executive needs to develop. It involves thinking through the requirements of the job and understanding the qualities (or Capabilities) needed to do the job.

Fig. 3.2 *Executive learning and development*

Thought patterns

Concerned with acquiring or 'bolting on' new knowledge

Applies to *Executive Understanding* – e.g., learning about new markets; cultures technologies

Behavioural patterns

Concerned with acquiring or 'bolting on' new behaviours

Applies to *Executive Understanding* – e.g., the improvement of behavioural skills such as negotiation; delegation etc.

Pattern modification (learning)

Extending patterns

Concerned with radical changes in thinking

Applies to changing the *Executive Mind* – e.g., results in paradigm shifts; a global mindset; customer focus.

Concerned with radical changes in behaviour

Applies to changing the *Executive Mind* – e.g., developing complex behaviours such as transformational leadership.

Reordering patterns

Pattern reframing (development)

Fig. 3.3   *Executive development*

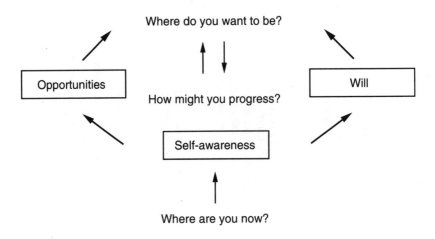

(2) *Where the executive is now.* This requires a degree of self-awareness on the part of the individual. The executive needs some sense of his or her personal strengths and weaknesses in relation to the Capabilities. Also important, is some understanding of which areas will be most critical to the executive's future progress.

(3) *How the executive might progress.* Executives need the will and motivation to reduce the gap between what is required for the role and the executive's current range of Capabilities. They can then seek opportunities both within the organisation and externally to enhance their effectiveness.

(1)   Understanding what has to be developed

One approach to deciding what the executive needs to develop is to first understand what the job requires and the qualities needed to fulfil these requirements. The resulting gap then becomes the focus of attention. We have suggested earlier (see Chapter 1) that the requirements of the senior executive role can be broadly grouped around the issues of Establishing, Enabling and Enacting. The qualities the executive needs can be seen in terms of the 11 Capabilities we outlined.

Both the requirements of the job and the qualities needed to perform in the role will need to be customised at an individual level. Nevertheless, the executive needs some general sense of how the Capabilities can be developed. We have therefore grouped these into four different categories which are outlined below:

(a) *Executive understanding.* Included in the first group are those Capabilities which are primarily concerned with executive knowledge and understanding. Namely, the Expertise, Organisational, and External Capabilities.

All of these seem to be important areas for the executive to grasp. For example, Evans (1992)[5] argues that it is vital not to lose sight of technical and functional expertise simply because other aspects such as leadership ability are more topical. Similarly, understanding the critical organisational components is important if executives are to implement change successfully. Moreover, increasingly, executives are being called upon to understand global issues – an aspect of the External Capability. Like other broad concepts, globalisation needs to be translated and understood within the requirements of the executive's own job. However, it has become a topic which cannot be ignored. Conger (1993) argues that future leaders will have to become globally aware. A survey by Harper (1992) found that globalisation of the firm's operations and international competition was the first or second most frequently cited issue of importance for the future. A different survey of nearly 1 500 managers in major US, European and Asian firms came to a similar conclusion.[6] It noted, however, that executives rated their company's effectiveness at developing a 'global orientation or mindset' last, out of a list of over 30 organisational competencies.

(b) *Executive behaviour.* The second group we identify covers those Capabilities concerned with improving executive behaviour and action; that is, the interpersonal Capabilities of Influence, Integration, and Leadership. Whilst all three are important, the need for effective leadership to transform organisations is increasingly seen as particularly critical at senior levels. However, improving these complex skill areas is a different (and frequently more difficult) process than improving executive understanding.

(c) *Executive mind.* As we discussed in Chapter 2, how executives think, their breadth and focus as well as the mindset they adopt, fundamentally influence how they operate at senior levels. The Cognitive and Maturity Capabilities are therefore included in this group. Executives need to be able to see how issues inter-relate, to think creatively and work outside traditional norms if they are to function strategically. For those moving from a senior, functional position into general management this may demand a radical reframing of an executive's thought patterns.

(d) *Self-directed development.* Ultimately, the Development Capability is not only about what is understood and applied, but how one goes about this process. Hall and Foulkes (1991) and McCall *et al.* (1994) maintain that because the business environment is changing so rapidly, executives have to be strong self-learners. Barham and Oates (1991) concluded that the 'international manager must know how to learn'. Several writers have found that the ability to learn from experience was a predictor of later acquisition of executive skills or of eventual executive success, or lack of it.[7] (However, again it is important to emphasise that if this learning process only results in pattern modification the executive may not develop fully.) As Figure 3.4 illustrates, self-directed development can be seen as the driving force for developing in the other areas.

This final category is concerned not only with executives' ability to understand their job, organisation and the business world: it is also about having the capacity to understand themselves. This involves awareness of strengths and weaknesses, the ability to seek out and use feedback and recognise one's personal limitations. This is usually a difficult process often involving pattern reframing. Nevertheless, according to Hall (1986), the ability to understand or at least review one's self-concept is critical to improving the adaptability of the executive.

More progress has been made in some of the categories identified above than in others. In the area of Executive Understanding, emphasising knowledge-based Capabilities, individual executives, corporations and development professionals have made great strides. Progress elsewhere has been less evident. This is partly because of the difficulties involved but also because less effort has been expended in these areas. While many skills can be learnt, how one develops the more complex leadership qualities needed to reposition organisations is less clear. While we can learn to think differently about some issues, reframing thought processes so that the executive can see the

Fig. 3.4 *What has to be developed – critical areas*

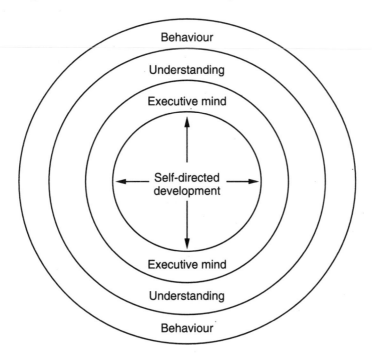

implications of a range of interrelated issues at several degrees of complexity is a challenge few have answers to. Moreover, self-directed development at senior levels is an area that has yet to be fully explored.

The organisational context

Development also has to be seen within an organisational context. At a senior level there is a need to balance corporate and personal development.[8] While individual needs must be met, development processes have to accommodate the necessity to achieve strategic goals and shape company culture. As a recent survey of executive education highlighted, companies are focusing more attention on linking the process of management and executive development with their firm's strategic imperatives.[9]

When outlining the factors that constitute a good executive programme, Kotter (1982) highlighted ones with a strong corporate emphasis; for example, the need to establish corporate identity, to communicate and implement corporate strategy, and to shape and manage culture and create strategic unity. Indeed, many CEOs have come to use executive education as an important tool for achieving their strategic agendas. Bolt (1993) reflects on how the programmes at Northern Telecom, Xerox and Motorola had an impact in terms of shaping the culture, and communicating and implementing corporate strategy. David Kearns, the former CEO of Xerox, used the company's Senior Management Programme to 'make the corporate strategy their strategy'. Robert Galvin, CEO of Motorola, used executive education to jolt his senior team into really reviewing the seriousness of the competitive threat represented by the Far East.

(2)   Where the executive is now – improving self-awareness

If personal development is to occur, executives must have some knowledge of their own specific strengths and weaknesses and consequently the gap between their ideal and the reality. Identifying the size of this gap can be problematic. Kotter (1982) found that many of the general managers in his study were 'surprisingly inarticulate' when asked about their strengths and weaknesses. Only two of the 15 general managers in his study gave answers which seemed to fit the facts he had gathered from other sources. All the executives felt they could manage anything successfully, displaying little conscious awareness of the specialised nature of their skills, knowledge and relationships.

Mumford (1988b) notes that many of the directors he surveyed lacked any help in establishing their actual levels of performance in required areas of competence. Equally, Kaplan *et al.* (1985) found a reluctance (and sometimes an adamant refusal) on the part of executives to admit weakness or acknowledge any need for improvement. We also found discrepancies between an executive's self-assessment of their performance and others' assessments. Our own research shows that only around 40 per cent of executives had a fairly accurate picture of themselves with respect to the Capabilities when we compared their assessments with those of their peers, staff members and senior managers.

This lack of awareness has consequences worth emphasising. To be unaware of the impact one has on others leaves the executive in a very vulnerable position. This is particularly true if an executive is promoted into a senior position based on their past successes – which may now be less relevant. For example, 'virtues' such as competitiveness, functional expertise and the ability to do everything alone become vices at board level where there is a need to work as a team member and manage through the structure.[10] McCall and Lombardo (1983) discovered that executives who 'derailed' often found themselves in a changed situation where strengths that had served them well earlier in their careers became liabilities later that threw them off-track. Moreover, Kotter (1982) sees the 'I can do anything syndrome' as a disease which only affects the strong and successful. Unfortunately, this disease often shows up when a person tries to do something in a very different environment. This can have a regressive effect on the careers of even very talented people.

In a later work, Lombardo and McCauley (1988) argued executive 'derailment' is associated with six basic flaws. These included problems with interpersonal relationships, moulding staff, not making strategic transitions, a failure to follow through and overdependence on a person or idea. Equally Kaplan *et al.* (1985) found the most common defects at a senior level included difficulty in thinking strategically; trouble adjusting to a job with huge scope and a proclivity for viewing all problems through the lens of one's speciality. A common theme they all mention is that executives must continue to be self-aware and improve once they reach a senior position. Otherwise, there is a danger that they will fail to make the transition into senior management which typically involves more highly challenging, ambiguous and complex tasks.

Individual hurdles to improving self-awareness

Why do some executives have difficulty coming to terms with their limitations? One factor relates to the process of introspection and reflection. Although assessing oneself is the first step towards improvement, getting executives to reflect on their own performance can be like drawing teeth. Kaplan *et al.* (1985) offer several possible reasons for this. Faced with staggering unremitting demands on their time, introspection is rarely a priority for executives. Furthermore, it does not solve immediate tangible problems like turning a plant around, improving profits or boosting productivity. Executives who do not see a connection between introspection and performance are understandably unwilling to put the time and energy that looking inward requires.

Executives also work in an atmosphere which makes self-development particularly difficult. Factors such as power, success, acquired expertise, personal ambition and the need to look highly competent, often act together to prevent the executive from achieving personal growth. This is related to a more complex factor: development often affects one's self-concept. In many ways a strong sense of self is crucial to the effectiveness and well being of the executive.[11] Without this, executives would not have the confidence to cope with the many demanding challenges they face. A sense of self provides individuals with boundaries, conviction, purpose, values, beliefs and guides their actions. However, our self-concept can also be tender and vulnerable and we build defences around it to protect ourselves.

Although these defences preserve our sanity they can also be the enemy of development.[12] They can prevent the executive from exploring new areas, taking risks, taking on new knowledge and tolerating ambiguity. They may also be less prepared to allow for mistakes and let go of things learnt previously – even although they are no longer relevant. The problem for senior executives is that these natural defences are compounded by other factors. As people in high positions continually draw fire, they learn to be 'thick skinned' and protect themselves from criticism. As managers become more able to shore themselves up, their motivation and ability to change diminishes.

If any real improvement is to take place, executives have to find ways to explore their strengths and weaknesses. If they do not know where their potential limitations lie, what gaps need to be reduced, or what strengths should be consolidated, they cannot exploit developmental opportunities. Indeed, without self-awareness, their chances of corporate survival may be severely diminished.

Organisational hurdles to self-awareness

Organisations can also prevent improvements in self-awareness. Executives who are not blinded by power, success and ambition and who wish to explore gaps in their performance are rarely in an environment which is conducive to doing this. At higher levels in the organisation there are much fewer people to confide in and, consequently, the potential for sharing and developing through others is more limited. Indeed, it can be difficult, if not dangerous, to talk about one's limitations in the competitive, and often political, climate in which the executive works.

Development can be inhibited by several organisational factors including the provision of a limited range of opportunities to experiment, a restrictive culture, the attitudes of one's senior manager, colleagues and staff, limited rewards for risk-taking and punishment for errors.[13] Indeed, Kaplan *et al.* (1985) argue that when an executive has problems, they are either moved, or people around them are moved, to new positions. Much less frequently do organisations attempt to create movement within the executive – that is, to encourage the executive's personal and managerial growth. If the company's culture neither tolerates failure nor promotes risk taking, high-potential managers become reluctant to accept developmental assignments. Thus real development, especially that involving the self-concept, tends to get lost in the day-to-day demands of running a competitive business.[14]

Balancing individual and organisational factors – feedback and appraisal

A major way of helping executives understand their strengths and weaknesses, at least in theory, is to provide performance feedback. The value of feedback in development is well recognised.[15] The formal method of doing this is through the performance appraisal process. Indeed, Longenecker and Gioia (1988, 1992) maintain that executives need more performance information than most other employees because of the sophisticated and more ambiguous nature of their jobs, and because their responsibilities and priorities change often. Moreover, there are serious organisational consequences of ineffective performance from senior managers. Their study found that executives did indeed want appraisals so that they could get feedback on how to improve, to talk about long-term and 'big picture' issues as well as review what they had done in the past year.

At the executive level, however, formal appraisals rarely seem to be well handled. Longenecker and Gioia found that upper level executives denigrated the appraisal process and that the quality of appraisals reduced as one rose in the organisation. Typically, performance appraisals at the executive level were done infrequently and irregularly. When they were done, they were very rushed and informal and tended to lack specific details about performance. Reasons for this included time pressure, a lack of conviction on the part of the superior that appraisals are an important and necessary part of managing people and the 'myth' that higher level people should be self-directive and therefore appraisals should be more or less unnecessary.

Mumford (1988b) also acknowledges the problems of performance appraisals at a senior level. Issues of status, skill, experience and competition for senior positions often prevent a proper process occurring. He admits, '. . . the bland assumption inherent in most of these appraisal processes, that needs will be properly identified and appropriate solutions defined, can only be put down to an unfortunate combination of naivety and ignorance'.

Clearly, not all appraisals are handled badly and some manage the process well. In a survey of CEOs, Harper (1992) found that nearly 30 per cent cited 'discovering and advancing new talent' and 'seeing people grow' as the most rewarding area of management, all of which implies some motivation to help executives review their performance. However, as we pointed out earlier, breaching the individual's self-concept is no easy process. One CEO in this study commented, '. . . Developing higher order competence in managers is incredibly frustrating. Most of them can't conquer their own fragile egos'. Executives often have the power to put themselves outside the appraisal system and only the most senior director can urge their participation.

This also applies to other forms of potential feedback. Great benefit can be derived (particularly on interpersonal issues) from others' feedback. However, it is a brave (some might say foolhardy) person who will point out an executive's limitations if he or she is in a less powerful position. Upward 'truth telling' is not a common activity in most organisations. Nor is this helped by the practice many executives adopt of surrounding themselves with compatible people who 'fit in'. Nevertheless, increasingly, 360-degree feedback (from senior managers, peers and staff members) is gradually taking hold in some of the more progressive organisations, particularly in the US. On balance, most executives who have undergone such a feedback process regarded it as beneficial. In our experience, it is not the feedback alone which is important but the opportunity to discuss its implications for the individual's development.

Thus, the need to have an accurate understanding of the executive's present qualities is important, but not straightforward. It requires both individual and organisational effort. Moreover, what works at more junior levels needs to be tempered for senior executives. For instance, most agree that more formal feedback mechanisms such as assessment centres at a senior level are of limited value. However, some companies have introduced the notion of what Iles (1992) calls 'development' centres. This concept is less concerned with assessment or rejection, but with helping managers identify strengths and weaknesses as well as development plans with no evaluative criteria attached. Also, the process is carried out in less threatening environments. Certainly such an environment is more likely to reduce the hurdles associated with improving self-awareness summarised in Table 3.1.

Table 3.1 Constraints on improving self-awareness

Personal hurdles	• Limited time to reflect
	• Trappings of power and success
	• Self concept vulnerability
Organisation hurdles	• Few people to confide in
	• Limited encouragement
	• Restrictive culture
Joint hurdles	• Inadequate organisational processes for giving feedback
	• Personal reluctance to seek feedback

(3) How executives can progress

Armed with some understanding of possible strengths and weaknesses the executive is potentially in a stronger position to exploit personal growth opportunities. Acting on this understanding, however, is an entirely different matter.

Will and motivation

In principle, self-directed development is premised on the individual being aware of performance gaps as well as having the will and opportunity to change. As we stated earlier, however, pattern reframing – the process of self-development – is a difficult route. It usually involves, at the very least, some degree of tension and sometimes a degree of distress.[16] Pattern reframing, as Braddick (1988) implies, requires the unlearning of old habits or patterns. This unfreezing process is often accompanied by tension.[17] Moreover, when individuals face new and difficult circumstances they may have to deal with shock, anger, bargaining and depression during the transition period.[18] (See also Chapter 9 which describes ways of managing oneself through such changes.)

Whilst there are important end benefits to self-development, the process can be very tough. When executives are called upon to look at the world in very different ways, review and possibly relearn complex and demanding skills – and to do this when the organisation is in difficulty – personal growth can be a hard experience. Reframing patterns of thinking or behaving demands not only an intellectual ability to review and reflect on one's actions, but a more fundamental degree of self-confrontation. Unless the individual is highly motivated, or has some strong external reward or encouragement to continue, the process will not occur.

Timing

It is also important to see personal development within a temporal context. Executives will be more receptive to personal change at some points than at others. For example, receptivity is usually higher when an executive takes over a new job. Gabarro (1987) notes how learning is considerable and novel at the start of a new job and becomes more incremental and routine as time passes.

Hambrick and Fukutomi (1991) argue that executives have a tendency to become more wedded to the correctness of their views with the passage of time. Beyond the early period in office, CEOs' commitment to certain ways of thinking and operating gradually increase. The longer their approach to running the firm has met with acceptable performance the greater their conviction of the enduring nature of their approach. This tendency can be reduced if there is pressure from owners or overseers on the CEO to perform, if the CEO's income is tied to the performance of the firm and if there is an assertive and diverse top management team.

THE NEED FOR A DEVELOPMENTAL PARTNERSHIP

Given the potential difficulties associated with development, it would seem that some serious consideration needs to be given to the type of help an executive can call upon. Clearly, no development can take place unless the individual wants it to occur. Ultimately, the process has to be personally driven. However, executive development may need outside intervention.

At one level, this may simply involve helping the executive to exploit potential learning opportunities better. A survey by Mumford (1988a) showed that many opportunities were lost because managers did not perceive in advance that the tasks they undertook were ones they could learn from. To be of benefit, projects had to be identified beforehand and discussed during the project or reviewed subsequently.

However, when radical change is required, others may need to step in and press for change. Without some external help the dice are certainly loaded against lasting growth taking place. McCall (1992) argues that organisations that consider development a priority and maintain the necessary developmental infrastructure will have a long-term business advantage. They need to know not only what executives must learn and develop, but also what types of experience will produce results, how to create these opportunities and help the executive make the most of them. Indeed, several writers point out that development requires the planned use of job assignments, relationships, risk taking and formal training.[19]

Below, we examine a range of developmental approaches – from those found through 'on-the-job' opportunities, to those which are less directly tied to the executive's current work tasks, or 'off-the-job' experiences.

On-the-job opportunities

Different experiences

Having a range of different job experiences is seen by several writers as critical for the executive's development. Kotter (1982) found that the most effective general managers had careers characterised by almost constant growth. They never stagnated in a job where there were few growth possibilities. Moreover, they were seldom moved too frequently or put into situations that were changing so rapidly that they could not learn and perform well. Evans (1992) also suggests that there is an optimum time in a job. He points out that, all too often, moves are made for 18 months to two years. Executives then develop an ability to start things off, but not implement and finish them.

While many note that exposure to a range of experiences is a key element, it is important to understand which activities are most conducive to development at a senior level. Career progression should not be assessed in terms of the number of promotions, functions worked in or training courses taken, but the extent to which job opportunities have allowed development to take place.[20]

Cross-functional experience

Conger (1993) argues that early on in their careers, executives should have cross-functional work experience. Raskas and Hambrick (1992) reviewed organisations engaged in what they call 'multifunctional management development'. They describe a range of approaches, from a programme of complete mobility across a range of functional areas (as employed at Hewlett-Packard) to providing managers with experience on multifunctional teams. Experiences such as these may also make executives more adaptive, increase their tolerance for change and help them understand the web of relationships which knit organisations together.

At the executive level, what might be called 'multi-unit' experience may also help. This involves exposing the executive to different Strategic Business Units (SBUs). As Gupta (1986) highlights, the higher one goes in the organisation, the more likely the executive is to manage several SBUs – which implies a greater number of different strategic contexts to understand. If the executive's work experience has been confined to one particular type of context (for example, creating new businesses or maximising short-term cash flow) there is greater potential for SBUs pursuing unfamiliar strategies to be either neglected or mismanaged (see Chapter 11). While Gupta points out there may be a mismatch at first between the executive and the strategic requirements of the job, the benefits include not only personal growth for the executive, but also the possibility of fresh ideas to revitalise a lacklustre business unit. Moreover, with an enhanced appreciation of the needs of different SBUs, executives may be better able to see synergistic benefits between SBUs, improve coordination and reduce conflict.

Building the job around the executive

An alternative, but less common, approach is to structure the job to suit the executive, rather than matching the executive to the job. This is a difficult notion for some. Forces inside organisations tend to push for conformity, uniformity and standardisation. Kotter (1982) suggests organisations create jobs for executives or break large divisions into two or more parts so that these new jobs can help develop others for the top job. It might mean divesting some divisions, or limiting the diversification strategy so that the CEO's job is more manageable.

Managerial responsibility

Executives' senior managers play an important part in the development process. They are in the best position to act as reviewer, guide, coach or appraiser. How well they do this, often influences the degree of learning the subordinate executive derives from various work experiences. Kotter (1982) notes that good management is particularly important at the start of the executive's tenure. It is at this point that new general managers need to get up to speed quickly and not be diverted. It is important to give managers space to work things out and to accomplish things for themselves.

Mentoring

A similar, but more targeted approach is that of mentoring. Lewis and Jacobs (1992) argue that mentoring and role modelling are extremely important ways of reinforcing the growth process. Mumford (1988b) argues the best kind of mentoring is a loose arrangement whereby each director is asked to pick up several managers at different levels of the organisation. They are expected to have informal discussions and talk with the executive about their development. This avoids the problems associated with formalising the process to the extent that it becomes an unwanted obligation.

Off-the-job approaches to executive development

There are, of course, a range of other options available, less directly tied in to the executive's current work tasks, but which provide a whole range of developmental opportunities. Some of these come through public courses, where the executive mixes with peers from other organisations, or through in-house programmes which concentrate on company specific issues. As Moulton and Fickel (1993) note, increasingly the distinction between the two is becoming more blurred. Educational institutions are entering into cooperative arrangements with their major customers in order to deliver more timely, relevant and appropriate offerings. Overall, the trend has been towards programmes which are customised, strategic and results oriented.[21]

Action learning

Nowhere is this trend more evident than in the area of Action Learning. Many writers see this as *the* trend for the future.[22] Indeed, in some companies, most notably General Electric, the move towards Action Learning has been thorough and forceful. Conger (1993) maintains the only barriers to its widespread use will be the cost and complex logistics involved.

Originally developed by Revans (1982), Action Learning now comes in several forms. However, the essence of the process is that managers pursue a work-based project of concern to both themselves and their organisation, using their colleagues as a resource to test out ideas, strategies and gain feedback. Consequently, Action Learning provides many potential areas for development through practically driven and directly relevant structured activities. In Action Learning, the curriculum is defined by the executive or the organisation. The process can be both an aid to problem solving and contribute towards the development of the individual. Proponents of Action Learning claim the process also helps executives deal with the issues of management of change and the development of managerial competencies. Conger (1993), for instance, argues that Action Learning should also be used to explore strategic issues.

Team based development processes

A different approach, but one which can be equally powerful, is where the senior team or a senior group take collective responsibility for their growth through team building activities or other collective processes. Done correctly, sometimes with outside help, a senior team can make tremendous leaps forward both at a personal and team level.

Clearly, what form this takes will depend on the needs of the individual and the group. The authors have been involved in several different kinds of intervention which have ranged from helping executives look at business and strategic problems differently, to helping develop team and personal-influence skills. The real advantage of such activities is that a collective commitment to strategic solutions can be made.

An alternative approach is offered by the 'Chief Executive Set', where half a dozen chief executives meet for one day a month for six months and use their own problems as the raw material for group learning.[23] The group operates as a problem solving/encounter group. The problems dealt with are important, large-scale, complex and strategic. These are usually ambiguous, confusing problems to which, initially at least, there are no clear-cut answers. Another avenue for growth is to seek involvement in external directorships or public committees.

Public courses and external providers

In recent years, public courses have received a mixed press. They have been criticised for stressing the intellectual, analytical and the short-term at the expense of interpersonal, intuitive and longer-term aspects of management.[24]

However, increasingly, public courses are becoming more responsive to customer needs. Moulton and Fickel (1993) cite a recent survey which showed that over 40 business schools in the US offered company specific programmes and that this trend was increasing. Business schools are also forming networks or alliances with each other to enhance their capacity to offer more internationally focused courses.

For example, The Global Leadership Programme developed by Noel Tichy of Michigan University attempts to teach an understanding of both global and strategic issues through international experiences. Participant teams travel to Brazil, India, China or other locations to explore new business opportunities and return to the US where their ideas are scrutinised by management. Indeed, several business schools have recently developed international programmes which give executives first-hand experience of different environments and issues. One such programme has been developed by the authors for Pacific Dunlop in conjunction with Melbourne Business School. One module of the programme is located in Hong Kong and involves visits to some of the organisation's major plants in China. Case studies (developed by a colleague at Harvard) explore the critical issues of managing the company's Chinese operations.

It is not appropriate to review here the vast range of public courses that are available. It is worthwhile emphasising, however, that executives should be clear about their objectives in attending a course, and whether these match the benefits the course is intended to provide. One of the major advantages of public courses is the opportunity for cross-fertilisation of ideas from people with different perspectives and experience. Educational institutions can play an invaluable role in helping executives avoid parochial beliefs and tunnel vision by bringing people together from different businesses and corporate settings, exposing them to a wide variety of issues, possibilities and ideas and challenging people's conclusions, ideas and opinions.[25] However, in our experience, many executives fail to benefit fully from public courses because they have not critically reviewed course objectives, how these relate to their real needs and the extent to which they can pursue the new knowledge they gain back at work.

Behavioural skills

There are many skill-based programmes offered by institutions which range from classroom-based approaches to outward bound courses. At a senior level, the outcomes of such programmes are less clear. If progress is made this may be more due to what happens after the programme rather than as a direct result of the programme itself. Conger (1993) argues that for interpersonal skill development to take hold, there needs to be active and persistent coaching – something most programmes neglect.

The development of a leadership capability is even more controversial. Some organisations, like the Center for Creative Leadership, have been working in this area for many years. The recent emphasis on improving executive leadership skills has seen many training institutions attempt to cater for these needs. However, it seems unlikely that external programmes alone, without job related experiences, can make dramatic and sustainable progress in this area.

Future directions

At the corporate level, Bolt (1993) sees executive education moving to a content which is unique to the organisation's needs, providing an avenue for executives to achieve strategic objectives. The focus of programmes at companies like Motorola, Xerox, Federated Department Stores, McDonalds and General Foods are aimed particularly at implementing business strategies and achieving corporate goals.

At the individual level, Mann and Staudenmier (1991) believe that in future there will be a greater emphasis on merging learning and work opportunities. Developing executives through mentoring relationships is one area of potential growth. There will also be an increase in one-on-one coaching and in providing courses that focus on solving specific problems facing the executive's business. Neglected in the past, more companies will make efforts to translate the content of executive education into specific development plans for individual executives, rather than leaving the creation of such plans to chance.

It is important to reinforce this last point. Ways should be found to help executives (and their staff) become better at self-directed development. This means helping executives take responsibility for their own development and helping them approach developmental opportunities, both formal and informal, in a more conscious and reflective way.

However, we still have some way to go in terms of being able to help executives develop the more complex interpersonal qualities as well as aspects such as intuition and mindset. As we search for solutions, we must also try to avoid the danger of becoming wedded to the latest management trend. In the same way that organisations involved in benchmarking are in danger of simply aping the best that is available, training professionals and executives may race to find new ways to do the same thing – that is, increase understanding rather than change patterns of thinking and behaving. Effort should be put into looking at ways of achieving sustainable change (Kaplan, 1992) and providing integrated programmes[26] – rather than simply searching for the next country to visit in order to create 'international managers.'

In general, therefore, we know much more about pattern modification than pattern reframing. We know more about providing opportunities to aid executive understanding than improving executives' capacity to act. Indeed, as the performance of some major corporations over the past decade has shown, we are more liable to bask in the shadow of our previous successes, than to reflect critically on our individual and collective limitations and do something about them. If ever there was a need for self-directed development both at the executive and corporate level the time has surely arrived.

SUMMARY

Increasingly, the capacity of organisations to learn and develop is viewed as a powerful competitive tool. However, if senior executives are themselves unwilling to adapt and change, such strategies are unlikely to succeed.

A number of different factors serve to make learning and development more difficult at senior levels. In the first instance, it is important to distinguish between the two. Learning involves the modification or acquisition of knowledge or new behaviours. Development is defined as the capacity to acknowledge, confront and change deeply-held patterns of thinking and behaving. Development is altogether a more profound and difficult process to undertake. It is also more likely to result in the dramatic changes in thinking and behaviour which 'learning organisations' need to demonstrate.

In order to develop, executives must think through the requirements of the job and the qualities that are needed. They must also be aware of their current position, their personal strengths and weaknesses and, as a consequence, the extent to which change and development needs to occur. In practice, however, such self-awareness is not always evident in senior executives. Indeed, previous successes often blind the executive to the need to continue to learn and develop in a senior management position.

There are other hurdles which can obstruct self-development. Power, acquired expertise, personal ambition and the need to look highly competent often act together to prevent the executive from achieving personal growth. Development can also be inhibited by restrictive organisational cultures which discourage risk-taking, are intolerant of mistakes and are overly competitive. Moreover, the formal mechanisms through which executives receive feedback are often inadequate.

While there are important end-benefits to self-development, the process is difficult and can produce a range of unsettling feelings. The individual needs the will and motivation to change if old habits or patterns are to be unlearnt. Given these difficulties, executives and those in charge of development in their organisations must think through the type of help they need. They need to work out what qualities executives must learn and develop as well as what types of experience will produce results. Thus, career moves need to be carefully planned to provide executives with a range of experiences and learning opportunities (see Figure 3.5).

Getting the most out of work based experiences can be structured through activities such as Action Learning. An equally powerful development experience can involve a team of executives learning

Fig. 3.5 *Progressing executive development*

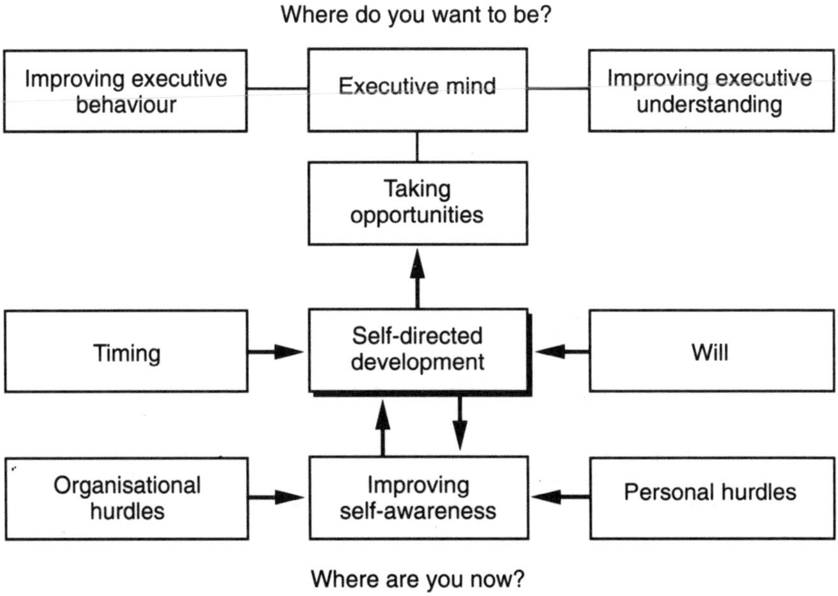

Where do you want to be?

| Improving executive behaviour | — | Executive mind | — | Improving executive understanding |

Taking opportunities

| Timing | → | Self-directed development | ← | Will |

| Organisational hurdles | → | Improving self-awareness | ← | Personal hurdles |

Where are you now?

together. Similarly, external programmes, be they company specific or public courses, continue to offer the executive a range of developmental opportunities. It is important to keep these in mind when exploring the other Capabilities in subsequent chapters.

NOTES

1. Peter Senge is currently the most well known of these. See also Brian Dumaine's article, 'Mr. Learning Organization', *Fortune*, 17 October 1994, which describes what companies like Ford and Federal Express are doing with Senge's work.
2. See McCall *et al.* (1994).
3. See Bolt (1993).
4. Comments by Edgar Schein at the symposium held by the ICEDR, Boston, Mass. October, 1994.
5. See Evans (1992) and also Kotter (1982).
6. See Ready (1994).
7. See McCall *et al.* (1994).
8. See Mann and Staudenmier (1991).
9. See Douglas Ready's editorial in 'Executive Education: Is it Making the Grade?', *Fortune Magazine* Supplement, 14 December 1992, 39–48.

10. See Braddick (1988).
11. See Jahoda (1958).
12. See Friedlander (1983).
13. Mumford (1988b).
14. See Hall and Foulkes (1991).
15. See Kirk and MacDonald (1989).
16. See, Kaplan, Drath and Kofodimos (1985).
17. Freidlander (1983) argues tension plays a central role in Piaget's, Kohlberg's and Silverman's theories of individual learning.
18. See Kubler-Ross (1969).
19. These include Kotter (1982), Hall and Foulkes (1991) and McCall *et al.* (1994).
20. See Evans (1992).
21. See Mann and Staudenmier (1991).
22. Including Mann and Staudenmier (1991) and Conger (1993).
23. See Braddick (1988).
24. Neither Kotter (1982), Mumford (1988b) nor Margerison and Kakabadse (1984) found evidence that training programmes after graduate school played an important part in helping the executives they surveyed.
25. See, for instance, Hollenbeck (1991).
26. The work being done by Quinn (1988) is a good example of an integrated approach. See also Hooijberg and Quinn (1992).

PART II

THE INTERPERSONAL CAPABILITIES: UNDERSTANDING AND MANAGING OTHERS

4 The Influence Capability: Influence, Power and Politics in Senior Management

INTRODUCTION

Yukl and Falbe (1990) argue that one of the most important determinants of managerial effectiveness is success in influencing subordinates, peers and higher level managers. At a senior level this is particularly important – indeed we believe the ability to influence people, situations and events is a fundamental prerequisite for those operating in the executive role.

Although a growing number support this view, the ability to influence others is one of the least researched and, for practising managers, the least deliberately developed skills. Influence – and the power one needs to exercise it – are amongst the more controversial areas of executive work because of their close association with political behaviour. While most executives know that politics exist within their organisation, few are willing to talk about it. Kanter (1979) has argued that power is a dirty word: 'It is easier to talk about money – and much easier to talk about sex – than it is to talk about power'.

Easy or not, however, executives need the knowledge and skills to use power and influence effectively. Without these, the executive is neither able to exercise effective leadership, nor able to protect themselves and others from the pressures and demands of competing groups.

In this chapter we explore what is meant by an Influence Capability. To do this it is important to clarify two aspects at the outset. The first is the difference between power, influence and politics. The second is the difference between formal Leadership (see Chapter 5) and the informal influence processes discussed here.

Power, influence and politics

Power has been defined in several ways. Here we take the view that power is a resource, while influence and politics are ways of interacting with others in order to get something done. Pfeffer (1992) sums up this distinction by noting that power is 'the potential ability . . . to get people to do things. Politics and influence are the processes, the actions, the behaviours through which this potential power is utilised.'[1]

Executives can influence others in a number of different ways. We view political behaviour as a form of influence which is covert. We also argue that political behaviour is not always devious and that it can be effective at senior levels.

Formal leadership and informal influence processes

Leadership is seen by most writers as a process of influencing staff in order to accomplish a task or goal. However, there are some differences in the way influence is exercised over one's staff, as distinct from influencing those who are outside an executive's formal area of control. With the former, one starts from a position of authority: influencing those the executive does not supervise either directly or indirectly is an entirely different matter.

Executives need to be able to influence a range of stakeholders, in addition to those they have formal authority over. Indeed, some of the executive's most critical relationships are with peers and higher-level managers and with other senior individuals outside the organisation. Usually, however, the power executives have over these players is more subscribed than with their own staff. When executives operate laterally we see this as exercising 'informal' influence. While some writers might also call this leadership, we believe there are differences between influencing peers and leading staff. Here we focus on the former; that is, the particular processes which are used for lateral and upward influence attempts (see Figure 4.1). We discuss leadership in the next chapter.

Power and informal influence processes colour many aspects of executive life. At a senior level they take on a particular importance for the following reasons:

Fig. 4.1   *Informal influence processes*

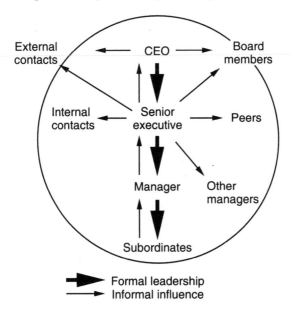

- Executives have to influence a wide range of people both within the organisation and outside it, and at many different levels, in order to move the organisation towards its goals.

- The typical manager is very dependent on a variety of people to perform his or her job effectively. As executives gain more formal authority in an organisation, the areas in which they are vulnerable increase and become more complex rather than the reverse.[2]

- Political behaviour is more frequently exhibited at higher levels of the organisation.[3] The environment is often ambiguous with a lot at stake; playing outside the normal rules is often 'a reality of relationships at the top.

INFLUENCE CAPABILITY – THE ESSENTIAL ELEMENTS

Executives need to understand the sources of power at their disposal and how to acquire and maintain these. They need to review their influencing skills and develop insight into others positions and political actions.

In this chapter we review each of these aspects in turn:

- *Understanding power*. One cannot begin to operate effectively in a senior role without having an understanding of power. Stewart (1993) notes that power battles are more common at senior management levels than they are lower down. Moreover, many well intentioned attempts to improve organisations are thwarted because of a lack of knowledge about patterns of power operating at the top level. Power cannot be ignored if we hope to understand and improve the functioning of organisations from within.[4]

- *Acquiring and maintaining power*. Executives need to complement their understanding of the nature of power with techniques which will help them acquire and maintain it. Without this, Kotter (1986) argues, the inevitable conflicts among interdependent and diverse groups cannot be managed in ways leading to creative outcomes. His belief is that the sheer volume of power orientated activity associated with executive work will continue to increase dramatically in the coming years. Indeed, the acquisition and maintenance of power may be the definitive feature of executive life.

- *Using influence*. If they are to be fully equipped for the senior role, executives need to go beyond power building and develop their capacity to influence others. For instance, arguably the most powerful person in the western world, US President Bill Clinton, has had great difficulty in influencing a range of groups and stakeholders to support his foreign policy and domestic reforms.

- *Having insight*. In order to influence others effectively, it is essential that executives have the ability to understand the motivations, hopes and fears of those around them. Understanding personal agendas, what is seen as acceptable or unacceptable behaviour by others and what reactions are likely in various circumstances, are critical insights. A lack of insight at senior levels when dealing with powerful others is akin to crawling in the dark – with a real likelihood of being trodden on.

- *Understanding politics*. Insight is particularly important when looking at organisational politics. Often misunderstood, politics is an influence process which few executives warm to. Nevertheless, executives must, at the very least, have an understanding of politics and the political capabilities of others. In some circumstances it may be impossible to act without such an understanding. Greiner (1986), for example, argues that large-scale, consultancy interventions will be doomed to failure unless the political dynamics among the company's senior executives are worked out.

- *Strategic influence.* In a survey by Gandz and Murray (1980), 89 per cent of respondents stated that successful executives must be good politicians. Politics, therefore, may be inevitable at a senior level – but the outcomes are not. Executives can choose how to respond to political behaviour and other influence attempts to influence, in ways which can aid or hinder both the organisation's and their own progress. In so doing, they must not get caught up in influence tactics aimed at short-term gains, but see these within a strategy of influencing others towards achieving their own and the organisation's longer term goals.

Understanding power

For some, power can be the source of tremendous benefit. It can aid in 'creating an active organisation, sustaining an active organisation and transforming an organisation in the direction of its fullest potential'.[5] McDonald (1972) has argued that 'only if the executive[s] know the alignment of the centers of real power can [they] operate effectively in and through the organisation.'

There are several typologies of power. The most popular is French and Raven's (1959) five power bases: coercive, legitimate, expert, reward, and referent or personal power. Information and connection power are often added to this list.[6] Writers have also looked at power in terms of where it ultimately comes from. In general, power stems from three areas; the organisation, the individual or a combination of both.

At a senior level, the power bases open to the executive are considerable. These have been drawn together in a typology outlined below which highlights four principle sources of power stemming from the organisation or the individual: Organisational Power, Network Power, Cognitive Power and Personal Power.

(a) Organisational power

Organisational Power is a product of the formal position the executive holds, sometimes known as 'legitimate' power. In addition, there is a wide range of potential power resources associated with one's position, namely:

- Position/Titles
- Authority/Rewards
- Control of scarce resources (for example, technology, finance, manpower)
- Power of dismissal
- Power to promote or reward
- Use of organisational rules/regulations and structure
- Control of decision making
- Access to power brokers through formal channels

Organisational power gives executives the formal authority to do such things as sign contracts to a certain amount, to make decisions over resources and to make demands on their staff. In addition, their position gives them the potential to decide the fate of others – by using rewards (material or otherwise) or through coercion. It also gives them a platform from which to exercise leadership over staff. As we discuss in Chapter 5, one's organisational position is not in itself a sufficient basis from which to exercise some aspects of leadership effectively – for example, an inspirational leadership approach. Nevertheless, it does give executives a strong starting position. At the very least organisational power gives the executive the opportunity to command the attention of staff.

However, increasingly, organisational power is being shown to have limitations and there is a danger the executive may rely too much on their position as a basis for influencing others. Often, coercion is not particularly effective (either with peers or staff) in the longer term. Punishment cannot be used indiscriminately on a mobile and educated workforce. Additionally, even for CEOs, the power to reward also has its limitations. Indeed, the 'power to reward appears increasingly circumscribed by obligations like affirmative action, by formalised compensation systems . . .'.[7] Instead, the trend is more towards using power which is derived from the person rather than the position.

(b) Network power

Network power is a product of both the executive's position and personality, and is particularly pertinent to senior executives. As

Kanter (1979) suggests, an important source of power derives from close contact with sponsors, peer networks and subordinates. Derived from formal and informal contacts both within and outside the organisation, this is an essential power base from which to get things done in an increasingly intricate and complex world. Kotter (1982) observed that networking was a key skill and practice of the most successful general managers. They spent significant amounts of time building and maintaining an extensive network of support for carrying out their agendas.

Byrum-Robinson and Womeldorff (1990) define networking as 'the ability to create and maintain an effective, widely based system of resources that works to the mutual benefit of oneself and others'. Networking includes:

- Developing contacts
- Membership of related organisations
- Links/access to power brokers through informal methods

Network power has tremendous potential. For instance, Sir Peter Ables, of TNT, derived much of his power from being an almost legendary behind the scenes deal maker. He is seen as having one of the best contact books in the industry:

> When I started out it was very hard for me to ring my peers in the transportation industry . . . I had to wait on people and knock on doors. Now I can lift the receiver . . . and people take my calls.[8]

(c) Cognitive power

An executive's intellectual capacities, such as knowledge and analytical ability, as well as other related cognitive aspects are also an important source of power. These include:

- Intellect
- Functional/Industry expertise
- Information
- Management and interpretation of meaning
- Interpretation of others' moves and motives
- Control of uncertainty
- Knowledge of the distribution of power

Cognitive power includes the notions of *Expert* and *Information* power which French and Raven highlighted. Expert power is to do with one's area of expertise and is usually derived from one's technical or functional ability. Expert power can be more important at different points in one's job or career. When the executive first moves into a new role, as Gabarro (1987) highlights, the individual's prior functional experience and industry background is often relied upon to prioritise and deal with issues. For example, when John Sculley (1987) moved from Pepsi to Apple computers, it was his knowledge of marketing which helped him make the transition.

Increasingly, however, the real challenge at senior levels is to learn how to manage the expert power of others. In the United States, it is estimated that one out of every four jobs now goes to a technical worker.[9] In many of the more 'high-tech' industries, executives are at pains to try to retain and motivate these highly mobile individuals, particularly when it comes to managing large-scale, technically complex developments. For many years, the major computing firms have had to carefully think through how to maintain the motivation of key product development staff in order to avert the threat of desertion to key competitors. This was a major issue for Intel senior executives in Silicon Valley when its revolutionary microprocessor, the Pentium, was being developed.[10]

Information power is derived from the possession of critical (and scarce) information. It is particularly valued in situations where one is negotiating or bargaining. Certainly, the senior executive cannot function without information; however, seniority does not always provide access to this power base. Lower-status employees, such as secretaries, can often tap sources of high quality information and use their information power to effect.

(d)   Personal power

Personal power is perhaps the least tangible power base of the four. It is concerned with the range of personal resources stemming from one's personality, and which exemplify the executive's unique approach. These can include aspects such as confidence and charm, but often include more powerful, dominant features as well.

When influencing peers, external contacts and higher-level managers, the use of charm, guile and assertiveness can produce considerable results. Indeed, in a *Fortune* poll of CEOs, personality was ranked amongst the three most important powerbases.[11]

Personal power includes:

- Gender
- Physical – sexuality/size
- Confidence
- Personality/charm
- Performance/reputation/judgement
- Personal reward in the form of praise or 'stroking'

An aspect of personal power is one's willingness to use it. In this particular poll, CEOs emphasised that they needed to be prepared to use the power at their disposal. While wealth and position are obviously key ingredients behind the success of executives like Kerry Packer, Chairman and Proprietor of Consolidated Press Holdings, on their own they are not enough. The MD of Packer's organisation argues:

> Lots of people have influence, but there are not that many people who actually have either the guts or the intellectual fire power . . . to get their way. Kerry is capable of seeing things very clearly – making a decision and then implementing it. An enormous amount of power derives from simply having the strength of character and will to do things.[12]

Acquiring and maintaining power

Power is not a static resource. As most managers know, the real power structure of an organisation is not found in organisation charts or job descriptions.[13] The informal organisation determines the relative power position of executives, and because this is constantly in flux, senior executive positions are highly volatile. Consequently, power can be gained and lost both in the short and long-term.

According to Kotter (1977), effective executives are those who are skilled in acquiring sources of power far beyond the formal power that goes with the job. Although additional bases of power are never freely granted, such executives manage to amass and construct power through constant attention, experimentation and observation. Thus, acquiring, maintaining and building power is a process that executives should actively pursue. Indeed, for Kotter, the effective executive becomes a full-time 'student' of power, seeking to develop it by:

- Acquiring information and ideas
- Creating good working relations
- Envisioning intelligent agendas for action
- Sharpening personal skills in diagnosis and interpersonal influence
- Constructing networks of cooperation
- Maintaining a good image and track record

Below, we explore how the different categories of power discussed above might be developed further.

Developing organisational power

There are two major ways to develop organisational power. One approach is to utilise the power that already goes with one's formal role. The second way is to attain other formal positions.

An executive's formal position carries with it many potential power bases. Frequently, some of these power bases are in a raw form and may need enhancing and reworking. For example, after a major promotion, executives often acquire a whole range of resources within a role, but these may not be fully understood or have the same impact until the executive can work out how they should be used. Moreover, executives' power to restructure organisations, to centralise or decentralise, can enhance or reduce their formal organisational authority. CEOs at many companies (including General Motors in the 1960s and Apple under John Sculley) use reorganisations to consolidate power. Indeed, a problem that continually faces many conglomerates is the relationship between corporate office and operating or business units. Power can be increased by centralising the organisation. The dilemma, however, is that in doing this it may reduce the divisions' capacity to respond quickly and appropriately.

Formal power can also be enhanced by acquiring roles which carry a range of decision-making powers and resource controls. One of the most powerful positions is where the role of CEO and Chairman are combined. Executives like Kerry Packer and Janet Holmes à Court have tremendous power because they can combine several executive positions into one role. Pfeffer (1992) personifies Robert Moses, Parks Commissioner for New York, as the most powerful public official in 20th Century United States. He notes that 'Robert Moses recognises the truth of the so called New Golden Rule: the person with the gold makes the rules'. Moses acquired 12 significant positions during his working life. Viewed in isolation, each of the 12 positions seemed of little importance; together they enabled Moses to accumulate resources and accrue the publicity and benefits needed to obtain a degree of power nearly unparalleled in public life.

Developing networks

Senior executives deal with many people in an organisation with whom they do not have a direct line relationship. Network building is, therefore, an important way of developing and maintaining links with others in the organisation. Some research suggests that women have less upward influence than men. The difference has been attributed to the less central positions women occupy in organisational networks and consequently less access to the main power holders in the organisation.[14]

Kotter (1982) maintains that far too many people ignore network management. The general managers he studied, all allocated significant time and effort early in their jobs to developing a network of cooperative relationships. Kotter found that the networks developed by these GMs often included hundreds or thousands of individuals. Moreover, these included subordinates, bosses, peers and outsiders such as customers, suppliers, the press and bankers. These executives created networks by:

- Focusing on people they felt dependent on or who they needed to implement their agendas
- Making others feel obliged to them
- Encouraging others to identify with them
- Establishing their reputation in the eyes of others
- Making others feel dependent on them
- Replacing or removing incompetent subordinates
- Changing suppliers or bankers or other outsiders

Kanter (1983) also argues that organisation members achieve major innovations through alliances, building coalitions and overcoming resistance. Developing and using networks demands subtlety and sensitivity. Kevin Gosper, a Vice President of the International Olympic Committee, a senior Shell executive and the Chief

Commissioner for Melbourne is someone who has access to an array
of powerful individuals in business, government and international
sport. When accessing top decision makers his experience shows,
'They almost without exception get back within 24 hours. It's better
not to call too often. It's better to have something to say. It's
important not to always ask for something. You won't last long if
you do.'[15]

Developing cognitive power

Cognitive power can be built up in very tangible ways. The most
obvious is by acquiring knowledge or expertise through some form of
qualification. Some qualifications also aid in improving thinking
processes, such as an Executive MBA program. Not only does this
enhance one's knowledge base, it also symbolises intellectual
capacity.

However, cognitive power is about something more than qualifications and functional knowledge. Less tangible, but critical, aspects
such as being strategically aware and having the ability to analyse the
external environment, are also important. Similarly, it is necessary to
be aware of how the organisation works and what the people within it
value and believe in. Indeed, some argue that an ability to interpret
the environment in a way which helps others understand and derive
meaning from it, is an essential element of effective management.

Developing personal power

Personal power is becoming an increasingly important asset as
management styles at senior levels become more participatory and
consensus oriented. Earlier a *Fortune* poll of CEOs was cited, which
identified personal power as the most important powerbase.[16] While
often described in terms of the popular notion of 'charisma', personal
power can be exhibited in a number of ways depending on the
particular style of the executive concerned. It is particularly useful
when organisational parameters are unclear and others need to be
persuaded to change a course of action or support one's point of
view.

Developing personal power, however, is less easy to establish than
the other three categories. As we note in Chapter 5, some executives
find it hard to see themselves as charismatic. Nevertheless, there are
many other personal power bases which can be improved and which
are within many executives' grasp. For example, one's communica-

tion and negotiation skills can be developed as well as one's capacity to be assertive and charming. Improving these alone will not necessarily build charisma but they can help the executive influence others in less dramatic ways.

In addition, performance and reputation, also sources of personal power, can be developed by being effective in one's job. Like the springboard diver who gets more points for performing more difficult dives, an executive can enhance his or her reputation by succeeding in more demanding roles, such as organisational restructuring or profit turnarounds. Pfeffer (1992) argues that many successful people (such as Henry Kissinger) consciously establish their reputation and performance early in their careers.

Pfeffer (1992) emphasises six individual characteristics important for acquiring power:

- Energy, endurance and physical stamina
- The ability to focus one's energy and avoid wasted effort
- Sensitivity to others
- Flexibility, particularly in the means to achieve one's goals
- Willingness to engage in conflict and confrontation – 'personal toughness'
- The ability to submerge one's ego to enlist the help of others.

In the discussion so far, the different sources of power open to the executive and how these might be developed have been described. Power gives executives a basis from which they can attempt to alter the attitude and behaviour of others. Whether they are successful or not depends on the processes they use to influence others. It is to this area we now turn.

Influence

Although the starting point in any influence attempt is to understand one's objectives, Cohen and Bradford (1990) argue that those engaging in influence processes are not always aware of precisely what they want. Requests can contain a cluster of needs (for example, a certain product, arranged in a certain way, delivered in a specified time). Executives, therefore, need to think through which aspects are more important and which can be jettisoned if necessary. Also, confusing the desired end goal with the means of accomplishing it, can lead to battles over the wrong things. Kanter (1983) reported that successful influencers in organisations were those who never lost sight of the ultimate objective, but were willing to be flexible about the means.

The means one uses are dependent on one's influence strategies. Kipnis *et al.* (1980) identify seven basic strategies individuals use to influence others. Namely:

Reason	Relies on data and logic
Friendliness	Uses interest/goodwill to create a favourable impression
Coalition	Mobilises others to support requests
Bargaining	Relies on negotiation and the exchange of favours/benefits
Assertiveness	Concerned with direct and forceful communication
Higher Authority	Calls on those at higher levels to support requests
Sanctions	Uses rewards and punishments derived from organisational position

Understanding one's predominant and preferred influence styles can help the executive improve their influence techniques. Both Yukl and Falbe (1990) and Kipnis *et al.* (1984) found reasoning to be the most commonly used strategy. Using three or four different strategies seems to be the optimum approach, rather than all of them. The choice will vary depending on the executive's objectives, their control of resources and expectations about the willingness of others to comply. Certainly, the executive should consider adopting a different strategy if their first influence attempt fails.

Lateral and upward influence

The level of person one is trying to influence is also an important factor to take into account. For example, Kipnis *et al.*, found that the use of sanctions was an unlikely strategy when influencing colleagues.

Cohen and Bradford's (1990) model is particularly helpful in looking at ways to influence others – particularly those at the same level – where the executive does not have formal authority at his or her disposal. They argue that all transactions within organisations are exchanges between people. An exchange can involve 'goods' (for example, money, personnel); services (for example, information, public support); or sentiments (for example, appreciation, praise). The exchange process is governed by the 'Law of Reciprocity' – the belief that people should be paid back for what they do, that one good or bad deed deserves another, and that one expects to be paid for resources provided.

The ability to influence is created by satisfying the needs and interests of others in the exchange of goods, services and/or sentiments. The exchange can be of tangible goods, such as a budget increase, new equipment, or more personnel; of tangible services such as a faster response time, more information or public support: or of sentiments such as gratitude, admiration or praise. Whatever form an exchange takes, unless the factors being traded are roughly equivalent over time, hard feelings will result.

To explain the process of exchange they use the metaphor of 'currencies'. Just as many types of currencies are traded in the world financial market, they are also traded in organisational life. In order to influence peers, the executive needs to recognise that many types of payment exist, broadening the range of what can be exchanged. Some of the major currencies that are commonly valued and traded in organisations are listed in Table 4.1.

Part of the usefulness of currencies comes from their flexibility. For example, there are many ways to express gratitude and give assistance. A manager who most values the currency of appreciation could be paid through verbal thanks, praise, a public statement at a meeting, informal comments to his peers and/or note to his boss. However, the note of thanks seen by one person as a sign of appreciation may be seen quite differently by someone else – perhaps as a cheap way to try to repay extensive favours and service. The currencies, therefore, have value not in some abstract sense but as defined by the receiver.

Cohen and Bradford also argue that trust is important. The greater the extent to which the influencer has worked with the potential ally and created trust, the easier the exchange process will be. Few transactions within organisations are once-off deals; who knows when the person may be needed again? Thus in most exchange situations two outcomes matter; success in achieving one's goals and success in improving the relationship, so that the next interaction will be even more productive. Although both task accomplishment and an improved relationship cannot always be realised at the same time, on some occasions the latter can be more important than the former. Winning the battle, but losing the war, is an expensive outcome.

Table 4.1 Currencies frequently valued in organisations

Inspiration-related currencies

Vision	Being involved in a task that has larger significance
Excellence	for unit, organisation, customers, or society
Moral/ethical	Having a chance to do important things really well
correctness	Doing what is 'right' by a higher standard than efficiency

Task-related currencies

New resources	Obtaining money, budget increases, personnel space, and so forth
Challenge/learning	Doing tasks that increase skills and abilities
Assistance	Getting help with existing projects or unwanted tasks
Task support	Receiving overt or subtle backing or actual assistance with implementation
Rapid response	Quicker response time
Information	Access to organisational as well as technical knowledge

Position-related currencies

Recognition	Acknowledgment of effort, accomplishment, or abilities
Visibility	The chance to be known by higher-ups or significant others in the organisation
Reputation	Being seen as competent, committed
Insiderness/ importance	A sense of centrality, of 'belonging'
Contacts	Opportunities for linking with others

Relationship-related currencies

Understanding	Having concerns and issues listened to
Acceptance/ Inclusion	Closeness and friendship
Personal support	Personal and emotional backing

Personal-related currencies

Gratitude	Appreciation or expression of indebtedness
Ownership/ involvement	Ownership of and influence over important tasks
Self-concept	Affirmation of one's values, self esteem, and identity
Comfort	Avoidance of hassles

Source: Cohen and Bradford (1990).

Trust is particularly important when influencing upwards, and research suggests that influencing one's boss depends heavily on aspects of personal power. In one study by Gabarro (1978) the single most important factor in determining how much influence a subordinate executive had over their boss was credibility – the degree of trust in a subordinate executive's judgement, recommendations and performance. Also important was the need to clarify, test or work through expectations. Where relationships between a senior executive and a senior manager were perceived to be less effective or satisfying, there had been a failure to address these issues.

Insight

Any influence attempt, at whatever level in the organisation, requires a capacity to work out where others are coming from, what motivates them and how they mentally view the world. Our research distinguished Insight as a separate Capability. Successful executives understand that other managers may have quite different perspectives and learn to live with and manage these differences. One of the reasons why Steve Jobs lost his position at Apple was because he was '. . . incapable of seeing the world from anyone else's perspective'.[17]

Insight is particularly important when it comes to influencing others. Executives need this quality to gauge others' power positions, their potential to use power and their skill at doing so. Pfeffer (1992) calls this 'sensitivity'. He argues, 'To be successful in getting things done in organisations, it is critical that you are able to diagnose the relative power of the various participants and comprehend the patterns of interdependence.'

Isenberg (1984) highlights this point when describing how senior managers think. He argues that a senior executive's conscious thoughts involve considerations like, 'Who are the key players here, and how can I get their support? Whom should I talk to first? Should I start by getting the production group's input? What kind of signal will that send to the marketing people?' Isenberg maintains that successful senior managers think a lot about interpersonal processes and the people they come in contact with. They try to understand the strengths and weaknesses of others, the relationships that are important to them and what their agendas and priorities are.

When outlining their exchange model of influence, Cohen and Bradford also highlight the need to understand the world of the potential ally. Without awareness of what the ally needs (or in their terms, what currencies are valued), attempts to influence the person can only be haphazard. Although they point out that this conclusion may seem self-evident, it is remarkable how often people attempt to influence others without adequate information about what is important to the potential ally. Instead they are driven by their own definition of 'what should be' and 'what is right'.

To make the exchange process effective, they conclude the influencer needs to:

- Think about the person to be influenced
- Know the world of the potential ally, including the pressures as well as the person's needs and goals
- Be aware of key goals and available resources that may be valued by the potential ally
- Understand the exchange transaction itself so that win/win outcomes are achieved

Insight is also important in a broader sense. Executives need insight in order to understand changes in the balance of power between their organisation and the outside world. For example, insight into customer needs, wants and purchasing power is as important as understanding the power of internal players. As a result, Kanter (1992) argues that the management of intercompany relationships is occupying more and more CEO time. There are multiple links with suppliers, marketing and manufacturing specialists and the like, who can all influence the success or failure of any given strategy.

Understanding politics at senior levels

We have highlighted how important it is to understand the motives of the person being influenced and to build trust. The reality, however, is that trust and mutually beneficial exchanges between people do not always occur. In part, this may result because the influencing strategy was not well chosen or executed – it may also be a product of other forces, particularly political actions. The implications of this are explored below.

While organisational politics is a topic of considerable importance, it does not sit easily in the minds of many writers, or executives.

Greiner (1986) argues that top management politics is a subject about which management scholars have been strangely silent. Additionally, the response of many managers to the subject of organisational politics – even from senior level executives – is often a negative one. More often than not the mere mention of the subject is enough to conjure up images of manipulation, deceit and dirty tricks. One long-serving executive in an oil company gave us his view of politics in his organisation; it was typical of many we interviewed:

> I'm not into politics . . . as a person I don't go for that kind of thing. I will not climb up the ladder unless I can do it by ability . . . I guess the longer I stay the more temptation there is to get the knives out like everybody else, but I don't particularly like that way of doing business. I've got enough problems without getting involved in that kind of thing.[18]

Other researchers have found a similar reaction. For instance, Cox and Cooper (1988) found that the CEOs they interviewed frequently denied any involvement in political activity, seeing it as detrimental to the organisation. Eisenhardt and Bourgeois (1988) point out that empirical studies have indicated that the view that politics interferes with effective management is common in organisations.

Despite its negative connotations, political behaviour is an important factor in senior executive life. Cox and Cooper (1988) believe that more people in their study engaged in politics than cared to admit. Pfeffer (1992, 47–8) has argued:

> . . . Your success in an organisation depends not only on your intelligence, industriousness and luck, but also on the match between your political skills and what is required in the position you occupy . . . My experience is that most people are neither very self-reflective about this particular dimension . . . nor very realistic in guiding their actions on the basis of it.

Managing political behaviour

The mystique and misunderstanding surrounding political behaviour is reflected in the attempts to define it. Some writers argue that all behaviour at all levels and in all circumstances can be regarded as political.[19] Political behaviour can either be generally supportive of longer-term goals and objectives or, as Kearns and Nadler (1992, 104–5) found at Xerox during the 1980s, it can work against them:

There are politics in any company or any family, but there certainly was a political issue at Xerox that affected the company in a most unfortunate way. There was tremendous competition for resources. Lots of tough fights and acrimony evolved, even at the field level . . . There were real hard feelings . . . In the end, we lost more than a few good people over it who simply wouldn't put up with it any longer.

As noted at the outset, political behaviour has been categorised as a form of influence that is covert in nature. It does not necessarily follow that political behaviour is therefore unsavoury or necessarily mischievous. It can, for instance, be organisationally concerned, or as political behaviour is often regarded, simply self-seeking.

Most agree that senior executives do affect political behaviour. Stewart (1993) argues that the chief executive and other top managers create conditions that encourage or discourage politics. How they do this is less clear. It is unclear, for instance, whether political behaviour is more likely in centralised situations with autocratic CEOs, or more likely in decentralised arenas where there is a degree of power sharing.

Several writers argue that decentralisation is more likely to give rise to politics.[20] Where the power of actors is roughly equivalent, individuals band together to influence decision processes. Where power is highly centralised, conflict is submerged and the use of power declines. However, Eisenhardt and Bourgeois's (1988) study of top management teams found that politics arise from over-centralisation, where the dominance of powerful CEOs, combined with a desire for control by top management teams, leads to politics.

Our experience has been that under certain conditions (that is, a relatively stable commercial environment, clear roles, access to resources and a capable CEO), negative political behaviour is less likely. However, stable environments are becoming rare and one can never completely control the behaviour of ambitious and powerful men and women in situations where the stakes are high. Consequently, whether 'good' or 'bad', politics in some form or other is a likely feature of executive life.

Influence and politics at senior levels: an explanatory model

Executives need to be prepared for the political actions of others. The following model brings together influence and politics to help executives anticipate and interpret the impact of their own and others actions in any influence attempt.

Four influence styles are illustrated in Figure 4.2. 'Diplomatic' and 'Devious' approaches are political in the sense that they are *covert* ways of influencing others. In contrast, 'Direct' and 'Destabilising' influence attempts are clearly visible and open to others. The essential point illustrated here is that while someone may act covertly, this may not necessarily lead to unhelpful or unsavoury outcomes. This depends on whether the influence attempts are seen as acceptable or unacceptable by the person the executive is trying to influence. Let us explore this point further by describing each of these positions in turn:

(1) *Direct.* Most influence attempts are Direct. As the matrix shows, these occur when someone adopts an open influencing style and whose objectives are seen to be acceptable. Our discussion of Kipnis's influence styles and Cohen and Bradford's exchange processes are usually centred around Direct influence attempts. This does not mean to say that the person being influenced fully agrees with what is being said or done, but rather that the influencer is operating within what is perceived to be the normal parameters of acceptable behaviour. For example, in Allison's (1971) description of the Cuban missile crisis, the various players relied on open and forthright discussion, with full information in meetings to influence decision making. Although there was conflict in this process and disagreement, influence attempts were open and acceptable.

(2) *Destabilising.* Alternatively, someone might do something which is open, but unacceptable to those they are trying to influence. For instance, an executive might try to invoke industrial relations laws to change conditions within the workplace. While this

Fig. 4.2 *Political processes*

Others' Reaction	Individual Style	
	Open	*Covert*
Acceptable	Direct	Diplomatic
Unacceptable	Destabilising	Devious

would be an open attempt to influence the regulatory climate, this could well be unacceptable to some trade unionists. In this case, the executive would need to be prepared for a reaction, and one which might not be very favourable. Here the influencer's attempt is called Destabilising.

When the executive has thought through some of the consequences of his/her actions, Destabilising behaviour can, in practice, help move organisations forward. The ex-CEO of the US telecommunications company, Ameritech adopted this strategy in early 1992 when appointing his successor.[21] At Palm Beach that year, Weiss convened a meeting of his top 30 senior executives (which included the seven-strong senior executive team) to discuss the organisation's future. After the formal presentations, Weiss stunned the group by inviting four relatively junior officers – not one a member of the august management committee – to meet with the CEO to find out how they would rebuild the company. Basically, Weiss did not feel that his senior team had the vision needed to cope with the changes which lay ahead. He needed to signal to them and others that the organisation was about to embark on a programme of significant change. Within months, most of the senior team had been eased into early retirement.

However, when the executive lacks insight or has failed to think through the consequences of their actions, Destabilising influence processes are of limited value. During a difficult time at Apple in the 1980s, Steve Jobs in a conversation with Del Yocam the senior executive who had run the Apple II division, illustrates this:

> Steve . . . said he wanted to run operations and he informed Del that he really was a much better operations person than Del was . . . Del asked him to repeat what he'd just said, so he did. After all, he was just repeating what should have been plain to everyone. But it wasn't plain to Del. Del was upset.[22]

(3) *Diplomatic*. Political behaviour is different from these open influence attempts. It is covert or concealed. If covert, but acceptable, then it is what we term Diplomatic in nature. For example, an executive might help someone get a new job by putting in a good word for them – but the individual in question is not aware of this action. Alternatively, an executive might be faced with trying to stop a major crisis between two departments. By putting pressure on one side, unknown to the other, the issue

gets resolved. Although this behaviour is not open, it is nevertheless acceptable to the other party. Like much of the work that goes on at a senior level, Diplomatic influencing strategies get the issues resolved in a way which benefits the organisation.

Pettigrew (1986) in his studies of ICI, describes this kind of behaviour as a form of 'unobtrusive power'. It is used by key executives, for instance, to lay the groundwork for major strategic organisational change. Unobtrusive power revolves around attempts to create agreement and legitimacy for certain arrangements, so they are not questioned by others. Conflicts are prevented by shaping the preferences, perceptions and beliefs of potential opponents in such a way that alternatives do not occur to them.

(4) *Devious*. Devious behaviour is different. It is both covert and unacceptable. Pettigrew's (1973) study also contains many examples of Devious political activity, such as controlling agendas, withholding information and forming behind the scenes coalitions. Myths can also be used to discredit opponents and to prevent or defeat potential opposition. However, while such activity can be self-seeking, this is not a condition of Devious behaviour. For example, a boardroom coup is often a product of Devious behaviour. The moves made by the boards of General Motors and IBM, for instance, would have been unacceptable to their respective CEOs, but seen to be in the interests of the shareholders. Devious behaviour is unsavoury when it is completely self-motivated and unacceptable to the target in terms of ends and means.

Thus, the matrix shows that influencing strategies can be open or hidden to those one is trying to affect. It reminds us that if we are open in our attempts to influence others we need to think through how our message will be received. Similarly, it demonstrates that covert attempts to influence others, that is, political behaviours, have the potential to be either positive or negative.

Strategic influence

Surviving and operating in the senior executive environment, however, involves more than understanding the difference between the political styles outlined above. It involves strategic influence; that is, an understanding of the issues and events facing one, and a plan to deal with these issues. To do this, the executive needs to draw and build on the concepts outlined in this chapter. The following factors are important when influencing others strategically:[23]

(a) Identifying the important players and their relative power positions
(b) Being aware of the disposition of the players to oneself or an issue
(c) Understanding the degree of interest the players have in an issue
(d) Understanding networks and relationships between players
(e) Using those networks to receive and give information
(f) Being prepared for critical events which determine or contribute to a significant outcome
(g) Understanding how the timing of those events can impact on outcomes
(h) Thinking through one's goals and tactics in light of this analysis

These are explored in turn below:

(a) *Important players and their power.* The executive needs to be aware of all those who have some degree of input on the issue in question and who can influence their role. Having identified the players it is then important to estimate their power.

(b) *Disposition of players.* Knowledge of the players and their relative power positions needs to be complemented with an awareness of their disposition. Disposition can be seen in terms of how favourable or unfavourable each person is towards you or an issue, and how predictable or unpredictable they are.

(c) *Degree of interest.* This is an estimate of the extent to which the issue or event is of interest to the various players one is trying to influence. For each player, an estimate has to be made as to whether the issue is a high, medium or low priority. It is unlikely that this assessment will be completely accurate, but it forces the executive to think more critically about the priorities of the other players.
     Figure 4.3 shows how disposition and degree of interest may be presented graphically. Disposition is shown in terms of two

Fig. 4.3 *Strategic influence mapping*

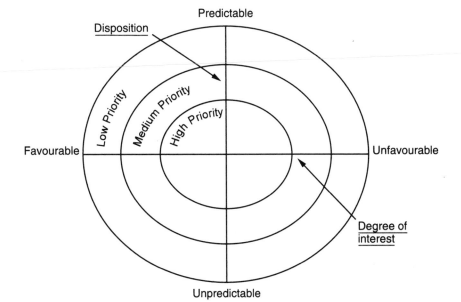

dimensions representing predictability and favourability. The three circles indicate the degree of interest, with those most interested closest to the centre.

(d) *Networks and relationships.* The next aspect to consider is how the players relate to oneself and each other. Networks are important for giving and receiving information on an ongoing basis. They are the arteries that transmit the informational lifeblood to the executive. Additionally, it is important that the executive considers how contact with one set of individuals may enhance or hinder relationships with others. The top team, for instance, will often be made up of a web of coalitions which disband, change and realign depending on the issue and event.

(e) *Using networks.* The executive also needs to cultivate these networks so that information about events can be given, mis-apprehensions rectified, feelings towards various issues under-stood and possible responses assessed.

(f) *Critical events.* These are opportunities or leverage points where one can move one's agenda forward or, if handled badly, risk having it damaged. This is particularly true of public relations issues where a crisis, badly handled, can wipe millions off the company's share price. Executives need to distinguish between events which demand a swift response and those which can be ignored without causing longer term difficulties.

(d) *Timing*. The time at which one acts or holds back is also crucial. Pfeffer (1992) outlines several considerations when determining when to act. Being early and moving first, is one aspect. Meeting deadlines is another. Delay may also be necessary. For example, Henry Kissinger was often late and also avoided meetings to get what he wanted – private audiences with the president.

(d) *Strategy and tactics*. Bearing the above points in mind, executives may be able to think through their influencing strategy and tactics more thoroughly. For Ryan (1989) strategies are long-term plans for achieving goals, while tactics are specific actions taken to influence particular events. Tactics include such things as impression management (to create favourable images), co-opting others to ones cause, controlling agendas to exclude others, flattery and ingratiation and making deals.

Application

These issues can be drawn together using a case study and cognitive mapping process. The case study involves a senior level manager called Cameron who is faced with the decision to relocate a large production facility. He feels the relocation must go ahead but has yet to reveal the decision to senior staff. Nevertheless, he has scheduled a date by which an announcement must be made. The senior people who will be most affected by the move are as follows:

- *John*, the CEO of the company
- *Richard*, the Finance director who has good relations with the CEO and several Board members
- *Alison*, an ambitious peer who also has the CEO's ear
- *Terry*, a senior manager reporting to Cameron who works hard, but has little contact with others in the department
- *Paul*, a senior manager reporting to Cameron who plays golf with the Finance Director

Having identified the players it is then important to estimate their relative power. One way of doing this is by drawing a circle to represent the relative power of various players. This can in itself help executives think about the power positions of their colleagues. Cameron sees the players he is dealing with as follows:

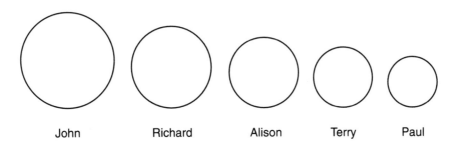

John   Richard   Alison   Terry   Paul

Figure 4.3 plots the players in Cameron's case in terms of their disposition and degree of interest. With Cameron at the centre, Alison and Paul are in the inner circle. Alison will be most affected by the move so has a high degree of interest. She is unfavourable and predictable in the sense Cameron knows she will oppose the move. Paul, whom Cameron has never got on well with, is also affected by the move and has a high degree of interest in it. He is both unfavourable and unpredictable. Terry also in the inner circle, is the only person definitely on side, as the relocation will take him nearer to his family.

The CEO (J) and Finance Director (R) have many competing demands, and place the relocation issue lower on their priority list. They are therefore positioned furthest from the centre. While both are favourable towards Cameron, he is unsure how either would react to the announcement. (As he cannot make a judgement, for this exercise, they are deemed unpredictable.) The map highlights that Cameron has few definite allies in this situation and many uncertainties.

Before announcing the relocation, Cameron would need to gain more information about his potential opponents. How difficult this might be is highlighted in Figures 4.5 and 4.6. Figure 4.5 shows Cameron's network relationships with the various players. The dotted line shows a weak relationship, the single line indicates limited contact, while the double lines indicate regular contact. As the

Fig. 4.4   *Strategic influence mapping*

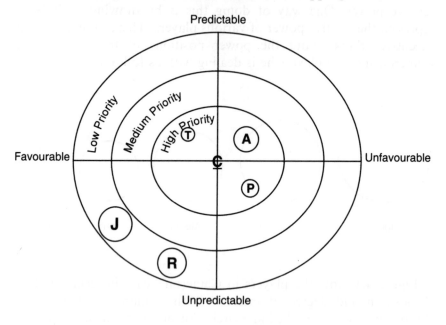

Fig. 4.5   *Strategic influence mapping*

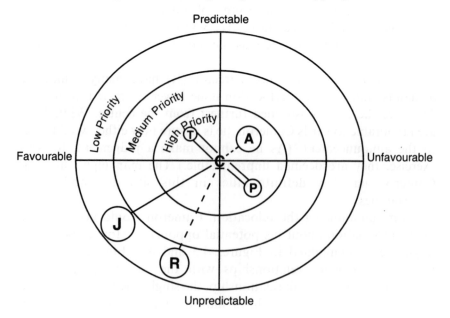

Fig. 4.6 *Strategic influence mapping*

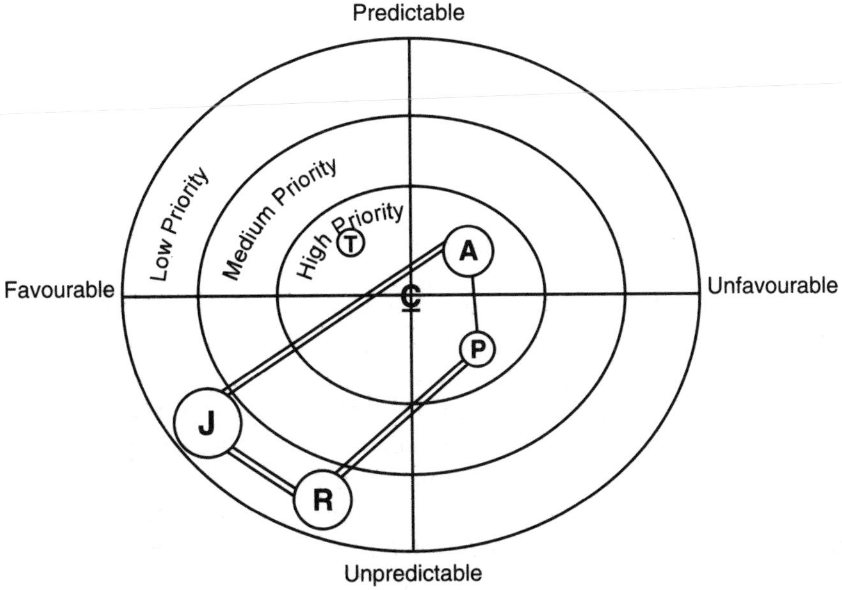

diagram shows, Cameron's links are less strong with some of the most powerful players.

Figure 4.6 shows the network relationships between the various players. Seen in this light there are a lot of powerful forces reigned against Cameron. By having to delineate his relationships with the other players (and his perceptions of their relationships with each other), Cameron may be forced to rethink his position relative to theirs. From this he may see that he needs to invest more in his network. He needs information on how several of the actors will react to the relocation. He may also need to prepare the ground in making the more important players aware of the positive aspects of relocation.

Additionally, Cameron should see the location in the context of his longer-term aims in influencing key players in the organisation. Handling the relocation is a tactical issue which may require him to gather and disseminate information to support his cause; he may need to use his networks to give and receive critical information and keep his options open so as to maintain freedom of choice. The announcement of the relocation is a critical event which needs to be managed; its timing may also be crucial. Whichever tactics he decides, he needs to have first mapped out the territory in the ways described above.

SUMMARY

The ability to influence people, situations and events is a fundamental prerequisite for those operating in a senior executive position. Executives have to influence a wide range of people, at many different levels, both within the organisation and outside it. Yet, influence – and the power one needs to exercise it – are controversial because of their close association with political behaviour. This chapter has looked at power, influence and politics at senior levels and explored why these are important to the executive.

Executives have a broad range of powerbases they can cultivate. Effective executives are skilled at acquiring sources of power that go beyond the formal power of their position. They also recognise that power can be gained and lost. From these powerbases they can attempt to alter the attitudes and behaviour of others. Whether they are successful or not depends on the processes they use to influence others.

The executive can choose between a number of influence strategies. The choice of strategy will vary depending on the executive's objectives, their control of resources and whether they think others will be willing to comply. Insight is therefore particularly important to cultivate. Executives must take time to understand others' motives, their agendas and what is important to them.

Even so, influence attempts can by stymied by political behaviour in the organisation. Political behaviour is often more frequently exhibited at higher levels in the organisation because executives have to operate in an ambiguous environment with other powerful individuals who have a lot at stake. Executives, therefore, must be prepared for the political actions of others. An explanatory model has been put forward to help executives anticipate and interpret the impact of their own and others' actions in any influence attempt.

Thus, executives can choose how to build power and use it to influence peers and colleagues. At the very least, they should be equipped with an understanding of the kind of influence processes which may be used. As will be seen from the next chapter, one cannot be a leader without power. Equally, one cannot be an effective executive if one does not understand the broader dimensions of influence and politics.

NOTES

1. There are two general approaches to looking at power and influence. The first sees power as formal authority, with influence as informal persuasion. Shea, former press secretary to the Queen, typifies this view when he argues, 'By and large, power is vested in a person's executive function. Influence depends on a person's capability to exert persuasion.' The second view is the one adopted here where power is a capacity to do something and influence the process of doing it.
2. See Kotter (1977).
3. Ferris and Kacmar (1992).
4. See Srivastva and Cooperrider (1986).
5. Srivastva and Cooperrider (1986).
6. See Hersey *et al.* (1979).
7. See Thomas Stewart's article, 'New Ways to Exercise Power', *Fortune*, vol. 120, no. 11, 6 November 1989, 46–51.
8. See Bruce Jacques and Rowena Stretton, 'The Power Brokers', *The Bulletin*, 19 March 1991, 32.
9. Louis S. Richman, 'The New Worker Elite', *Fortune*, vol. 130, no. 4, 22 August 1994, 46–54.
10. Malcolm Wheatley, 'Orchestrating the Big Project,' *Management Today*, May 1994, 50–4.
11. Thomas A. Stewart, 'CEOs See Clout Shifting', *Fortune*, vol. 120, no. 11, 6 November 1989.
12. *The Bulletin*, 19 March 1991, *op. cit.*, 36.
13. McDonald (1972).
14. See Brass (1985). Mainiero (1994) argues that political skill is particularly important if women are to advance their careers. See also Sinclair (1994).
15. *The Bulletin*, 19 March 1991, *op. cit.*
16. *Fortune*, 6 November 1989, *op. cit.*
17. Quoted in Pfeffer, (1992).
18. For fuller details of the research underlying this book, see the Appendix.
19. Mangham (1979).
20. See for instance, Pfeffer (1981).
21. Gary Samuels, 'A Meeting at the Breakers', *Forbes*, vol. 153, no. 13, 20 June 1994, 51–62.
22. Quoted in Pfeffer (1992, 214).
23. Several writers have written about issues explored here. See, for instance, Kakabadse (1984); Baddeley and James (1987); Ryan (1989).

5 The Leadership Capability: The Essentials of Leadership for Senior Executives

INTRODUCTION

There are few subjects which cause as much interest and concern as leadership. Whether we have the right political, religious and business leaders is a constant source of debate which pervades the popular media and our daily lives.

Developing leadership skills is critical for the senior executive, and in many organisations is a pressing requirement. In a survey asking what management talents were most urgently needed in their companies, CEOs singled out 'leadership' as the most important.[1] But developing leadership ability is problematic. Indeed, the outpourings on the subject of leadership over the years have prompted the comment, '. . . leadership is one of the most observed and least understood phenomena on earth'.[2]

Listed below are some of the main issues:

- *There is no universal agreement on how leadership is defined.* Bass (1990) notes that there are over 7500 published studies of leadership. There are probably almost as many definitions. Apart from the notion that leadership is an influence process involving two or more people, the definitions have little else in common.[3] There is also disagreement on whether there is a difference between leadership and management and what these differences might be.

- *There is no full agreement on what leadership involves.* Some see it as an inspirational process concerned with getting employees to go the 'extra mile'; while others see it as a more considered process involving an exchange relationship with clear goals and rewards.

- *There is confusion about which qualities are therefore most necessary for effective leadership.* Depending on the writer, leadership

126

can require everything from a range of superhuman qualities, down to one fundamental characteristic – such as cognitive ability.

- *There is doubt about which qualities can be developed.* The debate about whether leaders are born or made has raged for over 40 years and shows little sign of abating. While most writers seem to accept that there are some qualities like charisma, which no amount of training will develop, the notion that there are specific traits common to all leaders is widely questioned. As one recent study of 90 leaders noted, 'Our leaders were all too human; they were short and tall, articluate and inarticulate, dressed for success and dressed for failure, and there was virtually nothing in terms of physical appearance, personality or style that set them apart from the followers.'[4]

- *We only have a very limited understanding of what leadership at the top of organisations really means.* Despite all that has been written about leadership, until very recently the vast majority of leadership studies have been conducted on lower level managers.[5] How applicable such conclusions are to senior managers is uncertain.

Consequently, we need to treat the area of leadership with caution. There are many different interpretations of what leadership involves. In this chapter we identify those aspects of the leadership debate which seem most relevant to the senior executive and explore what is meant by a Leadership Capability.

LEADERSHIP AT A SENIOR LEVEL

Several recent studies have focused on what leadership involves for executives in senior positions. The principles which emerge from these are that:

(1) At a senior level it is not possible to divorce one's leadership style from the strategic context in which one is operating

Leadership exercised at the top has to be seen in relation to the external environment and the need to deal with the major issues facing organisations today. Whipp and Pettigrew (1993) cite one of the main weaknesses of the earlier approaches to leadership as being the search for almost universally applicable leader behaviour. Instead, they believe, 'The flow of alterations in both the organisation and the external competitive environment call for varying responses and, above all, different types of leadership . . . Different eras produce different leadership needs – leaders have to adapt accordingly.'

(2)   Leadership is concerned with change

Bennis (1993) argues that leadership is about innovating, initiating and creating. He believes that if senior executives are to ensure their organisations can compete successfully they must be at the forefront of change. In one study he highlighted how CEOs had become the 'Transformation Officer' of their organisations. Similarly, Kotter (1990) states, 'throughout the ages, individuals who have been seen as leaders have created change'. But it is successful change which is critical. Bennis (1993) notes that 47 per cent of the companies making up the 'Fortune 500' in 1980, were out of the list in 1990. He goes on to argue, therefore, that if organisations continue to act today the way they acted even five years ago, they are unlikely to last.

(3)   Leadership is intrinsically tied up with creating and communicating a vision or end state

It is imperative that leaders at the top define a vision which unifies and directs the whole of the organisation. Drucker has said that the first task of the leader is to define the mission.[6] Bennis found, 'every leader I talked with shared at least one characteristic: a concern with a guiding purpose, an overarching vision'.[7]

However, a vision that is not communicated is sterile. As Jung said, 'A dream that is not understood remains a mere occurrence. Understood it becomes a living experience'.[8]

(4)   Leadership is concerned with motivating and energising others to follow a route or path to achieve this vision

Managers need to motivate others and gain their commitment to the longer-term picture. At a senior level these tasks are particularly involved: typically executives will oversee large numbers of employees with whom they have only limited and indirect contact but whose working lives they influence to a very large degree. In this context, leadership demands careful thought and preparation as well as considerable personal drive from the individual involved.

(5) Leadership also entails enabling/empowering others to follow a particular path

In addition to motivating staff and gaining their commitment, staff also need resources and support to achieve and sustain progress towards achieving the vision. Senior executives have much greater control over resources than lower level managers. Providing the environment and resources to enable employees to achieve corporate goals is a critical leadership responsibility at this level.

(6) Effective leadership requires different approaches depending on internal circumstances and employee reactions

Executives are constrained by a range of factors in their operating environment which will affect the type of leadership approach adopted. In particular, leaders have to determine how quickly they can move the organisation forward and the appetite followers have for change.

Let us deal with some of these issues below in more detail.

(1) The strategic context of leadership

Miller (1990) argues that to pursue a narrow strategy based on past successes, rather than present imperatives and the needs of the market, can result in organisational decline. Rothschild (1993) argues that there is a need for a different type of leader at each phase of the business life cycle. He describes four different types (see Figure 5.1):

- *Risktakers.* Risktakers are needed when the business or institution is in a period of rapid growth. Risktakers are revolutionaries and creators, whose special talent is leading new businesses or institutions. Steve Jobs, one of the founders of Apple, is an example of this type of leader.

- *Caretakers.* A different kind of leadership is necessary to nurture a more orderly, evolutionary growth and long-term prosperity. These leaders add structure and stability to the organisation.

Fig. 5.1   *The four faces of strategic leadership*

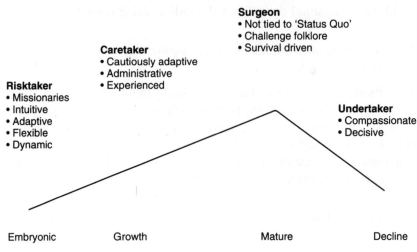

Source: Rothschild (1993)

- *Surgeons.* Surgeons are necessary when a mature institution or business slows down. It needs a different type of leader who is able to restructure the organisation. They are able to separate the strong from the weak and to focus on those parts that can survive and grow. Rupert Murdoch of News Corporation is an example of someone who can use this style effectively.

- *Undertakers.* Undertakers are required when things are terminal. They are necessary when the organisation must either be closed down or dismantled completely, so that independent existence ceases.

Although Rothschild does not provide any consistent research support for his typology, nevertheless, his different leadership types typify a growing attempt to understand how leadership relates to different strategic contexts.

Nahavandi and Malekzadeh (1993) provide another example of this type of approach. They relate different leadership qualities to two commonly used strategic classifications. Miles and Snow's (1978) classification uses the concepts of defender/analyser/prospector, while that of Porter (1980) relies on the concepts of cost leadership and differentiation.

The 'defender' and 'cost leadership' approaches are low risk strategies that are production and efficiency orientated and focus on well defined markets and domains. Both strategies require centralised control and autocratic decision making and mechanistic structures in order to succeed.

In contrast, 'prospector' and 'differentiation' strategies are high risk, innovative and R&D oriented, and focus on growth and marketing opportunities. These strategies require decentralised control, participative decision making and organic structures.

Getting the wrong focus for the strategic context or not changing to take into account different circumstances can prove disastrous. In the 1970s, Rank Xerox hired key ex-Ford employees to help introduce much needed controls and discipline into the company. However, while increased control was needed, their input was of little use to a company which should have been concerned primarily with increased differentiation and product improvement. David Kearns, the ex-CEO comments, 'Rather than buy into the culture that was there, the Ford men began to change it. For instance, the rigid managerial structure they subscribed to was driven by cost savings and not by what the customer wanted. It was something that Xerox was not used to. In the long run, it was not wholly helpful to the company'.[9]

Thus, leadership requires not only an understanding of the strategic context, but also, and more critically, the ability to align the company's practices to that environment. More work needs to be done in identifying the relationship between leadership qualities and the external context of the organisation. (Some of these issues are explored further in Chapter 11.) However, at the very least, senior managers implementing radical organisational change need a different leadership emphasis to that employed when maintaining or consolidating a company's activities.

(2)   Leadership and change

Kouzes and Posner (1987) found that managers who were asked to identify their own personal leadership experiences talked about significant change and about ventures into new territory. For Bennis, managing change is the ultimate leadership challenge of the Nineties.[10]

Transformational leadership

The emphasis amongst writers concerned with senior managers has been on their ability to handle radical or transformational change. It is, in fact, the external context which has largely given rise to this emphasis. If organisations are to cope with the increasing challenges resulting from global competition, they need to improve their practices radically and on a continual basis. Hence the growth of 'transformational leadership' approaches.[11]

Transformational leadership is about transforming organisations. It is concerned with the ability to motivate staff to commit themselves to a performance that exceeds expectations. Examples of transformational leaders include Michael Eisner at Walt Disney, Jack Welch at General Electric and Bill Gates at Microsoft.

For example, Michael Eisner transformed Walt Disney Corporation from a conservative firm into an assertive, proactive one. He took Disney into live action movies (some R-rated), developed new cartoon characters, syndicated a business show for television, introduced a TV channel, and licensed new products. This was a risky path for Eisner and one that veered from a course the company had followed for 40 years. Eisner brought in a work ethic, a style and a vision that has helped put Disney back into the forefront of entertainment.[12]

In order to transform organisations, leaders need certain qualities. Bass (1985) sees these as being:

- *Charisma.* The leader is able to instil a sense of value, respect and pride and to articulate a vision.

- *Individual attention.* The leader pays attention to followers needs and assigns meaningful projects so that followers grow personally.

- *Intellectual stimulation.* The leader helps followers rethink rational ways to examine a situation. They encourage followers to be creative.

In addition, transformational leaders need assessment skills, communication abilities and sensitivity to others. They must be able to articulate their vision, and they must be sensitive to the skill deficiencies of followers.

Many of the qualities evident in transformational leaders are also found in other leadership approaches concerned with radical change.

These include 'visionary leadership' and 'charismatic leadership'. Conger (1989) provides an example of one approach to 'charismatic leadership'. His framework involves four stages (Table 5.1).

- In Stage 1 the leader continuously assesses the environment, adapts and formulates a vision of what must be done. Here the leader's goals are established.

- In Stage 2, the leader communicates his/her vision to followers, using whatever means are necessary.

- Stage 3 is highlighted by working on trust and commitment. Doing the unexpected, taking risks and being technically proficient are important at this stage.

- In Stage 4, the charismatic leader serves as a role model and motivator. The charismatic leader uses praise and recognition to instil within followers the belief that they can achieve the vision.

Although not categorised as 'charismatic leadership', the theory developed by Kouzes and Posner (1987) also emphasises vision and motivation. They found that leaders who accomplished extraordinary things followed five crucial practices, namely:

Table 5.1 Stages in charismatic leadership

Stage one	Stage two	Stage three	Stage four
Detecting unexploited opportunities and deficiencies in the present situation	Communicating the vision	Building trust through technical expertise, personal risk-taking, self-sacrifice, and unconventional behaviour	Demonstrating the means to achieve the vision through role modelling, empowerment, and unconventional tactics
	Articulating the status quo as unacceptable and the vision as the most attractive alternative		
Sensitivity to constituents' needs			
Formulating an idealised strategic vision	Articulating motivation to lead followers		

Source: Gibson *et al.* (1994), adapted from Conger and Kanungo (1988)

- Challenge the process (that is, challenge the status quo)
- Inspire a shared vision
- Enable others to act
- Model the way
- Encourage the heart (that is, motivate and keep everyone going)

Thus, the various 'radical change' theories do have differences, but in general transforming organisations is about having vision, inspiring others, change and innovation, empowerment, creating commitment, stimulating extra effort and generating empathy with others.

(3)   Creating and communicating a vision

As in Conger's model, one of the first requirements for transforming organisations is through the expression of a shared vision of what the future might be. Most writers seem to agree that there is a distinction between creating a vision of the desired future and how this is articulated and communicated.

Creating the vision

Kouzes and Posner (1987) argue that leaders must have a vision. By this they mean they must be forward looking and have a clear sense of the direction they want to take their organisations. A vision is about possibilities, desired futures and expresses optimism and hope. It lends itself to visual imagery, implies some kind of ideal, implicitly involves choice and is unique.

Javidan (1991) sees it similarly, pointing out that visioning depends on:

- Understand existing realities; that is, where the organisation currently stands, including its culture, history and, if a division, where it fits into the whole.

- Developing a clear sense of direction for the organisation. An executive's views of the future direction should be based on some deeply held personal values and ideas. A vision is not a set of goals, but a set of ambitions that once internalised by subordinates, create a powerful intrinsic motivation to work in that direction.

There is some confusion as to how specific the vision should be. Javidan concludes that while leaders are clear about their vision, they do not provide a detailed account of the direction they are advocating. Instead, they tend to use broad descriptions to communicate their ideas. For instance, Jack Welch's vision for GE was expressed as follows:

> A decade from now I would like General Electric to be perceived as a unique, high spirited, entrepreneurial enterprise . . . a company known around the world for its unmatched level of excellence. I want General Electric to be the most profitable, highly diversified company on earth with world quality leadership in every one of its product lines.[13]

Just as important, however, is that the vision stretches staff. A vision which is easily attainable is unlikely to motivate. Again, Welch illustrates this point:

> Another thing I've learned is the value of stretching the organisation by setting the bar higher than people think they can go. The standard of performance we use is: be as good as the best in the world. Invariably people find the way to get there, or most of the way . . . unless you set the bar high enough you will never find out what people can do.[14]

For Senge (1990b) it is about 'creative tension'. This 'comes from seeing clearly where we want to be, our "vision", and telling the truth about our "current reality". The gap between the two generates a natural tension.' Learning how to use this tension and the energy it creates can help individuals, groups and organisations move more reliably towards their vision.

How much of the vision is developed exclusively by the leader or in consultation is debatable. A vision usually starts with one individual. However, many writers agree that the refinement and development of a successfully implemented vision is more likely to involve informal consultation and reality testing with key staff. Kotter (1982) has highlighted the essential nature of networking at a senior level in order to both receive information and test out ideas. Senge (1990b) also believes that for staff to be committed to a vision, it must be shared and built on personal visions. Visioning, he emphasises, is also an on-going process.

Communicating the vision

The factor that singles out the true executive leader is the ability to communicate this vision in a meaningful way. Jack Welch argues that, 'Yesterday's idea of the boss, who became the boss because he or she knew one more fact than the person working for them, is yesterday's manager. Tomorrow's person leads through a vision, a shared set of values, a shared objective.'[15] Several factors should be born in mind:

- *Clarity*. To communicate effectively leaders need to be clear not only about their vision statements, but also the values from which these derive. Kouzes and Posner (1987) showed that if senior managers clarify their values it produces significant pay-offs for their subordinates and their organisations.[16] Welch notes, 'You need an overarching message, something big but understandable. Whatever it is, every idea you present must be something you could get across easily at a cocktail party with strangers. If only aficionados of your industry can understand what you're saying, you've blown it'.[17]

- *Complementarity*. Leaders need to show how the vision will benefit the people they are addressing. When people understand their leader's beliefs and find their personal beliefs align, they are more likely to work hard to help the organisation achieve its goals. Clarity (people knowing what their organisation stands for), consensus (as to what the organisation's values are) and significance (people feel these values are worthwhile) are three essential factors for aligning leaders' values with those of their followers.[18]

- *Use of language*. Language has the ability to stimulate and motivate by appealing to people's emotions not just their intellect. Ever since Aristotle, alliteration, irony, imagery, and metaphor, have been used to provoke identification and emotional commitment amongst listeners. The speeches of leaders such as Churchill and Martin Luther King allowed their listeners to see the visions as if they were real. Analysis of Lee Iacocca's leadership in the Chrysler turnaround suggests that much of the power of his strategic initiative resided in his use of metaphors to unite stakeholders behind him.[19]

- *Credibility.* However, no amount of clever language will inspire others if the words are hollow. A leader's commitment to the vision must be credible. Credibility is a difficult quality to pin down, but it boils down to how one expresses the vision and demonstrates one's personal commitment to it. For instance, James E. Burke, ex-CEO of Johnson and Johnson, set up a series of meetings called the 'Credo Challenge' during which time he would tell his directors:

  > If you do not really believe in the Credo [mission] and you aren't urging your employees to abide by it, then it is an act of pretension. In that case, you should take it off the walls of your office and throw it away' . . . The assignment was to come out of the meeting either recommending that we get rid of it, change it, or commit to it as it is.[20]

- *Leading by example.* Credibility is also established through what leaders do as well as what they say. Much of what a leader does sends symbolic messages. The way leaders spend their time is carefully observed by subordinates. Kouzes and Posner (1987) believe that leaders should set an example to others by behaving in ways which are consistent with their stated values. It is of little use talking about trust, openness and honesty unless, as Welch notes, 'you do what you'll say you do, consistently, over time'.[21] An executive who focuses time and energy on accomplishing the organisation's values and goals sends strong and consistent signals concerning the behaviour expected of subordinates.

  Some of the most powerful messages can be accomplished through examples which involve personal sacrifice. This is especially true if an initiative involves some risk to one's career, status or position. Take Lee Iacocca for example who cut his own salary to $1.0 dollar a year:

  > I was the general in the war to save Chrysler . . . I began by reducing my own salary to $1.0 a year. Leadership means setting an example . . . I didn't take $1.0 a year to be a martyr. I took it because I had to go into the pits. I took it so that when I went to Dave Fraser, the union president, I could look him in the eye and say: 'Here's what I want from you guys as your share' . . . I wanted our employees and our suppliers to be thinking: 'I can follow a guy who sets that kind of example' . . .

people accept a lot of pain if everybody's going through the chute together.[22]

Other factors which may be relevant, include the leader's reactions to critical incidents (particularly in times of stress), what leaders reward and what issues they give feedback on and are consequently emphasising. Non-verbal elements such as gestures, timing, movement and props are also able to evoke responses. For example, in the early days at Apple, Steve Jobs organised the company office as a circle of work sections around a central foyer. In the foyer stood a grand piano and a BMW because Jobs believed people got ideas from seeing great products.[23]

In sum, the media of communication are many and varied. In developing and communicating a vision, the leader is 'managing meaning'. In other words, they are interpreting the environment and developing possible organisational responses to it. The vision, the organisation's response to the environment in the longer term, is conveyed by the leader through both what is said and the actions taken. Indeed, effective leadership involves understanding, not just that a vision has to be communicated, but how this is going to be accomplished and reinforced over time.

(4) Motivating and energising staff to achieve the vision

Energising through inspiration and charisma

As the previous section highlights, there is a close relationship between communicating the vision and motivating staff. Motivation involves a range of factors including both external rewards (such as pay and promotion) and the internal satisfaction people feel as a result of praise and the feeling of a job 'well done'. However, it is unlikely that transformational change will occur without a leader who has the ability to motivate staff in a magnetic and inspiring way. Some writers see this as 'energising' – the generation of high energy and excitement in getting staff to work towards a vision. Others use the word 'charismatic' – indeed, most of the radical-change leadership approaches emphasise inspirational or charismatic-like qualities in their leaders.

Max Weber (1947) first suggested that some leaders have a list of exceptional qualities – a charisma – that enables them to motivate followers to achieve outstanding performance. Several individuals such as Winston Churchill, John Kennedy and Martin Luther King had qualities which helped them have a strong impact. In the business arena, Sam Walton of Wal-Mart is considered by many to have charismatic qualities. He worked hard to explain his vision of retailing and serving the customer. He visited Wal-Mart stores to reinforce the message to employees that customer service is the first, second and third priorities for the firm in order to become recognised as a top retailer. As people responded to his vision and goals, Walton kept up a fast pace to meet other people and express his viewpoint. He paid attention to his employees and his customers – the human assets of business. Walton had a gift for making other people feel good about working for him and buying his products and service.[24]

Charisma, however, is a slippery concept. Empirical studies which have examined charismatic leaders have not produced a universally accepted set of behaviour and attributes. Moreover, charisma has several potential downsides which are frequently glossed over in the more popular management texts. Drucker claims 'charisma becomes the undoing of leaders'.[25] Indeed, there is a void in understanding the extent to which charismatic leaders can be harmful in expressing visions that are unrealistic or inaccurate in the way they attack a crisis or problem. The notion of the charismatic leader does not distinguish between moral, immoral and amoral intentions. For instance, Lee Iacocca is often cited as a charismatic leader with integrity. Other leaders, however, are not always seen so favourably. For instance, John De Lorean was able to raise hundreds of millions of dollars for his failed automobile venture because of his powers of persuasion and impression management.

Lord King of British Airways used a forceful personality to get staff to use questionable methods to pursue his aims. In encouraging staff to 'do something about Branson' of Virgin Airlines, he allegedly presided over a regime which deliberately followed a strategy of 'dirty tricks'. This involved painting Virgin as a dangerously overstretched airline headed by an irrational eccentric who indulged in a range of physically and morally dangerous pursuits. The intention was to get investors to lose confidence in Branson. With the strategy made public, the threat of substantial financial damages and the potential damage to BA's reputation, BA and Lord King apologised unreservedly for any injury caused to Richard Branson.[26] However, it still resulted in a $US1 billion lawsuit against BA.

Therefore, while charisma can result in heroic self-sacrifice in the service of a beneficial cause, it can also lead to high energy in the service of dangerous values. Several writers, including Conger (1990) and Kets De Vries (1989), have written about this 'darker side' to leadership.

Even if we accept these downsides, is it possible to develop charismatic qualities in executives at senior levels? As charisma is quite often associated with almost superhuman qualities, many executives find it difficult to imagine themselves being this way. One way round this is to emphasise what the leader must do – rather than focus on what they are. It may be more practical to focus on the actions which are needed to get employees to commit to changing themselves and their organisation, rather than cultivating a charismatic approach which does not fit easily with the personal style of the individual executive.

Take for example, the approaches adopted by Nelson Mandela and F. W. de Klerk. Ten years ago, few would have believed that in May 1994 a new South Africa, free of apartheid, would be born without civil war. The two men most responsible for this achievement, Mandela and de Klerk, achieved an exceptional outcome. But both are very different men and while Mandela might be seen as charismatic, the term is less easily applied to de Klerk. Yet de Klerk has inspired a white minority in a strong power position to relinquish that power for the good of all. Both have inspired different sections of the community and in different ways. Moreover, while Mandela has always been seen as a symbol of change, de Klerk was initially seen as a strong conservative and an unlikely radical. Inspirational approaches therefore, can be adopted by those who have not been blessed with overtly charismatic qualities.

This is also the case, at a less exalted level, in the corporate world. In the mid 1980s David Hancock, the MD of Apple UK, knew the company was losing its hold on the UK computer market and that members of his new executive team were not pulling together or giving each other support. Rather than give up on their business objectives, Hancock decided to challenge the team to climb the highest mountain in Africa arguing that if they could do that they would have the confidence to climb any mountain in business.

The challenge resulted in a group of 14 people – all but one non-athletes – climbing 19 000 feet to the top of Mount Kilimanjaro in Tanzania in a six-day trek through bad weather. 'Some literally clawed their way to the top; others moved just 10 feet at a time before collapsing to reach the summit.' Commenting on the experience, one manager said:

> Anybody who climbs Kilimanjaro who hasn't climbed more than two floors of steps in his life before gets great confidence. There's a much greater sense of understanding and a willingness to talk with each other today . . . [Afterwards] our business planning meeting was like telepathy. It was like brothers and sisters coming together.[27]

After their climb, this British subsidiary began to turn in record results.

An executive does not have to get his or her staff to climb mountains to be inspirational. But this example shows how being inspirational can be achieved in different ways, by what you do and the actions you take and encourage. The Apple executive helped his staff change their perception of what they were capable of. He inspired them to have a go, established a high level of confidence and helped them draw on their abilities and energy and to develop mental resilience. This was achieved by encouraging them to believe in themselves and their ability to overcome personal (as well as external) limitations.

Motivating through rewards

However, moving staff towards a vision is not only about inspirational appeals. Indeed, not everyone responds to inspirational messages in the same way, and sometimes not at all. Staff can be motivated without being inspired and there are other ways a leader can and must motivate others.

For example, Nadler and Tushman (1990) highlight another type of leadership behaviour which they call 'instrumental leadership', which relies on more traditional methods of motivation. In particular, executives have to focus on how key constituent groups (such as individuals within the senior team) behave in ways needed for change to occur. They emphasise that leaders need to clarify what needs to be done and build in measurement criteria and administer rewards so that individuals understand what behaviours are necessary to achieve corporate goals.

As Kouzes and Posner (1987) note, it is important that people know what is expected of them, that they are provided with feedback on their performance and that rewards are related to meeting the agreed standard. They argue that leaders should celebrate achievements, particularly behaviours which reinforce key organisational values. They also argue that leaders should make recognition public and be personally involved in the reward process. 'Leaders are always on the lookout for people who are doing the right things in the right way so they can celebrate the victories.'[28] This not only reinforces good behaviour, it also helps build relationships and support networks. They argue that good leaders don't maintain their distance but build genuine personal relationships between members of the team and the leader.

However, we also motivate staff through 'negative rewards' and fear. Few writers concerned with transformational leadership dwell on such processes. Nevertheless, as we noted at the start of the chapter, some external circumstances require leaders to downsize and close organisations. In order to improve GE's performance, Jack Welch had to do the '. . . hard structural work. Take out the layers. Pull up the weeds. Scrape off the rust'.[29] It is unrealistic to ignore the use of negative rewards and their consequences in these circumstances.

(5)   Empowering and enabling others to achieve a vision

A critical aspect of radical-change leadership approaches is empowering individuals to achieve the vision. Empowering staff has motivational consequences. However, like other aspects of leadership, the concept of empowerment is much used but not easily defined. According to Conger (1989) empowerment, 'is based on the premise that employees should be provided with various opportunities to develop and maintain their sense of self-control, competence and purpose'. It is a process of 'changing the employees internal beliefs . . . to increase their sense of self determination and to help them feel more powerful'.[30]

For other writers, empowerment is also about self-control and self-determination, but frequently much more as well. Bennis (1993) believes empowerment:

. . . involves the sense that people are at the centre of things rather than the periphery. In an effectively led organisation everyone feels he or she contributes to its success. Empowered individuals believe what they do has significance and meaning. Empowered people have both discretion and obligations. They live in a culture of respect where they can actually do things without getting permission first from some parent figure. Empowered organisations are characterised by trust and system-wide communication.[31]

Javidan (1991) adds several additional factors to the empowerment list. He argues that successful executives empower their subordinates by;

- Helping to develop a sense of ownership among employees by helping them understand their role and how they are contributing to the accomplishment of organisational goals.
- Helping employees build self-confidence by emphasising training and development.
- Encouraging employees to take responsibility and express their views and concerns.
- Providing the support needed to get the job done. Leaders ensure subordinates receive resources to perform their task. They also provide emotional and intellectual support. They are good mentors who help subordinates learn the ropes and avoid mistakes.
- Rewarding and recognising accomplishment. 'They also act as a cheerleader for their troops by trying to catch them when they are doing something right'.

From this we can see that empowerment has become a general concept to describe ways of generating high performance amongst employees in changing environments. At a senior level, however, the concept of empowerment needs to be further refined. Through their control of resources and the influence they have on the overall culture and configuration of the organisation, senior executives are in a much better position than lower level managers to enable employees to achieve work goals. Enabling others involves 'resourcing'; that is, providing people with the resources, tools and equipment to do the job. It also involves actions which 'endorse' the efforts of others in pursuit of the vision: for example, providing a supportive environment and culture and the encouragement of productive working relationships within the organisation.

These concepts are described in more detail below.

Resourcing

In the same way that a mountain climber (however enthusiastic and motivated) would not be expected to scale a mountain without adequate equipment, leaders need to ensure that followers have the necessary resources, tools and training to achieve the vision of their organisation.

There are dangers in executives using inspirational communication techniques and intrinsic rewards like praise and encouragement, which energise staff towards trying to achieve a vision, only to fall short in providing the tools to get the job done. In an analysis of why Xerox became uncompetitive in the 1980s, Kearns described how the previous CEO had outlined a vision for the company which in the end proved too ambitious to resource and carry out:

> Xerox employees heard this catchy 'architecture of information' phrase over and over again. But they never saw any true manifestation of it. All they saw were copiers . . . Quite simply [the vision] was too big for us. Too many ideas were coming at us to be properly dealt with . . . We just couldn't afford all the new ideas we were developing. So we did a number of things half-baked . . . As a result our goal of being seen as an office systems company, and not just a specialist in copiers, was not realized.[32]

Kanter (1977) argues that the key factor in leadership is the ability to obtain for the group, for subordinates or followers, a favourable share of the resources, opportunities and rewards available through the organisation. Finance, time, and a whole range of material resources come under the resourcing category. Key staff need to be given the flexibility to reward their employees in a way that contributes to corporate goals. If staff immediately below the leader are constrained in the way they can reward good performance, then it makes their job much harder to keep employees on track over the longer term.

Another critical aspect of resourcing is providing the appropriate human capital through recruitment and transfer of people within the organisation. Indeed, some senior executives regard the decisions they make about who they recruit into their organisation as one of their most important responsibilities. For it is through their immediate staff that much of the vision and values are translated into action. Theodore Roosevelt has said, 'The best executive is the one who has sense enough to pick good men to do what he wants done', although he also added the caveat, 'and the self-restraint enough to keep from meddling with them while they do it'.[33]

Endorsing

In addition to being provided with concrete resources, employees also need help in less tangible ways. They need to have the leader's endorsement and protection to help them in their pursuits. To do this it is necessary to create an environment and supporting infrastructure that allows this to happen. This includes protecting staff from the hassles, politics and interventions of 'powerful others'. Steve Jobs exemplified this approach when he talked of protecting his staff from 'the corporate noise'.[34]

One of the most debilitating aspects of corporate interference is having to cope with unnecessary bureaucracy. Katz (1974) argued 20 years ago, that leaders should create a work atmosphere where individuals are protected from bureaucratic pressures. In such an environment, employees know that when rules and procedures become an obstacle, they can depend on their leader to remove or lessen them. Peters and Waterman (1982) were equally concerned with this issue in highlighting a 'simple form – lean staff' as one of the eight characteristics of excellent companies.

Endorsing is also about creating a positive atmosphere which encourages behaviours that will help the organisation achieve its goals. As Sir John Harvey-Jones has pointed out, it is those at the top who set the general tone of the organisation which enhances or inhibits innovation and organisational learning and development.[35] The kind of environment generated is critical and there are a range of views on what this should be. Bennis (1993), for instance, sees the key to competitive advantage in the 1990s as a leader's ability to create an environment that generates intellectual capital. Effective leaders will be those who are best able to facilitate and orchestrate ideas, whatever their source.

Certainly, to compete effectively, leaders need to create a work environment which encourages innovation, new ideas, methods and risk-taking. The work environment has to be challenging and dynamic. Employees need to feel they can challenge work processes which prevent change and re-engineer routines which stultify.

Encouraging a challenging and dynamic environment is demanding. James E Burke, when CEO of Johnson & Johnson, described the situation at his company:

> We have some very tough meetings, very open and often emotion filled. It is a style of management that I have always encouraged . . . By putting a lot of contention into our system we get better results . . . I don't think it bruises people to argue and debate. You'd be surprised how easy some of our young people find it to politely say, 'You know you're wrong . . . you don't have the facts . . . I do . . . and here's the evidence to prove it' . . . To suppress talented people from speaking their minds is to deny your most important resource . . . ideas.'[36]

Equally important is the need to be tolerant of failure – to have enough patience to permit the growth of an environment of genuine risk-taking and initiative. Managers who are punished for embarking on new projects which fail, sends a strong signal to others that creativity is hazardous. An answer is to treat each failure as a learning experience. Effective leaders help subordinates find out why initiatives failed and how to avoid such failure in the future.

James Burke at Johnson & Johnson had just such an experience as a young executive in the mid-1950s. He developed a children's chest rub which was safer and easier to use. The product failed. The secretary of 'General' Robert Wood Johnson (the CEO at the time) summoned Burke to the General's office. He felt he was going to be fired but was surprised that the General wanted to do it himself. In the room the General said, 'I understand that your product failed'. Burke replied, 'Yes sir, that's true'. Picking up a piece of blue paper, the General said, 'furthermore, I understand it cost this corporation $865 000'. Burke said, 'Yes sir, that's right'. The General stood up, held out his hand and said, 'I just wanted to congratulate you. Nothing happens unless people are willing to make decisions, and you can't make decisions without making mistakes'. . . But he quickly added: 'If you make the same one again, you're through, but that doesn't mean that you should stop making mistakes'.[37]

(6) Different leadership approaches and different circumstances

At the start of the chapter, the need for different leadership approaches in different external environments was discussed. While much of what has been outlined above could be seen as critical to executives in a leadership role, not all aspects may be applicable in all environments. What of the 'Surgeon' that Rothschild identified? What of the circumstances where downsizing is needed? Are inspiration and empowerment appropriate in this context?

Certainly, some flexibility is necessary as the task faced by top executives when leading change can be very difficult. It is not unusual for even the most adept leader to find that various opposing elements will frequently work against the change attempt, actually inviting failure rather than promoting success. Indeed, it has long been recognised that change is often met with considerable resistance from within the organisation.[38] (We explore this further in Chapter 9.)

Contingency approaches

Consequently, it is worth looking in more detail at the different leadership approaches needed in different circumstances. Indeed, for the past 30 years leadership studies have been dominated by 'contingency' theories emphasising such flexibility. These say that leadership is about working out what needs to be done in any one situation and adapting one's leadership style accordingly. Under this scenario, being a born leader is less important than being able to develop a range of skills and use these to manage different situations.

An example of such an approach, and one which has enjoyed considerable popularity, is Situational Leadership.[39] As the name implies, Situational Leadership encourages leaders to adapt their behaviour to different situations. The leaders' behaviour is a combination of giving instructions on how to carry out a task (Task Behaviour) and giving interpersonal support (Relationship Behaviour). Thus, a leader can take a very precise, factual and task-orientated approach or be very interpersonally sympathetic. They can also combine both approaches giving rise to four different styles of Telling, Coaching, Participating or Delegating.

The decision about which of these four styles to use, depends on how able and motivated the followers are; known as their degree of 'maturity'. Those who are mature (that is, willing and able) require a 'delegating' style, while staff at the other extreme, lacking both motivation and ability, require a more 'telling' style (see Figure 5.2).[40]

For the senior executive, such theories have limitations. Largely used with lower level managers, these approaches have tended to emphasise face-to-face interactions or group situations. The majority

Fig. 5.2 *Situational leadership*

Style of leader

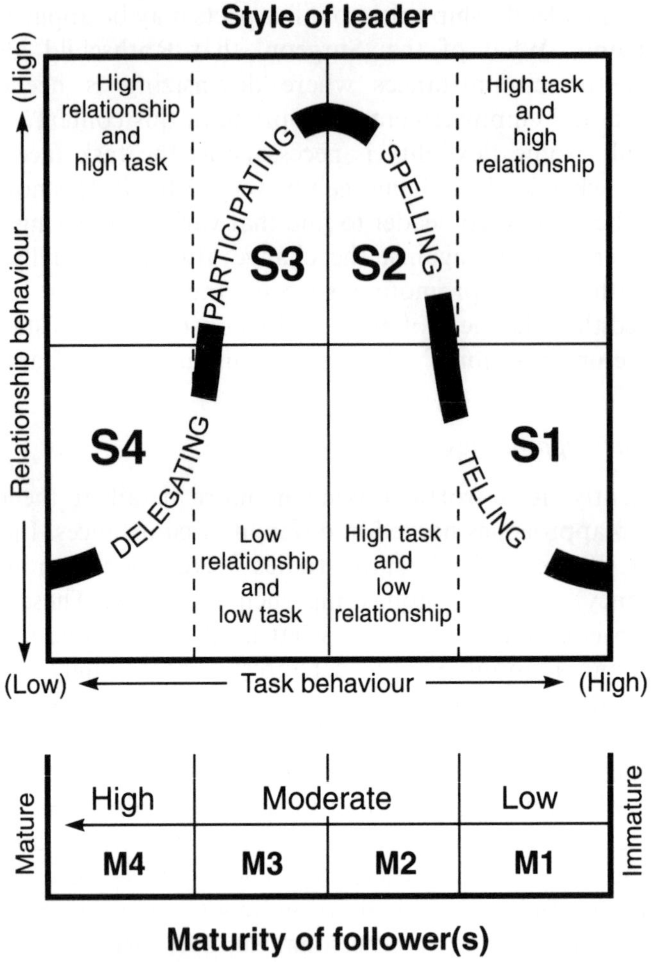

Source: Hersey and Blanchard (1982)

do not usually incorporate the broader perspectives needed at senior level, including acknowledgment of the external, strategic context, or ways of 'enabling' employees.

However, Situational Leadership does have relevance for senior managers. It highlights the different ways executives can manage one to one, or small group relationships. Moreover, transformational leadership approaches tend to emphasise a positive, inspirational and frequently 'uplifting' experience. Theories such as Situational Leadership highlight the point that more directing or autocratic styles may be appropriate in some situations.

While it makes sense for the executive to try to adapt their style to different situations, in practice there will be constraints on how much impact they can have. Yukl (1994) notes that their discretion can be limited by both internal and external factors.

The internal factors he cites include

(a) The degree of power the CEO has in relation to other major stakeholders including the board and coalitions of managers or trade unions.
(b) The financial condition of the organisation.
(c) The culture of the organisation. A traditional bureaucratic culture with standardised ways of doing things may have an inertia which is difficult to overcome.

The external environment includes factors such as

(a) The type of markets the company is in. Managerial discretion is greater in a growth industry, with differentiated products and little competition.
(b) The degree of power held by external stakeholders. There is less discretion when a few clients account for sales or the organisation has a single source for raw materials.
(c) The political/legal limitations. The more environmental regulations, safety requirements and legal obligations, the less the discretion.

SENIOR EXECUTIVE LEADERSHIP – A CONTINGENCY MODEL

Whilst the kinds of factors Yukl has identified may inhibit what the leader can do, few leadership models seem to take such external and internal variables into account. Indeed, Ropo (1989) goes further arguing that, 'although an implicit notion of change and flexibility is inherent in most situational leadership models . . . the issues of time and processes have been totally neglected . . . leader behaviour of managers is abstracted from their contextual settings and investigated in reductionist terms as if it had no past and future.'[41]

We put forward a contingency model below which attempts to address some of these shortcomings and brings together the essential items of the Leadership Capability. Firstly, the model acknowledges that leadership is concerned with change and that this needs to be viewed in relation to the strategic context of the firm. This can be radical change or more incrementally driven.

In addition, the leader has to balance the external requirements with the possible reactions of employees he or she is trying to lead inside the organisation. If leadership is about change then follower-ship is also about change. Thus, the senior executive has to account for employees' disposition to change. The model emphasises either an adverse or favourable disposition to change. Combining these two dimensions gives rise to four leadership styles illustrated in Figure 5.3. These are called Inspiring, Directing, Involving and Guiding.

Inspiring

Faced with an external environment that requires radical change, an organisation needs to transform itself. This can be achieved through the transformational leadership models described above. But to do this employees, at the very least, have to be marginally disposed towards considering the necessity to change. No matter how skilful leaders may be, they are constrained by the reactions of followers. It is the disposition of followers as well as the skills of the leader which

Fig. 5.3 *Senior executive leadership model*

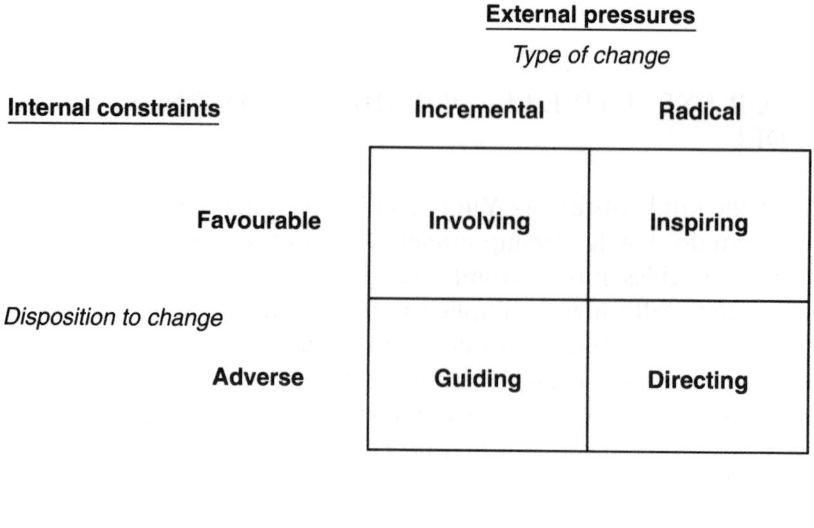

	External pressures	
	Type of change	
Internal constraints	**Incremental**	**Radical**
Favourable	Involving	Inspiring
Disposition to change		
Adverse	Guiding	Directing

provide the potential to bring about fundamental change and in a relatively short space of time.

The need to change radically and the positive disposition of one's employees give the leader the opportunity to be Inspiring. An Inspiring style emphasises radical change, which generates dedication and high energy from employees. (This is similar to Rothschild's 'Risk Taker' mentioned earlier in this chapter.)

Inspiring is most appropriate during the growth phase of a company or where a radical reorientation is necessary (but not downsizing). In these circumstances, the leader communicates a clear vision, energises staff through inspiring them and enables them to achieve the vision through providing the resources and a dynamic environment. For example, Steve Jobs did this at Apple. He provided the vision, the resources and an enabling environment by hiving off the Mac team from the rest of Apple. He had the personality and provided the ingredients for an Inspirational style to work. However, the staff on the Mac team were recruited very carefully and scrutinised in particular for their attitude towards what Jobs was attempting to do.

Directing

No matter how radical the change required, it may not always be possible to introduce this with the full commitment of the workforce. Whilst it is certainly more desirable to have the full backing of one's employees, there are many circumstances where they will not be disposed to change. This can occur when staff may lose privileged positions as a result of change, or do not see (and have no intention of seeing) the need to move out of established work patterns.

In this case, a more Directing leadership style is necessary. Here, compliance from staff may be the best that can be achieved. (Rothschild's 'Surgeon' or 'Undertaker' would apply here.) The emphasis is on making the most efficient use of the remaining resources and endorsing behaviour which contributes to the turn-around. One of the conclusions from a study of executives which identified what made the world's most competitive companies successful, was a need to 'Understand that change creates tension – acceptance that not everyone is able to adapt or wants to adapt: those who can't adapt or won't adapt will have to go'.[42]

Welch of GE illustrates the need to Direct:

You've got to be prepared for massive resistance . . . Incremental change does not work very well in the type of transformation GE has gone through. If your change isn't big enough, isn't revolutionary enough, the bureaucracy can beat you. When you get leaders who confuse popularity with leadership, who just nibble away at things, nothing changes.'[43]

Involving

Radical change may not always be necessary. Organisations sometimes go off course, but do not require a radical overhaul. Change can be evolutionary as at IBM in the 1980s, Shell and Merck. Moreover, radical change may subsequently require a process of building, particularly if the organisation has been traumatised. Consequently, a more Involving leadership style may be appropriate. Here, as with Inspiring, staff are not antagonistic to change. They may be fearful and worried, and may need reassurance, but they do not have entrenched antipathy to change possibilities. In this case the vision is clear and there is a positive environment. However, the change process is more considered, the time scale less pressing and the activities of the organisation less frenetic. The leader has time to review and develop enabling structures, such as the organisational culture and support systems, in order to reinforce the new direction.

An Involving approach is also important when an organisation is consolidating its position after initial growth. (This is the Caretaker style outlined by Rothschild.) Indeed, ignoring the need for such an approach when the strategic context requires it can prove disastrous. One of the reasons why the American airline People Express failed to stay in business was partly due to the CEO, Don Burr's constant striving for growth, when consolidation was necessary. Moreover, it is no less a leadership task to keep organisations moving forward when products are in mature markets. Indeed, knowing when not to intervene in a radical way is a critical leadership quality.

Guiding

Finally, there are also circumstances where radical change may not be necessary, where time may be on one's side, but the reaction of employees to change is adverse. This might occur in bureaucratic organisations, both in the public and private sector, or in large-scale capital intensive industries where radical, overnight change may not be appropriate or possible. Instead, the leader may be constrained by the inertia of the organisation.

In these circumstances, change comes from Guiding employees to achieve 'small wins'. If there are entrenched views or conflicting values, then no vision, no matter how well communicated, is going to transform the organisation. Here the leader needs to implement change through 'instrumental' methods, by giving clear rewards for behaviour which aligns with corporate goals.[44] Again compliance may be the best that can be achieved.

Changing style

But can leaders change their style in the ways encouraged by contingency theories? There is evidence to suggest that this is not easy. Churchill, for example, was a much more effective leader during war-time Britain than when the country was at peace. Some senior executives (like Al Dunlap, during his time at Consolidated Press Holdings in the late 1980s) pride themselves on their ability to implement change in a forceful, Directing way and are unlikely to be as effective as Inspirational or Involving leaders. Clearly, it is more appropriate to fit these leaders to the circumstances rather than expect them to adapt.

However, it does seem possible for senior executives to adopt a range of styles and indeed, it is important that they do. Companies and the products and services they produce go through cycles of growth and decline. As conditions change, executives need to have the capacity to respond to different circumstances. In conglomerates, leadership may involve an Inspiring approach in some areas of the business, and Directing or Guiding in others. Philip Brass, CEO of Pacific Dunlop, a very diverse organisation with 47000 employees, has to constantly shift between leading growth, consolidation, decline and divestiture.

Sir John Harvey-Jones during his period as Chairman of ICI (1982–1987), illustrates how senior executives can adapt their style. He implemented widespread changes in what was a monolithic organisation. He streamlined the board, reduced corporate head-quarters staff from 1200 to 400, restructured the organisation, providing economies of scale saving £50 million per year. He changed the culture and diversified the company, reducing dependency on the UK market which had previously left the company vulnerable.

To do this, Sir John had to use the full range of styles outlined above. He Inspired many, but he also met with resistance. 'As fast as Harvey-Jones could excite people in middle and lower management, their bosses were just as swift in killing that new energy'.[45] Consequently, Sir John had to use more Guiding and Directing styles in order to achieve a 25 per cent reduction in the company's UK workforce during the 1980s. The overall result of the changes was strong internal morale and a new direction for the company.

SUMMARY

Despite the vast range of studies on leadership, there is very little agreement as to the qualities needed for effective leadership. Moreover, until very recently the majority of leadership studies have been conducted on lower level managers.

Nevertheless, from the research that has been carried out, certain principles have emerged. At a senior level, the issue of leadership style cannot be divorced from the strategic context of the firm. Leaders may need to take a very different approach in a firm which is undergoing radical organisational change versus one which is consolidating or maintaining its business.

Despite the need to take context into account, in recent years the transformational approaches to leadership have received most attention. These involve using vision to inspire others and gain commitment, empowering others to act and 'go that extra mile'. Of these, the capacity to create a vision which unifies and directs the organisation is of central importance.

Executives must also have the capacity to communicate, motivate and energise others to achieve the vision. Whilst charisma if often cited as the inspirational quality leaders need, in practice executives can motivate others in a number of ways. More traditional or 'instrumental' approaches, which involve clarifying goals and building in measurement criteria to reward success, also have their place. Senior executives must also ensure followers have the necessary resources to do the job and help create an environment and culture which is supportive of the end vision.

Thus, the leadership task at senior levels is complex and demanding and even the most adept leader can face resistance. Flexibility is therefore the key. Executives may well have to adapt their behaviour to different situations. Furthermore, when choosing between different leadership approaches they must take a range of internal and external variables into account. A Contingency Model for Senior Executive Leadership has been presented to help executives think through their approach.

Strategic imperatives will influence the rate of change that is required. Ultimately, success will depend on the leader aligning external requirements with internal constraints and opportunities. Having done this, the test is then whether the leader can move on to let others take their place as circumstances change, or change their style as new imperatives appear.

NOTES

1. See Louis Richman's article 'CEOs To Workers: Help Not Wanted', *Fortune*, 12 July 1993, 56–7.
2. J. M. Burns (1978) *Leadership,* New York: Harper & Row.
3. See Yukl (1994).
4. See Bennis and Nanus (1985).
5. See Sashkin and Burke (1987).
6. Warren Bennis quoted Drucker in his article, 'Managing the Dream: Leadership in the 21st Century', *Training: The Magazine of Human Resources Development*, Lakewood Publications, May 1990.
7. Bennis (1990).
8. Quoted in Bennis (1990).
9. Kearns and Nadler (1992).
10. See Warren Bennis, 'The Chasm Between Management and Leadership', *Healthcare Forum Journal*, 1993 in 'Insights on Leadership', documentation for the University of Melbourne Top Management Forum, December 1993.
11. Transformational Leadership was originated by Burns (1978) and developed by writers such as Bass (1985) and Tichy and Devanna (1986).
12. Gibson *et al.* (1994).
13. Cited in Aguilar (1988, 90).
14. Noel Tichy and Stratford Sherman 'Jack Welch's Lessons for Success', *Fortune*, 25 Janaury 1993.
15. Tichy and Sherman (1993).
16. Kouzes and Posner (1987).
17. Tichy and Sherman (1993).
18. This is drawn from Kouzes and Posner (1987), although the last of their three factors is 'intensity'.
19. Westley and Mintzberg (1989).

20. See Horton (1986).
21. Noel Tichy and Stratford Sherman, 'Jack Welch's Lessons for Success', *Fortune*, 25 January 1993.
22. Iaccoca and Novak (1984).
23. See D. Wise, 'Apple's New Crusade', *Business Week*, November, 1984.
24. Gibson *et al.* (1994).
25. Gibson *et al.* (1994).
26. See Gregory (1994).
27. See Sculley (1987, 483).
28. Kouzes and Posner (1987).
29. Tichy and Sherman (1993).
30. Conger (1989).
31. Quoted in excerpts from 'An Invented Life – Reflections on Leadership and Change', documentation for the University of Melbourne Top Management Forum, December 1993.
32. Kearns and Nadler (1992).
33. Quoted in documentation for the University of Melbourne Top Management Forum, December 1993.
34. From the video 'In Search of Excellence', based on the book by Peters and Waterman (1982).
35. From the BBC video series 'Troubleshooter'. Sir John argues it is the person at the top of the organisation who sets the tone, when interviewing the CEO at Triang in the UK.
36. Horton (1986, 15, 16).
37. Horton (1986, 25).
38. For instance, Lewin (1947) and Kotter *et al.* (1979).
39. See Hersey and Blanchard (1982). Despite the limited empirical support for the Situational Leadership model, it has enjoyed tremendous popularity worldwide.
40. Hersey and Blanchard now call their four styles S1 – Directing, S2 – Coaching, S3 – Supporting and S4 – Delegating. They have also replaced follower 'maturity' with 'readiness'. Nevertheless, the principles of their theory remain largely the same.
41. Ropo (1989) quoted by R. Whipp and A. M. Pettigrew, 'Leading Change and the Management of Competition', in J. Hendry, G. Johnson and J. Newton (eds) (1993) *Strategic Thinking, Leadership and the Management of Change*, New York: John Wiley, 1993.
42. 'What Makes the World's Most Competitive Companies So Competitive?' Conclusions of executives who participated in the Management Frontiers Competitive Leadership Study Tour, Europe/USA, September–October 1991.
43. Quotes from Tichy and Sherman (1993), cited in an article entitled 'Jack Welch's Lessons for Success', *Fortune*, 25 January 1993, 64–8.
44. Guiding has some similarities with 'instrumental' leadership mentioned earlier and the 'transactional' leadership approach. This is particularly true in situations where the leader gives benefits to staff (such as a definition to

the situation and direction) and they reciprocate in terms of increased responsiveness to the leader. It involves winning (eventually) acceptance for the direction one is proposing and getting followers sufficiently motivated to pursue it.

45. See *Sir John Harvey-Jones,* Case 9-490-013, Harvard Business School, 1989, 9.

6 The Integration Capability: The Design and Development of Senior Teams

INTRODUCTION

As executives rise up the organisation, they need to rely on others to a greater extent to get things done. The Integration Capability concerns the executive's ability to work with various individuals, groups and departments in order to produce effective results. Executives need to recognise when such groups – be they formal teams, or larger business units – are not working effectively and how to correct this. To do this they need to get other managers on their side to design and create new and more effective structures.

The skills needed to integrate are most evident and at their most demanding when working with the top management team. Consequently, in this chapter, our major focus is to explore the particular knowledge and skills needed to work with (and, where necessary, lead) other executives on the senior team.

TEAMS AT THE TOP

Teamwork has long been recognised as something of value and worthy of development within work organisations. In general, effective teams make qualitatively better decisions than individuals, can produce more creative solutions and provide a camaraderie and satisfaction that is not available when working alone.

Teamwork is particularly important at the top of the organisation. Hambrick (1987) argues that the strategic success of business depends not just on one person, but on the entire Top Management Team. If the aptitude, values, skills and knowledge of the .Top Management

Team do not fit with what is required by the competitive environment, or if they do not mesh with each other, the business may encounter serious problems.

However, despite the importance of senior teams to the strategic management of the organisation, what makes for an effective senior team is controversial. While we know a lot about, for instance, sports teams, social groups and lower level work teams, much less is known about the Top Management Team. Indeed, many writers shy away from giving prescriptions about the ideal top team.

Although some characteristics of lower level work groups have applicability to the top team, it is dangerous to assume that all teams are the same. Ancona and Nadler (1989) see the senior team differing from other teams in several ways.

- *The external environment is more salient.* Customers, competitors, financial markets, and a range of stakeholders have an impact on team functioning. Understanding and managing the environment is a critical task of the team.

- *The tasks they carry out are more complex.* The team must cope simultaneously with managing internal processes, external relationships, organisational leadership and strategic decision making.

- *There is a likelihood of intensified political behaviour.* Because of the nature of the senior team environment (with powerful executives and often very high stakes) the likelihood of political behaviour is more pronounced than in other teams.

- *The team has increased visibility.* The team's actions and dynamics are observed critically by others in the organisation. Symbols are important and seemingly inconsequential actions can have a major impact.

- *The CEO is in a unique role as team leader.* In almost all organisations, the CEO is the one who hires and fires and is the ultimate arbiter of conflict: a major disagreement with the boss means there are only limited avenues of escape for the subordinate executive.

Given these features, working within and managing a senior team is challenging and often difficult. Katzenbach and Smith (1993a) argue that the complexities of long-term challenges, the heavy demands on executive time and deep seated individualism of senior people can work against teamwork at senior levels.

Managing these issues is an important part of the executive's Integration Capability. Effectiveness in this area depends on understanding several factors, which are explored in this chapter. They are:

- *The nature of top teams.* The notion of the Top Management Team has gained general recognition in recent years, but there are differing views as to what this means. Understanding the different kinds of team at the top helps considerably in managing these entities.

- *Teamwork at senior levels.* The senior executive team can have considerable impact on the performance of the organisation. Before trying to build an effective team however, executives need to look at the strategic context in which the team will be operating and develop a realistic picture of the degree of teamwork required.

- *Team purpose, process and design.* Where teams are needed, managers need to consider the purpose or focus of the team and how they process issues and interact. They also need to pay attention to design aspects such as how the group organises itself, how members are rewarded and so forth.

- *Team performance and development.* Team development takes time and effort. Executives embarking on initiatives to build their team need to understand the different types of senior team which exist, the consequences of teams underperforming and estimate the potential of their team to develop.

Understanding the nature of top teams

In recent years, the term Top Management Team has been used to denote the 'dominant coalition' or senior group of managers at the top of the organisation who are collectively responsible for, and influence, the strategic direction of the firm.[1]

Not all Top Teams are the same, however. Some writers view the Top Management Team as being the six or seven key senior executives responsible for the major business units within the firm. Other writers and CEOs have included anything up to 40 or more executives in their definition of the Top Management Team. Clearly, these differences in size and representation will have implications for how a team operates and is managed.

In fact, several types of executive team can be identified at the upper levels of the organisation (Figure 6.1). At the top is the Board of Directors, and below this the senior executive team. In some companies both the Board and this senior team will be largely indistinguishable. In addition, there may be several senior 'teams' immediately below the executive team which are also influential and form part of the 'dominant coalition' or senior group of managers running the organisation.

The Top Management Team or dominant coalition, particularly if it is a large group, has to be managed differently to a smaller executive team. The emphasis here will be on ensuring the group communicates the vision and general direction of the company, encourages company values and acts as a leadership role model. This will demand broader integration and alignment skills rather than the degree of teambuilding that may be necessary with the smaller executive team. Within the dominant coalition, the emphasis will be on winning cooperation from other executives, usually in a series of one-on-one, or smaller group negotiations. Typically, executives will form temporary alignments depending on the issues involved, and

Fig. 6.1 *Top teams*

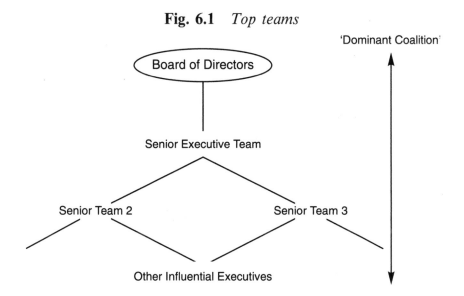

whilst commitment to the group may be high, in effect this is a group of cooperating executives rather than a closely knit team.

There is nothing wrong with such an arrangement. Indeed, as Katzenbach and Smith (1994) point out, the top managers at many of the world's most successful companies, such as General Electric, JP Morgan and Hewlett-Packard operate explicitly as a more loosely connected senior group. Moreover, Sir John Harvey-Jones, when CEO of ICI, illustrated the importance of managing the dominant coalition effectively. He had the ability to focus key executives throughout a vast organisation on the overall group strategy and to get the senior group to work cooperatively in a competitive environment. As a consequence, he was able to transform a 'sleeping giant' into a more dynamic organisation. Despite considerable challenges (including retrenchment and quite radical changes in the way ICI operated), he maintained the cooperation of his top management group, merging and integrating their interests with those of the organisation overall.

Teamwork at senior levels

Improving and managing a senior executive team is more exacting. Indeed, it is important to consider whether a close-knit senior team is necessary at all, or whether the organisation is best served by the looser relationships noted above. Despite the exhortations from many quarters about the importance of having teams, the reality is that teamwork is often difficult to develop. Sinclair (1992) argues that without considerable thought, some teams can actually be detrimental to the individual and the organisation. Certainly, there is plenty of evidence to suggest that teams can perform poorly. In a study of 26 top-level corporate teams, fewer than 45 per cent of the interactions were described as teamwork.[2] Although the team option promises greater performance, it also brings more risk and executives must be brutally honest in assessing the trade-offs.[3]

The senior team does not have to reach some textbook ideal: there are several levels below perfection where the team's contribution can still be beneficial to the corporation. However, the necessity for a team varies, and in some instances, if a senior team is not in place and operating well, the company may be vulnerable. In order to decide the degree of teamwork necessary and what form it should take, two factors are important. The first of these is the external strategic context within which the organisation finds itself. The second is the degree of internal dependency between the different parts of the business.

External context

Two general approaches have been taken to linking the top team with the external context. The first of these, led by Hambrick and Mason (1984), has tried to link the strategic thrusts of the business with the demographic characteristics of top team members, such as education, functional expertise, age, length of time in the job, and so forth. This work has given insights into the strategic paths chosen by some companies and also offered clues about the type of executive best suited for a top team in pursuing a particular strategy. For instance, Miles and Snow (1978) found that firms which compete successfully by continual product innovation have relatively heavier representation of marketing and product development specialists within their top teams.

It is not unusual to find companies reengineering the composition of their senior team in order to take advantage of new strategic realities. For instance, in the early 1990s,[4] in order to help transform itself into a marketing – led organisation with a reputation for quality, the MD of British Telecom, Michael Hepher, embarked on a programme of steadily filling the top executive posts with outsiders who 'valued customer responsiveness and appreciated the need for change'. BT's management board was renamed the group quality council. By 1994, only two of its nine members were career BT executives: the other seven were from companies such as IBM, Black & Decker and from US regional telephone companies with more market focused backgrounds.

In addition to the detailed assessment of demographic characteristics, a second, broader approach has attempted to identify the kind of top team needed when organisations face either a stable or rapidly changing external environment. In a stable environment, a high degree of teamwork may not be necessary. However, in fast changing and complex environments, there is a much greater requirement for executive teamwork to solve the challenges facing the organisation. An executive in the telecommunications industry commented, 'In an industry like ours which never stands still, the manager that does it himself rather than involve other managers is at the crux of the problem . . . unless they can see the benefits of teamwork and see success outside of themselves the whole stack of cards will fall over.'[5]

Internal dependency

The second major aspect affecting executive teamwork is the extent to which members need to work together. If the tasks which the team have to perform involve a great deal of interdependency and cooperation, then a high degree of teamwork is essential. Several writers argue that an organisation which has high interdependence between units requires considerable coordination between executives.[6]

However, companies following a strategy of unrelated diversification, for instance, may offer only limited opportunities for teamwork. For example, the CEO of a large mining conglomerate in Australia tolerates a fairly small amount of cooperation between members of the senior team. Each executive is responsible for sizeable parts of the business, but operates largely autonomously due to the very diverse nature of the company's mining and exploration interests. Here, the senior team is seen primarily as a vehicle for information sharing at senior levels. Developing a stronger team in these circumstances is both difficult and unnecessary.

However, no matter how difficult, where the degree of internal interdependence between units is strong and the organisation is faced with a changing external environment, there is a much greater need for a highly interactive team that can discuss issues in some depth. Indeed, the consequences of not having teamwork in such an environment can be disastrous. Hambrick (1987) highlights how a company attempting an aggressive product innovation strategy in the medical instrument industry found that the heads of marketing and R&D, while both very strong in their own areas, were not compatible or sufficiently compromising with each other. The strategy floundered and the executives had to be replaced.

FACTORS AFFECTING SENIOR TEAM PERFORMANCE

External changes and internal coordination are the starting point for assessing the extent to which an executive team needs to be developed. The performance of the team will then be determined by several factors (see Table 6.1). These are explored further in the chapter as follows:[7]

Table 6.1 Senior teams – performance factors

Team purpose (what is focused on)	Team process (how people interact)	Team design (how the team is structured)
Action focus • Share information • Discuss issues • Make decisions	Team skills • Communication • Give/receive feedback • Individual mgt. styles	Personnel structure • Team membership • Individual Capabilities • Beliefs about teams • Teamwork skills
Time focus • Past vs present • Short vs longer-term	Team stages • Forming • Storming • Norming • Performing	Reward structure • Team rewards • Individual rewards • Power/status
Issue focus • Operational vs strategic • Problems vs puzzles	Team politics • Hidden agendas • Executive dual role • Succession • Power plays	Operating structure • Location • Frequency of meetings • Other factors impacting the group

- *Team purpose.* The extent to which the team concentrates on the right issues and produces positive outcomes.[8]

- *Team process.* How members relate, the extent to which they understand and manage team behaviour, and their satisfaction with the team.

- *Team design.* The membership of the team, the rewards for teamwork and the opportunities to meet as a team.

Team purpose

Team purpose refers to the focus of the senior team. Katzenbach and Smith (1993a) argue that too often teams at the top confuse the broad mission of the total organisation with the specific purpose of the executive team. For a real team to form there must be a team purpose that is distinctive and specific, which requires its members to role up their sleeves and accomplish something beyond individual end products.

Our research on senior executive teams suggests that executives need to consider three aspects of Team Purpose. These are a team's focus on Action, Time and Issues.

Action focus

Senior teams must agree whether their function is simply to share information, to discuss problems, or to take decisions and then act upon them. Teams will not take decisions on everything facing them and there will be several problems which cannot be resolved in the short-term. However, it is important to ensure that the team does resolve difficulties and does not resort to putting contentious decisions to one side. Easy as it sounds, in many cases senior teams do not take the time to sort out their decision making role and frustration can result.

Time focus

Executives are often encouraged to analyse their past performance and then make adjustments to bring in better results. In some senior groups, however, the past is all that is reviewed. It is not unusual to find senior groups spending a large percentage of their time concentrating on past financial or sales data which are of limited use to the future management of the business. One executive of a European based manufacturing company we interviewed said:

> We were dragged together for the meeting every couple of months
> . . . that really is John's chance to berate everybody for their
> financial performance. Tell us about Spain, will you bring Sweden
> in on time? Will you get the dollars in? It serves a very good
> purpose but there should be another forum..which isn't concen-
> trating on the day-to-day results . . . one where we discuss
> strategically, without any pressure, how we can manage the
> business better.[9]

Issue focus

In principle, the senior team should be focusing on critical issues which involve collective involvement. Two factors in particular may sidetrack the team from achieving this focus.

The first is the drift towards reviewing individual issues. These issues, confined to an individual's area of responsibility, are usually of no concern of the senior team. Casey (1985) calls these 'simple puzzles'. Typically, simple puzzles are technical issues from one functional or business area. They can be solved by a member of the management team on their own, without any help from their peers or colleagues. In teams which are functioning effectively, simple puzzles are quickly delegated to the individual concerned. When management groups are struggling to become a team, however, everyone may feel an obligation to get involved in everybody else's business with dire consequences – both in relation to the decisions taken and the emotions released. This is because the question, 'Do we need to be a team for this work?' has never been asked.

The second obstacle is to concentrate too much on internal, organisational issues at the expense of addressing the external demands of the market place. This may occur because information about market trends is less easily available. In addition, it is often easier to review the more immediate, concrete issues as opposed to the more ambiguous problems senior teams often face. Decisions about operational matters often have fairly clear measurement criteria: one knows relatively easily if output in the factory has declined or employee turnover has increased. Measuring the effectiveness of strategic and longer-term approaches is almost always less obvious. Indeed, senior teams may be drawn into concentrating on operational issues, precisely because of the ambiguity, uncertainty and lack of immediate feedback on longer-term issues.

Rover, the UK car manufacturer, decided to come to grips with this problem in the late 1980s. It created flatter management structures with responsibility for operational issues devolved further down the organisation. 'The move created a team of top level managers . . . to think about the next 10 years.' As a result 'significant change' resulted from the strategy team's work.[10]

Casey (1985) talks of senior teams dealing with real 'problems'. While the solution to a puzzle exists somewhere (such as trying to produce a leak-proof battery), a problem is so difficult that nobody knows what the answer is. Problems cannot be neatly categorised as production, finance or personnel puzzles. Problems are large, ambiguous and unprecedented; some are insoluble. Real problems include: what happens if a mining company's mineral reserves run out with the possible collapse of a whole community built around the mine; or more generally, how to generate a long-range plan in conditions of maximum political, fiscal, economic and social ambivalence.

Casey (1985) argues that all management groups face problems, but very few face up to them. A useful starting point is to decide what problems the team should be tackling. This will vary depending on the context, but in our view most senior teams need to address (to some degree) the kinds of issues listed below:

- Objectives and purpose of the organisation
- Resources available to meet these objectives
- Future threats and opportunities for the organisation
- The impact of influential actors and groups on the business
- The establishment of appropriate organisational structures
- The implications of cost management (both reduction and expenditure) for business survival and development
- Development of an appropriate strategy

In essence, therefore, senior teams must define their purpose and the extent and nature of their decision making. Until these aspects are clarified they have little chance of being able to identify their responsibilities and thereby measure their achievements – far less understand and learn where they may be going wrong.

Team process

If teams are to find solutions to problems, executives have to be able to explore and manage the dynamics of the group – or what we call Team Process. This covers such things as how open members are, how conflict is resolved, and the degree of support, cohesiveness and trust shown by team members.

While much research has been done on team processes at middle and supervisory management levels, much less has been achieved at the upper management level due to the problems of accessing senior teams for research purposes. Teamwork is, nevertheless, an area most senior managers will be conscious of and, increasingly, assessed upon. When managers try to gauge whether they have an effective team or are 'good team players' they need to consider a range of behaviours. For example, who listens, who blocks, who dominates meetings of the senior team? Does everyone participate and if not why not? Who reduces tension and who keeps the group on track? Who maintains motivation and morale? All of these are Process issues. Usually, they are the kind of problems which are relatively easy to spot but hard to tackle and do something about. A typical situation is illustrated by an executive in the electronics industry:

> There's a lot of time wasted by these two guys throwing rocks at one another. They don't get on. They always have different views and their management styles are totally different. It's a real issue for the rest of us but I guess we ignore it and hope it might go away.[11]

Several factors are important in looking at Team Process and what affects it. Below, team skills, stages in a team's development and the use of power within the team are discussed in more detail.

Team skills

One obvious influence on team behaviour is the skills individual senior executives bring to the team. However, it is rare for these to be given much consideration. It is even more rare for senior executives to spend time developing their team skills. Often, it is assumed that because executives have developed a range of interpersonal abilities they will also be able to use these effectively within the executive team. As we noted earlier, there are substantial differences between senior teams and those at other levels in the organisation. As a result, executives may be unprepared for the dynamics with which they are confronted.

Ancona and Nadler (1989) believe teamwork at senior levels demands sophisticated social skills: executives must be able to negotiate and compromise, pool information from multiple sources and blend analysis and action. They must have the ability to listen and possess skills of inquiry and compromise. Usually, it is not that executives lack these skills, rather they tend not to consider how to adjust their skills to suit the dynamics of the senior team.

Stages of team development

The skills that are needed will differ depending on what stage the team is at in its development. Little empirical work has been done on this issue at a senior level. However, Tuckman's (1965) model has some applicability to senior teams. Tuckman argued that to become fully effective, a group experiences different stages of development (see Figure 6.2). Not all groups go through the stages in exactly the same way, or experience each stage with the same degree of intensity.

Fig. 6.2 *Team development wheel*

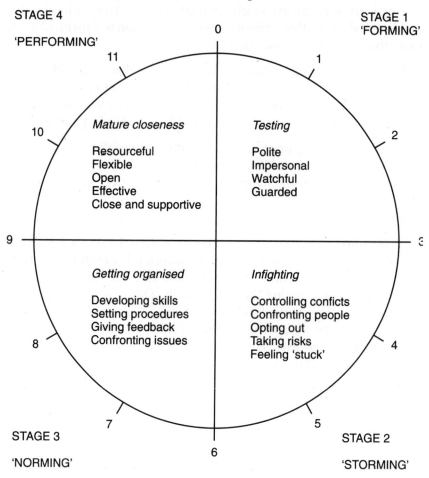

STAGE 4

'PERFORMING'

STAGE 1

'FORMING'

0

11

1

10

2

Mature closeness

Resourceful
Flexible
Open
Effective
Close and supportive

Testing

Polite
Impersonal
Watchful
Guarded

9

3

Getting organised

Developing skills
Setting procedures
Giving feedback
Confronting issues

Infighting

Controlling conficts
Confronting people
Opting out
Taking risks
Feeling 'stuck'

8

4

7

5

STAGE 3

'NORMING'

STAGE 2

'STORMING'

6

Source: Based on Tuckman (1965)

The first stage (Forming) is usually evident when groups first meet. Here individuals test each other out and remain watchful, guarded and inhibited. Groups at this stage are characterised by polite behaviour and avoidance. However, some groups never get past this stage. Senior groups and Boards which meet infrequently and do not have individuals who are committed to team activity can remain in this category indefinitely. For example, this kind of behaviour typified meetings of the senior team at the telecommunications company, Ameritech. According to the then CEO, William Weiss:

... the management committee's meetings were the most civil, uninteresting, unconstructive kinds of meetings you could have. You did not get varying points of view. If you didn't like what the boss wanted to do, you sat on your hands. You didn't do things with your heart, so nothing ever got done very well.[12]

To progress, many groups go through the Storming stage. This is often the point where real development of interpersonal processes takes place. It is here that members will try, as Kofodimos (1991) suggests, to understand their own style and the style and contributions of others. Defensive communication, which inhibits team interaction, might also be addressed at this point. Storming is the most difficult stage, in part because team members feel they are getting nowhere, and because moving on demands skill and emotional energy. Not all team members will have the skills to handle the more difficult issues and some may be afraid to raise them because of possible conflict. Furthermore, individuals may not be fully committed to the team or fully understand what being in an effective team means. For these reasons, a team may often fail to complete this stage in its development.

A real danger with senior groups is that they get into the Storming stage with comparative ease and then have difficulty in getting beyond personal antagonism, mistrust and miscommunication. Nevertheless, handled correctly, a team can develop to the Norming stage. At this point the team is able to establish procedures and solve issues. Although some teams may swing back into Storming behaviours from time to time, conflicts will usually be resolved sufficiently to allow the group to get through its agenda successfully.

If the team wishes to achieve more and progress to the Performing stage, considerable amount of time and effort is usually required. It is at this stage that quality interactions occur and the team is resourceful, flexible, open, close and supportive. Table 6.2 highlights the kind of behaviours exhibited by a team in this quadrant.[13]

Power and hidden agendas

While teams may benefit from exploring defensive communication, it is unlikely that Team Process problems are always a product of poor interpersonal skills. When assessing how best to develop a team it is important to identify whether executives need to listen and be more honest and trusting in their interactions, or whether it is the use of

Table 6.2   Characteristics of an effective team

1	Clear purpose	The vision, mission, goal, or task of the team has been defined and is now accepted by everyone There is an action plan
2	Informality	The climate tends to be informal, comfortable, and relaxed There are no obvious tensions or signs of boredom
3	Participation	There is much discussion and everyone is encouraged to participate
4	Listening	The members use effective listening techniques such as questioning, paraphrasing, and summarising to get out ideas
5	Civilised disagreement	There is disagreement, but the team is comfortable with this and shows no signs of avoiding, smoothing over or suppressing conflict
6	Consensus decisions	For important decisions, the goal is substantial but not necessarily unanimous agreement through open discussion of everyone's ideas, avoidance of formal voting, or easy compromises
7	Open communication	Team members feel free to express their feelings on the tasks as well as on the group's operation There are few hidden agendas Communication takes place outside of meetings
8	Clear roles and work assignments	There are clear expectations about the roles played by each team member When action is taken, clear assignments are made, accepted, and carried out Work is fairly distributed among team members
9	Shared leadership	While the team has a formal leader, leadership functions shift from time to time depending upon the circumstances, the needs of the group, and the skills of the members The formal leader models the appropriate behaviour and helps establish positive norms
10	External relations	The team spends time developing key outside relationships, mobilising resources, and building credibility with important players in other parts of the organisation
11	Style diversity	The team has a broad spectrum of team-player types, including members who emphasize attention to task goal setting, focus on process, and who question how the team is functioning
12	Self-assessment	Periodically, the team stops to examine how well it is functioning and what may be interfering with its effectiveness

Source: Parker (1990)

power to attain their own ends (or block the advancement of others) that is really preventing 'open communication' taking place.

At a senior level, each executive on the management team will have sizeable personal interests to represent, build and protect. Pursuing these interests can be done quite openly or, alternatively, as 'hidden agendas' concealed from other team members. Hidden agendas are personal, unrevealed issues which individuals try to satisfy at the expense of the team. They come in various forms – including rivalry, status disputes and one-upmanship – and can be a product of different circumstances. A common problem stems from an executive's 'dual role'. Steele (1983) notes that the executive plays two roles; one as the head of a specific, differentiated unit or function, and the other as an executive of the whole organisation. Consequently, the issues the executive may want to pursue within the senior team will not always have the wider organisation's interest at heart.

At AT&T, the CEO gets round this problem by asking his executive team to wear two hats:

> I say, 'Come to our management meetings and represent your businesses. But there are times when I ask you to put on *my* hat on behalf of the shareowners and help me make decisions that cross business-unit boundaries.' It's complicated even further as we globalize our businesses. We want the people in Country X to make decisions that respond to that marketplace and yet still remain accountable to the business units.[14]

However, while executives need to be encouraged to take these multiple interests into account, the reality is that power and politics (see Chapter 4) will also frequently play a part in senior teams. After all, they are composed of men and women with arguably the most power within an organisation. Unless the power plays of others are acknowledged and some attempt made to minimise these, it is likely that team effectiveness will be impaired.

The power of the CEO

The CEO is usually the most influential figure within the senior team and (particularly where CEOs combine the role of CEO/Chairman) also at Board level. From the perspective of the Board of Directors, the CEO is particularly powerful. In Lorsch and MacIver's (1989) study of Directors of US corporations, a number of constraints on directors' ability to govern in a timely and effective way were highlighted. Among these was the superior power of management and, in particular, that of the CEO/Chairman. Indeed, the CEO emerged as having more influence than directors on the majority of Board issues. Consequently, there is a high responsibility on the CEO to make the executive team and the Board work effectively.

Clearly it is not his or her responsibility alone, and in some cases the balance of power appears to be shifting. The appointment of more outside directors to boards in the US, for example, together with their willingness to play a more active role, has meant that CEOs appear to be more willing to listen.[15]

Moreover, the CEO's power is not unlimited.[16] According to Greiner (1986), the CEO's immediate subordinates often have great political skill and frequently use it. In one financial services company we investigated, one powerful executive on the senior team largely disregarded the CEO and the other team members. This executive was able to disrupt the senior team consistently because his area and its importance to the company overall was perceived to outweigh the positional power of the CEO. Relying on a high degree of functional expertise, long service and the profits his organisation contributed, the executive consistently put his people's interests before those of the company. Clearly, in this instance, the CEO was prepared to limit his own power of dismissal.

Succession

In general, however, the CEO's impact is considerable – particularly in relation to succession issues. Whilst a smooth transfer of power is desirable, more often than not CEOs fail to have the necessary plans in place for this to occur. In a survey of 348 large US companies, the recruitment firm Korn Ferry International found that only 34 per cent of Chief Executives had identified their successors either publicly or privately.[17] Yet, even when the necessary planning has been done, problems can occur. The death of Time Warner's chairman and founder, Steve Ross, in late 1992, was immediately followed by an internal clash amongst senior management. That clash led to a significant shake-up of Time Warner's board – even though the chief executive, Gerald Levin, had been hand-picked by Ross long before.

Ancona and Nadler (1989) highlight the possible problems resulting from the way succession is managed. The appointment of the CEO and the high stakes this involves, can easily shape members' relationships and, hence, team processes. They highlight two particular succession scenarios.

The first is what they call the 'executive selection' scenario. This occurs at the end of a CEO's term where the team can become an arena for assessing, selecting and preparing potential successors. The executive team becomes the setting for an executive 'horse race' which creates an inherently competitive win–lose situation that motivates individuals not to collaborate. Members perceive that their individual stakes are more important than those deriving from the success or failure of the team – at least in the short-term. Thus, competitive, non-collaborative and, in some cases, destructive behaviour is encouraged. Reginald Jones at GE, Ted Brophy at GTE and Walter Wriston at Citicorp all created structures of this kind in the early 1980s.

The second scenario is that of the new CEO. Here the aftermath of the succession decision can create interpersonal dynamics that make teamwork difficult or impossible. Candidates not appointed as CEO may feel wounded and attempt to prove (consciously or not) that a poor choice was made. In the new situation, team members may be anxious about their position and their evolving relationship with the new CEO who, until recently, may have been their peer and possibly a competitor. This situation is compounded if there is the possibility of a deputy being appointed, with a secondary succession scenario developing. Clearly, such situations can create significant problems for senior teams.

Team design

The design and structure of the senior team can also have a significant impact on how well the team performs. Below we review some of the issues to consider when selecting, organising and rewarding the members of a senior team.

Personnel structure

Personnel structure is concerned with who is on the team, and the kinds of technical, cognitive and personal qualities they bring to it. Earlier, we noted the research into senior teams which has attempted to identify the critical demographic factors which affect company performance. For instance, Wiersema and Bantel (1992) argue that firms most likely to undergo changes in corporate strategy have teams which have a lower average age, higher team tenure, higher educational level and higher academic training in the sciences than in other teams. Norburn and Birley (1988) argue that top management teams which exhibit a preponderance of functional experience, multiple company employment and wider educational training will outperform those that do not.

However, most writers agree that other factors such as psychological and personal attributes, as well as intellectual and physical characteristics should be considered when looking at team membership. In demonstrating the importance of different roles played by individuals within teams, Belbin has shown how an emphasis on functional expertise may be too limiting when looking at team composition. Belbin's (1981) typology identified the importance of eight team roles, while Margerison and McCann (1984) have developed alternative profiles within their Team Wheel framework. In addition, Nutt (1990) has looked at top team building using the personality variables identified by the Myers-Briggs Type Indicator (outlined in Chapter 2).

Hambrick (1987) argues that there is a danger in being too narrow in structuring the team. He outlines very broad areas of managerial 'wherewithal' but then leaves it to the general manager to identify specific dimensions for profiling the team. These broad areas are:[18]

- *Values.* The fundamental perspectives that team members should have in terms of ethics, hard work, wealth etc.
- *Aptitudes.* The personal capacities of team members such as creativity, intellect, tolerance for ambiguity and interpersonal awareness
- *Knowledge.* Including the necessity for in-depth familiarity with certain industry, technical or functional area issues, legal or regulatory factors and market place trends
- *Cognitive Style.* The need to include a mix of executives with orderly/analytic approaches with those who are nonlinear and intuitive thinkers
- *Demeanour.* An intangible aura or style which includes qualities such as enthusiasm, warmth, poise or staleness

Personnel structure and diversity

How similar the team should be in terms of the above characteristics is controversial. Hambrick (1987) argues that compatibility of executives is an important factor in organisational success. Indeed, Bettenhausen (1991) argues that most demographic studies have found that executives with very different backgrounds can hinder group and organisational performance, especially in times of crisis and rapid change. Some caution is necessary here as the pressure to conform and accept the dominant beliefs and perspectives of the group can, in themselves, take senior teams down blinkered paths. Nevertheless, Bettenhausen's review of the research in this area, concludes that it is better to have a compatible group than deal with the problems of getting consensus from individuals with divergent perspectives.

In some circumstances, executives may have less flexibility over who sits on the executive team and the issue may be more about how to learn to manage differences than attaining homogeneity. This is particularly true where executives are part of internationally based teams. As organisations move to compete on a global basis, the need to understand and manage different perspectives is becoming increasingly important. Some companies have shown they are equal to this task. For example, senior executives from the Wellcome Foundation are improving their global efficiency through the use of transnational teams in their drug development process.[19] However, research into how cultural, racial or ethnic differences affect group behaviour is in its infancy, particularly at a senior level.

Reward structure

Given the demands on senior executives' time, there have to be compelling rewards to get individuals to commit themselves to the senior executive team. These rewards can come in various forms. If the senior team is seen as being powerful and effective, membership may be reward in itself. Alternatively, one's personal values or preferences towards teamwork may increase one's personal commitment to the team. In the absence of such incentives, the most effective approach is when individuals are directly evaluated for their contribution towards some team or group results. Typically, however, rewards are weighted in favour of departmental or business unit success, rather than the senior team. In these circumstances, when forced to choose, executives are less likely to work on issues which are perceived to have less direct benefit to them.

There is, however, a shift in many organisations to build in performance standards which emphasise teamwork rather than individual success.[20] For some organisations the introduction of a team emphasis at a senior level has been a necessary step to get different functional heads to discuss and implement customer focused strategies. Jack Welch, General Electric's CEO, is unequivocal about the importance of teamwork to his organisation. But there is also a very harsh negative reward for those who cannot take on team values in GE:

> . . . When you make a value like teamwork important, you shape behaviour. If you can't operate as a team player, no matter how valuable you've been, you really don't belong at GE. To embed our values, we give our people 360-degree evaluations, with input from superiors, peers and subordinates. These are the roughest evaluations you can get, because people hear things about themselves they've never heard before. But they get the input they need, and then they get the chance to improve. If they don't improve, they have to go.[21]

Operating structure

Operating structure is concerned with how the team manages and organises itself, and the factors which facilitate the work of the team. Two areas are worth emphasising.

The first is concerned with the 'ground rules' that the team sets itself. Sometimes these are so obvious that they are sometimes ignored at a senior level – with frustrating results. Seemingly routine items such as having an agenda, reading minutes before the meeting and allocating duties, all help team members organise themselves for the task at hand. These issues can cause frustration and difficulty if they have not been established in the first place, or are not adhered to.

The second area has to do with those aspects which help improve and maintain contact between members. These include the location of team members and the frequency with which they meet. A team that meets infrequently or provides little opportunity for members to meet formally or informally outside of meetings may have a greater degree of difficulty in building rapport and effective team processes. One manager we interviewed could see quite clearly the consequences of not getting these factors right. He said of his own team:

> It's very difficult to get them all together at one place at one time . . . consequently we only meet once every 2 or 3 months. It then

becomes a discussion about 'where are we with X, Y, Z country and what happened to that performance figure' . . . (Instead) we need to free up enough time to think more strategically and critically.

Katzenbach and Smith (1993b) argue that busy executives and managers too often intentionally minimise the time they spend together. Successful teams are given time by the wise team leader to learn to be a team. Such an approach is used by Claude Bebear, the somewhat unorthodox Chairman of France's Axa insurance group, one of Europe's biggest and most rapidly growing insurance companies.[23] Bebear uses a number of techniques to help prepare his senior managers for a much more competitive environment. For example, in order to plan the company's strategy for entering the Chinese market he set up six competing teams to present to the organisation's strategy committee. They then went on a seven-day trip to China and spent the final night on China's Great Wall listening to a chorus of opera singers. Senior managers have been exposed to several other adventure workouts to help improve communications and consolidate team spirit – including a week in tents in the Sahara desert, a train journey around Europe and a Caribbean island trip.

TEAM PERFORMANCE AND DEVELOPMENT

In this chapter we have examined a range of factors to do with Team Purpose, Process and Design. Design issues help managers select the team and work out how best to organise and reward its members. Whilst these are important building blocks, the focus of the team (Team Purpose) and how team members work with each other (Team Process) are critical to assessing how a senior team is performing and what it needs to develop.

Executive team model

Based on our own and earlier research into top teams, we have combined the dimensions of Team Purpose and Team Process to produce an Executive Team Model (Figure 6.3) explained below.

Fig. 6.3   *Executive team model*

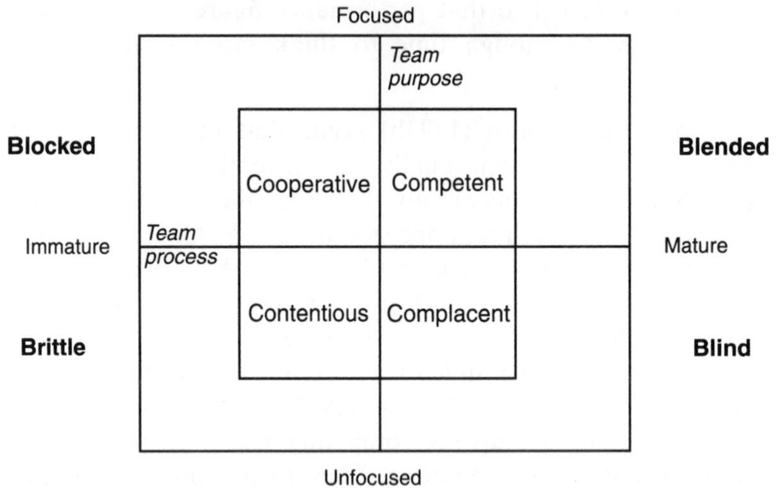

In terms of Team Purpose, those teams which are dealing with the right issues and making positive decisions (within their own particular strategic context) are described as 'Focused'. Teams which instead concentrate on short-term or operational issues and are indecisive are described as 'Unfocused'. The more Focused the team, the more the team will be dealing with what Casey calls 'problems' rather than 'puzzles'. Similarly, in terms of Team Process, if members can understand and manage group behaviours the team is called Mature. Where members have much more difficulty with each other the team is Immature.

We use this model to help executives identify the predominant behaviour within their senior team. Many find they can relate their performance to one of the quadrants in Figure 6.3, although rarely is this on the outer reaches of the matrix. Consequently, below we explore the four central quadrants of the four major team types – Blended, Blind, Brittle and Blocked.

The Blended team

This team is both high on Purpose and Process. It is the most effective type of senior team. Team members are capable of appreciating and discussing the key business issues and interacting positively with each other.

In practice, few senior teams operate consistently as truly Blended teams. More commonly, the team is '*Competent*' – serious problems are tackled and interpersonal processes are reasonably good. Although most immediate problems will be addressed, the team may get sidetracked into concentrating unnecessarily on technical or operational aspects. Some issues may simply be left in the 'too hard' basket.

While Blended teams are hard to develop, Competent teams are within the reach of most senior executives. Certainly, in contrast to the other three major categories of teams, they are much more effective. Organisations that are faced with a changing external climate and have a strong need to coordinate across business areas will find such teams make a strong contribution.

The Blind team

This is low on Purpose, but higher on Process. Here, the senior team interacts well, but in so doing loses its focus on the objectives and purpose of the team. Industrial history is littered with failed organisations which have had senior teams operating in this category. Even blue chip companies can become Blind for a period of time. For example, Exxon's inability to achieve success outside the oil industry has been blamed on the extreme homogeneity and long tenures in the oil industry of Exxon's Top Management Team.[24]

Less dangerous, but having similar weaknesses, is the '*Complacent*' team. This team is characterised by harmony rather than conflict. It has established good working patterns, is businesslike, well organised, but limited. In a stable environment, where the emphasis is on dealing with internal issues of coordination and interdependence the team will operate quite adequately. The danger is that the team concentrates too much on maintaining the status quo. Although the team is not Blind, its excellent puzzle-solving ability may distract it from some of the real problems which make the team complacent. In a more demanding strategic environment the team needs to be prepared to tackle ambiguous, but more critical, business problems.

The Brittle team

This team is very low on both the Purpose and Process dimensions. This team will avoid the fundamental issues facing the organisation, and outright antagonism will be evident within the team. Such teams may fold easily under pressure.

Some teams may be less extreme than this but still fall within this quadrant. We call teams which are hampered by overt or subdued conflict '*Contentious*'. Until the team can improve the interpersonal processes of its members, little more than puzzle solving will be achieved. Functional or operational puzzles will be concentrated on because these are the most tangible and allow the team to get something done. When the team does get round to tackling problems, the personal agendas and frustrations will usually surface. The team either has to develop into one that performs better or resort to a looser group arrangement.

The Blocked team

This is higher on Purpose but low on Process. With a Blocked team, members are able to appreciate and discuss the key business issues, but face difficulties in the way they interact.

Again, the less extreme version is the '*Cooperative*' team. While the Cooperative team concentrates on problems, it often pulls back from discussing the really difficult issues as a team. If they are tackled, antagonism and point scoring is more likely to result. Because the group 'gets by', members will be content with maintaining the status quo. However, there is likely to be noticeable political behaviour and feelings that the real decisions are often made outside the team.

Margaret Thatcher's Cabinet is an example of a team in this quadrant. Her style was to have consensus behind her conviction.[25] When Thatcher was on top, the Cabinet tackled important issues under her guidance. When Thatcher lost her edge, the poor Cabinet dynamics prevented most of the members (Whitelaw was perhaps the exception) from helping her and the team regain its focus.

This type of team can survive adequately if certain team members (who have the expertise) are allowed to get the job done. Many senior teams, in our experience, fall into the 'cooperative' category. Perhaps the major reason for trying to improve the interpersonal processes within this kind of team is because, frequently, the pattern of the team members' relationships is reflected within the organisation as a whole. This will give rise to problems of coordination between different functions. Over time, with teams such as these, it becomes increasingly difficult to solve problems which cross functional or business areas.

Teams may not fall neatly into this Executive Team Model on all issues and at all times. It is meant to highlight the predominant behaviour of the senior team and the implications of this. Improvement comes from understanding where the team is and developing better team Processes or clarifying the Purpose of the team (see Table 6.3).

Table 6.3 Developing senior teams

Type of senior team	Typical behaviours	Ideas for development

The brittle team
• Weak on purpose
• Weak on process
	Guarded
	Untrusting
	Self-oriented
	Ill-disciplined
		Recommend external facilitator
		Build teamwork skills
		Develop strategic focus
		  • External orientation
		  • Organisational coordinatión

The blocked team • Strong on purpose • Weak on process	Unwilling to confront Issues decided outside team Avoids interpersonal issues Defers to powerful members	Recommend outside facilitator Giving/receiving feedback Pay attention to power dynamics Demonstrate impact on organisation
The blended team • Strong on purpose • Strong on process	Give/receive feedback Open communication Regular progress reviews Aware of external issues Realistic/thoughtful	Maintain performance Integrate new team members Build in regular views Use as role model for other teams
The blind team • Strong on process • Weak on purpose	Rule bound Threatened by feedback Ponderous/complacent Slow External issues ignored	Giving/receiving feedback Support/counsel individuals Reframe perceptions of organisation's situation

TEAMWORK AT BOARD LEVEL

In recent years, the performance and contribution of Boards of Directors has come under heavy scrutiny given the poor performance of some major corporations. In terms of what has been written, however, the primary focus has been to outline the responsibilities of directors with regard to the strategic development of the business and, in particular, their legal obligations.[26] There has been far less discussion about how directors actually work together when they meet, and the particular difficulties they face as groups.

Despite the strategic importance of the Board to the organisation, in practice boardroom agendas are easily diverted onto more routine issues. Indeed, many writers such as Drucker (1973) have been prompted to comment that 'Board meetings rarely go beyond . . . trivia'. The reasons for this situation again lie in issues to do with Team Purpose, Process and Design.

In their study of corporate governance, Lorsch and MacIver (1989) specify a number of constraints directors face in trying to carry out their legally defined responsibilities. They include such things as the directors' psychological reasons for serving, the limits on their time, how well they understand their role and responsibilities as directors and the relationships they have among themselves and with the CEO-chairman. In particular they explore how power is exercised at Board level and the difficulties Boards face in operating effectively:

> . . . essentially directors are at a disadvantage . . . The CEO-Chairman usually has greater knowledge and information and controls both the meeting agenda and the discussion process. Often, he has been instrumental in selecting the other directors. In truth, other than their legal mandate, the directors' only power advantage is their capacity to act as a group by reaching a consensus, but doing this requires group cohesion and time for discussion, often scarce commodities in the typical boardroom.[27]

A team that meets infrequently, has members who display varying levels of commitment and who are not interdependent, cannot be expected to perform well without some consideration of team process issues. At Board level, however, norms exist which inhibit real changes in behaviour. Lorsch and MacIver found a number of subtle rules were observed. For example, CEOs tend to canvass opinions in advance of meetings rather than encourage open discussion and run the risk of disagreement. For their part, directors tend not to:

- Openly criticise the CEO on any issue
- Articulate the key issues on their minds
- Assert leadership over other directors
- Consider their responsibilities to constituencies other than shareholders

Their evidence suggests that as a result of such practices, important issues are not discussed openly or in a timely fashion at Board level. More importantly, such norms stultify the processes needed to improve communication and decision making. In companies that are not in difficulties, Boards who work according to norms such as these may not cause damage. In organisations facing crisis or needing to embark on major change, a Board which is unable to focus and make considered decisions on the problems at hand will be a serious handicap. Changing behaviour in all senior teams is difficult. But, if any group needs development it must be the Board that is poorly focused and immature in its interactions.

SUMMARY

Senior executives have to learn to work with and integrate a variety of groups in the organisation. This chapter has focused on the knowledge and skills needed to work with and manage other executives on the senior team.

Senior teams differ from other teams in an organisation. They have to handle complex tasks dealing simultaneously with internal processes and external relationships. They also have to take into account the interests of a broad range of stakeholders – from customers and competitors and employees to the Board of Directors. Moreover, the actions and dynamics of a senior team are highly visible to the rest of the organisation.

Given these features, teamwork at senior levels is demanding and often difficult to achieve. As team development takes time and effort, executives have to weigh up the degree of teamwork required before taking steps to improve an executive team. For example, does the strategic position of the firm demand a strong team? To what extent do members of the team need to work together?

Those interested in developing a senior team must consider three principle factors. The first is the extent to which the team is concentrating on the right issues and producing positive outcomes, that is, Team Purpose. Senior teams have to agree whether their function is simply to share information, discuss problems or take decisions. Easy as this sounds, many senior teams fail to take this critical step.

The second area of importance is Team Process. This is concerned with such things as how members relate, how open they are and how conflict is resolved. The extent to which team members understand and manage team behaviour is influenced by a number of factors such as the skills of team members, the stage a team is at in its development and the political dynamics of the team.

Executives must also create structures which will help teams operate effectively. Team Design involves looking at factors such as the composition of the team, how often team members meet and how the team is organised and rewarded.

An Executive Team Model has been put forward to help executives assess how well a team is performing currently and what it needs to develop. It does so by combining the dimensions of Team Purpose and Team Process. Finally, the particular challenges associated with teamwork at Board level have been examined.

NOTES

1. The 'dominant coalition' and 'upper echelons' are explored further in a paper which gave rise to several research trends investigating the Top Management Team. See Hambrick and Mason (1984).
2. See Lefton and Buzzotta (1987).
3. Katzenbach and Smith (1993a).
4. 'A Long and Winding Road: Should BT go Down the Superhighway?', *Financial Times*, 31 July 1994.
5. For fuller details of the research underlying this book, see the Appendix.
6. See for instance, Shea and Guzzo (1987) and Ancona and Nadler (1989).
7. The team model discussed in this chapter which combines the notion of Team Purpose and Team Process first appeared in Dainty and Kakabadse (1992).
8. Ancona and Nadler (1989) highlight two major factors in looking at team performance. Namely:

   (1) *Production of results*: This reflects the team's ability to meet the demands of its role. At the executive level this includes producing consistent positive results (earnings, growth, returns etc.) and maintaining organisational performance in the face of strategic and organisational changes. It also includes the quality of decision making, the

ability to implement decisions, the outcomes of teamwork in terms of problems solved and work completed, and finally the quality of institutional leadership involved.

(2) *Maintenance of Effectiveness*: This includes the team's ability to satisfy members' needs, members' ability to work together over time and the team's ability to adapt to new demands or situations.

9. For fuller details of the research underlying this book, see the Appendix.
10. See Jane Bird, 'The Rover Route to Computing', in the Managing IT series, *Management Today*, October, 1993, 92–6.
11. For fuller details of the research underlying this book, see the Appendix.
12. See Stratford Sherman's interviews with four leading CEOs in 'A Master Class in Radical Change', *Fortune*, vol. 128, no.15, 13 December 1993, 40–4, William Weiss' comments were on p. 430.
13. Many writers outline similar characteristics to these in portraying the effective team. This table is adapted from Parker (1990).
14. See David Kirkpatrick, 'Could AT & T Rule the World?', *Fortune*, vol. 127, no. 10, 17 May 1993, 19–27.
15. See Thomas A. Stewart, 'CEOs See Clout Shifting', *Fortune*, vol. 120, no. 11, 6 November 1989, 54.
16. See for instance, Bantel and Jackson (1989) and Finkelstein (1992).
17. Cited in 'Who Inherits the Crown?, *Financial Times*, 8 August 1994.
18. These aspects are also elaborated further in Hambrick and Mason (1984).
19. Charles Snow, *Transnational Teams in Global Network Organizations*, Conference Proceedings, ICEDR Research Symposium, October, 1994.
20. See 'The Best Practices Report: An Analysis of Management Practices that Impact Performance', published jointly by Ernst andYoung and the American Quality Foundation, 1992. The report is based on a survey of 580 organisations worldwide.
21. *Fortune*, 13 December 1993, 41.
22. For fuller details of the research underlying this book, see the Appendix.
23. See Richard Lapper's profile of Claude Bebear in 'Modelnetics of Life', *Financial Times*, 26 August 1994.
24. Hambrick (1987).
25. Quoted by Casey (1985).
26. See Davies (1991).
27. Lorsch and MacIver (1989, 13).

PART III

THE DIRECTIONAL CAPABILITIES: UNDERSTANDING AND MANAGING THE JOB

7 The External Capability: Understanding and Managing the External Environment

INTRODUCTION

Unless senior executives grasp and understand the significance of changes occurring in the external environment, they risk putting their organisation's long-term survival at risk. This is an obvious statement, but one which is frequently forgotten.

The fastest growing airline in history was People Express. In three years the company went from nothing, to flying to 33 American cities, with 66 aircraft in service, nearly 6000 staff and carrying 9.1 million passengers. By 1987, three years later, it had failed. PE was not run by inexperienced newcomers; it was run by a group of senior executives who had vast experience and successful track records in the American airline industry. The company failed for several reasons – most notably because senior management took their eye off the external ball. They underestimated the competition and failed to foresee the impact information technology would have on the airline industry.

During the 1980s, People Express was in good company. Many blue chip organisations also lost the external plot. In the US, the American auto industry performed poorly and, most importantly, failed to recognise and act on the threat from their Japanese competitors. The adoption of a 'Maginot type mentality' by names such as General Motors, Ford and Chrysler meant that Detroit 'effectively conceded a permanent share of the US market to the Japanese who reinvested more in American plants'.[1] In the copying industry, companies like Rank Xerox also felt the heat. Xerox's CEO, David Kearns, said of the organisation in 1982:

I came to the conclusion that the trends affecting Xerox were so ominous that if something revolutionary weren't done the company would surely go out of business. The institution was

191

more than threatened; it was terminally ill. Clearly from everything I could see in the market place the scales had tilted against us.[2]

External understanding and the senior executive

In contrast to People Express, Xerox survived and prospered because its senior executives were able to understand the changes in the external market and respond to them effectively. The need to do this at the top is critical. Clearly, some kind of external focus (in terms of market and customer awareness) is also important at lower levels in the organisation and in particular functional areas (for example, in Marketing and Business Planning). However, at senior levels executives must have a holistic understanding of the external environment and the changes that are occurring within it. Moreover, they must be able to translate this understanding into a viable direction for their organisation.

What does this involve? A complex environment requires sophisticated and complex methods of analysis. In large organisations this analysis is frequently carried out by business planners. However, it is not the planners who make the critical decisions: ultimately it is up to top management to guide the direction of the company. Senior level managers therefore need some mental tools to help them do this.

This chapter is not a substitute for a text on strategic management – although the frameworks are drawn from that discipline. It is concerned, rather, with helping executives maintain external vigilance which, indeed, is the essence of an External Capability. The frameworks which can help with this process are outlined in Figure 7.1. These are concerned principally with two aspects. The first is understanding the context in which the firm is operating, which involves some degree of comparative or competitive business analysis. The second involves understanding the strategic options open to the organisation in the longer term. In this chapter, therefore, we will explore the following topics:

- *Business environment.* The executive needs to be aware of those changes within society and the economy which will affect their business now and in the future. Moreover, it is global, not simply domestic changes, which need to be monitored.

- *Industry Environment.* The executive needs to be aware of the major forces within an industry which could affect the organisa-

Fig. 7.1 *External understanding*

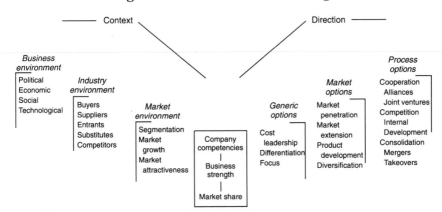

tion's long term ability to remain competitive. These include such things as changing customer needs, the activities of competitors, the possibility of new entrants and the potential for substitute products.

- *Market and company environment.* Within the industry environment, the executive needs to be aware of the principles of market segmentation and the characteristics of the markets within which they operate. Equally important is an understanding of the company's core competencies which will enable it to compete.

- *Generic options.* Understanding the environment and the company's place within it are only part of the picture. Also necessary is an awareness of the broad basis on which the company intends to sustain its competitive advantage. Principally, this is seen in terms of an emphasis on cost, differentiation of products or services, or some combination of the two.

- *Market options.* The executive then needs to understand how these generic options might be translated into specific product strategies such as product development, market penetration and diversification.

- *Process options.* Finally, the executive must be aware of ways to achieve long-term viability through competitive approaches and cooperative ventures, such as alliances or joint ventures, or by consolidating through mergers and takeovers.

Before we go any further, it is important to stress that, at the end of the day, it is the way the executive thinks about external issues – as well as what they think about – which is important. All the frameworks in the world will not help the executive who lacks the capacity to have Breadth and Focus (see Chapter 2).

For example, in the early 1990s when the Chairman of Samsung tried to educate his senior managers about the difficulties they faced in the American market, he organised an on-site visit to Los Angeles to help bring the message home.[3] There he demonstrated how US buyers and sellers were largely ignoring Samsung products. However, rather than creating a sense of urgency Samsung managers continued to be complacent and inward looking. The Chairman had to go further if the organisation was to achieve its goal of becoming one of the world's ten largest technological powerhouses. He decided to invest in a $100 million training programme which involved sending executives abroad to learn about other cultures and to help develop innovative ways of thinking in the organisation as a whole. Thus, for Samsung and many other organisations, the pitfalls of operating in the external environment are often a problem of a lack of perception, rather than a lack of analysis.

This lack of perception has been highlighted by writers such as Zahra and Chaples (1993). They outline six potential blind spots or flaws in competitive analysis which the executive needs to guard against. In summary, these involve:

- *Misjudging industry boundaries.* It is important not to be restricted by assumptions about the extent of the industry one is in. Critical here are, domain (where does the industry begin and end); customer groups (sectors to be served); customer functions (needs and purchasing patterns) and critical technologies (production, marketing and administrative systems).

- *Poor identification of the competition.* This involves having an exclusive focus on well known companies while ignoring other potentially viable firms, or emphasising a regional identification of the competition, when a national or international focus is necessary. For example, during the 1980s Xerox only saw IBM and Kodak as rivals when Japanese companies were its closest threat.

- *Overemphasis on competitor's visible competence.* Typically, manufacturing companies focus on their competitors' finance, R&D and production functions when other areas such as product design, logistics and human resources do not receive the same attention.

- *Overemphasis on where/how rivals will compete.* Executives sometimes get caught in the trap of focusing on those markets where the organisation currently faces stiff competition, and ignoring those which competitors may tackle in the future.

- *Faulty assumptions about the competition.* Underestimating rivals' competence can create and reinforce faulty assumptions about these companies. For many years, almost any product which came out of Asia was not given a second's thought by complacent Western companies.

- *Paralysis by analysis.* While effective competitive analysis requires extensive data collection, it does not require obsessive data collection. As Sutton (1989) has observed, 'one of the main inhibitions to competitive analysis is that there is far too much information and it's hard to separate the essential from the inessential'.

The frameworks described below are often used to help sharpen executives' awareness of their external environment. Clearly, as with all such sorting mechanisms, frameworks simplify and have their limitations. Used as a starting point, however, they may help focus and structure executives' thinking about their firm's competitive position.

THE BUSINESS ENVIRONMENT

Many of the changes occurring daily in the world are of enormous proportions. There have been massive readjustments in the world geopolitical environment, with a radical change in the balance of the global superpowers. Downturns in the economic environment have resulted in recession and layoffs for literally millions of employees. Shifts in social and political systems, including destabilisation and conflict, have often left idyllic areas of the world ravaged by war. There are continual technological breakthroughs in a vast range of areas from medicine, to data processing and fibre optics.

Some of these issues will be of passing interest but others will have considerable implications for how business is transacted. Changes in the superpower balance affect trade agreements; national conflicts can both close down and open market opportunities. Economic recession and growth affect interest rates and exchange rates, which can have a very direct impact on an enterprise's operations. Changes in technology, which may seem to have no relevance to one's own industry, can wipe out corporations which are too slow or unwilling to adapt.

Some, if not all of these factors, have affected German industrialists in recent years. A global downturn, the costs of reunification and the rising economic power of Asia combined in the early 1990s to halt German industry in its tracks. High labour costs have had to be reduced in order to make individual firms more competitive internationally. For Bayer, one of Germany's largest chemical companies, regulatory changes across Europe have had a particular impact. A succession of cost-cutting healthcare reforms by European governments has resulted in a shift by doctors towards prescribing cheaper copies of brand name drugs.[4] Bayer and its rivals, BASF and Hoechst have since had to take up positions in the fiercely contested international market for out-of-patent generic drugs.

Changes in an organisation's external environment may be of little relevance, others may provide new opportunities or turn out to be major threats. Macro changes also have micro consequences and the executive needs to keep a handle on trends which, at the outset, may seem far removed from the day-to-day running of the business. Moreover, increasingly these trends need to be assessed on a global basis. For instance, executives in the electronics, software, multimedia and biotechnology industries must monitor the actions of many firms around the globe.[5]

One way of analysing the broader environment is through what is called a 'PEST' analysis. This involves looking at Political, Economic, Social and Technological changes.

Social and political issues

Social and political issues can have a significant long-term impact. In some instances it may be necessary to monitor these issues on a continuous basis. The oil industry, for example, has to be particularly sensitive to environmental issues. Royal/Dutch Shell has operations around the world with activities which span the exploration of oilfields to the distribution of petrochemicals and their derivatives.

During the 1980s, Shell International expanded its Public Affairs division to analyse and monitor developments in a range of areas. In addition to the usual cadre of press officers, Shell employed staff to maintain contact with United Nations agencies and committees and maintained at least one full-time specialist academic in Middle East affairs. Intelligence was then passed on to Shell's Planning function to incorporate in divisional business plans.

There are a range of political and social issues which can affect an organisation. These may include such things as:

- Government impact on the company (for example, policy, taxes, laws)
- International rulings (for example, safety, quality)
- Demography (for example, employment trends, labour market)
- Sociological changes (for example, expectations, life-style, social values, mobility)
- Environmental concerns

For most enterprises, social and political changes take some time to filter through. It is therefore important to stand back from the detail and recognise broader trends and correctly interpret their significance for the sector or industry one is in. For example, over the past ten years entertainment and recreation have claimed a steadily increasing share of consumer spending in the US. Today, entertainment and recreation are being viewed as the growth industries of the 1990s – not health care or the car industry – as was once believed.[6]

Economic and technology issues

By contrast, some economic changes can have an almost instantaneous and devastating affect. The OPEC oil crises of the 1970s and the stock market crash on Black Friday in 1987 are just two examples of global economic changes that have had a far reaching and intense impact. More recently, the emergence of low-cost production locations in Eastern Europe has created a whole new market reality for organisations such as Siemens, Europe's largest electrical and electronics company.[7]

Similarly, the pace of technological change is causing the boundaries of industries (for example, entertainment and computing) to be redrawn. The structure of these industries is also changing. At one time, companies like IBM and Digital Equipment designed and built their computers from the bottom up. Customers were tied into the whole package from one manufacturer. Today, says Andy Grove, CEO of Intel, 'Everybody's products have to work with everybody else's products or they don't sell.'[8] As a result, the industry has now moved from being vertically aligned to a horizontal structure. Intel foresaw, and indeed encouraged, this trend by producing processing chips which work on any IBM-type personal computer, no matter who builds it.

THE INDUSTRY ENVIRONMENT

An assessment of the broad business environment needs to be complemented by an evaluation of the specific industry environment in which the firm operates. Michael Porter's (1980) Competitive Forces Model is perhaps the best known framework for this kind of analysis.

Porter's competitive forces model

Pearson (1990)[9] points out that the model focuses on two key issues:

- The factors that determine the long-term profitability of an industry
- The factors that determine a firm's competitive position in the industry

Understanding the forces which affect competition and consequently the degree of competitive rivalry within a particular industry is the central theme of Porter's model. The model (Figure 7.2) emphasises five factors; competitive rivalry and the four forces which affect it; that is, new entrants, suppliers, buyers and substitutes. Let us look briefly at each of these in turn.

New entrants

As mentioned earlier, a failure to identify future competitors and new entrants is often cited as a potential blind spot for executives.

Fig. 7.2 *Competitive forces model*

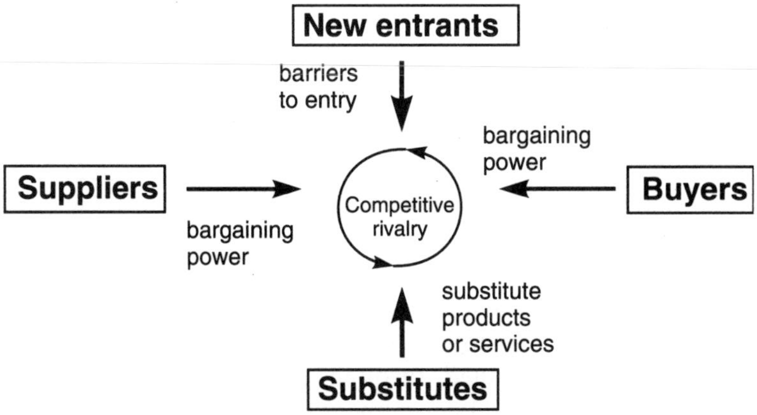

Source: Adapted from Porter (1980)

According to Hamel and Prahalad (1989), executives typically focus on the existing resources of the firm's current competitors.

Such a perspective, they argue, is a poor indicator of future industry leadership. In particular, it has caused many companies to ignore potential foreign rivals. In 1970 Komatsu was less than 35 per cent as large as Caterpillar (measured by sales); Honda was smaller than American Motors; and Canon was feeling its way in the reprographics industry against giants like Xerox. By 1985, Komatsu was a $2.8 billion company. By 1987, Honda manufactured almost as many cars worldwide as Chrysler, and Canon had matched Xerox's global market share. As Hamel and Prahalad note, 'assessing the current tactical advantages of known competitors will not help you understand the resolution, stamina and inventiveness of potential competitors'.

Another assessment which needs to be made is to determine what barriers to entry new companies face. Some of the most common ones according to Johnson and Scholes (1993) are as follows:

- Capital requirements of entry
- Economies of scale enjoyed by existing competitors
- Legislation/Government action
- Cost advantages enjoyed by existing competitors – learning curve benefits
- Existing product differences

- Strength of existing product brand loyalty
- Access to appropriate technology
- Access to long-term supplies of raw materials

Understanding the intentions of new entrants can demand some degree of lateral thinking. Hamel and Prahalad (1989) point out that during the 1970s both Kodak and IBM tried to match Xerox's business system in terms of segmentation, products, distribution and pricing. As a result, Xerox had no trouble decoding the new entrants intentions and developing countermoves. Canon, on the other hand, changed the terms of competitive engagement. While Xerox built a wide range of copiers, Canon standardised machines and components to reduce costs, distributed through office product dealers, and appealed to secretaries and department managers, rather than selling to the heads of corporate duplicating departments. Competitors who tried to match Xerox's business system found that the barriers to imitation were high; IBM withdrew from the photocopier business, while Kodak remains a distant second to Xerox. Canon dramatically reduced the barriers to entry by changing the rules of the game. This also short-circuited Xerox's ability to retaliate quickly against its new rival.

Substitutes

The second important set of factors in Porter's model is substitute products. For Johnson and Scholes (1993) the major issue posed by substitutes is the extent to which an organisation can legitimately regard itself as operating in a discrete market with a limited number of like competitors as opposed to having as potential competitors a wider range of substitute products. This threat of substitutes depends on;[10]

- Relative price of substitutes
- Technical comparability of substitutes
- Costs of switching
- Speed of technological development in 'substitute' industries

The threat from substitutes may take different forms. One form may be the substitution of one product for another. Another stimulus for substitution may be an event such as the recession which reduces disposable income and therefore spending patterns across a whole range of activities. Thus, the traditional holiday budget may become the more transferable 'leisure dollar' which can be spent on a variety of products from video rental, home computers and other forms of recreation and entertainment.

The threat of substitute products can revolutionise an industry. Zahra and Chaples (1993) note that the American newspaper industry is currently in a state of disarray because of the success of cable television. It has taken nearly a decade for well-established giants such as the New York Times, the Washington Post and Chicago Tribune to fully come to terms with the notion that newspapers have competing substitute products in the form of broadcast and telecast media. Cable has forced a redefinition of the whole newspaper industry.

Johnson and Scholes (1993) highlight several questions when considering substitutes:

- To what extent is there a danger that substitutes may encroach upon an organisation's activities?
- What steps can be taken to minimise the risks of such substitution – perhaps through differentiation or low cost profiles?
- Is there the possibility that one's own products could find new markets as substitutes for some other product?

Suppliers

It is important to assess the position of one's suppliers and the amount of power they have over you. Many companies have underestimated the power of suppliers and their potential to emerge as major forces within their industry.

The case of Intel, the world's largest semiconductor manufacturer, and Compaq, the most profitable PC manufacturer, helps illustrate this point. In 1994, Intel started an $80 million advertising campaign to persuade consumers and businesses to buy personal computers based on its latest microprocessor, the Pentium. The Pentium has the power to take full advantage of multimedia PC applications, such as games which incorporate sophisticated video graphics. Intel's biggest customer, Compaq Computer, had meanwhile built up huge inventories of lower performance PCs (based on older Intel micro-processors) which it was also trying to sell. A senior executive of Compaq's European operations said, 'What upsets us generally is that a component supplier should try to influence the end-user. The end-user market is not their business. They are interfering.'[11]

Interference or not, Intel's capacity to shift the PC market rapidly from one generation of microprocessors to the next – or effectively move forward into its customer's sphere of business – is a strategic move many organisations need to be concerned about. Had Compaq senior executives thought through the following criteria, they might have recognised the potential power Intel had to disrupt their existing business franchise.

For example, they needed to consider the following aspects:

- Degree of monopoly power in the supplier industry
- Degree of differentiation of the supplier's product
- Cost of switching from one supplier to another – for the supplier and for the firm in question
- Importance of volume to the supplier
- Importance of the supplier's product to the industry

According to Johnson and Scholes (1993), supplier power is likely to be high where there is a concentration of suppliers, when there are high 'switching costs' to move from one supplier to another and when suppliers have the potential to integrate forward if they are dissatisfied.

Buyers

Porter also singles out buyers as another group which, in aggregate terms, can determine the potential profitability of an industry. Again Porter argues that it is important to understand the power buyers have relative to the firm.

In the UK retail food industry, major firms such as Sainsbury, Tesco and Argyll constantly juggle the prices of thousands of different products to maintain the loyalty of the average British shopper. More recently, competition has intensified with the prospect of discount warehouses (like Costco from the US) setting up shop in locations around the UK.[12] In late 1993, Sainsbury, the retailer with the largest market share, cut prices on 300 of its basic own-label products. Senior management argued they would, however, still be able to compete on quality as well as price. Major stores like Sainsbury's carry a broad product line, elements of which can be discounted whenever customer buying patterns require. Investment in Electronic Point of Sale technology gives them the capacity to respond to buyer demand almost instantaneously. Competitors in the industry (particularly the discounters) carry a much smaller product range and have a much narrower distribution base. For the time being, therefore, stores like Sainsbury can reduce the likelihood of customers shopping around.

The possibility of buyers switching to substitute products is clearly not the only factor in assessing buyer's power. Other factors which affect the power of buyers, according to Pearson (1990), include:

- Buyer volume
- Availability of substitute products
- Costs of switching
- Concentration of buyer's industry
- Price sensitivity
- Product differences
- Buyer information

Johnson and Scholes (1993) point out that buyer power is likely to be high where there is a concentration of buyers, there are alternate sources of supply (because the product is undifferentiated between suppliers), and where industrial buyers pose a threat of backward integration.

Competitive rivalry

The four forces described above (that is, new entrants, substitutes, suppliers and buyers) will affect the degree of competitive rivalry within an industry. According to Pearson (1990), competitive rivalry depends on factors which fall into three main groups:

- The rate and shape of market growth
- The degree to which products and firms are differentiated from each other
- The extent to which firms are committed to the industry

All three factors critically affect the degree of industry rivalry. For example, with no growth, little differentiation and a high degree of commitment, there is likely to be intense competition over market share, breaking out into intermittent price wars and reducing industry profitability. The airline industry is a classic example of this situation. In the USA in 1993, only one carrier made a profit, Southwest. With overcapacity in the industry, little differentiation in the product and high barriers to exit, the cut-throat price wars have left the industry with $10 billion dollar losses in the three years since 1990 – more than the industry earned in the last 60 years.[13]

By avoiding this rivalry, for example by differentiating the product or by avoiding a head on conflict with a competitor, it should be possible to enjoy less competition and consequently achieve higher prices and profit. Indeed, even in the unattractive airline industry, Southwest has managed to do this with a short flight, no frills service, which is contrary to the normal formula.

Porter's model helps the executive think through the structure of an industry and the relative power of the firm with respect to the major players within it. In order to focus the executive further, Johnson and Scholes (1993) suggest thinking through the following questions:

- What are the key forces at work in the competitive environment? These will differ by industry. For example, for grocery manufacturers the power of retail buyers is of extreme importance. For computer companies the growing power of chip manufacturers such as Intel is crucial. In a deregulated public sector organisation, new entrants with more commercial experience might be the central problem.

- Are there underlying forces – perhaps identified by the PEST analysis – which are driving the industry? For example, government constraints on expenditure may affect the availability of sufficiently educated staff or finance for future investment.

- Is it likely that forces will change and, if so, how? For example, a company with a strong market position within a given country will have built its strategy on that market strength. However, if forces for globalisation in the industry are occurring, strength in the national market might become much less important. Bass in the UK, and Coors in the US, both successful brewers concentrating on the domestic brewing market, have had to review their strategy faced with the increasing internationalisation of their industry.

- Are some industries more attractive than others? Some industries are intrinsically more profitable than others because, for example, entry is more difficult, or buyers and suppliers are more powerful.

Competitors

Additionally, any attempt to understand the industry environment requires a thorough review of competitors. Zahra and Chapels (1993) believe that a firm's competitors are those companies who currently (and those who have the potential to) offer a product targeted to a specific segment with the goal of satisfying a specific need. However, Johnson and Scholes (1993) take a broader view that all organisations (public or private) are in a competitive position in relation to each other, in so far as they are competing either for customers or, perhaps in the case of public services, for resources.

Porter (1980) suggests that a detailed analysis of competitor capabilities is needed. The following factors should be assessed:

- Competitors' products
- Dealer/distribution networks
- Marketing and selling activities
- Operations
- Research and engineering capability
- Overall costs
- Financial strength
- Organisation
- Management ability
- Corporate portfolio
- Personnel turnover
- Relationships with government bodies, etc.

Most writers also emphasise the necessity to go beyond assessing the characteristics of the competition, to consider their potential actions and response. Questions which help with this include: 'What are competitors likely to do next? How will they go about it? What methods will they use? Where will they focus their activities? Are they desperate? How seriously should we take them? What is their likely response to any moves we make? How fast can they grow? Can they sustain it?'

Again, any check-list should not be taken at face value. The executive needs to use these pointers to investigate their own way of thinking about their competitors. One can have a list of questions and still make false assumptions about the competition. Indeed, Hamel and Prahalad (1989) argue that few Western companies have an enviable track record anticipating the moves of competitors because of the widespread focus on existing resources of present competitors. The only companies seen as a threat are those with the resources to erode margin and market share in the next planning period. In a rapidly changing world, clearly there is a great need to continuously update one's assessment and challenge one's assumptions about where the true forces of competition lie.

For example, Heineken has earned the accolade of being the world's first truly global brand of beer. Over many years, the Dutch brewer has developed a network of relationships with brewers and distributors in 150 countries. To stay ahead of its closest rivals in the US – organisations like Miller Brewing (a unit of Philip Morris) and Anheuser-Busch – it is having to expand into Asian and Central European markets. Closer to home, Heineken is challenging the assumption that European drinkers will only drink local beers. In order to defend its Number 1 position in Europe, the company is teaming up with competitors with the aim of getting them to brew Heineken themselves. Eventually, the goal is to make Heineken as dominant in Europe as Budweiser is in the US.[14]

THE MARKET AND COMPANY ENVIRONMENT

Segmentation

An industry can be assessed in very broad terms (for example, transportation), or more narrowly (rail distribution). However, because customers have different needs, an industry or market is usually thought of in terms of smaller sections, or market segments. While not explicitly singled out for attention within Porter's model, a recurring implication throughout is the importance of identifying the different market segments within one's competitive environment.

As Johnson and Scholes (1993) point out, the extent to which an organisation has located and exploited a clear market segment is likely to affect its vulnerability to substitutes, its bargaining power with regard to suppliers and buyers, the threat of entry into its market area and the degree of competition it faces. An industry with little segmentation is more likely to be characterised by a greater degree of rivalry. Consequently, market segmentation can help executives think through how this rivalry might be reduced. For example, by first targeting the budget customer and flying on peripheral routes, People Express found a market segment which protected it from retaliation by the major US airlines.

Segmentation is the process of seeking the smallest set of groups within a market that are:

- Distinctive – so that it is possible to justify a separate approach
- Substantial – so that it is worth the additional cost
- Measurable – so that decisions are based on more than guess work
- Durable – so that there are good chances of future financial returns
- Identifiable – so that the group can be reached through targeted efforts

In principle, markets should be broken down into segments in a way which help one understand the external environment and improves one's ability to respond. Again, however, this analysis should not be static. Industries change and market segments change. For example, during the past two decades the electronics industry has grown rapidly to include semiconductors, connectors, office equipment, measuring and testing tools, office automation, audio and video products, electronic games and toys, home computers and home automation products. Each field can be viewed as a market segment or a distinct industry in its own right. When companies compete in an industry similar to the electronics industry, the likelihood of misjudging boundaries increase because the segments are related. Consequently, while defining segments is important this should not be a static or rigid assessment, particularly when participants in one segment may opt to penetrate others, sometimes without being detected.

Thus, a market can be segmented in various ways, and each different basis of segmentation could give rise to a different assessment of potential opportunities. As a result, it is important to think through factors such as the segments which are growing; segment size; the degree of competition within a segment; and whether some segments help identify new opportunities to differentiate ones product. Some of the bases of market segmentation are outlined in Table 7.1.

Table 7.1　Bases of market segmentation

Type of factor	Consumer markets	Industrial/organisational markets
Characteristics of people/organisations	Age, sex, race Income Family size Life-cycle stage Location Lifestyle	Industry Location Size Technology Profitability Management
Purchase/use situation	Size of purchase Brand loyalty Purpose of use Purchasing behaviour Importance of purchase Choice criteria	Application Importance of purchase Volume Frequency of purchase Purchasing procedure Choice criteria Distribution channel
Users' needs and preferences for product characteristics	Product similarity Price preferences Brand preferences Desired features Quality	Performance requirements Assistance from suppliers Brand preferences Desired features Quality Service requirements

Markets and positioning

The analysis so far has concentrated on understanding the major external factors. However, it is important to locate one's own enterprise or Strategic Business Unit in relation to these factors.[15] One way of doing this is through portfolio analysis and, in particular, the use of a popular tool called the Boston Matrix. The matrix has been criticised for its simplicity, but it provides a clear outline of several fundamental issues and forms the basis of more involved models (one of which is described later).

The matrix singles out two important factors which determine the long term profitability of a business; that is (a) rate of growth of its market and (b) the share of the market (segment) that the business has relative to its largest competitor. The two dimensional matrix is presented in Figure 7.3. By contrasting these two dimensions, four possible positions are produced. The product can either be a 'Cash Cow', a 'Star', a 'Question Mark/Problem Child' or a 'Dog':

- *Cash cow*. The Cash Cow has a high market share in a mature market. It needs minimum updating or marketing investment, provides a regular return and is the mainstay of the business.

- *Star*. The Star has a high market share in a growing market. Apple's original Macintosh Personal Computer is an example of a Star. While a Star demands considerable investment, product promotion and so forth, to gain market share, it also yields high returns.

- *Question-mark*. The Question Mark is also in a growing market but with a low market share. Usually they take a lot of time, effort and resources even though their future is unclear. Most new products are Question Marks. The difficulty is to decide how much investment is required to make them a success.

- *Dog*. The Dog has a relatively low market share in a low-growth market. It is a prime candidate for divestment. Dogs should be minimised and certainly not retained without a reason. Nevertheless, they may be necessary, for instance as part of a range to sell on other products, as publicity for a company, or because the service is required by statute, as with some public services.

The Boston matrix is basically concerned with two aspects. The first is to ensure that the activities which make up the company's portfolio are complementary. The other is to assess whether this produces a balanced portfolio over time through the management of cash flows. Thus, as Pearson notes, cash is invested in Stars to convert them into tomorrow's Cash Cows. It is extracted from Cash Cows to fund Stars. Dogs are divested, and Question Marks are either converted into Stars or liquidated.

The matrix has several problems. It only considers market growth and market share, it is difficult to assess precisely what is high or low on either of these dimensions, and the original emphasis on cash is only one critical resource which has to be balanced. Moreover, it only indicates four strategies – invest, hold, harvest or divest. But it does

The Directional Capabilities

Fig. 7.3 *Boston matrix*

RELATIVE MARKET SHARE

	High	Low
High MARKET GROWTH RATE	Star	Problem child or question mark
Low	Cash cow	Dog

Source: From original research by the Boston Consulting Group

provide a starting point in looking at a Strategic Business Unit's (SBU) place within the external market. It can also be used as a basis for more involved models which bring together some of the external methods of analysis outlined so far.

Market attractiveness and business strength

The Directional Policy Matrix is a development of the Boston Matrix and explores the relationship between the market environment and the SBU. It maps SBUs according to (a) the attractiveness of the industry or market it is operating in, and (b) the competitive strength of the SBU. Thus, market attractiveness replaces market growth, and business strength replaces market share. Each business is positioned within the matrix according to a series of indicators of attractiveness and strength.

Market attractiveness

In assessing market attractiveness it may be useful to use the tools considered earlier in this chapter. These should help highlight factors which are most relevant to the organisation and its market. (Table 7.2 highlights factors Johnson and Scholes (1993) believe are most typically considered.)

Table 7.2　Indicators of market attractiveness

- Market size
- Market growth rate
- Cyclicality
- Competitive structure
- Barriers to entry
- Industry profitability
- Technology
- Inflation
- Regulation
- Workforce availability
- Social issues
- Environmental issues
- Political issues
- Legal issues

Source:　Johnson and Scholes (1993)

Business strength

In looking at business strength the executive has to assess the company's core or competitive competencies. There are several ways of doing this including value chain analysis and resource analyses. In principle, the concern is to understand the company's strengths and weaknesses. In Table 7.3 Pearson (1990) highlights 13 factors used by Readymix, an Australian company, when considering its business strength.

An enhancement of this process, and one which is becoming increasingly popular, is external benchmarking. During the 1980s, benchmarking was an important step in Xerox's recovery. As the CEO at that time explains:

> The monopoly environment that Xerox thrived in encouraged internal competition, but not external. We would measure the quality of a new Xerox machine according to the specification of older Xerox copiers. Those specifications didn't mean very much if other companies were producing something altogether better . . . Benchmarking was one of the first concrete things we did to get Xerox on its feet and moving again.[16]

Again, this process is not straightforward. Zahra and Chaples (1993) warn against the dangers of inflexible commitment to such

Table 7.3 Aspects of business strength

---

1   Relative market share
2   Change in relative market share
3   Profitability
4   Distribution
5   Product differentiation
6   Vertical integration
7   Management calibre and depth
8   Company reputation and image
9   Process economics, plant age, obsolescence, etc.
10 Plant capacity
11 Feedstock availability and price
12 Investment intensity
13 Product R&D and technical competence

Source: Pearson (1990)

things as key factors of success in an industry, particularly when these are based on historical indicators. Whilst companies which meet these are often considered viable members of an industry, the industry will continue to evolve. Companies therefore need to keep abreast of changes to these success factors and try to anticipate change where possible.

Pearson (1990) outlines a business strengths/market attractiveness matrix (see Figure 7.4). Johnson and Scholes point out that some analysts also choose to show graphically how large the market is for a given business unit's activity, and even the market share of the SBU (see Figure 7.5). This matrix provides a useful way of directing a manager's attention to key forces in the environment and raises questions about appropriate strategies for different business units and the portfolio as a whole.

STRATEGIC DIRECTION

It is appropriate now, therefore, to turn to the question of the strategic direction of the firm and its long-term aims and intentions. Typically, achieving long-term aims involves finding a fit between current resources and future opportunities. Hamel and Prahalad (1989) suggest that to cope in an international environment and to go some way towards attaining global leadership, something more is

Fig. 7.4 *Business strength – market attractiveness matrix*

100%

Invest to maintain dominance	Invest and grow	Dominate or divest
Invest and grow	Invest and grow	Improve performance or withdraw
Earn and protect	Earn and protect	Phased withdrawal
Earn and protect	Phased withdrawal	Divest

MARKET ATTRACTIVENESS

0%

100% BUSINESS STRENGTH 0%

Source: Pearson (1990)

Fig. 7.5 *Market attractiveness/SBU strength matrix*

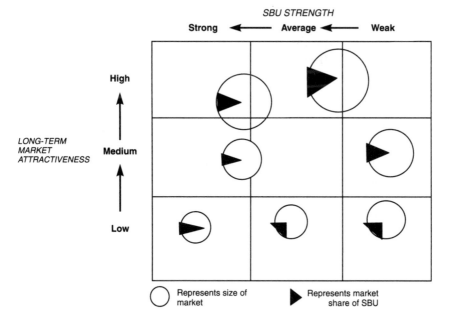

SBU STRENGTH

Strong ← Average ← Weak

High

LONG-TERM MARKET ATTRACTIVENESS   Medium

Low

○ Represents size of market   ▶ Represents market share of SBU

Source: Johnson and Scholes (1993)

needed. They outline the notion of strategic intent which is about ambition, challenges which stretch the organisation and novel approaches which change the way the competitive game is played. They argue that for smart competitors, the goal is not competitive imitation but competitive innovation, the art of containing competitive risks within manageable proportions. Strategic intent involves folding the future back into the present. The important question is not, 'How will next year be different from this year?', but 'What must we do differently next year to get closer to our strategic intent?'

While Hamel and Prahalad argue that a 10–20 year quest for global leadership cannot be planned in the traditional sense, they also argue that it is unlikely that one will fall into a leadership position by accident. It is important, therefore, to have clear objectives and specific ends (reducing product development times by 75 per cent for example) although perhaps using less prescriptive means.

In order to achieve one's longer-term position (be it global leadership or something less ambitious), some understanding of strategic principles is necessary. Although Hamel and Prahalad encourage the executive to go beyond traditional strategic models, it is nevertheless important to have some frameworks for understanding the means by which a business will achieve its competitive advantage.

Two frameworks are discussed. The first draws on Porter (1980) and is to do with the generic strategy one adopts. The second, drawing on Ansoff (1965), is the alternative directions the organisation may chose to develop within its generic strategy.

GENERIC OPTIONS

Porter argues there are three fundamental ways that a firm can achieve sustainable competitive advantage. The first of these, 'cost leadership', can be achieved by adopting the average market price and achieving the lowest costs. The second involves accepting industry average costs and achieving the highest product price through 'differentiation'. The third, called 'focus', is concerned with whether these two strategies are applied across a broad front, or are focused on a limited segment of the market.

Cost leadership, differentiation and focus are the only competitive strategy options available in Porter's model. (These are shown in Figure 7.6 and described in more detail in what follows.) Any other

Fig. 7.6   *Competitive strategies*

Low cost	Differentiation	
Overall cost leadership	Differentiation (value added)	**Broad – Industry wide**
Cost based focus	Differentiation based focus	**Narrow – Selected market**

Source: Porter (1985)

strategy, he argues, will fall between two stools and be likely only to result in average industry profitability.

Cost leadership

A low-cost, industry-wide producer is aiming for cost leadership. This does not mean a low quality product, but one that in Demming's terms would be seen as 'fit for purpose'. Cost leadership has come to mean many different things. A firm which is accounting dominated and constantly emphasises efficiency, is frequently referred to as having adopted a cost leadership strategy. This is not necessarily correct. In the 1970s, the adoption of financial models at Xerox as a result of the influence of ex-Ford personnel resulted in the company losing touch with its customers. The strategy of cost leadership applies to businesses which attempt to become the lowest cost producer in an industry.

There are many criticisms of this concept. For example, it argues that in an industry there can be only one cost leader. Thus, those coming second best will almost certainly be forced to reduce market share or stand making losses. As an industry-wide strategy it is problematic, arguably for almost everyone except one firm. Consequently, it is more likely to be sustainable in market segments. For example, People Express was successful as an extremely low-cost carrier on regional airline routes in the US. When the company attempted cost leadership as a national carrier it met much fiercer competition and in the end this became impossible to sustain.

Another criticism is that a focus on cost reduction and efficiency, at the expense of other factors, may become a dangerous end in itself. The approach which has been commonplace amongst many American and British companies tends to emphasise accounting practices and place the greatest attention on production costs, rather than any strategic factors. While this focus may be effective in the short-term, it may inhibit investment in new plant and technology which in due course results in firms losing their ability to compete effectively.

Perhaps the major criticism is Porter's use of 'cost leadership' and 'low price' as though they are interchangeable. Cost is an input measure while price is an output measure. In itself, low cost gives no competitive advantage. It only has benefit, and enhances competitive advantage, if it is either accompanied by price leadership or provides a means of achieving or enhancing output in some way. For instance, many Japanese companies achieve cost leadership so they can implement a customer orientated strategy aimed at achieving long-term growth and profitability. This is a key point. Often, Japanese companies will reinvest the margins they make into Research and Development. They invest heavily in coming up with the next generation of products so that once the competition catches up they can bring new products onto the market, attract high margins and the cycle goes on. Thus, not only are they able to satisfy customer needs through the provision of additional features, improved quality or some other form of product differentiation, they are also able to stay ahead of the competition.

As this example shows, and Johnson and Scholes (1993) note, it may be more useful to think of 'cost-based' strategies, rather than cost leadership, the benefits of which (for example, such as increased margins or surplus, low prices or efficiency) can be used to achieve competitive advantage.

Differentiation

By contrast, differentiation is looked on much more favourably by strategy commentators. It is concerned with providing a product or service that is in some way differentiated from competitive products. The key issue here is to establish in what way the product or service adds value and hence differentiates itself from other products in the market. The basis of the differentiation does not appear to matter; it may be to do with the product, its quality or with customer service.

It is important, however, that the basis for differentiation is related to customer need. Customers have to perceive it as something for which they will pay a premium price. Differentiating oneself from the competition is of no use in itself. It is only of use if the customer perceives and values the differentiation. The most successful differentiation strategies are those where the point of differentiation perceived and valued by customers, coincides with the organisation's distinctive competence. It may be skill, knowledge or an organisational competence at fast delivery. Distinctive competence is the key to effective competition in specific market areas or niches.

Differentiation also has its problems, however. Porter (1980) defines differentiation in terms of the ability of a firm to price higher than its competitors. He argues that a product or service which offers something unique, or is of greater value than the competition, should merit a higher price. However, this neglects the possibility that a firm may choose to offer a differentiated product at a similar price to competitors in order to increase market share and volume. Thus, businesses may, by keeping down costs relative to the competition, reinvest in unique features and therefore achieve differentiation. Consequently, some argue, a firm could simultaneously follow a low-cost strategy and yet seek differentiation which contradicts the dangerous position of getting 'stuck in the middle'.

Combining cost leadership and differentiation

Although there are dangers in being stuck in the middle, many companies, such as Proctor and Gamble and Philip Morris, compete successfully by combining some form of cost-based strategy with differentiation. Moreover, many writers see advantages in looking at the various possibilities of combining the two approaches. An illustration of this is the strategy matrix presented in Figure 7.7 based on Bowman's (1992) ideas.

This matrix contrasts the dimensions of price and perceived added value[17]. It is based on the notion that customers choose purchases either because the price of the product is lower, or because the product is seen to have a higher perceived added value. These dimensions are underpinned by the notions of cost and differentiation. Bowman's approach is to translate these concepts into several

Fig. 7.7   *Strategy matrix*

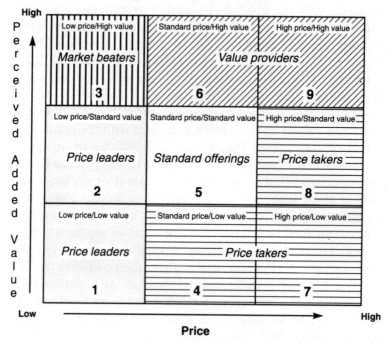

Source: Based on the work of Bowman (1992)

strategic options. These have been adapted and grouped into five areas: Standard Offerings, Price Takers, Price Leaders, Market Beaters and Value Providers.

Standard offerings

A standard price/standard value approach is highlighted in Sector 5. This emphasises that it is possible to be 'stuck in the middle' unless the executive thinks clearly about their underlying bases of competing. Many companies provide standard offerings but few can sustain such an approach over the longer term. A company in this sector is vulnerable as competitors could either marginally lower their price or increase the value of their products.

Price takers

Equally vulnerable strategies fall into sectors 4, 7 and 8 of the matrix. In sectors 4 and 7 a standard price/low value or high price/low value approach is taken. These positions are sustainable but usually only if the firm is in a monopoly position. To remain successful in these sectors legislation, or high economic barriers to entry, would need to be evident to prevent the erosion of market share.

Similarly in Sector 8, with a strategy of high price/standard value the firm may need some monopolistic benefits to sustain its position. Airline companies in America and Australia before deregulation enjoyed just such a position. A company may also be able to maintain this position through strong brand loyalty. In slow changing industries this may not be problematic, but in more dynamic markets an aggressive competitor with a more attractive offering may make quick inroads.

Price leaders

What Bowman (1992) calls 'priced based' strategies are evident in sectors 1 and 2. Sector 1 is concerned with a 'cheap and nasty' option which entails low price/low added value and focuses on a price-sensitive segment. Sector 2, on the other hand, is concerned with a low price while maintaining a product or service of standard value. This may be difficult to sustain if competitors can also reduce prices. Both sectors necessitate some degree of cost-based leadership. As noted previously, this is more easily achieved in a focused market rather than on an industry-wide basis.

Market beaters

A Sector 3 position requires a strategy which both provides high added value to the customer and maintains relatively low prices. It is a demanding strategy, but one which companies like the furniture retailer IKEA have been pursuing successfully for years. It demands a low-cost base and an ability to meet demanding customer needs. It is also attractive as an entry strategy in a market with established competitors. Many well known Japanese firms in the automotive and electronics goods industries have used this strategy to penetrate and retain markets on a global basis. Once thought of as an almost unattainable strategy, it is now almost common-place amongst some manufacturers.

According to Hamel and Prahalad (1989), companies need to adopt ambitious stretch targets and a sense of 'strategic intent' to help build such leadership positions in an industry. Some Japanese competitors have employed this strategy to devastating effect. Again, listen to the words of Xerox CEO, David Kearns, when comparing the competition's product offerings to those of Xerox in the early 1980s:

> The unit manufacturing cost – in other words, the cost to get a machine to the dock for shipping – of Japanese companies was about two thirds of ours. That statistic was absolutely astonishing. When we understood that, we were terrified. We had no idea they were making machines that much cheaper. That was no gap. That was a chasm.[18]

Value providers

Sectors 6 and 9 are the result of differentiation strategies. In both cases a high value product is being offered either at a standard price (sector 6) or premium price (sector 9). The aim here is to achieve higher market share (and therefore higher volumes than competitors) by offering better products or services at the same price; or enhanced margins by pricing slightly higher. Sector 9 (high price/high value) is usually pursued within a particular market segment. Porche, for instance, offers a product with higher perceived value often at a substantially higher price.

It is questionable whether competitive advantage through differentiation can be achieved on a static basis. In many markets, customer values change and therefore the basis of differentiation needs to change. The implication is that a business must therefore keep its strategy under constant review and continue to innovate. This is perhaps best illustrated by the constant outpourings of new product offerings from the automobile and PC manufacturers.

Accordingly, to pursue this kind of strategy it is important to:

- Be clear which market segment the firm is competing in
- Monitor market changes
- Understand stakeholder expectations

MARKET OPTIONS

The generic strategies outlined above need to be complemented by an understanding of some of the options available in relation to various market segments. It is of little use having an underlying generic strategy if this is forgotten when the executive looks at the specific approaches that might be taken in developing products and markets. This perspective can be helped by considering Ansoff's (1965) matrix. This looks at several different options, including whether to capture more of the present market, move into new markets or diversify.

Ansoff matrix

The matrix posits two dimensions (see Figure 7.8): the first is concerned with markets and whether these are new or existing, and the second is concerned with products and, again, whether these are new or existing.

Market penetration

The top left-hand box of the matrix is concerned with existing products in existing markets. When one attempts to improve one's position with the same product in the same market, this is called Market Penetration. This is possibly the safest option because there is existing knowledge about the customer benefits provided by the product, and the capabilities of the competition. The low cost/high value added, or 'Market Beater' tactic mentioned earlier, will arguably make the most inroads into the market.

Other responses are also possible. One option may be *Withdrawal* which may be necessary for several reasons – from poor performance

Fig. 7.8 *Directions for development*

PRODUCTS

	Existing	New
Existing	Market penetration	Product development
New	Market development	Diversification

MARKETS

Source: Adapted from Ansoff (1965)

to the need to change the company's product portfolio. Also of importance is *Consolidating* one's position. This may be needed because of an increase in competitor' activity, a declining market and the need to maintain market share, or changes in the internal competencies of the firm. During the 1980s, after a period of massive expansion, People Express arguably needed a period of consolidation in order to restructure and iron out some of the organisational problems the company faced.

Market development

The bottom left-hand corner of the matrix is to do with Market Development, and is concerned with taking existing products into new markets. The main advantage associated with this position is that the strengths and limitations of the product are known. The real challenge lies in understanding the new market one has targeted. This can pose problems, particularly if those markets are overseas with different tastes, norms and standards.

One way of reducing the risks of entering a new market is to form joint ventures with companies already operating there. Since the late 1980s, Unilever, Nestle and Procter & Gamble have done just this to help establish a foothold in China.[19] They are working through joint ventures with local state-owned companies, and taking larger majority stakes in each successive venture as their experience grows. It is a slow process, however. Nestle negotiated for 13 years before signing its first deal to set up a manufacturing plant for powdered milk. The logistics of organising local supplies of raw materials and promoting and distributing products in China are also proving problematic. While these issues are being ironed out, local competitors are starting to improve the quality of their offerings and competition is increasing. Overall, there appears to be no easy way to reduce the risks – but the strategy of these major firms is unchanged. They will persist rather than miss out altogether on a potential market of over 1.2 billion people.

Product development

This is concerned with selling a new product to an existing market. In many industries, and particularly where product life cycles are short, product development is essential in order to survive. In many ways, product development may be fraught with more difficulties than market development. Developing a new product can be expensive, time consuming and promises few guarantees. Kotler (1988) points out that most new products never reach the market and if they do, relatively few succeed.

Diversification

Despite the difficulties associated with these three approaches, a strategy of Diversification is easily the most fraught with danger. (The label 'suicide square' which is sometimes applied to this position on the matrix gives some flavour of the challenges and dangers involved.) The understanding one needs to place a new product or service successfully in a new market is clearly enormous. Such a process demands a considerable amount of analysis of customers and markets before attempting it. Indeed, it may be better to diversify initially through other means – for example, by taking either a Product or Market Development approach.

Some of the pitfalls of diversification are illustrated by Chrysler during the 1980s.[20] Of all the major US car producers, Chrysler diversified the most aggressively. During the 1980s, under the direction of Lee Iacocca, Chrysler made several major purchases – including four rental-car companies, a small defence electronics firm and even flirted with the possibility of buying the brokerage house, E. F. Hutton. Iacocca tried to bring together these and other somewhat disparate assets under a holding company with three subsidiaries: Chrysler Motors, Chrysler Financial and Chrysler Technologies. In the end the grand plan floundered. After the acquisition of Gulfstream Aerospace for $637 million, Chrysler began to learn more about the defence industry and realised it could not compete. Moreover, during the diversification programme the car side of the business started to deteriorate. By 1988 it had decided to abandon its diversification strategy and was trying to rescue its core business.

Diversification should not be dismissed as a viable strategy simply because of the difficulties involved. Honda was ignored by US firms partly because of its diversification strategy. For two decades Honda entered a series of seemingly unrelated businesses; automobiles, lawn mowers, marine engines and generators. Honda was able to grow because it competed differently, emphasising different managerial and manufacturing philosophies.

It is worth emphasising that the market or product development options highlighted by Ansoff have to be related to the generic strategies outlined earlier in this chapter. Thus, taking a new product to a new market would be underpinned by the broad cost/differentiation approach adopted by the company based on its core competencies. It is easy to make mistakes here. People Express in the US (as did Compass in Australia) subsequently aimed their low-cost airline service at the business customer. While they had some initial success, People Express's strengths lay in a low cost/low price service. Selling on price to a market segment requiring a high quality service was always going to face problems. These became exacerbated as the major airlines (whose generic option lay in a higher value service) began to improve the quality of their own service.

PROCESS OPTIONS – STRATEGIC ALLIANCES

The emphasis in this chapter has been on competition and, as Ohmae (1982) has commented, without competition there is no need for strategy. Increasingly, however, the complexities of global competition are demanding a more sophisticated and flexible approach. Rather than viewing competition as a warlike zero-sum game, organisations are being encouraged to explore the continuum between competition and cooperation. An increasingly popular example of this is the use of strategic alliances.

There has been a huge increase in the number of strategic alliances in recent years. In the five years to 1995, Bleeke and Ernst (1995) calculate that the number of domestic and international alliances formed by American companies has grown by more than 25 per cent annually. IBM alone has over 400 strategic alliances worldwide and no sector of the economy has been left untouched by such collaborative developments.

Strategic alliances are having an impact in different ways. Hamel and Prahalad (1989) argue that through licensing, outsourcing agreements and joint ventures, it is sometimes possible 'to win without fighting'. For instance, in the early 1980s, Matsushita established a joint venture with Thorn in the UK, Telefunken in Germany and Thomson in France which allowed it to quickly multiply the forces arrayed against Philips in the battle for leadership in the European VCR business. Indeed, alliances can change industries. For years pharmaceutical companies fiercely jockeyed for position and ignored the threat posed by young biotechnology companies. However, recognising the potential of these companies, some pharmaceutical corporations have formed strategic alliances with start-up biotechnology firms – an alliance which has profoundly transformed the pharmaceutical industry.

Alliances can help reduce market complexity and uncertainty, give companies access to new markets and acquire emerging technology or special expertise. While the potential benefits can be great, overall, however, alliances are not particularly successful. Bleeke and Ernst (1993) suggest that upwards of 60 per cent of all alliances fail. The median life span for alliances is only about seven years, and nearly 80 per cent of joint ventures – one of the most common alliance structures – ultimately end in a sale by one of the partners.[21]

Studies suggest there are two areas which are critical to develop if an alliance is to be successful. The first is to examine the potential business outcomes of an alliance. Bleeke and Ernst (1995) argue that different types of alliance create greater hurdles to success than others. For example, managers who choose direct competitors as partners in order to create short-term synergy tend to make the worst alliance partners. Instead, they should consider either acquiring such competitors or partnering with companies that focus on different business or geographic markets. The best type of alliance involves two strong and complementary partners that remain strong during the course of the alliance. These mutually beneficial relationships are likely to last much longer than seven years. Dow Corning is more than 50 years old, Fuji Xerox is more than 30 and Siecor – an alliance between Siemens and Corning – is more than 15 years old.

The second area of consideration is the way the alliance is managed – in particular, the interpersonal relationships between those responsible for developing and maintaining the venture. Spekman *et al.* (1994) found that both the business and interpersonal processes must be attended to throughout the different stages of the alliance life cycle.

Considerable energy is needed to build and nurture interpersonal relationships, and this can take a lot of time. Alliances are so central to the strategy of Corning, the $3 billion a year glass and ceramics manufacturer, that the corporation now defines itself as a 'network of organisations'. The company's success comes from working with a very long-term perspective. Vice chairman, Van Campbell says:

We're looking only for lifetime associations, because you have to invest an enormous amount of energy to make a partnership work. You not only have to deal with the business: you also constantly have to deal with the relationship you have with the partner – nurturing and maintaining high level contacts, so that when you deal with items of substance you will be dealing with friends, people you understand and respect. A partnership that is only going to last 5 to 7 years, simply doesn't warrant that kind of investment.[22]

A central stumbling block to the success of an alliance is lack of trust. A mindset of collaboration, rather than acquisition and control, is what is required. Philip Benton Jr, President of Ford, argues that the need for trust is why American companies have to lengthen their time horizon on alliances. 'It's absolutely essential to start slowly to build trust. The first time two companies work together, the chances of succeeding are very slight. But once you find ways of working together all sorts of opportunities come up – and the likelihood of severing that relationship and starting the whole process over again becomes remote'.[23]

The need to retain flexibility is also important. Researchers in this area highlight how even the most successful alliances change considerably over time, and that different skills may be needed at different points in the relationship. While joint efforts need clear ground rules, they also need flexibility and adaptability from all partners.

Kanter (1994) argues that whatever the duration and objectives of an alliance, being a good partner has become a key corporate asset. She calls it the company's 'collaborate advantage'. In the global economy, a well-developed ability to create and sustain fruitful collaborations gives companies a significant competitive edge. She argues that North American and European companies lag behind their Asian counterparts who are most comfortable with relationships and the interpersonal aspects of alliances.

SUMMARY

The frameworks outlined in this chapter are designed to help structure executives' analyses of their firms competitive environment. A number of techniques and frameworks have been highlighted to help the executive focus on important trends in the business, industry and market environments.

The bases on which organisations choose to compete have been reviewed using Porter's Competitive Forces Model. Several additional frameworks are also used to help the executive think about the markets in which they operate and market segmentation. Executives have several options for building sustainable competitive advantage. These have been discussed in the chapter in terms of the generic options of cost and differentiation; market options and product strategies; and process options through competing, consolidating as a result of mergers and takeovers, or cooperating through alliances.

While most of the chapter has been devoted to these aspects, the way executives think about the external environment is as important as what they think about. The External Capability requires the executive to think outside their own mental frames of reference and look at the industry through the eyes of the customer and the competition. Executives need to guard against competitive blindspots by provoking debate within their organisations to maximise their own and others' exposure to different perspectives.

The approach one takes to the external environment has significant implications for the kind of organisation one builds. It affects both the culture and structure of the organisation. The External Capability must therefore be complemented by an awareness of how the organisation operates and its capacity to grow and develop. These points are examined in more detail in the next two chapters devoted to the Organisational Capability.

NOTES

1. See Alex Taylor III, 'US Cars Come Back', *Fortune*, vol. 126, no. 11, 16 November 1992, 24–53.
2. Kearns and Nadler (1992, 133).
3. Laxmi Nakarmi and Robert Neff, 'Samsung's Radical Shakeup', *Business Week*, 28 February 1994, 35–7.
4. Nick Hasell, 'The View from Bayer', *Management Today*, November, 1993, 61–4.
5. Zahra and Chaples (1993).
6. Ronald Grover, Joseph Weber, Richard A. Melcher, 'The Entertainment Economy', *Business Week*, 14 March 1994, 36–42.
7. Aziz Panni, 'Sea Change at Siemens', *Management Today*, March, 1994, 51–4.
8. Edmund Faltermayer, 'Andy Grove: How Intel Makes Spending Pay Off', *Fortune*, vol. 127, no. 4, 22 February 1993, 25–7.

9. This chapter draws extensively on Europe's best selling strategy text by Johnson and Scholes (1993) and also Pearson (1990).
10. Pearson (1990).
11. Louise Kehoe and Alan Cane, 'Chips Down for PC Partners', *Financial Times*, 20 September 1994, 19.
12. Peter Wilsher, 'Whose Hands on the Housekeeping?', *Management Today*, December 1993, 38–43.
13. See Kennith Labich, 'What Will Save the US Airlines', *Fortune*, vol. 127, no. 12, 14 June 1993, 50–3 and Wilton Woods, 'Goodbye Hub and Spoke?', *Fortune*, vol. 128, no. 15, 13 December 1993, 72–3.
14. Julia Flynn and Richard A. Melcher, 'Can Heineken Stay on the Top Shelf?', *Business Week*, 1 August 1994, 32–4.
15. Pearson (1990) points out that there are an infinite number of ways of defining SBUs, and no clear guideline as to which is best. They can be defined according to:

- Product groups
- End-user groups
- Distribution channels
- Geography
- Technology
- Original equipment/replacement parts
- Custom/standard parts
- Manufacturing/marketing dominant
- Established business/development business

Kevan Scholes points out that there is a danger in confusing SBUs with organisational structure. He argues that an SBU is a bundle of products and services and the market segments they serve. However, this particular strategic focus may, or may not, be reflected in the structure of the organisation. For example, several market segments could be serviced by one particular functional area.
16. Kearns and Nadler (1992, 123).
17. Johnson and Scholes (1993) have converted Bowman's original term of 'use value' to 'added value' which is used here.
18. Kearns and Nadler (1992, 122).
19. Roderick Oram, 'A Consuming Interest in China', *Financial Times*, 28 September 1994, 17.
20. Alex Taylor III, 'Lee Iacocca's Parting Shots', *Fortune*, vol. 126, no. 5, 7 September 1992, 34–8, and another article by Taylor, 'U.S. Cars Come Back', *Fortune*, vol. 126, no. 11, 16 November 1992, 24–53.
21. Bleeke and Ernst (1995).
22. See Stratford Sherman's article, 'Are Strategic Alliances Working?', *Fortune*, vol. 126, no. 6, 21 September 1992, 33–4.
23. *Fortune*, 21 September 1992, *op. cit.*

8 The Organisational Capability – Design: Designing Corporate Systems and Structures

INTRODUCTION

In the past decade, organisations have focused on downsizing, right-sizing, re-engineering and a host of other changes in an attempt to improve productivity and competitiveness. Indeed, it is estimated that corporate America spends around $10 billion a year on restructuring.[1] All this activity poses considerable challenges for senior level managers. They have a particular responsibility to direct and implement structural changes in their organisation. Ultimately, their goal is to emerge with a capable organisation – that is, one which can adapt more quickly than its competitors to the full range of external and internal threats.[2]

The reality, however, seems to be rather different. A recent study of organisations in the US highlighted that fewer than half of the firms which downsized their operations subsequently raised their profits.[3] Those who did, did not start to see real benefits until three years after the cuts. Moreover, 40 per cent of executives in this study said they were unhappy with the results of their restructuring activities.

Clearly, selecting and designing appropriate organisational systems and structures is not easy. In this chapter, we focus on the know-how individual executives need to do this effectively. In the previous chapter we explored issues to do with understanding the external environment: in effect, these often provide the reasons *why* an organisation should change. In order to respond, the executive needs to be able to develop the organisation's internal work processes, structures and systems. What we call an executive's 'Organisational Capability' is concerned with this. It consists of two major aspects:

- An understanding of the key components of the organisation and the way these can be configured to best respond to external demands.
- An understanding of how to manage, change and develop organisational components to create an organisation which is able to respond effectively.

In this chapter we will be concerned with the first of these two aspects – that is, knowing *what* elements of the organisation to change. In Chapter 9 we will explore *how* the executive goes about the change process. Thus, Chapters 7, 8 and 9 are related as they look at why organisations should change, what needs to be changed and how to go about this.

MAJOR ORGANISATIONAL COMPONENTS

There are several major components of an organisation that the senior executive needs to understand and manage. In particular these include:

- *Key tasks and work processes*. The key work activities and underlying processes which need to be carried out in order to meet the organisation's strategic goals.

- *Individual competencies*. The principle skills, attitudes and disposition needed by individuals within the organisation to perform key tasks.

- *Critical technology*. The technology that is needed both now and in the future to enable individuals to operate effectively.

- *Organisational structures*. The appropriate kinds of structures which will help the organisation achieve its aims.

- *Organisational systems*. Coordination and control systems to help ensure the organisation operates efficiently.

- *Organisational culture*. The informal processes which will shape general ways of behaving, acting and thinking within the organisation to support organisational goals.

In this chapter, we have decided to focus on the last three items – the broad elements of organisational design, the formal structures and systems; also the key informal components of the organisation, often referred to as organisational culture. This does not mean that the rest are unimportant or that they are completely excluded from the discussions which follow. It is essential that the senior manager understands what individual competencies (functional and business knowledge, personal and interpersonal abilities) are needed in the organisation. It is also essential that the executive appreciates the overall tasks which need to be performed and the processes which support these. Moreover, executives need some understanding of how technology can both assist and constrain the organisation.

In what follows, however, we will be focusing more on the structure and culture of the organisation, for it is these elements which are particularly important at senior levels. As Braddick (1988) notes, managers often reach board level because they are very self-sufficient. As a result, they may not find it easy to manage indirectly through others using the structures, culture and work processes within the organisation. However, before we look at these in more detail it is worth considering three related issues.

Executive mindset

The first of these is concerned with executive mindset (explored in more detail in Chapter 2). The mindset of those who direct (as well as those who are affected by) organisational change can have a profound influence on the success of any reorganisation or restructuring. Some thought therefore needs to be given to the way the executive and his or her staff think about and view their organisation.

Often, employee morale will suffer as a result of some structural change to the organisation. Indeed, long after a restructuring, employees may still be questioning the need for change. For example, despite the scale of the downsizing at IBM in the late 1980s and early 1990s, CEO Lou Gerstner, found that a 'mainframe mindset' – that is, a belief that big computers will one day reassert their dominance – still haunted the company.[4]

At British Gas, Europe's 13th largest company, breaking down entrenched attitudes within the workforce is one of the most critical challenges facing the organisation.[5] A public utility for many years,

British Gas is transforming itself in order to fend off competition in the domestic markets and compete in the international gas industry. To do this the company embarked on a massive restructuring exercise shedding around a third of its workforce. In the early 1990s, British Gas disbanded its regional structure in favour of five national business units. In the process, management and supervisory layers were reduced from around 13 to just five or six. The decision to move away from a 'command and control' management style towards a more empowering culture was greeted with suspicion and incredulity at many levels. The challenge of trying to change an essentially bureaucratic and risk-averse organisation into one which is more commercially minded is formidable. The new Chairman and CEO, however, are in no doubt that the new strategy and structure will be worth very little unless this is accompanied by a change in thinking throughout British Gas.

Picturing the capable organisation

If we accept that some kind of mental shift in thinking and outlook has to take place, then it is critical that executives spend time and effort building a picture of what the organisation will look like in the future. For it is this picture which will motivate and inspire others to make the transition. The picture should, of course, be related to the overall strategic aims of the organisation, to choices about what business to be in and the type of goods and services to be provided.

Hamel and Prahalad (1994) believe that the greatest competitive advantage a company can have is a vision of the future. Rather than contemplating downsizing, re-engineering and other restructuring exercises dealing with present realities, organisations should spend time thinking hard about where they will be a decade hence. For example, IBM spent $6 billion a year on R&D but failed to see that the market was moving from mainframes to personal computers. Around the same time, the founders of Apple were tinkering in a Californian garage with what was to turn out to be Apple's first PC. According to Hamel and Prahalad, the difference was that Apple's founders had a dream of a computer for every 'man, woman and child' in America. Building on their earlier, influential ideas about the need to identify an organisation's core competencies, the authors argue that a company which thinks about its future will not necessarily be concerned with releasing one world-beating product, but will nurture those competencies which will help it dominate a market.

While it is clearly better to have a picture than not, identifying the kind of organisation one needs in the longer term (particularly under conditions of great uncertainty and change) is less straightforward than some writers acknowledge.

Take for example, the notion of the learning organisation. Increasingly, major corporations are attempting to create structures and processes within their organisations which will help them learn from experience as they reach out to achieve their strategic goals. According to Senge (1990a) the emergence of a learning organisation requires a climate created by five disciplines; systems thinking, personal mastery, mental models, shared vision and team learning. Of these, systems thinking is the cornerstone of the five disciplines and is a framework for seeing interrelationships and patterns of change rather than static snapshots. This approach to organisational learning has its roots in the work of writers such as Argyris and Schon (1978).[6]

There are many emerging developments in the area; for instance, Watkins and Marsick (1993) suggest that to facilitate organisation-wide learning, six action imperatives are important, namely:

(1) Create continuous learning opportunities
(2) Promote inquiry and dialogue
(3) Encourage collaboration and team learning
(4) Establish systems to capture and share learning
(5) Empower people towards a collective vision
(6) Connect the organisation to its environment

As yet, however, few organisations can claim to have mastered such principles. A recent research study examined 20 development projects being undertaken at Digital, Kodak, Ford and Hewlett-Packard.[7] It showed that managers seldom realise that the learning to be gained from carrying out a project could be more important than the new product or process itself. For example, few of the projects in the study were formally audited after the event, and as a result the lessons learnt were not translated and applied to other projects.

If organisations have difficulty in learning from individual projects, it may take even longer for systems to emerge which will allow learning to be applied across different functions and businesses. A true picture of what a learning organisation looks like has therefore yet to emerge. According to Lessum (1993, viii);

> Whenever I am asked to provide an example of an authentic learning organisation, that is one that is wholly engaged in the process of individual and collective learning, I am lost for words. Such an entity does not exist, not withstanding the abundance of wishful thinking around us.

Alternatively, Ulrich and Lake (1990) suggest that rather than trying to pursue an ideal lasting image, executives should establish a process for ongoing organisational design. Under these circumstances the emphasis is on the principles which enable the organisation to move forward. This does not negate the need to consider the type of systems and structures required, but rather keeps the focus on using organisational design as a way of contributing to the company's strategic path. Thus, these authors argue, the executive should aim to develop an organisation which:

- Has budgets and programs in place which support the strategy
- Has a strong organisation wide commitment to the chosen strategy
- Links motivation and reward structures directly to achieving the targeted results
- Creates an organisation culture and a working environment that is in tune with the strategy
- Installs policies and procedures that facilitate strategy implementation
- Develops an information and reporting system to track progress and monitor performance

Formal vs informal organisation

The third issue to consider is the potential difficulty (or ease) with which the 'formal' and 'informal' aspects of an organisation can be changed. The former refers to items which have been deliberately set up such as financial and IT systems, organisational reporting relationships or the structure of an organisation. These are easier to change than informal aspects such as values and culture. The formal aspects are concrete, can be drawn on pieces of paper and discussed. It is obvious when they have been installed or removed.

Informal aspects are less tangible and more ambiguous. Indeed, they often only make themselves apparent under pressure or when novel situations arise.

Because the structure and systems of an organisation are more apparent, formal aspects are relatively easier to change. Also, as they can have a fairly immediate impact on organisational effectiveness, they are important levers for the senior executive. Changing organisational structures, systems and rewards can produce benefits like saving money, channel energy and help realign organisations. They also send symbolic signals about who and what are important. They can also cause massive problems.

For example, a major reason for the poor performance of the automobile manufacturers in the USA in the 1980s was because they tried to diversify, neglected day-to-day activities, and sent mixed messages to managers with 'grandiose but botched reorganisations'.[8] One of Jack Smith's first tasks when he took over as president of GM in 1992 was to undo the massively flawed reorganisation which the company had lived with for eight years. He said, 'It is tough to operate when the structure isn't right. It just stops you cold.'[9]

However, even getting the structure correct may not be enough. When Lou Gerstner arrived at IBM in 1993 with $14 billion losses in hardware profits, he concluded that the company was out of touch with the market.[10] What he found was a ponderous bureaucracy, out-of-date procedures and turf wars between different product divisions. Under his tenure, the size of IBM's legendary salesforce was dramatically reduced from a peak of 150 000 in 1990 to around 70 000 in 1994. Those who remained had their roles redefined and refocused around customer needs. The salesforce was reorganised into 14 industry-specific teams. Steps were taken to consolidate product groups to help stop internal bickering between divisions for sales. Compensation systems were changed to reflect the emphasis on providing customer solutions rather than products. Commissions were then tied to both customer satisfaction and profitability. Clearly the use of all these different levers – structure, size, and reward systems – will impact on the activities of IBM in the 1990s. But is this enough? Only if the informal elements of the organisation also change – including the arrogant mindset on the part of many salestaff, the bureaucratic mentality of the organisation and if the potential threat of competitors is acknowledged.

The informal aspects can be easily overlooked in organisational realignments. We will discuss whether, and to what degree, culture can be managed later in this chapter. Suffice to say that executives need to recognise the interrelationship between the formal structural aspects of the organisation and the informal behavioural processes which underpin them. Decisions about structure must be tempered by an understanding of how that design will impact on the interpersonal and power relationships within the organisation. As many executives will know, it is little use changing to a new structure when it may be blighted by the power plays and conflicts of uncooperative individuals.

Design considerations

For many years now the call has been for flatter work structures. As Ulrich and Lake (1990) point out, some organisations have found that when they remove several layers of management they become more flexible, provide employees with more autonomy over their work and are more responsive to customer needs. However, a flatter work structure (that is, an increase in the span of control) is only one element of understanding organisational design. In looking at the overall form of the organisation, several other factors need to be considered, namely;

(1) How internally efficient or externally responsive does the organisation need to be? Usually, this is not an 'either or' decision but a continuum. Internal efficiency enables the organisation to reduce costs through economies of scale or develop products and services through focused effort. Responsiveness is the degree to which an organisation can respond to external changes or the detailed requirements of customers. Whether efficiency or responsiveness are primarily emphasised, will depend on the strategic thrust of the company.

(2) What degree of centralisation or decentralisation is required? To what extent is decision making generally pushed down to lower managerial and staff levels in the organisation? Where are operational and strategic decisions made?

(3) What is the optimum size for the organisation? Large organisations can exploit such things as economies of scale, large

distribution systems, widespread brand identity. However, as organisations increase in size, they emphasise predictability, formalised roles and control systems.[11] To respond effectively, it is frequently necessary to create small and dynamic organisations or divisions.

(4) How internationally focused should the organisation be? Organisations face the dual challenges of maintaining market share and consistency in a domestic market while branching into global markets. To do so, organisation structures must maintain existing manufacturing and distribution systems while complementing them with strategic alliances and global organisation structures.

ORGANISATIONAL STRUCTURE

The issues raised so far are an important backdrop to looking at organisational structure and design. Organisational structure is the skeleton of the organisation and determines the form it will take. Organ and Bateman (1986) describe it as the formal, systematic arrangement of the operations and activities that constitute an organisation and the interrelationships of these operations to one another. Miles (1980) sees structure as the systematic patterns of differentiation and integration of organised activities. Thus, structure both differentiates the elements of an organisation and simultaneously integrates them. As Nadler and Tushman (1988b) note, this involves choice in grouping some resources in order to gain economies of scale, benefits of specialisation, and/or integration. But it also requires structural linking mechanisms to help knit interdependent areas together.

By arranging the organisation into different forms or groups, the executive is providing the core framework within which all other design decisions are made. Grouping puts some tasks, functions or disciplines together and draws others apart – it focuses the organisation.

The principal groupings executives use to structure their organisations are outlined below. Typically, these emphasise particular work activities, external factors such as products, customers or location, or a combination of these.

Grouping by internal activity – the functional structure

This form combines people in terms of the same functions, disciplines, skills or work processes (see Figure 8.1). Reporting relationships and responsibilities are clearly identified. Such a structure enables expertise to be developed and economies of scale to be exploited. It is particularly advantageous where stability is needed and centralised decision making is necessary.

Organisations grouped this way can, however, be less responsive to clients, markets and users. Senior managers at Electrolux, the Swedish household appliances multinational, have grappled with just this problem. In 1994, a strong, functional structure separated its sales and marketing organisation from its product development and factory units.[12] Bridging these different organisational units to provide an integrated response to customers had, in the past, proved problematic. Indeed, the gulf between them has made the company slower, less innovative and less cost-efficient than it should have been. As a result, it has been hampered in its bid to compete against rivals like Germany's Bosch Siemens and Whirlpool Philips in the US.

Companies which need to respond in diverse ways or with different products may therefore find functional structures too restrictive. While senior executives may be able to maintain operational control more easily, under more dynamic circumstances executives can be dragged into sorting out operational issues and become overbur-

Fig. 8.1   *Functional structure*

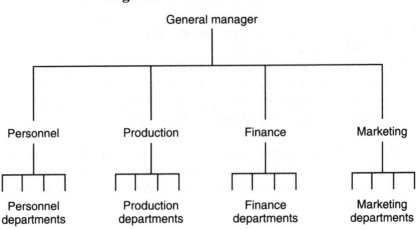

dened. It is rarely found as the dominant structure of large companies, although it is very common as a component of other structures.

Grouping by external focus – divisional structures

This form of organisational structure combines people in terms of an external emphasis, such as similar products or services, markets or market segments, or geography (Figure 8.2). Whatever the basis of the grouping – product, customer or location – each division is able to concentrate and respond more quickly to the specific problems with which it is faced.

The major advantage of the divisional structure is its responsiveness and increasingly it is the preferred option for multinationals who want to cut complexity and costs and improve the speed of their competitive response. The downside is that divisionalisation can lead to a fragmented focus, with functional expertise spread across geographic or product lines and low economies of scale. However, this depends on how the organisation is split. Divisionalisation along product lines can lead to a degree of concentration and economies of scale in the production of one product, yet still give the organisation overall flexibility in its product emphasis and portfolio. Ulrich and Lake (1990) argue that between 1955 and 1975 the majority of Fortune 500 companies shifted to a product organisation. Product groupings are also forming the basis of many companies current attempts to cope with globalisation.

Fig. 8.2 *Divisional structure*

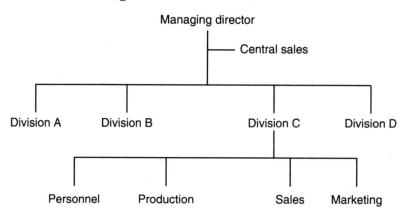

Multinational companies often follow a divisional structure which has several layers. For example, a company might be broken into a number of divisions based on broad products/markets. Within each of these divisions there may be separate businesses, which in turn may have their own divisional structures. At some level in the organisation a division may then be split into functionally based departments dealing with the specialist tasks of that business.[13]

Groupings based on diversity – matrix and integrated structures

The third type is where the groupings are based on several dimensions, for instance a combination of product and functional structures, or a combination of product and geographic location. The purpose of this kind of structure is to balance responsiveness and efficiency. A matrix structure is one where there is a fairly equal balance between these two and an equal sharing of responsibility for performance (Figure 8.3).

The advantages of the matrix organisation are that it allows for resources to be shifted across product lines, and is helpful in situations where scarce technical expertise needs to be strategically allocated among a number of projects or programmes. The draw-

Fig. 8.3 *Matrix structure*

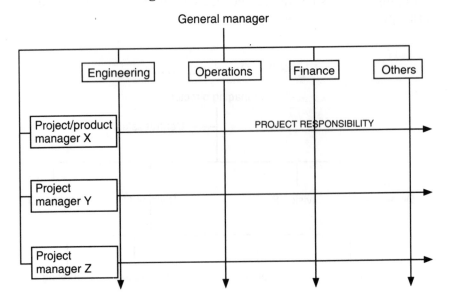

backs are that it is complex and requires voluntary problem resolution at the general manager level, which may slow down decision making. Maintaining a balance of power between the product, functional, or regional managers is often difficult and time consuming. Given these difficulties, the trend is for firms to move away from matrix structures. Only a minority of companies in any industry are following the lead of ABB, the Swedish Swiss engineering firm which has succeeded in making its matrix structure work.[14]

In the early 1980s, Peters and Waterman (1982) concluded that matrix structures were largely unworkable. However, many of the problems with matrix structures arise because organisations fail to pay attention to the informal cultural aspects which are necessary to integrate and bind together these particular configurations. As Organ and Bateman (1986) point out, the establishment of a matrix structure should be preceded by a comprehensive programme of organisational resocialisation of norms and attitudes. Furthermore, they argue that matrix structures do not seem to work well in climates which emphasise legitimate authority and specific individual roles.

In practice, the aim should be to create a set of groupings which best facilitate the organisation's operations. While matrix structures in their pure form may be problematic, many corporations combine internal activity, external focus and balanced matrix groups, to create more integrated and complex structures which are more appropriate to organisational needs. Often these integrated structures get around the problem of dual authority by making the responsibility for various activities clear. Figure 8.4 shows a combination of product and functional groupings which combine some degree of responsiveness in some areas with functional expertise in others. The range of structural combinations discussed so far is highlighted in Figure 8.5.

Corporate focus – centralisation vs decentralisation

It is worth discussing at this point an aspect of organisational design which has considerable implications for organisation structure – namely, whether to centralise or decentralise.

Goold (1991) cites three reasons why organisations decentralise: to help ensure that strategies are based on detailed knowledge of specific markets and products; to increase business level ownership of strategy and to reduce the load on senior management at the centre. He argues that decentralisation only works well if the centre knows when the businesses are on track with the strategy (and intervenes

Fig. 8.4 *Integrated structure*

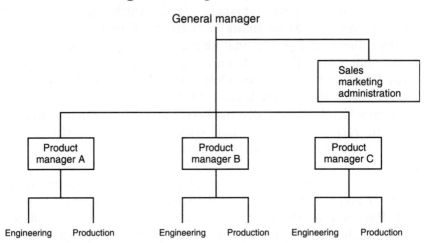

when they are not). Similarly, for their part, the business heads must know what will be counted as good performance by the centre.

The extent to which organisations fulfil these conditions varies enormously. Indeed, what types of decisions and where they are made is often a source of tension between the centre and the separate business units, particularly in large divisionalised companies. It is important to note in discussing this relationship that divisionalisation does not mean decentralisation. While a divisional structure facilitates autonomous decision making, as will be seen below, there are nevertheless a range of decision making possibilities within this organisational structure. In fact, different assumptions about what 'divisionalisation' means can sometimes add to the tension.

Goold argues that the centre's role can be seen from three different perspectives (see Table 8.1). At one end of the spectrum is the holding company, or what Goold and Campbell (1988) call a situation of 'Financial Control'. Here, at the extreme, the corporate centre is no more than a shareholder in a variety of individual, unconnected business operations, which it buys and sells. Assuming the centre is confident in the management team, operational and most strategic decisions are left to senior management in the operating companies.

The centre's main tasks are to sanction expenditure, agree targets, monitor performance and to reorganise management teams that are performing poorly. Hanson Trust and BTR are good examples of this

Fig. 8.5 *Organisational structures*

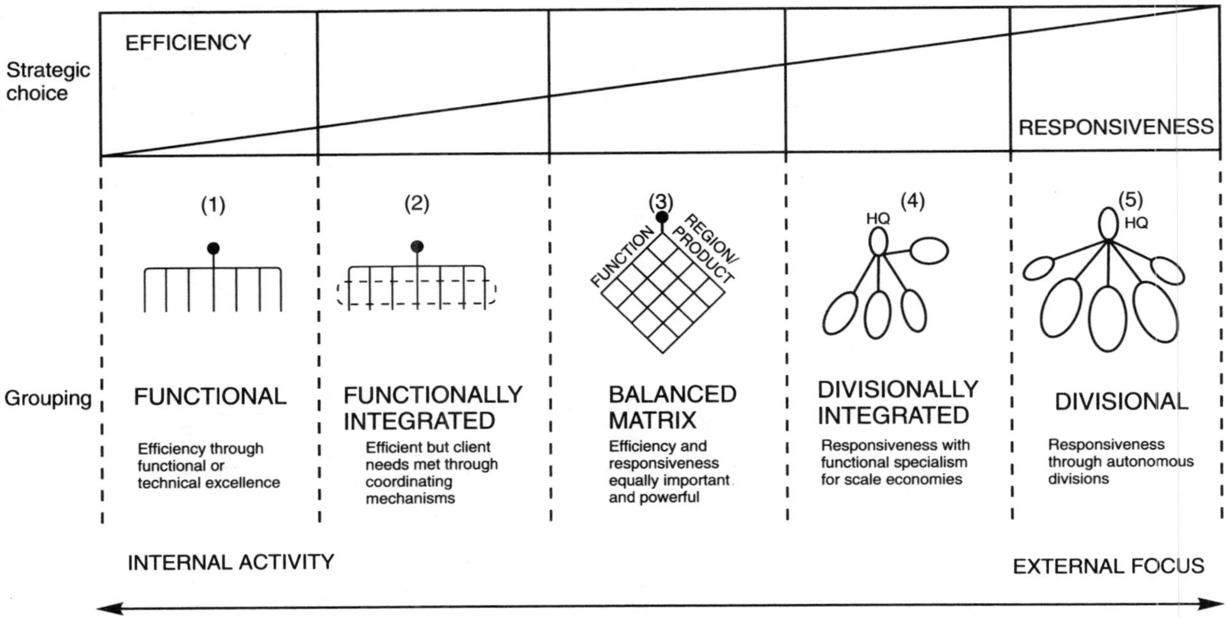

Strategic choice	EFFICIENCY				RESPONSIVENESS

Grouping

(1) FUNCTIONAL — Efficiency through functional or technical excellence

(2) FUNCTIONALLY INTEGRATED — Efficient but client needs met through coordinating mechanisms

(3) REGION/PRODUCT / FUNCTION — BALANCED MATRIX — Efficiency and responsiveness equally important and powerful

(4) HQ — DIVISIONALLY INTEGRATED — Responsiveness with functional specialism for scale economies

(5) HQ — DIVISIONAL — Responsiveness through autonomous divisions

INTERNAL ACTIVITY ←————————————————————→ EXTERNAL FOCUS

Table 8.1　Corporate focus

Centralised	Controlled initiative	Decentralised
Strategic planning	Strategic control	Financial control
Centre sets detailed business plans	Centre reviews business unit proposals	Centre agrees expenditure
Centre maintains a thorough review process	Centre and unit negotiates business plan	Centre agrees targets
Clearly defined procedures	Centre allows independence within an overall strategy	Centre monitors performance

Source:　Based on the work of Goold and Campbell (1988)

approach. In 1994 BTR had a skeleton staff at its London headquarters of around 80 people whereas worldwide there were around 130 000 BTR employees.[15] In addition to managing the organisation's statutory obligations, the centre steers the development of the group, and sets managers stretching financial targets to achieve. Senior managers at BTR exercise strict financial controls on BTR operations. Subsidiary managers are expected to provide themselves with whatever services they need.

There are several advantages associated with decentralisation. Most decisions which impact on the running of the business are left to those executives closest to the customer. Where there are problems, the centre will bring in expertise to help revitalise the business. In some cases strict short-term financial targets are applied, but in others such as the Australian based conglomerate Pacific Dunlop, some protection may be given to allow businesses to sort out their operational base in the longer term. Also, as banker, the centre may be able to get much better financing, spread risk across many business ventures and divest itself of individual companies easily.

At the other extreme is the centralised approach, where the centre participates in and influences the development of business unit strategies. It does this by establishing demanding and thorough review processes for business plans and making strong contributions to strategic development and thinking. Goold and Campbell (1988) call this 'Strategic Planning'. Companies in this category would include IBM and Canon, the camera and office equipment company. The main benefit of operating in this way comes from the high levels of control and coordination which the centre is able to exert over strategy.

In the middle of the continuum is 'Strategic Control' where the focus is on independent business units, leaving as much initiative as possible to unit management within an overall strategic framework. The centre concentrates on reviewing and criticising unit proposals, rather than on advocating particular ways forward. Here, the advantage is in giving decision-making responsibility to those who are most capable. The problem, however, is that this may result in frequent negotiation, a continual balancing act and tension between the centre and the rest of the organisation. This relationship needs to be considered carefully, as Goold *et al.* (1994) emphasise how hard it is for a parent company to add value to the operating businesses and how easy it is to damage them.

More recently, organisations have reconfigured the relationship between the centre and the operating businesses under what is called a 'federalist' approach. Handy (1992) identifies certain key principles which distinguish this particular organisational structure. Under federalism, the centre exists to coordinate, not control. Power is seen to reside with the constituent parts of the organisation (as opposed to being delegated from the centre as is the case with decentralisation). Thus, there are many centers of power and expertise. Business units are interdependent and, when appropriate, can take advantage of each others' skills, know-how and resources. In order to do this, they need to develop a common language, values and ways of doing business. They need to be able to 'talk' to one another with ease. As a result, information technology plays a key role.

Federalism allows organisations to break themselves down into smaller units and still benefit from economies of scale by devolving appropriate functions to the centre. Thus, organisations can be both big and small, they can access a range of markets and be both a global and local player. They are, however, according to O'Toole and Bennis (1992) 'devilishly hard to manage'. As Handy notes, federalism is not simply about how an organisation is structured – it involves adopting a whole new management philosophy. 'It relies as much on influence, trust and empathy as on formal power and explicit controls.'

New trends and challenges

As we have just seen, advances in technology, the opening of new trading markets and the relentless trend towards globalisation are all important factors influencing the way organisations are configured and managed.[16] One of the major challenges for the senior executive in the future is to create organisational structures (and compatible systems and work processes) which can accommodate dynamic, global industries.

The move towards globalisation has long been evident in companies such as Volkswagen, Toyota, General Electric, Hewlett-Packard and Xerox. Today, the trend is escalating with more companies joining the ranks of those that have streamlined their domestic operations and are now looking for efficiencies abroad. In the process, traditional corporate structures are giving way to new ways of configuring the organisation.

At the corporate level, the challenge is to develop organisational groupings on a global scale which maximise the organisation's competitive advantage. At the business unit level, the emphasis has also been to create more responsive structures. The trend has been away from what Burns and Stalker (1961) call a 'mechanistic' structure based on specialisation, hierarchy and detailed policies and procedures. Instead, organisations are moving to more of an 'organic' organisational form with an emphasis on expertise, changing responsibility (depending on the task) and judgement, rather than detailed rules.

In this section we look at some of these newer organisational structures.

Boundaries and the network organisation

The trend towards network organisations has been spurred by the rethinking of traditional organisational boundaries. Boundaries both integrate and separate organisations from their environment. A boundary is an organisation structure or a set of norms which puts parameters around the organisation and influences how it relates to the external environment. It can also apply to relationships internally between divisions and to sections of organisations.

One of the main reasons why some organisations prefer more fluid, organic boundaries is to improve their responsiveness. Thus, networks of alliances are being formed both within and outside organisations to draw upon the expertise, know-how and technology needed to compete in rapidly changing markets. Organisations must have the capacity to network with a range of potential collaborators and suppliers if they are to cope with the rapid changes and demands of markets in the 1990s. (See Chapter 7 for a discussion of strategic alliances.)

Boundaries can help organisations by acting as a buffer, by filtering and coding inputs. They can also protect the integrity of the organisation, preventing it from being absorbed by the environment or from losing the distinctive character that distinguishes it from other organisations. Boundaries also have their downsides. In the same way that the individual can become very narrow, boundaries (for instance, in the form of a rigid structure or an inflexible culture) can equally prevent the organisation from adapting to its environment successfully.

This struggle is very evident at Samsung, the giant Korean manufacturer of semiconductor memory chips where the culture of the company has created boundaries which are difficult to penetrate. In its drive to become a truly global organisation, Samsung has adopted a major diversification programme establishing manufacturing facilities in markets such as China, Thailand and Mexico.[17] More controversially, it also earmarked at least $5 billion to enter the passenger car business in 1997. In addition, major management reforms have been introduced to reduce bureaucracy within the organisation and shift the focus from quantity to quality. However, while these may be very necessary, fundamental changes to the intangible boundaries which determine how the company relates to its environment may be harder to engineer. Changes in structure are essential, but at Samsung the organisation has been torn between its traditional commitment to growth, and Chairman Lee's goal of promoting quality when the latter may mean losing market share. This change in emphasis is proving hard for executives to adopt, and Lee is concerned that the group is psychologically ill-prepared to compete in a global market.

Technology

Information technology continues to have a profound impact on how organisations change and develop.[18] Desk-top computers, computer-aided manufacturing, electronic mail, video conferencing are all innovations which have changed the manner and speed at which traditional management activities are organised and carried out. For some, the impact of technology has been threatening: it has meant broader access to information and helped erode traditional power-bases within the organisation.

Other organisations (such as IBM and Digital Equipment) are using technology to create flexible work arrangements which negate the need for staff to work together in one physical location. In 1994, Reuters Holdings was credited with taking this concept a stage further by employing consultants from a range of organisations around the world to work on a project designed to increase the user-friendliness of Reuters' products.[19] Highly specialised consultants from organisations like Microsoft and Logica were linked together by technology to collaborate from remote locations on this one project. The pool of consultants used could change, grow and reduce depending on the progress being made. As a result, huge savings were made in direct salary costs, benefits, office rentals and recruitment charges. In addition, each consultant could access their own organisations' resources to bring added value to the project.

High customer – responsive structures

Experiments with boundaryless organisations are often aimed at creating organisational structures which improve responsiveness to the customer. Ulrich and Lake (1990) give a good example of this with their 'customer management organisation'. This has greater external focus and emphasis on the customer than the traditional structures discussed earlier. This structure is characterised by three fundamental management processes:

(1) A focus on flow, not function. Work flows are analysed in terms of customer needs, not in terms of the functional area handling each part of the process. A customer manager diagnoses and responds to customer requirements and then matches customer needs with organisation competencies (see Figure 8.6). As will be seen later, a manifestation of this has risen in the form of process re-engineering.

(2) A dependence on dynamic teams rather than fixed hierarchies. The customer manager ensures continuity between the organisation and its customers. The customer manager has to extract resources from within the organisation to focus on customer

Fig. 8.6 *Flow of customer–management organisation*

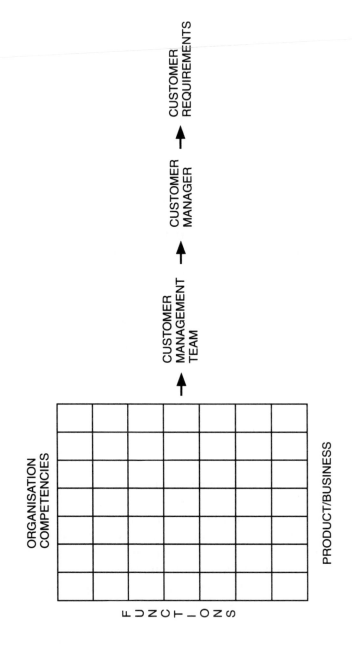

Source: Ulrich and Lake (1990)

needs. Since customer requirements vary, the composition of teams may also vary.

(3) Fluid rather than a fixed boundary of the organisation. The customer manager and customer management team have a dual role. They are part of their own organisation but spend so much time in the customer organisation that boundaries between the two are nearly invisible. For example, in some divisions of Hewlett-Packard, engineers spend as much time in customer offices as their own, and product design is based largely on customer input.

In addition, there is a flexible boundary around the customer management team itself. Customer requirements may be met not only by organisation members, but also by managers drawing on resources which are outside the current boundary of the organisation. The organisation is permeable because ownership of resources is less critical than ensuring that customer needs are satisfied.

Process re-engineering

Re-engineering is a very practical process which highlights some of these customer focused principles.[20] It involves a total rethink of the company's operating procedures with all work processes analysed in detail. Managers are encouraged to sit down with a blank sheet of paper and redesign processes with the customer as the focal point. Filling in the sheet begins not with, 'how do we want the customer to deal with us?' but rather, 'how do *they* want to deal with us?' Re-engineering therefore demands a fundamental shift in thinking. It starts from the future and works backwards, as if unconstrained by existing methods, people or departments.

Done well, process re-engineering delivers extraordinary gains in speed, productivity and profitability. In Europe, it is estimated that around 56 per cent of companies with turnovers of more than $250 million have re-engineering projects underway.[21] Union Carbide has used this process to get $400 million out of fixed costs in just three years. GTE expects re-engineering to deliver huge benefits to its telephone operations – in some cases doubling revenues or halving costs.

However, according to the co-founder of the movement, Michael Hammer, there are many pitfalls to overcome. Companies often get bogged down in analysis and fail to institute sufficiently radical change. Similarly, it is difficult to maintain a customer focus and avoid thinking along internally focused, organisational lines. The management of such a process is complex:

> ... Re-engineering entails sweeping change to an organisation. When a company's operating procedures are rethought from the ground up, virtually every other aspect of the company is called into question: the content of people's jobs, the structure of the organisation, the mechanisms for reward and compensation, even the cultural norms that govern attitudes and behaviour.[22]

Unfortunately, re-engineering initiatives have become synonymous in many managers' minds with headcount reductions and cost cutting. One of the reasons for this is because managers often focus on the more obvious and tangible levers (such as changing work processes and structures), and neglect other important and related informal aspects such as the attitudes and values of those affected by the change. Indeed, a recent study of over 100 European organisations showed that many organisations prefer not to use the term re-engineering when introducing new work processes.[23]

Designing an organisation structure

There are several techniques which may help the executive design an appropriate organisation structure. One way is through decision tree analysis.[24] Another, outlined by several writers, emphasises a five-step approach.[25] These methods have to be seen within the context of the company's strategic objectives and the need to develop an organisation which has a true competitive advantage. The five steps are:

(1) *Specify the key tasks to be done.* Define which work activities are critical to the accomplishment of business goals.

(2) *Define optional areas where tasks can be performed.* These include:

- Headquarters
- Geographic area
- Group level
- Division/Business Unit
- Outside (via subcontractors)

By identifying the key tasks and where they can be performed a responsibility matrix (see Table 8.2) can be created which provides a process for deciding how work can be allocated. One axis defines the key tasks; the other is used to describe the locations where those tasks could be carried out.

(3) *Define the criteria for the responsibility matrix.* The next step is to decide where responsibility for each work activity should be located. Such decisions should be made with a view to achieving competitive advantage in the eyes of the customer. For example, the executive has to consider whether the customer's preference is for lower cost and, if so, whether the organisation can be grouped to achieve economies of scale. If the emphasis is on providing customised service and a high degree of personal contact, then more externally focused groupings would be appropriate.

(4) *Assign tasks to specific locations.* Decisions also have to be made as to which level of management is responsible for accomplishing certain tasks. In a highly centralised organisation, many responsibilities would be located at corporate headquarters. In a decentralised organisation responsibilities would be mainly at the Group or Divisional level. Where possible, responsibilities should be allocated bearing in mind the longer term strategic objectives of the organisation.

Table 8.2   Responsibility matrix

Key tasks	Where work can be performed				
	Corporate	Geographic	Group	Division/ business unit	Outsource
Research					
Design engineering					
Manufacturing engineering					
Quality assurance					
Manufacturing					
Purchasing					
Distribution					
Finance					
Sales and marketing					
Human resources					

Source: Ulrich and Lake (1990)

(5) *Prepare reporting relationships and establish a process for re-evaluation.* This is where the structure of the organisation is then developed. Whatever form is established, however, it should not be cast in stone. Organisations need to be able to respond with a different configuration if customer requirements change fundamentally. Some of the major variables affecting the choice of organisational structure are outlined in Figure 8.7.

ORGANISATIONAL SYSTEMS

Having defined the organisational structure, it is important to consider what systems should be in place. If structure is the basic skeleton, the systems are the arteries, muscles and veins running through the organisation which tie it together and control and coordinate activities.

There are several different kinds of system including financial, information, staffing and reward systems. Some of these coordinate and facilitate activities within the organisation. For instance, standardising work procedures, outputs (through product and service specifications) and skills and supervision are, in effect, ways of coordinating activities across an organisation.

Other types of system, control and measure activities. Most executives are more than aware of the need to have effective control systems in place. In a recent survey of Times 1000 companies, executives were interviewed to discover how management practices had changed since the early 1980s.[26] At a senior level, there was a widespread reluctance to dilute or weaken hierarchical control. Executives would selectively take on board some aspects of new-wave management theories, but essentially keep the processes of 'command and control' intact. One of the underlying reasons for this was the extent to which executives ultimately felt accountable for their own and others' actions.

However, the increased emphasis placed on executives to energise and empower staff means that control methods need to be rethought. Too much control stifles initiative and reduces the flexibility that is needed for organisations to respond effectively to the rapid changes in the market place. Thus, increasingly, executives need to balance their leadership skills with an understanding of the control systems which set parameters, measure performance and reward individuals.

Fig. 8.7 *Variables in organisational structure*

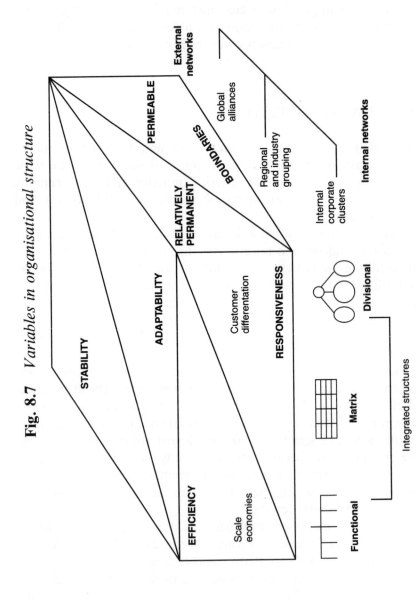

Source: Adapted from Limerick and Cunnington (1993)

The use of controls

While balance is important, the fundamental responsibility of the senior executive is to ensure that adequate parameters and measurement of activities are evident within the organisation. Control in organisations involves influencing people to act in particular ways and to focus on particular outcomes. It gives organisations direction and, used in the appropriate manner, is a key mechanism for ensuring that the organisation achieves its strategic goals. Indeed, without effective control systems no organisation can survive.

Control comes in various forms:

- Financial   for example, budgets and variance analysis
- Targets   for example, production or sales targets
- Resources   through investment funds, personnel
- Supervision   through immediate physical presence
- Technical   technology and associated design of work
- Structural   hierarchy of authority, rules, career structure
- Rewards   tying reward to performance
- Professional   internalised ethos associated with the occupation
- Cultural   internalised commitment to organisational objectives

It is worth making the distinction between general and detailed control.[27] General control refers to the compliance of the workforce with the overall direction of the organisation; detailed control refers to the control of specific work tasks. The two forms of control are largely independent. For example, there may be a high level of general control at the same time that there may be chaos with regard to a particular task. Similarly, control over a particular task can be accompanied by a lack of direction from the top.

The senior executive needs to be particularly concerned with general controls. A typical example would be resource allocation. At a corporate level the executive can use investment funds to control how separate parts of the organisation support the overall strategy of the business. Changes in resource allocation can be used to aid strategic change. At the business level resources can and should be allocated to those particular activities which most add value and contribute to the success of the business strategy: for example, through approaches aimed at cost advantages or differentiation.

Johnson and Scholes (1993) outline several guidelines for the design of control systems:

- Distinguish between various levels of control – strategic, management or operational control
- Create responsibility centres – this can be in terms of revenue, cost, profit or investment
- Select key factors and collect relevant information
- Allow diversity in control
- Avoid misleading measurements
- Beware of negative monitoring

The use of rewards

When designing or modifying organisations, executives need to bear in mind that people will concentrate on what they are rewarded for. Reward systems are also important for maintaining and sustaining an organisational system in the longer term. In principle, reward systems should be used to influence the behaviour of people within the organisation towards achieving and working on the most important issues. Although this may sound obvious, many companies continue to extol the virtues of long-term growth and yet tie reward systems into the achievement of short-term financial or sales targets.

Reward systems come in various forms including monetary, non-monetary (for example, promotion, status) and intangible rewards. They can be used for different outcomes and at different levels of the organisation, including obtaining a short or long-term focus, risk-taking and contributing to group (as against individual) pursuits.

They are also symbolic. For example, there has been considerable debate over what seemed to be an inverse relationship between increases in CEO pay and the profitability of several Fortune 500 companies. In the UK, after a decade of privatisation, Lord Parkinson admitted that others had done 'rather better' out of the programme than had customers. For example, the heads of Britain's 12 electricity boards each had a compensation package worth more than $2 million – six chiefs made over $4 million. In late 1994, the head of British Gas announced his salary would almost double to more than $1 million.[28] Whether these executives deserved the money or not is less important than the messages that were being sent to lower level employees about reward and effort.

ORGANISATIONAL CULTURE

Whilst acknowledging the importance of rewards, not everyone is motivated or guided by external motivators. Moreover, organic structures require flexible and productive behaviour. If the reward systems being used are too restrictive, people may not respond with the creativity and initiative that is often required.

Indeed, in today's climate of rapid change, there are many instances in organisations where people need to be self-regulating, creative and persistent. Under these circumstances, staff need to operate according to certain predetermined, principles which guide decision making and behaviour. Thus, it is important to explore the general patterns of thinking and behaving which typify an organisation. Although appropriately designed systems can facilitate these aspects, ultimately, whether staff perform often depends on the culture of the organisation.

Deal and Kennedy (1982) view culture as the glue which binds the organisation together. Schein (1984, 1986) identifies three elements which are possibly the most consistently used guidelines for exploring the nature of culture. These are outlined below.

Basic assumptions

These refer to the basic assumptions and beliefs about the organisation. At times, these may be so taken for granted that they reside at a largely unconscious level in people's minds. That is, they are not easily articulated by individuals because they have become the unquestioned basis on which people think and act. Basic assumptions, which Schein sees as the essence of culture, are likely to exist in relation to:

- The need for hierarchy
- The trustworthiness of people
- The basis of competitive success
- The identity of the market in which an organisation operates
- The competitive nature of the market
- How conflict is to be treated
- The importance of consultation

Values

By contrast, the espoused values of an organisation are much more evident. People express views about how and why things are done.

The extent to which these are accurate depends on whether people's behaviour matches up to them. For example the senior managers in an organisation may express the view that they reward innovation and risk-taking. However, if an individual's experience is different to this then they may believe the real rewards go to those who play it safe and by the rules.

Artefacts

These are more concrete than values, and include such things as the language, myths, rituals and ceremonies that are used in an organisation. Artefacts can be interpreted to give clues about the values and beliefs which underlie them.

Language highlights which ideas, functions, groups and so forth are influential within an organisation through the use of such things as jargon, in-jokes and technical terms. Myths or stories, on the other hand, shape beliefs through the retelling of some event in an organisation's history. Often these glorify 'heroes' or portray 'villains' in ways which reinforce cultural traits. Rituals are routinised activities which maintain cultural values. Drinks on a Friday night, birthday celebrations and retirement parties are rituals of this type. Indeed, there are a wide range of artefacts, such as promotions, condemnations, and office privileges, which either reinforce or highlight discrepancies between real and espoused values.

Culture is as much a controlling experience as it is an energising one, however. Often this notion is misunderstood: control is often associated with authoritarian cultures. However, when the culture of an organisation is widely shared, points everyone in a similar direction and puts strong pressure on group members to conform, it exerts, in effect, a controlling influence. Indeed, particularly under highly uncertain and ambiguous conditions, a strong culture can often be the only form of control that works effectively.

Kanter argues that, despite the popularity of empowerment strategies, this cannot mean setting everyone loose to do whatever they want, however they want to do it.[29] Organisations, therefore, must solve the control problem: how to get guidance and coherence in light of complex activities, diverse people and the need for speed and innovation. Certainly, given that rules cannot cover all contingencies, there is considerable value in having a set of generally held principles which enable employees to make decisions.

However, even this may not be straightforward. While many see culture as a unifying force, others see organisational culture as being characterised by diversity and even inconsistency. Moreover, different cultures can exist within an organisation based on factors as diverse as background, gender and occupation. Indeed, the challenges experienced by giants such as IBM, Hewlett-Packard, British Telecom and many others when trying to change their culture, raises the question of whether a strong, cohesive culture is necessarily a strength.

One of the reasons why some of the larger companies fail to rectify their organisational shortcomings (in some cases, almost to the point of collapse) is because the culture which kept the organisation going has also been intolerant of those challenging the status quo. As a consequence, the trend is more towards developing adaptive or flexible cultures. Kotter and Heskett (1992) demonstrated that highly profitable companies like Pepsi, Wal-Mart and Shell have adaptive cultures which serve the interests of all three of their main constituents – customers, employees and stockholders. Ideally, there should be at least a tolerance for constructive friction – where a strong corporate culture is maintained, but where the core beliefs and assumptions are continuously subjected to critique.

Thus, while ambiguous, culture is something which can be identified. The trend is towards creating cultures which can adapt and learn and which are supportive of the overall strategic purpose of the organisation.

SUMMARY

This chapter has looked at the kinds of issues senior executives should be aware of when designing organisations. In particular, it describes different types of organisational structure and the relationship with organisational systems and culture.

Ultimately, the mindset and attitudes of those affected by a change to the structure of an organisation can have a profound affect on its success. Executives therefore must spend time and effort understanding how the organisation is viewed and appreciate the interrelationship of key organisational elements. Formal aspects such as financial systems, reporting relationships and the structure of the organisation are more apparent and therefore easier to change than informal aspects such as values and culture. Often, the temptation is to focus on the more formal and concrete levers within the organisation and neglect the less tangible, but powerful, aspects such as norms and values.

There are several kinds of groupings which form the basis of most organisational designs. Typically, these emphasise either particular work activities, or external factors such as products, customers or location, or a combination of these. However, a range of influences – for example, advances in technology and the move towards global industries – are forcing organisations to create more fluid, customer-focused organisation structures. A five-step approach to designing an appropriate organisational structure has been outlined.

Consideration also has to be given to the systems within the organisation which control and coordinate activities. A delicate balance needs to be achieved between empowering others to act, and maintaining controls which set parameters, measure performance and reward individuals. Finally, the executive needs to be aware of the dominant culture of the organisation and ascertain whether it is supportive of strategic goals.

Understanding organisational components is one side of the executive's Organisational Capability. The next challenge is to develop and change these components to meet the vicissitudes of an increasingly complex and dynamic world. How the executive might do this is explored in the next chapter.

NOTES

1. 'When Slimming is Not Enough', *The Economist*, 3 September 1994, 63–4.
2. See Ulrich and Lake (1990).
3. American Management Association study referenced in *The Economist*, 3 September 1994, *op. cit.*
4. *The Economist*, 3 September 1994, *op. cit.*
5. Robert Corzine, 'Fuel for a More Fiery Future', *Financial Times*, 3 October 1994, 13.
6. See, for instance, Argyris (1977) and Argyris and Schon (1978).
7. See Bowen *et al.* (1994).
8. Alex Taylor III, 'US Cars Come Back', *Fortune*, vol. 126, no. 11, 16 November 1992, 24–53.
9. *Fortune*, 16 November 1992, *op. cit.*
10. Ira Sager, 'The Few, The True, The Blue', *Business Week*, 30 May 1994, 56–8.
11. Kelly and Amburgey (1991).

12. Christopher Lorenz, 'How to Bridge Functional Gaps', *Financial Times*, 25 November 1994, 10.
13. Johnson and Scholes (1993).
14. *Financial Times*, 25 November 1994, *op. cit.*
15. Geoffrey Foster, 'The Central Question', *Management Today*, April 1994, 56–61. See also Ashridge Strategic Management Centre study, *Effective Headquarters Staff*, 1993.
16. For a comprehensive study of these trends see Bartlett and Ghoshal (1989).
17. John Burton, 'Samsung Drives towards Globalisation', *Financial Times*, 25 October 1994, 21.
18. See Thach and Woodman (1994).
19. Desmond Dearlove, 'Cherry-Picking Top Talent', *Financial Times*, 16 November 1994, 14.
20. The most influential book on this subject is Hammer and Champy (1993).
21. Survey by Computer Services Corporation cited in Peter Bartram's article, 'Re-engineering Revisited', *Management Today*, July 1994, 61–3.
22. Article by Michael Hammer and Steven Stanton, 'No Need for Excuses', *Financial Times*, 13 October 1994.
23. Findings from an independent study, *The Cobra Report* published by Adaptation Ltd. cited by Christopher Lorenz, 'Putting Re-engineering into Perspective', *Financial Times*, 21 October 1994.
24. See, for instance, Duncan (1979).
25. Originally outlined by Beckhard and Harris (1977). It has been developed by Ulrich and Lake (1990).
26. Research project funded by the Chartered Institute of Management Accountants by Mahmoud Ezzamel, Simon Lilley and Hugh Wilmott (Manchester School of Management) referenced in their article, 'Be Wary of New Waves', *Management Today*, October 1993, 99–102.
27. Dunford (1992).
28. Peter Ellingsen, 'More Major Blundering', *The Age*, 1 December 1994, 17.
29. See Moss Kanter's Editorial, 'Discipline!', *Harvard Business Review*, January/February 1992, 7–8.

9 The Organisational Capability – Change: Managing Organisational and Personal Change

INTRODUCTION

The scale and pace of organisational change that senior executives are involved with is daunting. Jack Smith, CEO of General Motors, had to turn round GM's core car and truck business from the brink of financial collapse when he took on the job in 1992. To do this, Smith and his senior executive group had to 'rightsize' an organisation with a worldwide payroll of over 700 000, initiate a massive cost-cutting programme and streamline GM's operations.[1] The story at IBM was even more ambitious. Expected to lead the biggest corporate transformation of all time, CEO Lou Gerstner and the top executives on his Worldwide Management Council had to cut 170 000 jobs worldwide and reduced expenses by \$4.8 billion in order to begin the process of making IBM more competitive.[2]

This story of corporate renewal is being repeated in many other corporations in the US and Europe and, increasingly, in Japan. Although much has been written about the techniques which can be used to implement change successfully, however, the process is not straightforward. Keichel (1987)[3] has suggested that only ten per cent of Fortune 1000 corporations have strategies which are fully implemented and work.

One of the factors affecting the success of a change programme is the role and contribution of those in the senior management group. For large-scale change to be successful, it must have the backing of these key executives. Attempting change programmes without their support often results in inconsequential change, or the abandonment of the change programme altogether.

The senior executive, therefore, needs to have the capability to manage change. Indeed Morgan (1988) argues that:

Managers of the future will have to become increasingly skilled in managing transition. They will have to recognize flux as the norm and develop mindsets and skills that allow them to cope with the continuous flow of new ideas, products, technologies . . . In some cases, they will have to deal with crisis as a norm . . .

In this chapter we explore the other side of the executive's organisational capability which is concerned with change. We help executives identify when change needs to occur and review strategies for managing the change process.

A framework for change

The effective management of change involves developing an understanding of the current state of the organisation, creating an image of the future state and moving the organisation through a transition period.[4] This process is explored in this chapter through the framework outlined below. Change processes are frequently far from logical or orderly, particularly where radical change is being undertaken. Consequently, the framework is offered as an aid to understanding organisational change rather than as a blueprint for action. The major issues which need to be considered are:

Why is change necessary?

(1) Diagnosing the present condition and problem(s)
(2) Identifying whether there is a need for change
(3) Determining change goals and the new state or condition after the change

What needs to be changed?

(4) Specifying which components need to change to achieve the new state
(5) Identifying the impediments to change

How should change occur?

(6) Selecting a change strategy
(7) Implementing the change strategy

(8) Establishing systems and processes to maintain the new situation
(9) Evaluating the change effort

In this chapter we explore each of these aspects in turn.

WHY IS CHANGE NECESSARY?

(1) & (2)   Diagnosing problems and identifying the need for change

To help identify whether there is a need for change, the executive needs to consider the extent to which the organisation's internal competencies match the demands of the external environment. The greater the match – or 'fit' – the more likely it is that the organisation is producing goods and services at a quantity and price the market wants.

There are several clues which help indicate a potential mismatch. These include;

- A decline in financial indicators of effectiveness
- A change in other indicators such as market share
- Increased turnover of key personnel
- Lowering of results on quality indices
- Increased client complaints
- Increasing morale/stress amongst employees

Often, however, there are earlier warning signs of potential problems – if executives are alert to them. For example, there may be benchmarks in other industries which the executive can use as reasons to initiate change. In the early 1990s, Boeing decided to compare its manufacturing performance to that of other organisations – like GE – and found it sorely wanting. Despite occupying the Number 1 slot in its own industry sector, Boeing had an expensive and out-of-date design and manufacturing process which resulted in an 18-month production cycle for some of its aircraft. The price of new aircraft was so high that airlines put off buying replacements and simply repaired older planes. To help improve their competitiveness, Boeing management overcame resistance and initiated a massive change programme to automate and streamline the design and production processes. Instead of a two-year wait, the delivery time for certain aircraft was reduced to just eight months. Pricing was also more competitive which helped stimulate business for replacement aircraft.[5]

Having decided that change of some kind is needed, a more difficult question is to decide 'how much change?' and 'what kind of change?' Logically, this depends on how great a mismatch there is between organisational performance and market or customer demands. Usually, only incremental or evolutionary change is necessary when there are minor disparities between the two. When the organisation is markedly out of 'fit', however, not only may revolutionary or transformational change be needed, but a 'refit' may be appropriate. This may involve, as Hamel and Prahalad (1989) argue, redefining the firm's strategic intent in order to find and build new ways of competing.

It is also worth noting that the external environment may facilitate or impede change, as well as drive it. For instance, when implementing changes at ICI in the 1980s, John Harvey-Jones was helped by a complex set of outside forces which worked to prepare the company for change. The policies of the Thatcher administration made it more socially acceptable to impose changes at the industrial level. Moreover, increased levels of unemployment drained the power base of the trade unions making it easier to introduce changes on the shop floor.[6]

Thus, judgements about the need to change depend on the executive's ability to read trends in the external environment and gauge whether the organisation can respond. In turn, this demands more than strong powers of analysis. At a more fundamental level, the mindset executives adopt as well as their capacity to accept changing realities is also important. Commenting on his own experience at General Electric, CEO Jack Welch notes:

> There's a very fine line between self-confidence and arrogance. Success often breeds both, along with the reluctance to change. The bureaucracy builds up. The people begin to feel they are invulnerable. Before they know it, the world changes and they've got to react.[7]

(3) Determining change goals and the new end state

Many writers emphasise that executives need to identify clearly the kind of organisation they are trying to create – in as much detail as possible. Beckhard and Harris (1977), for instance, argue that executives should specify the expected organisational structure, reward system, personnel policies, authority and task-responsibility distributions, managerial styles and roles, performance review systems and performance outcomes. They argue that by defining explicitly what the organisation should look like, the end-picture will serve as a descriptive guide for determining the change strategy.

However, the level of detail one can provide depends on the kind of change process being undertaken. If the executive is attempting incremental change, it may well be possible (and necessary) to itemise in detail the objectives and changes that are required. When more fundamental change is required, the executive may need to be content with using a more flexible picture which is broadly concerned with the firm's strategic intent. Moreover, as we highlight later when discussing the change process, often precise detail cannot be established until the change process has begun.

The real value of trying to identify a purpose and end-picture may lie in the process itself – rather than the accuracy of the outcomes. The process may help focus attention on the organisation's limitations. It may also clarify the particular competencies, systems and processes the organisation can build on to help bridge the gap between the current reality and the desired end state.

It is essential to think critically about these issues. The senior executive has a responsibility to initiate changes which will assist in developing an organisation's competitive advantage. Many new approaches, such as Total Quality Management (TQM), the trend towards flatter organisation structures and the creation of 'learning organisations' have undoubted benefits – but they are not appropriate in all circumstances. In 1992, the American Quality Foundation and Ernst & Young released *The Best Practices Report* which assessed the impact of different management techniques on a firm's performance.[8] They evaluated over 900 practices in 580 organisations in Europe, Japan and North America. They found that lower performing companies had to stay focused on the basics and not be distracted by trends and fashions in management practices. Some of the high-profile management practices – such as benchmarking, employee empowerment and externally oriented planning tools – appeared to work best for higher performing firms.

According to one of the authors of the report, those that performed best were the ones who spent time evaluating their approach and then kept at it. 'They don't lose sight of what they are focusing on because some new idea has come along. Instead they evaluate the ideas critically; think about them. If they decide to use it, they graft it on top. They don't use it instead of what they were doing before.'

For middle performing companies, the report found that a quality strategy is crucial. Again, however, caution needs to be exercised if, for example, a company is basing its change strategy on something like process re-engineering. John Hagel of McKinsey notes, 'We did an audit of client experiences with process engineering. We found lots of examples where there were truly dramatic impacts on processes – 60 to 80 per cent reductions in cost and cycle time – but only very modest effects at the business unit level, because the changes didn't matter to the customer.' He also cites the case of a computer company which was 'convinced that customers needed more expertise from its sales force, poured tens of millions of dollars into re-engineering its selling operations, training people in consultative sales techniques and outfitting them with costly electronic gear. It turned out that most customers didn't care. What mattered to them was price'.[9] In this case the bridge was built without the end-picture in mind.

WHAT NEEDS TO CHANGE?

(4)   Identifying the key components of change

Executives also need a realistic picture of their *current* position before they embark on major change. This involves reviewing those aspects of the organisation which are most likely to be significantly affected and identifying the changes which need to occur if the goals are to be reached.

Major leverage points

The key components of the organisation may be used as a starting point. In the previous chapter, six critical areas were identified; key tasks and work processes, individual competencies, technology, organisational structures, systems and culture. Identifying such components is useful in highlighting what some writers call leverage points.[10] Leverage points not only identify where to intervene, but also highlight where change may evolve from internally. These components are, of course, interdependent. Consequently, change in one area will probably result in compensatory or retaliatory changes in another.

Technical vs. people factors

One particular area of interplay is critical. This is between what can broadly be called the technical factors, (tasks, technology, structure and systems) and the people factors (individuals and culture). It is unclear whether changes in the way organisations work can be achieved by first changing the people, or the technical factors. Most change programmes focus on changing individual attitudes, but Beer *et al.* (1990) believe this approach is fundamentally flawed. They argue that the most effective way to change behaviour is to put people into a new organisational context, which imposes new rules responsibilities and relationships.

What is clear is that fundamental change is unlikely to occur without some change on *both* fronts. Yet it is not unusual to find organisations attempting to change attitudes, opinions or value systems, independent of the formal structure of the organisation (for example, the reward system, hierarchical arrangements, reporting relationships) or vice versa. For example, since the privatisation of British Telecom in the early 1980s, the company has reduced significantly the size of its workforce and adopted a number of initiatives such as multi-skilling, performance targets and TQM to improve service levels. Despite significant progress on all these measures, however, on the people side, poor morale continued to affect key organisational groups – particularly those with customer contact. At one particular meeting workers complained of, 'job insecurity . . . they also complained about lack of trust, excessive use of outside contractors, "flavour of the month" organisational reforms [and] the disappearance of pride in working for BT'.[11]

As Katz and Kahn (1978) argue, 'The major error in dealing with problems of organisational change, is to . . . confuse individual change with modifications in . . . organisational variables'. Organ and Bateman (1986) argue that, ultimately, the issue is not so much which of the two strategies is more effective, but in what sequence. The best approach is to aim at both changing the people and technical factors in alternating, overlapping phases.

Depth of change required

It is very easy to change many things superficially, without changing anything fundamentally. Take for example, the problems experienced by Chase Manhattan Bank in the late 1980s, 'Many present and former executives . . . refer to frustrations at Chase because management repeatedly tried to solve fundamental problems by merely reshuffling the way the company was organised'. According to a former senior employee, 'Almost every 18 months there's been a reorganisation and an announcement is made that a new strategy is in place. But almost always it's just a change in the organisational chart. Rarely is it a business strategy.'[12]

Executives therefore have to judge the depth of change that is required. Not all changes demand a fundamental overhaul of the organisation. Indeed, minor changes take place on a continuous basis in any large organisation. Some writers, such as Nadler and Tushman (1990), see this as a predominant characteristic of organisations. Organisations evolve as a result of relatively long periods of continuous and incremental change. As a consequence, most design changes maintain the congruence and consistency of the organisational system. As minor changes in the environment occur, or as an organisation grows in size and scope, the design is altered to maintain the 'fit' mentioned earlier. Levy and Merry (1986) argue along similar lines. They see many changes within organisations as being to do with 'first-order' change. This is used to describe an intervention which may change systems, structures or people to improve the effectiveness of the organisation – but which largely leaves the underlying infrastructure and core patterns of behaviour and thinking intact.

There comes a time, however, when major fundamental reorganisations must occur which disturb the organisational equilibrium. Here, fine tuning is inappropriate: the need is to transform. This is 'frame bending'[13], transformational change, or what Levy and Merry (1986) call 'second-order' change. It involves alteration of the system's basic governing rules and is a multi-dimensional, multi-component and multi-level alteration that shifts the system irreversibly to a new and revolutionary paradigm.

Many mistakes have been made because executives have failed to work out whether first or second-order change is needed. When organisations have been very successful in the past, this judgement is even harder to make. Talking about the experiences of transforming General Electric, CEO Jack Welch comments:

When it's been so easy for so long, some people can never get around to facing reality. That's why you see so many businesses making incremental changes when they get into trouble: They can't believe that the situation is probably ten times worse than they've admitted to themselves. . .[14]

Level of management involved

It is also important for the senior executive to be aware of the level of management being targeted in the change process. Change is often aimed at the lower or middle levels of the organisation. However, frequently, organisations get into trouble because senior staff do not get behind the change strategy. It is hard to make progress if the troops change but the old guard remains in control.

Particular attention needs to be paid to other powerful executives in senior management positions. Senior level managers often have enough power and ability not only to block major changes occurring in the organisation overall but can also shield themselves from personal change. Many are particularly adept at appearing to give new initiatives their support but then withdrawing it in more subtle ways – for example, by not following through, allocating insufficient resources and so on.

In some circumstances it may be possible to remove entrenched sources of resistance. More often, the senior power brokers either need to be won over or worked around. In practice, this often demands considerable skill. When Xerox was embarking on its quest for improved quality, initially it was particularly difficult to engender support and ownership from key executives at the top – despite the backing of the then CEO, David Kearns. Those charged with the responsibility of getting the quality programme up and running had to estimate the power of the senior people running the organisation to find out who would commit and who wouldn't. They decided that most senior managers were only lukewarm to the idea – it was their next level reports who were most supportive. Kearns observed, 'Rickard knew that if the quality programme, so amorphous to many managers, was going to get anyplace in the organization, he would have to play on the support of the princes and, for the time being, to dance past the kings'.[15]

Scale of change – department, company or industry?

The scale of change also needs to be considered. Often, it is easier to use some part of the organisation to pilot change, at least in the initial stages, rather than involve the organisation as a whole. In a study of 12 major change programmes, Beer *et al.* (1990) found that successful transformations usually started at the periphery of the corporation in a few plants and divisions far from corporate headquarters. One of the challenges for top management is to then find ways to replicate this change company wide. Increasingly, however, the type of changes that are needed go beyond the scope of individual firms and involve changing the way an entire industry does business.[16]

(5) Impediments to change

There will always be unpredictable factors in the environment that hamper the change process. While some of these are outside the executive's control, others could be managed better. Alexander (1989) conducted a survey of 93 private-sector firms which highlighted the organisational problems executives encounter when trying to implement such things as a new product launch, starting up a new plant or facility or making an acquisition. Overall, some 76 per cent found that implementation took more time than had originally been allocated. Other issues highlighted by companies were:

- Major problems surfaced that had not been identified beforehand (74 per cent)
- Co-ordination of activities (for example, by task force, committees, supervisors) not effective enough (66 per cent)
- Competing activities distracted attention from the change effort (64 per cent)
- Insufficient skills/abilities of employees involved with the change (63 per cent)
- Inadequate training and instruction of lower level employees (62 per cent)
- Uncontrollable factors in the external environment (e.g., competitive, economic, governmental) having an adverse affect (60 per cent)

Some of these factors – for example, setting aside adequate time, better coordination of activities, better training and instruction – are ones that the individual executive can control. Other aspects not mentioned above – such as the need to establish an end-picture and appropriate organisational structures – can also be managed. However, there are other impediments which while less controllable than these factors, nevertheless deserve no less consideration. These are individuals' feelings towards change.

Coping with resistance

Change can prompt a range of negative responses which may result in resistance. Reflecting on what he had learnt as CEO of GE during the 1980s, Jack Welch comments:

> . . . one of the big lessons is that change has no constituency. People like the status quo. They like the way it was. When you start changing things, the good old days look better and better. You've got to be prepared for massive resistance.[17]

Resistance is often seen as a consequence of fear of the unknown and feelings of being threatened. In a worldwide survey of top executives,[18] 92 per cent itemised the 'fear factor' and human resistance as an obstacle to implementing strategic change. Kotter and Schlesinger (1979) see resistance as one of the key variables to manage. They put forward a number of options executives can use for dealing with resistance to change. Importantly, these serve to emphasise that involvement may not always be the best tactic to use. Moreover, they highlight the likely consequences of adopting one strategy versus another (see Table 9.1).

The skills needed to cope with resistance are very different to those needed to analyse and develop an initial change strategy. During organisational change, executives have to manage people who may be in a state of emotional upheaval as well as those who are motivated to act politically. They also need to give careful consideration to the very different agendas various groups within the organisation may have as the change process unfolds.

Gaining stakeholders' support

The previous point highlights the issue of stakeholders. Many writers emphasise the need to get the support of key power groups within an organisation in order to build a critical mass in favour of change. Nutt (1989) argues that successful implementation of change often depends on obtaining the involvement, cooperation, endorsement or consent of power centres that will operate the plan, be served by it, or be influenced by its operation. He argues that implementation 'short cuts', using tactics which minimise the manager's involvement, are a key source of failure.

Beckhard and Harris (1977) agree that key personnel must be on board, including the top team, if change is to be implemented effectively. However, in addition there are a range of key individuals

Table 9.1   Options for dealing with resistance to change

Approach...	Commonly used	Advantages	Drawbacks
Education & communication	Where there is a lack of information or inaccurate information and analysis	Once persuaded, people will often help with the implementation of the change	Can be very time consuming if lots of people are involved
Participation & involvement	Where the initiators do not have all the information they need to design the change and where others have considerable power to resist	People who participate will be committed and any relevant information they have will be integrated into the change plan	Can be very time consuming if participators design an inappropriate change
Facilitation & support	Where people are resisting because of adjustment problems	No other approach works as well with adjustment problems	Can be time-consuming, expensive and still fail
Negotiation & agreement	Where someone or some group will clearly lose out in a change, and where that group has considerable power to resist	Sometimes it is a relatively easy way to avoid major resistance	Can be too expensive in many cases if it alerts others to negotiate for compliance
Manipulation & co-opting	Where other tactics will not work or are too expensive	It can be a relatively quick and inexpensive solution	Can lead to future problems if people feel manipulated
Explicit & implicit coercion	Where speed is essential, and the change initiators possess considerable power	It is speedy and can overcome any kind of resistance	Can be risky if it leaves people mad at the initiators

Source: Kotter and Schlesinger (1979)

and groups whose commitment to any new ideas, to providing resources and to carrying out the new process, is vital. The executive must ensure that they have the support of a critical mass of key individuals if the change process is to be successful.

Mindset – 'unfreezing, changing and refreezing'

As mentioned earlier, there are a number of different strategies executives can use to overcome resistance and gain the commitment of others. Choosing an effective strategy depends, in part, on the executive's understanding of other people's mental disposition towards change. This is illustrated by a model, first advanced by Lewin (1947), which has formed the basis of many subsequent explanations of individual reactions to the change process. While the model has been developed by others, the principles Lewin advocated have enduring relevance. His three-step model consists of unfreezing, changing and refreezing.

The 'unfreezing' process involves helping individuals unlock their current mental approach towards doing things. They need to be prepared to accept new ideas and behaviour, which is helped by adopting a more flexible mindset (see Chapter 2). They need to be able to listen to new information, be more aware of problems and open to different ways of solving them.

Involvement may be a means by which this is achieved but, often, more hard hitting approaches are necessary. For example, Goodstein and Burke (1991) highlight how, in the British Airways change effort, the unfreezing process involved a massive reduction in the workforce from 59 000 to 37 000 people. Often the need to change only becomes apparent when dramatic changes such as these occur. Indeed, as Organ and Bateman (1986) point out, there are a range of forces at work in the organisation which serve to maintain people's current attitudes and behaviour. The culture of the organisation, the ways things get done, and the sorts of behaviour which are rewarded can all provide people with the ammunition they need to resist change. Certainly, in the longer term it is unlikely that substantive change will occur without altering these factors.

A mindset which is 'unfrozen' offers the possibility that new learning can take place. At this point, people need some assistance. They need some concept of what is expected of them, be given opportunities to experiment with new approaches and have incentives for doing so.

Finally, there is a process of 'refreezing' or consolidation. In other words, new patterns of behaviour and thinking must be supported by social cues and formal and informal reward systems so they become more natural processes. It is easy for failure to occur at this stage. It is not unusual to come across executives who promote a new organisational picture, but who fail to evaluate critically what is condemned and encouraged within the organisation, and how this contributes or detracts from achieving the end state. During the 1980s at British Airways several devices were used to reward and reinforce changes in behaviour. People exemplifying the new values were more likely to be promoted; there were 'Open Learning' programmes for new staff as well as 'Top Flight Academies' that included executive and senior management training; the performance appraisal system was changed to reflect both behaviour and results; and BA symbols were changed, including new uniforms, refurbished aircraft and a new corporate coat of arms.[19]

While Lewin's model may simplify the complexities associated with change, unsuccessful efforts to induce significant and lasting change can often be traced to failure in one or more aspects of his model. The organisation may fail to alter in any significant way the forces maintaining old behaviour and attitudes; it may fail to offer a clear, satisfying alternative and allow adequate learning and experimentation to take place; or it may fail to reinforce the new learning.[20]

Time

In a turbulent world, an increasing impediment to successful change is the time available to implement it. Executives are both hampered by external pressures to solve problems quickly and by the time it takes for some changes to succeed. Vandermerwe (1991) found that insufficient time is one of the major reasons for the failure of change interventions. Most of the executives in this study concurred that strategic change always takes longer to implement than originally anticipated. The reasons were because top management did not understand how long various implementation tasks would take to complete and tended to downplay the likelihood of potential problems occurring.

Delays in implementing change can result in considerable cost to an organisation. When he took over the job of CEO of IBM in early 1993, Lou Gerstner commented on how, in his first month of taking office, the number one message he heard was 'to fix what needed to be done quickly'. He said, 'The adjustment period that IBM has been going through in trying to deal with changes in its markets is now carrying into its second or third year. The longevity of the change is as dysfunctional as the seriousness of the change.'[21]

Indeed, companies who can manage change and time effectively can gain considerable competitive advantage. For instance, Singapore Airlines became a world-class airline in just ten years. From 1974 to 1984, total revenues grew sixfold from $400m to $2600m. Nevertheless, staff numbers only increased from 5000 to 10 600, giving Singapore Airlines one of the highest levels of productivity in the airline industry. Increasingly, it is those executives who can engineer change in shorter time frames who have the competitive edge.

HOW SHOULD CHANGE OCCUR?

(6) Selecting a change strategy

Before selecting a change strategy some thought must be given to assessing the present state of the organisation and identifying change goals. Three areas in particular, then need to be reviewed – the style, depth and method of change.

Style

In Chapter 5 we argued that successful change demands capable leadership. Providing a vision of the future end state, articulating that vision and energising and enabling staff to achieve the vision are all important. However, different styles may be needed for different change strategies. Of late, collaborative approaches and participative leadership have received most emphasis. Indeed, in many studies of the change process, one of the major reasons why change interventions falter is because of a lack of two-way communication and a lack of participation and involvement.

While involvement is important – particularly if the retention and motivation of ·staff is critical – it is not universally applicable. For instance, Dunphy and Stace (1992) argue that in the major (predominantly US) tradition there is often an implicit assumption of harmony of interests among the organisational stakeholders and a downplaying of conflicts of interests. Yet, in some cases significant conflicts of interest may only be resolved by autocratic or even coercive solutions.

Depth

Consideration also needs to be given to the depth of change. This has been discussed earlier. Will the change be incremental or more transformational in nature? This may be difficult to establish for it requires a critical review of what really needs to happen within the organisation. First-order change (which Nadler and Tushman (1990) argue may be large and significant) usually occurs within the existing framework of the organisation and may leave the basic support systems and ways of thinking within the organisation untouched. Transformational change fundamentally redefines what the organisation is, or changes its basic framework. Implementing transformational change requires a lot more skill, determination and effort than incremental change.

Methods

A third important area to consider is the methods that might be used to change the organisation. Organisational Development (OD) has been used by many organisations to initiate incremental change. Although there are a broad range of intervention strategies that fall under this overall heading (see Table 9.2), OD tends to emphasise team development and cultural change through collaborative approaches. The emphasis is on creating trust, openness and constructively handling conflict.

Indeed, the overwhelming emphasis in the literature in this area is on developing trust and reducing anxiety through communication and participation in the change process. There is little question that OD in general, and participatory based approaches, can have tremendous benefits. Companies like British Airways have used OD interventions with considerable success and Sashkin and Burke (1987) conclude that when applied properly, OD has had substantial positive effects on performance. However, OD has its limitations. The major criticism is that it tends to gloss over the reality of organisational politics and tends to take a naive and limited view of conflict resolution. Thus, it is important to review a range of methods and their consequences in the light of what the executive is trying to achieve in the change process.

Table 9.2   Thirteen major 'families' of OD interventions

---

1   *Diagnostic activities*: Fact-finding activities designed to ascertain problems. Traditional data-collection methods – including interviews and questionnaires are commonly used

2   *Team-building activities*: Activities designed to enhance the effective operation of system teams

3   *Intergroup activities*: Activities designed to improve effectiveness of interdependent groups. The focus is on joint activities

4   *Survey feedback activities*: Analysing data produced by a survey and designing action-plans based on these data

5   *Education and training activities*: A wide range of possible activities designed to improve skills, abilities, and knowledge of individuals

6   *Structural activities*: Activities designed to improve the effectiveness of the technical or structural aspects affecting individuals or groups Examples include job enrichment, matrix structures and MBO

7   *Process consultation activities*: Activities on the part of the consultant that help managers understand and act on human processes in organizations, such as leadership, cooperation and conflict

8   *Grid organization development activities*: Activities developed by Blake and Mouton, constituting a six-phase change model involving the entire organisation

9   *Third-party peacemaking activities*: Activities designed to manage conflict between two parties, and conducted by a third party, usually a skilled consultant

10   *Coaching and counselling activities*: Activities that entail working with individuals to better enable them to define learning goals, learn how others see their behaviour, explore alternative behaviours, and learn new behaviours

11   *Life-and career-planning activities*: Activities that help individuals identify life and career objectives, capabilities, areas of strength and deficiency, and strategies for achieving objectives

12   *Planning and goal-setting activities*: Activities that include theory and experience in planning and goal setting. They may be conducted at the level of the individual group, and total organisation

13   *Strategic management activities*: Activities that help key policymakers identify their organisation's basic mission and goals; ascertain environmental demands, threats, and opportunities; and engage in long-range action planning

---

Source: French and Bell (1983)

Contingent approaches

Increasingly, writers are emphasising the need to look at a range of different methods and to see these in the light of different levels at which change is aimed. Nadler and Tushman (1990), for instance, when targeting stakeholders suggest participation as the first strategy, then bargaining with incentives, then isolation and finally, if none of these work, removal.

One way of looking at a range of methods in relation to different circumstances is provided by Dunphy and Stace (1992). Their contingency approach combines different styles with differences in the depth of change (or what they call 'scale of change') mentioned above. From this one can draw several conclusions about the methods that might be most appropriate. Combining incremental and transformational change with collaborative and coercive styles gives rise to four approaches outlined in Figure 9.1.

- Type 1. *Participative evolution* emphasises incremental changes achieved by collaborative methods. It is most appropriate where only minor adjustments are needed (first-order change) or where

Fig. 9.1 *The Dunphy/Stace change matrix*

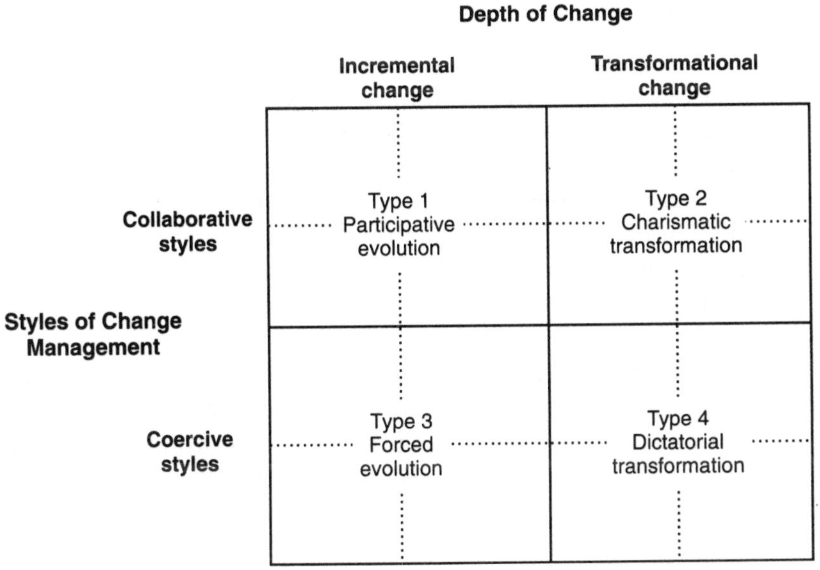

Depth of Change

	Incremental change	**Transformational change**
Collaborative styles	Type 1 Participative evolution	Type 2 Charismatic transformation
Coercive styles	Type 3 Forced evolution	Type 4 Dictatorial transformation

Styles of Change Management

Source: Adapted from Dunphy and Stace (1992)

an organisation is out of 'fit', but time is available to change and key interest groups are in favour of this. The style is best in periods of stability and steady growth and is personified by IBM during the early 1980s.

- Type 2. *Charismatic transformation* also emphasises collaborative approaches but under different circumstances to a Type 1 scenario. Here, time is not on the executive's side and radical, or second-order change is needed because the organisation is out of 'fit' with the environment. Participation is possible because key stakeholders support the need for radical change. This approach, however, also requires inspirational leadership at the top. Chrysler under Iaccoca and Honeywell in the 1980s are examples where this approach has occurred.

- Type 3. *Forced evolution* The methods needed to implement change in these circumstances are more autocratic, top down, and in some cases, coercive. This approach is necessary where change needs to occur, time is less pressing, but key stakeholders are opposed to change. This approach is appropriate in situations where the organisation is characterised by, for instance, entrenched middle management or union groups who have rejected participation and may have moved into unresponsive or even spoiling tactics. Sectors of the Australian Electricity Generation and Supply Industry have used this approach.

- Type 4. *Dictatorial transformation* is necessary when the organisation is out of 'fit', there is no time for extensive participation and no support within the organisation for radical change – but radical change is vital to organisational survival and fulfilment of its basic mission. In this case, the methods used have to be radical in order to achieve the revitalisation of the organisation. Rupert Murdoch of News Corporation is an example of someone who uses this approach.

Dunphy and Stace (1992) argue that these different approaches should be used depending on differing circumstances. Moreover, organisations can alter their change strategy. For example, a Type 4 style (used initially to turn a company around) may need to be replaced by a Type 1 style (where collaborative and involving approaches are necessary) to build the organisation back up. The danger is in using one style when another is more appropriate; for instance a Type 1 approach when radical change is needed, which may result in time delays and more coercive methods being used later on.

(7) Implementing change

Having worked out the change goals and the strategy to be taken, the executive has won half the battle – and possibly the easy half. The much more difficult process is to put these into effect. Pettigrew and Whipp (1991), for instance, highlight 34 characteristics which make a difference in the management of change. They see the management of strategic change as a long-term process with action taken simultaneously and sequentially on many fronts and levels by several actors. Indeed, at companies like ICI and British Airways, multiple interventions were initiated rather than just one.

Whichever change strategy one adopts, it helps to know something about the possible reactions people may have. The Transitions Curve[22] highlights the stages individuals and organisations may go through during times of change.[23] By making these stages more concrete and apparent, it is easier to map out and recognise possible reactions at each stage (see Figure 9.2). From this one can then begin the process of managing oneself and others through the highs and lows.

The Transitions Curve is made up of two axes; it contrasts individual certainty and competency against the dimension of time. As can be seen from the shape of the curve, the individual needs to be prepared to experience some uncertainty as well as a loss in competency before a complete transition can occur. The mindset one adopts will have an important bearing on one's ability to move through the change process successfully.

The overall process has two important sequences. The first of these, the Recognition stage, is concerned with coming to terms with the kind of change that is needed. The second stage, called Development, is concerned with exploring the change process. These are explained in more detail below.

First stage: recognition

(a) Stimulus Initially there will be some kind of stimulus, such as a downturn in profits or the loss of key personnel, which will cause the executive to consider whether change is necessary. It can be both internal and external to the firm. The nature and degree of the

Fig. 9.2 *Transitions curve*

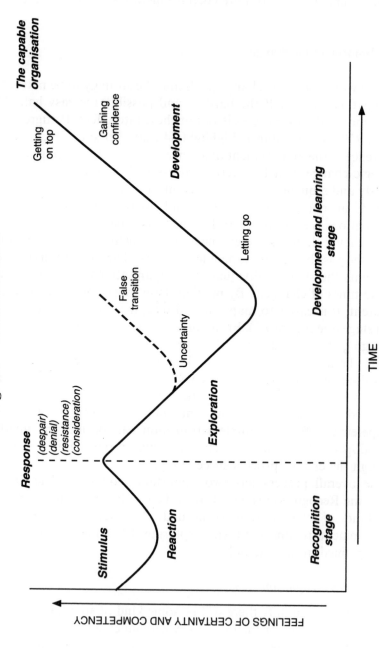

Source: Adapted from Parker and Lewis (1981)

stimulus has implications for the degree of change one may have to undergo.

(b) Reaction   A stimulus will usually give rise to some kind of reaction, however it is unlikely that one's initial response will give rise to anything deeper than first-order change. Even if a major catastrophe is facing the organisation, it will take time for individuals to come to terms with it. Consequently, a more superficial response is more usual at the beginning. Indeed, this may be all that is necessary. If the threats are more fundamental, however, change needs to go further.

(c) Response   Several responses are possible at this next stage. We have identified four which are related to the mindsets we describe in Chapter 2. These are Despair, Denial, Resistance, or Consideration:

- *Despair* occurs when the individual, senior team or organisation recognises that the threats are much greater than first thought and demand a much greater response, but do not believe that they can do anything about them. Despair is most closely related to the Despondent mindset.

- *Denial* is where an individual or group will be aware of changes to some extent, and may have gone through an element of change, but will deny that any further change is necessary. Jack Welch experienced this at GE:

    The changes are always bigger than you initially sense. In the beginning of something like the defence industry downsizing, people are in denial – they can't get themselves to believe how big the change will be.[24]

    A company which has been extremely successful in the past may express this by adopting an 'arrogant' mindset (see Chapter 2). Having made some changes, a degree of complacency may set in. Giants of the industrial world including IBM, GM, Ford and Caterpillar have suffered from this type of response.

- *Resistance* is reflected in a response of extreme caution, doubt or fear as described earlier. Resistance occurs when people have become comfortable in their work patterns and believe they may lose out in any fundamental reorganisation. This type of response is associated with what we call a Conservative mindset. Although the individual may acknowledge that all is not well, there will be a whole range of stalling tactics and outright resistance to putting the problem right. Here, logical argument is unlikely to be effective as it is the individual's negative mental set and emotional response which is behind their resistance to change.

- *Consideration* is a response which indicates a preparedness to look at the need to change and what this might entail. At this point the individual may begin to recognise the nature and level of change that may be necessary. Those with what we call a Capable mindset tend to be prepared to respond in this way.

However, there may be others who are slower to respond (or 'unfreeze', using Lewin's terminology) and it is the executive's responsibility to get them to listen. This may be possible with persuasion, but it usually involves stronger measures. Rarely do individuals or organisations begin to consider the enormity of the changes needed for second-order change, unless the threat to the organisation is very real and very great. As AlliedSignal's boss, Lawrence Bossidy says, 'To inaugurate large scale change, you may have to create the burning platform. You have to give people a reason to do something differently.'[25] Thus, the feedback given to individuals at this point has to be strong enough to overcome responses which are resistant or ones of denial.

There are many different ways of doing this. For example, executives often have to create a sense of urgency. Hallmark cards needed to get their managers to take on board process re-engineering, but to do this they needed to be knocked out of their comfortable belief in themselves and their unassailable market position. A video of customer reactions was shown to the top 40 executives about how Hallmark brought new products to market. First, small retailers talked about slowly falling store traffic. Then a senior vice-president of Wal-Mart, a significant customer, delivered the message that he hoped their companies could continue to do business. Apparently, 'By the time the lights went up the temperature in the room had fallen 20 degrees.'[26] As Harvey-Jones puts it, people need to develop the feeling that the present is more dangerous than the future.

Second stage: development and action

Exploration This is the point at which the implications of the changes which need to occur take hold. Before they can move on, individuals need to explore the limitations of their past behaviour and seek new ways of doing things. This is the period where individuals need to take risks, to experiment and to accept some mistakes. It is about pattern reframing (see Chapter 3). As a consequence, the executive needs to provide support, incentives, encouragement, involvement and a strong vision and inspiration to keep the momentum going.

It would be foolish for the executive to specify in great detail the new behaviours needed. Instead, people need to be prepared to take a critical look at the way things get done and to abandon old ways of thinking and operating. However, it is only unhelpful behaviour and thinking that has to change – not everything else. As Goodstein and Burke (1991) note, for change (rather than chaos) to occur, individuals and organisations must have some key, valuable aspects from the past that they can hold on to. In other words, change should occur from starting points that have some familiarity and leverage individual and organisational strengths. The executive should be trying to provide paths or 'strategic bridges' between their current assets and those which may be of potential benefit. Consequently, the kind of bridges that are built, which course they take and what load they carry are the constructive processes that the executive has to encourage and nurture.

When one takes a really critical look at how an individual or company operates, often this results in feelings of declining competency and uncertainty. Indeed, if there are no feelings of uncertainty, nor some degree of discomfort, it is unlikely that real learning is taking place. Those who try out new ways and can accept mistakes as part of the learning process are more likely to get through this stage quicker. Either way, it will require considerable mental resilience and persistence to push the changes through. Moreover, the temptation to go back to old ways of working and give up on the process is often very real.

Development   If individuals or organisations as a whole are to learn and develop, it will take place during this phase of the Transitions Curve. To progress, people not only have to be prepared to consider new ways of operating, they must also discard old patterns of thinking and behaving before they genuinely can try to adopt different approaches. (This is explored in more detail in Chapter 3). At first, change of this kind may be far from easy. However, as people realise they are getting runs on the board, that the new ways of working are yielding results and that they are beginning to take control of a different kind of destiny, things can take off. As confidence returns learning often accelerates.

Full transition   As the organisation or individual begins to master most aspects of the situation they move to the top of the Transitions curve. They experience feelings of rising certainty and capability. Although the environment will continue to change, the challenges which emerge will be coped with in a different and more productive way.

(8) & (9)   Establishing maintenance systems and evaluating the change effort

Having gone through a period of change – and in some cases quite traumatic change – it is easy to feel exhausted or become complacent. There is a real danger that having achieved a major organisational transformation, capability then gives way to complacency; exhilaration to fatigue; strategising to habituation. Outwardly, organisations may show few signs of this malaise, but underneath openness and responsiveness is diminished.

For example, by late 1994, two and a half years into Jack Smith's tenure as CEO of General Motors, the organisation was on the road to recovery with its core car and truck business rescued from the brink of financial collapse. Despite the turnaround, some of the old behaviours remained. According to one report, 'some managers still exude the same mixture of arrogance and infallibility that got GM into trouble in the first place'. A senior GM executive commented, 'I constantly worry that we will slip back into the complacency that got us into trouble in the past. We work every day at disabusing people of the notion that we have this thing fixed.'[27]

Increasingly, the challenge is to sustain and extend the change process. The bad news is that even organisations who have made it through second-order change are unlikely to be able to rest in the pressurised economic climate of the 1990s and beyond. The good news is that some companies are finding ways to maintain their momentum. At GNB Technologies, the third largest worldwide lead–acid battery producer, it is through a 'stay hungry' campaign which gets associates to think constantly in terms of new ways to improve. 3M uses stretch targets to boost flagging sales – in 1994, some 25–30 per cent of its revenues were from products introduced in the past five years.[28]

As Kanter (1988) argues, the challenge is to build into organisations the capacity to improve and change direction as conditions change. Jack Welch of GE sums this up in his answer to people who ask of him, 'Is the change over? Can we stop now?' – 'You've got to tell them, "No it's just begun".'[29]

SUMMARY

Despite the complexity of the change process, there are many aspects of organisational change which executives can influence. To do so, they must be able to identify when change needs to occur, understand what the process involves and develop strategies for managing the change process. This chapter has been structured around these three key issues.

Increased personnel turnover, client complaints, a decline in market share and overall profitability are just some of the clues which might indicate that change has to occur. Depending on the organisation's 'fit' with the environment, first or second-order change may be required. Having decided that change is necessary, executives must then determine what the new organisation will look like. They must work out which parts of the organisation will be most affected by the change process and the depth and scale of change that is required.

Executives experience a range of issues when implementing change: often, unexpected difficulties crop up and the process takes longer to implement than executives originally anticipate. In addition, change can prompt a range of negative responses which may result in resistance. Consideration therefore has to be given to the concerns and agendas of key stakeholders in the organisation. Executives must also understand and learn to manage their own and others reactions to change. The Transitions Curve is used to illustrate the feelings individuals may experience during times of change.

Ultimately there is a tremendously responsibility on senior management to initiate changes which will progress the organisation and to handle the change process well. Their decisions and actions can influence not only whether organisations survive, but in some cases, entire industries. Change is the arena where executives' leadership skills, ability to handle conflict and manage powerful stakeholders are put to the test. However, the biggest challenge may be how they handle their own responses to change. Unless they can manage these well, their ability to manage others during times of change will prove a great deal more difficult.

NOTES

1. See Alex Taylor III, 'GM's $11,000,000,000 Turnaround', *Fortune*, vol. 130, no. 8, 17 October 1994, 38–54.
2. Stratford Sherman, 'Is He Too Cautious to Save IBM?', *Fortune*, vol. 130, no. 7, 3 October 1994, 46–55.
3. Quoted in Payne and Lumsden (1987).
4. See Nadler and Tushman (1988b).
5. Shawn Tully, 'Why To Go For Stretch Targets', *Fortune*, vol. 130, no. 10, 14 November 1994, 95–100.
6. *Sir John Harvey-Jones* Case 9-490-013, Harvard Business School, 1989.
7. Stratford Sherman, 'A Master Class in Radical Change', *Fortune*, vol. 128, no. 15, 13 December 1993, 40–4.
8. See 'The Best Practices Report: An Analysis of Management Practices That Impact Performance', published jointly by Ernst & Young and the American Quality Foundation, 1992. The report is based on a survey of 580 organisations worldwide.
9. See Thomas Stewart, 'Reengineering – The Hot New Management Tool', *Fortune*, vol. 128, no. 4, 23 August 1993, 24–9.
10. Leavitt (1964) was possibly the first person to discuss leverage points when he identified task, technology, people and structure.
11. David Goodhart, 'Bad Connections at BT', *Financial Times*, 7 November 1994, 8.
12. 'Chase Tries Again, But Does it Have Time?' *The Age*, 3 October 1990.
13. See Nadler and Tushman (1988a).
14. *Fortune*, December 13, 1993. *op. cit.*
15. Kearns and Nadler (1992).
16. See Myron Magnet's article, 'Meet the New Revolutionaries', *Fortune*, vol. 125, no. 4, 24 February 1992.
17. See Noel Tichy and Stratford Sherman, 'Jack Welch's Lessons for Success', *Fortune*, vol. 127, no. 2, 25 January 1993, 64–8.
18. See Vandermerwe and Vandermerwe (1991).
19. Goodstein and Burke (1991).
20. Indeed, similar principles have been outlined by other writers such as Barczak, Smith and Wilemon (1987) who advocate a process of pattern breaking, experimenting, visioning, bonding and attunement.
21. David Kirkpatrick, 'Lou Gerstner's First 30 Days', *Fortune*, vol. 127, no. 11, 31 May 1993, 41–3.
22. This diagram is derived from work outlined in Parker and Lewis (1981).

23. Several writers have written about the transitions process including Kubler-Ross (1975), Adams, Hays and Hopson (1976), Parker and Lewis (1981) and Hambrick (1991).
24. *Fortune*, 13 December 1993, 41.
25. *Fortune*, 13 December 1993.
26. *Fortune*, 23 August 1993.
27. *Fortune*, 17 October 1994.
28. *Fortune*, 14 November 1994.
29. *Fortune*, 13 December 1993.

10   The Actioning/Structuring and Expertise Capabilities: Energy, Purpose and Focus in the Senior Executive Role

INTRODUCTION

No matter what the capabilities of the executive, unless they can translate these into effective action they are of little use. Ultimately, it is what senior executives do, the actions they take, the results they achieve, which are important.

How executives translate their ability into action is through the Capability we call Actioning/Structuring. It is this Capability which correlated most highly with effectiveness in our own research. It is concerned with the energy and focus needed to be effective in a senior executive role. The Actioning part of this capability is concerned with the capacity to sustain high work loads, maintain motivation and persist. The Structuring aspect reflects how the executive channels this energy and the personal and organisational structures and systems needed to achieve both short and long-term goals. During his time in Australia as Managing Director of Consolidated Press Holdings, Al Dunlap exhibited this combination of qualities. One of Dunlap's great strengths was seen to be his:

> . . . ability to reduce complex problems to very basic components and to prioritise these. He can also totally avoid distraction until each of these issues are resolved. He will reduce some complex multi-million situation to say 5 points. Then he won't rest until each of these points have been dealt with and will require similar dedication from those around him until those goals have been accomplished.[1]

In addition, the executive's Expertise Capability plays an important part in providing the knowledge needed to help focus on the appropriate issues and cover the essentials across a range of functions. This includes functional expertise, but also includes the ability to see beyond specialisms which are too narrow. Gilbert (1991) quotes Michael Johnson, financial vice-president and CFO of AT&T's general business systems division. He believes that the extraordinary competitiveness of contemporary business means decisions have to be broad based. 'Those people who cannot crawl out of their speciality to a greater understanding of business as a whole will be confined to lower levels', Johnson maintains. 'Today, every piece of information, whether it be accounting, manufacturing or marketing, has to be examined in the light of what it means to the organisation as a whole.' As one executive we interviewed said, 'Like everything else, the higher you go up the tree, the less specifics you need to know. Probably the less you know about a function the better.'

These two Capabilities will be discussed in this chapter. We start with the Actioning/Structuring Capability and explore the link between maintaining energy and drive and channelling this within a system, structure or plan which focuses the executive on issues of importance. As Drucker (1955) notes, 'Planning and doing are separate parts of the same job; they are not separate jobs. There is no work that can be performed effectively unless it contains elements of both.'

THE ACTIONING/STRUCTURING CAPABILITY

Executive drive

The ability to get things done and operate with a great deal of energy and persistence is essential at a senior level. Cox and Cooper (1988) point out that most studies show top executives work very long hours and there are many examples of this. Jack Smith head of GM arrives at his desk at 7.30 a.m. and typically remains there until 6.30 p.m. A couple of days a week he tries to skip lunch and work out in a small gym in the building, but he says 'Usually I just skip lunch and don't work out'. At home in the evening, Smith spends another 90 minutes going through the mail. 'You can really get some tough days when you have a tremendous demand on your time', he says. 'You don't have time to breathe; you don't have time to think. I don't think that's good. That's overload.'[2]

According to Jim Cannavino, IBM's strategy chief, CEO Lou Gerstner, 'reads a stack of stuff that is probably half his size everyday'. Gerstner packs his calendar with visits to IBM locations and customers around the world. He is so busy that John Thompson the executive responsible for a range of products including mainframes and minicomputers recently had to wait a month for a routine meeting with him.[3]

As both examples indicate, hard work can also have its downsides. This is highlighted more sharply by a manager in our study who said, 'The problem with the high energy, dynamic types like myself and the (MD) is we love working harder and that's the problem. You know we love putting in silly long hours and getting there early and working ourselves too hard, whether it's on the squash court or at work. But it is not always very productive. It makes you feel better but it doesn't really do a lot for the business. It's been a lot of fun, but we need to stand back and say hey, how can we lift our eyes up from the table and think about generating new ideas.'

Hence, it would seem that not only is hard work part of the executive role, it also has to be channelled. (How this is done will be dealt with later in the chapter.) Nevertheless, maintaining high energy day in and day out can be a challenge. This is especially important when sales have been declining for some time, targets are not being achieved, and new products are failing. It is also important that the executive has the energy to persist given the many hurdles faced each day. Indeed, one of the most important qualities of the executive may be their ability to maintain momentum, persist and see issues through to resolution. Consequently, understanding what motivates the executive and how they can re-energise themselves through lean times is important.

Executive motivation is not well understood, however. It is often assumed that high salaries and the power of the position are the most important attractions. Research suggests, however, that this is a limited view of what motivates many executives. Cox and Cooper (1988) found that while most MDs in their study clearly enjoyed the money and status associated with their position, they all maintained this was secondary to other motives. Additionally, Mumford *et al.* (1987) did not find that the main motivating drive of directors was financial reward.

Executives' needs and motivation

Motivation studies of executives have largely been concerned with itemising executives' needs. These have usually drawn on Herzberg *et al.* (1959) or Maslow (1954) who argued that we have a hierarchy of needs with lower-level needs like food and shelter needing to be satisfied first. As these lower level needs are satisfied, the higher order needs (such as self-actualisation, challenge and achievement) become more significant. The studies indicate that senior executives are largely motivated by the higher-order needs or 'motivators'. These needs include self-realisation and autonomy,[4] self-actualisation,[5] challenge,[6] enjoyment of the job and achieving objectives.[7]

Nevertheless, it would be rather limiting to ignore the potential impact that money, power and status may have in motivating the executive. Mills (1985), for instance, found that pay is important for managers as a way of recognising and rewarding performance and for overcoming and responding to challenges. McClelland and Burnham (1976) have demonstrated how power, affiliation and achievement have different motivational consequences. Clearly, if executives did not in some way see the exercise of power or influence and the need to achieve as important, most would never survive in the role. Moreover, different factors may be important at different times. Early on in an executive's career, status, money and promotion may be much more significant. However, as Ancona and Nadler (1989) have highlighted with regard to succession issues, it would be short-sighted to assume that promotion was not a highly motivating (and at times demotivating) factor for many who seek the top job, even right to the end of their careers.

It is important to try to work out what motivates the executive so that drive and energy can be maintained. However, the subject is complex. While, in general, intrinsic and higher-order needs seem to be more significant than external material rewards, it is necessary to look beyond the executive's needs in order to get a more comprehensive view of executive motivation.

Self-concept motivation

A greater understanding of executive motivation can be gained from looking more broadly at the executive's self-concept. This is concerned with how the executive views himself or herself in terms of their self-identity. An individual's self-identity is a product of many factors, partly their needs, but also social background, experience, values and beliefs.

Values are a central part of an executive's self-concept. The importance of values in the decision making process was emphasised in Chapter 2. However, as values are concerned with what we value and what guides us, consequently they impact on what drives us. We can value getting ahead, achievement, hard work, power, integrity and so forth. As Covey (1989) notes, values, which are part our mental maps of the world, are part of our internal frames of reference. They interpret what is happening to us and they contain standards, principles or implicit criteria that govern our actions.

Our self-identity is tied up with what we do. Executives who spend a great deal of time tied up in their work will often express their talents, opinions, beliefs and creativity through their work. Even executives who lead a more balanced existence and have other outlets such as family, leisure or artistic pursuits, will nevertheless have a large part of their self-identity tied up with work. We often communicate to others who we are by stating what work we do, what work title we have, what company we work for and what resources we manage.

If work allows us to express our values then our drive is likely to be high. If we are not able to express what is intrinsically important to us, or our work role conflicts with our values and feelings of self-worth, then we will be less motivated. It is important, therefore, that executives understand what they value personally.

Often, however, individuals do not have a clear picture of the values they hold and how their self-identity might be fully expressed. Sufficient time may not have been devoted to clarifying our mental maps, what we stand for, what drives us and keeps us focused or knocks us off track. As well as guiding us, our values can act to constrain us. If, for instance, we value technical excellence, then we may get caught up in issues we should leave to others. It is no wonder that many companies have difficulty in building truly effective top teams if, as Cox and Cooper (1988) claim, executives value independence and self-reliance. The 'people' values of Don Burr, CEO of People Express during the 1980s, blinded him to other priorities in the market place. Those who value achievement may pursue concrete outcomes which give them a sense of achievement (for example, short-term goals) rather than less tangible outcomes (developing business strategies) which may be equally significant.

At other times we may ignore our values or what enhances our self-worth. Many executives, realising that they cannot fulfil themselves in the way they would wish through work, opt for the material rewards – the mink handcuffs which ultimately never fully maintain their true drive and peak performance. Moreover, in tough times, when there is less to draw on personally, maintaining a high degree of motivation may be impossible.

Thus, executives should try and surface their ultimate drivers. Unless these are acknowledged, they may have difficulty in understanding how to maintain their own motivation and will have real difficulty motivating others through general approaches that are based on values. Executives need to be aware of their 'value maps' as these can also direct them along paths and in patterns which may be too comfortable and narrow. Consequently, without understanding these more fundamental drives, any externally imposed structure (such as a personal planning system) will be very limited in focusing the executive and facilitating action.

Converting energy into action

Our fundamental drives and motivations are only part of the story. Executives use a whole range of internal (that is, cognitive maps) and external (for example, planning) devices to structure their world. The executive needs ways of facilitating and channelling energy into effective action both in the short and long term. Executives like Al Dunlap (noted earlier) and Paul Simons, Chairman of Woolworths Australia, are examples of executives who are able to focus, prioritise and take action on important issues. This is not necessarily typical, however. The more usual scenario is highlighted by one manager who commented:

> It's difficult to keep a focus on what's really important. Before you came this morning, I was just sketching the four things I thought were important and I could have put another 104 things down easily. It's difficult to keep a real focus. You can only keep so many things in the shop at once and obviously the day-to-day operational things drive out the longer term issues.

Despite the myriad number of approaches designed to help employees better manage themselves and their time, problems still persist even at senior levels. Why is this? While we know we need to focus on what is critical, how do we decide which these issues are? An executive may be focused, but if it is on the short rather than the long-term, or on detail rather than the big picture, then the principle of 'focus' is a limitation rather than an advantage. The ex-CEO of General Motors, Robert Stempel, for all his talents, was criticised for getting lost in the detail and deliberating on problems for too long.[8]

Internal and external maps

The notion of cognitive maps has been raised earlier and in Chapter 2. These are patterns or mental charts of various aspects of our world which act as our guides to it. Some of these charts are very accurate, some inaccurate, some are very rigid and others very fluid. Some are based on fundamental concepts such as beliefs or values which can guide all aspects of our lives. Others may be more superficial and applied to particular contexts such as work. The mental maps we might use to structure the work environment can be concerned with:

- Time (for example, today, next quarter, next year)
- Ends (for example, meeting financial targets)
- Means (methods of increasing profitability or sales)

Maps can also be about people, things or events. They can also be:

- Prescriptive (what should be)
- Descriptive (what is)
- Predictive (what will be)

Many of our mental maps are a combination of these items. More frequently, however, they emphasise some items to the detriment of others. For example, time may be spent figuring out how to meet this quarter's budget forecast rather than predicting the outcomes of technological developments ten years hence.

Structuring is concerned with producing external frameworks, schemas, plans or charts which partly translate our mental maps into concrete form, but also add to them, to give us a sense of our world and provide direction. External plans and charts should sharpen and extend our internal maps. However, as noted earlier, frequently we do not fully understand the mental maps we use. While these maps may help us understand the world and bring order to it, they also, often unconsciously, work to exclude many items.

It is therefore very easy to create plans for both ourselves and others which look good on paper but bare little relationship to how we really see the world and what we believe is important. When executives take on more complex roles but cling onto charts which are no longer relevant because of changes in their job or the environment, the results can be disastrous. Hence the importance of data gathering and thinking issues through, not only in the first months of a senior role as Gabarro (1988) and Kotter (1982) highlight, but also at regular times throughout our worklife.

Managing the environment

The job environment contains a myriad of potential stimuli. How we respond to these depends on whether we have personal structures or maps which help us respond effectively. The reactive manager reacts to events as they occur and is *managed by* them. The proactive manager responds to events earlier and *manages* them. Traditional writers exhort executives to become more proactive, although in the senior role – which is often described as a reactive environment – this may be more than a little difficult.

A reactive environment implies little or no choice. However, as writers such as Stewart (1982) point out, executives do have choice. How much choice depends partly on the environment and partly on the executive's own perceptions, or cognitive maps. While an executive may be under pressure to act quickly this does not mean they have to give knee-jerk reactions. Just because the environment is outwardly chaotic, does not mean the executive needs to be in chaos. The point is not that executives should try to bring complete order to an environment that by nature is dynamic: rather, they should look for ways of managing themselves better within that environment. As Kotter (1982) has highlighted, effectiveness is possible from seemingly ineffective behaviour. This is because the successful executive *does* give considered responses and uses the environment to pursue their maps, agendas or plans, rather than try to completely reorder the environment to fit the plan.

Consequently, while one cannot have control over everything, one can develop better ways of responding to events. An extreme example would be some of the coping mechanisms used by prisoners of war, or hostages who have been completely at the mercy of their captors. The

Second World War, Vietnam and more recently the Iranian hostage crises have produced outstanding examples of heroism. John McCarthy,[9] a British journalist who was held hostage in Beirut for five years, has described how even in situations where one has little control over whether one lives or dies, one can still manage one's mental response to this situation.

Domains of interest and areas of response

Different ways of managing the environment can be illustrated by first considering one's Domain of Interest – that is, everything that impinges on one's work or organisation (Figure 10.1). Some of the factors that make up the executive's Domain cannot be controlled, such as interest rates. These would be placed towards the outer edge of the Circle. Other events which can be controlled (for example, a forthcoming staff meeting to discuss the performance of one's business unit or organisation) would occupy a more central position.

The executive has to map out the extent of their Domain of Interest. This is what was called Establishing in Chapter 1 – the process of locating the executive, the position of the business and all the important factors within the environment. Clearly, one can have different Domains of Interest and different Establishing processes (for example, for the business as a whole, or within a particular market, or personally within one's job).

Fig. 10.1   *Managing the environment*

Domain of Interest

Establishing

Loacating oneself and one's business within the environment and identifying influential factors and critical issues

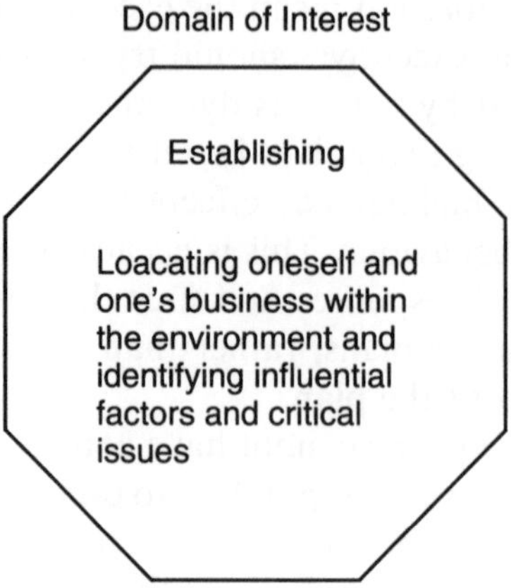

One can then identify within the Domain of Interest an Area of Response (Figure 10.2). The Area of Response is the area that the executive can affect, either directly or through indirect means. The executive has a direct affect through the actions taken to maintain or progress the organisation or through what we term the Enacting process. Executives influence the situation indirectly through the infrastructure they put in place to help others achieve organisational goals – that is, through the Enabling process (see Figure 10.3).

Fig. 10.2   *Managing the environment*

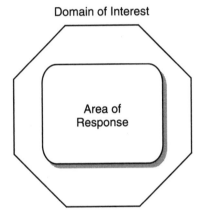

Domain of Interest

Area of Response

Fig. 10.3   *Managing the environment*

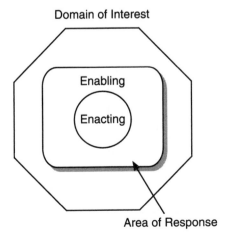

Domain of Interest

Enabling

Enacting

Area of Response

The Area of Response is where executives should be devoting their time and energy. However, this does not mean that they should neglect what seems on the surface to be a black hole of unpredictable events which swirl around outside the Area of Response, but which are still important and within the Domain of Interest. For example, trade agreements or exchange rate fluctuations cannot be controlled by most executives, although they will impinge on many businesses. Does this mean they are unmanageable?

Clearly, these cannot be managed in the way executives manage a meeting to review their organisation's performance. However, events which are outside the executive's control can be managed by reviewing and preparing different responses to them. By so doing the executive is extending their Area of Response and creating a potential competitive advantage (Figure 10.4).

Hamel and Prahalad (1994)[10] illustrate this by highlighting how many senior executives fail to develop any kind of considered response to future changes which will affect their company. They ask senior executives three questions:

(1) What percentage of your time is spent on external rather than internal issues? For example, understanding the implications of new technology versus debating corporate overhead allocations.

Fig. 10.4 *Managing the environment*

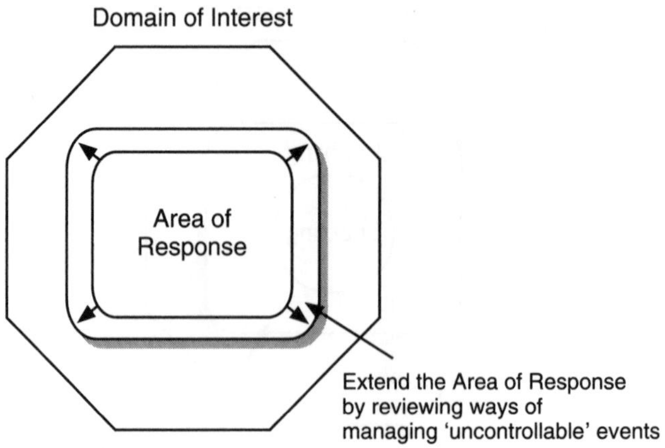

Domain of Interest

Area of Response

Extend the Area of Response by reviewing ways of managing 'uncontrollable' events

(2) Of this time, how much is spent considering how the world could be different in five or ten years? – as opposed to how to win the next big contract or changes in competitors pricing.

(3) Of the time devoted to looking outward and forward, how much is spent consulting with colleagues on how to build a deeply shared, well tested view of the future?

They find that about 40 per cent of senior executives' time is spent looking outward (1). Of this, about 30 per cent is spent looking three or more years into the future (2). Of this time spent looking outward and forward, only 20 per cent is spent attempting to share one's understanding with colleagues and build a collective future picture (3). This means that less than 3 per cent (40% × 30% × 20% = 2.4%) of the executive's time is spent considering the corporate perspective. In some companies the figure is less than 1 per cent.

While the future cannot be controlled, those executives who are reviewing future scenarios in some depth are more likely to be able to manage and forge a distinctive competitive position and take the competitive high ground. Executives and senior teams who are not considering external future scenarios are giving up any real attempt to manage their destiny to competitors who are devoting time to these issues. At a time when the actions of some large companies can change the structure of an industry, to not extend one's Area of Response is potentially very dangerous.

Thus, it is possible to extend one's Area of Response by developing more sophisticated maps to manage the uncontrollable. The more senior one becomes, the larger one's Area of Response will be. However, if the executive's impact on their Area of Response is largely through Enacting (that is, through their own actions rather than indirectly through Enabling others to act) then they must seriously look at their role and how they are operating within it.

Managing within the area of response

As mentioned earlier, within the Area of Response the executive Enacts or Enables. While Enacting involves the maintenance or progression of the organisation and Enabling is concerned with building the infrastructure, what an executive actually does in the role can be somewhat different. There may be many behaviours or actions which neither maintain, progress, build or even have a neutral impact on the organisation.

Fig. 10.5 *Managing within the area of response*

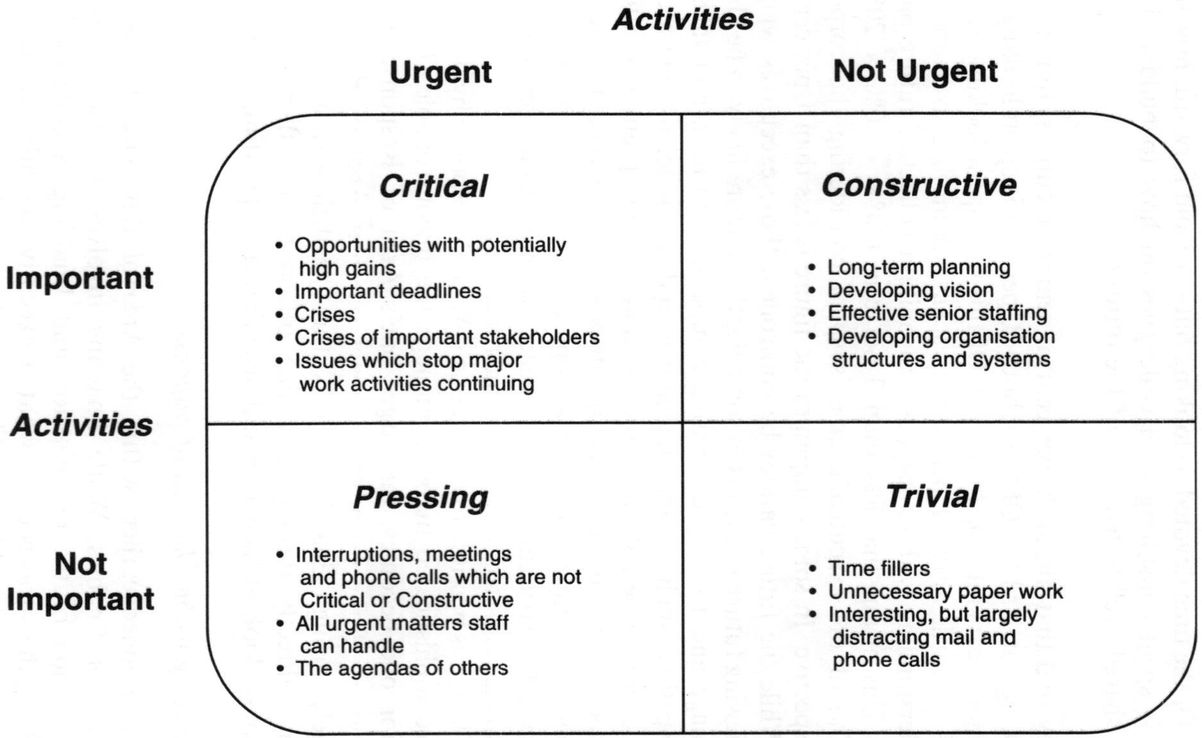

Activities

	Urgent	**Not Urgent**
Important	**Critical** • Opportunities with potentially high gains • Important deadlines • Crises • Crises of important stakeholders • Issues which stop major work activities continuing	**Constructive** • Long-term planning • Developing vision • Effective senior staffing • Developing organisation structures and systems
Not Important	**Pressing** • Interruptions, meetings and phone calls which are not Critical or Constructive • All urgent matters staff can handle • The agendas of others	**Trivial** • Time fillers • Unnecessary paper work • Interesting, but largely distracting mail and phone calls

Activities

To help assess where the bulk of one's energy is focused, it helps to have some kind of sorting mechanism. The matrix illustrated in Figure 10.5 assesses an activity in terms of four factors – whether it is urgent, or not urgent; important or not important. An urgent issue requires an immediate response. An important issue contributes to the executive's critical goals.

These factors can be combined to produce four types of activity – Critical, Pressing, Trivial and Constructive (Figure 10.5). A Critical activity is one that is both urgent and important and demands immediate attention (top left-hand corner of the diagram). At a senior level there will be many items which fall into this category. Indeed, frequently, the problem executives face is how to cope with an overwhelming number of urgent and important issues. Many executives we spoke to, often found that almost everything they do falls into this quadrant.

Executives have to engage in activities which build the organisation and infrastructure to Enable others to move the organisation forward. This is what we have called a Constructive activity – those issues which are not urgent but important (the top right-hand corner of the diagram). Constructive activities are usually initiated by the executive. They involve long-term planning, developing a vision, reviewing alternative future scenarios, effective staffing at the senior level, changing organisational structures to make them more efficient and ensuring the correct financial, information and reward systems are in place. Because they are often not pressing, less concrete and visible and sometimes involve longer-term paybacks, they are usually much harder to tackle. Ultimately, no business or executive can survive without a great deal of time being spent on Constructive activities.

In the early 1990s, a study by McKinsey advocated that senior executives should set aside time devoted to attend to activities like long-term decision making and strategic thinking.[11] The report recommended at least two 'CEO time alone' sessions a week, each for two hours. It also suggested allocating time for various roles over a 12-month period, such as blocking out 900 hours for strategic development. This would seem to contradict other research which suggests that effective senior executives spend most of their time interacting with others on brief, fragmented activities.[12] Indeed, some argue that without a constant stream of interruptions, the executive is not able to build up the networks and gather the information vital to perform the senior role.[13]

However, these issues have to be seen in the light of whether the activities the executive undertakes are Critical or Constructive. Interruptions are essential for network building and are Constructive ways of ensuring that the executive both has the information to operate, but more importantly that the executive's agenda is being disseminated throughout the organisation. What is important is who is interrupting, and whether these are Trivial or Constructive in outcomes rather than in the nature of the interaction. Moreover, there will be moments when executives need time to themselves, for report writing, for instance. They should therefore set aside 60 to 90 minutes of private time, when least interruptions are likely to occur – which for most executives is first thing in the morning.

Thus, in theory, the executive should stay away from the lower part of the matrix – from the Pressing and Trivial activities – as these are not important. In concentrating on the top half of the matrix, executive effort should largely go into Constructive activities, which enable others to operate effectively. While Critical activities can never be eradicated, they are likely to be reduced if time and effort is devoted to Constructive activities. For instance, plans may have been developed which can help manage potential Critical activities early, or an effective senior team may have been built which allows some of the Critical activities to be shared.

However, while this sounds fine in theory, why in reality is this map, at best, only partially adhered to by many managers? Why did Shaw and Nadler (1991) find in their survey, that over half the respondents felt that managers in their company worked hard but rarely accomplished the important work that needed to be done. Why is it that often managers work hard, but the outcomes are less than satisfactory?

Work planning

Shaw and Nadler (1991) argue the solution lies in looking at those factors which affect what they call the executive's capacity to act. What inhibits action to solve key organisational problems? Part of the issue is to do with follow through. Problems are identified, solutions generated, but somehow they do not get implemented or are implemented inefficiently. Another part of the issue is that key organisational problems are not addressed in the first place. The problems are not identified, or they are acknowledged but treated as a given, or less significant problems are worked on because the pressure is not there to look at important problems. Over time, urgent problems, or ones that can be resolved in a structured fashion, drive out the vital business issues.

Planning is the traditional solution to some of these problems. Executives reading this book will be familiar with a range of planning processes hence our intention is not to review these here. However, there are several points worth emphasising in terms of the ways plans are used and viewed.

Personal planning

The traditional view of how one keeps oneself focused on Critical and Constructive activities is by setting long, medium and short-term goals and creating plans to accomplish these. At a personal level, these are often translated into daily and monthly plans where ways of achieving short and longer-term goals are listed and prioritised – in a sense they are formalised cognitive maps.

For a plan to be successful, Noon (1985) argues that four criteria must be met:

- It needs to be flexible
- It must be directed at definable and achievable objectives
- It must concentrate on the effective use of resources and use of time
- Planning must be reviewed constantly and adapted

Possibly more important is why managers do not adhere to their plans. Noon (1985) argues it is due to several reasons, including:

- A lack of commitment to a manager's plans – overtaken by crises
- Absence of a general strategy for the managers job and performance
- Lack of objectives, or objectives which lack definition
- A tendency to over-plan and become bogged down in detail
- Over reliance on experience, becoming short sighted

Formal planning

These pointers are also important when looking at more formal strategic planning processes. However, if executives have difficulty sticking to their own personal plans, adhering to broader, more strategic structures which others usually impose, is riddled with potential hurdles.

Davies (1991) points out that strategic planning is a process which relates to the company as a whole. It is a process which touches and individually involves all parts of the business. Each unit produces a plan which is part of a hierarchy of plans consolidated into a corporate plan for the organisation as a whole. This hierarchy of plans should be developed within a framework set by the corporate centre, in order to ensure consistency of direction, assumptions and action.

The corporate plan is comprised of the strategic plans of each level of operation down to the smallest, viable business activity or SBU. Such a hierarchy might comprise major subsidiary companies, divisions within such subsidiaries and SBUs in those divisions, indicating three levels of consolidation up to corporate level. Within each strategic plan there may be another hierarchy – marketing plans, manpower plans, manufacturing plans, R & D plans and so on.

As many executives know, this is a complex process fraught with difficulty. Anthony *et al.* (1993) argue that research shows that planners have difficulty in developing practical or realistic future scenarios. Personal biases and assumptions often place stumbling blocks in the way of accuracy and reality. Moreover, distilling perceptions of the scenarios into useful information to enable the formulation of realistic goals, objectives and action plans is even more difficult. Strategic managers may develop a strategic plan based solely on the extrapolation of past and present situations, which may not be at all appropriate given today's rate of change.

However, one cannot do away with planning processes. Such planning is essential in order to provide structure for many people working in complex environments. The essential point is that such plans are only of use if line managers who have to deliver the planned results have an input in their production. While planning departments have been scaled down in many organisations, nevertheless parts of the planning process, such as forecasting, data collection, analysis, and programme suggestions are often delegated to others. Therefore the senior executive, must at the very least, be able to establish ground rules and broad objectives, and should be involved in directing the planning activities.

Planning involves discussion, ideas and models. However, it is the action that arises from the plan which is critical. Hence, this is why many writers now emphasise that it is the planning process which is more important than the plan. It is the process through which assumptions, ideas and personal cognitive maps are shared and commitment is made. It is through the planning process that individual mental models are likely to be surfaced and come together. The closer these are, the more likely that the department, company and conglomerate will be heading down the same path. It is less likely that a plan or structure produced by someone else, whether it is corporate planners, the CEO or the top team alone, will ever work if it is not shared before it is formalised. Although this seems common sense, it has not always been common practice.

Reconciling personal and formal plans

This last point highlights the inherent problem of structuring one's own and others' environments. The challenge is to reconcile different individual maps within a very diverse and complex reality. No plan can bring order to chaos. However, it can bring understanding, shared perceptions and a structure which guides within a dynamic environment.

Kotter (1982) sees the executive's personal agendas (a conscious mental map which is sometimes written, sometimes not) and formal plans as both being different, but necessary. Kotter found that the general manager's agendas always included goals, priorities and strategies that were not in the written documents. The executive's agenda and the formal plan were not incompatible, but different in several ways. They were different in terms of the financial emphasis. The formal plans tended to be written mostly in terms of detailed financial numbers; the executive's agendas were less detailed in financial objectives, but more detailed in terms of strategies and plans for the business or the organisation. Agendas and plans were also different in terms of their timescale; the formal plans usually focused entirely on the short and moderate run (three months to five years), whereas the executive's agendas tended to focus on a broader time frame, including the immediate future (1–30 days) and the longer term (5–20 years). Additionally, they were different in terms of their precision; formal plans tended to be more explicit, rigorous and logical, especially regarding how various financial items fit together, while the executive's agendas often contained lists of goals or plans that were not as explicitly connected.

Seen in this light, formal plans can complement the executive's personal plans. They can help the executive think strategically and communicate the thrust of the organisation to others. They can encourage the executive to think longer term and explore the key issues of the business. However, if the planning process is highly bureaucratic, it is less likely to produce good results.

The importance of vision

If the executive is to take action, give considered responses rather than knee-jerk reactions, prioritise and use structures to enable others to operate more effectively, something more fundamental has to occur. A personal and organisational vision, a theme which runs throughout this book, is a fundamental prerequisite to help guide the executive's action and progress.

Shaw and Nadler (1991), however, found that less than half the people they surveyed believed that their fellow managers had a clear sense of vision and purpose. Without this, dealing with the unrelenting pressure to balance conflicting priorities becomes a chaotic melee. Without a fundamental guide and purpose, there is a much greater likelihood that the executive will be managed by events, rather than be in a position to respond effectively.

Personal vision

At a personal level, an end state or picture is critical to enable the executive to assess what is important, what can be put to one side, and whether the executive is making progress. Establishing a personal vision, which takes into account the fulfilment of personal values, has been advocated by several writers as a way of achieving and maintaining focus. Garfield (1986), for instance, found that success-ful people have a sense of mission that helps them mobilise their inner resources. Covey (1989) has argued that we must get to our very centre and understand how we might deal with our vision, our values and what guides us.

Several writers (including Covey) argue that the best way to do this, is to 'begin with the end in mind'. This is a process of thinking of ourselves in several years time, or even at the end of our life and trying to imagine what ideally we would like to have happened during that period. What would we have liked to have achieved – what is our end vision? Anthony *et al.* (1993) see this as a process of mental imagery. Imagery has been used to improve sports performance for several years. In the same way, if executives can imagine themselves in a future scenario they can identify more vividly some of the assumptions and beliefs they may hold which are relevant to the organisation, environment or their future. By placing oneself in a future scenario, tacit knowledge becomes available. With this picture in mind we then have a frame of reference, a set of criteria by which activities can be examined. If an activity does not contribute to achieving this end-picture, then decisions on how to handle that activity become clearer. Thus, by keeping the end-picture in mind, executives can ensure that what they do each day contributes to it.

Business vision

The same principle can be applied to a business or corporate vision. Unless the organisation has some broader and longer-term purpose and a set of guiding philosophies by which it might be achieved, then it too may be swayed by very powerful and more focused players in the competitive environment.

As Shaw and Nadler (1991) argue, it is important to ensure all managers possess and understand a clear vision and strategy for their company. However, as Hamel and Prahalad (1994) explain, that vision is not some dream or blinding insight. They use the term 'industrial foresight' to describe an end-picture which is based on a very thorough understanding of the trends in the economic environment and which uses creativity and imagination to turn these into competitive opportunities.

However, according to Bartlett and Ghoshal (1994), the outcome of this process, should not then only be expressed in financial terms. Although achieving acceptable financial objectives is clearly important for a company's survival, a target Return on Investment (ROI) rarely galvanises others into action. If people are to expend the extraordinary effort required to realise company targets, they must be able to identify with them personally. One disaffected manager is quoted as saying, 'It's fine to emphasise what we must shoot for, but we also need to know what we stand for'.

If an organisation is to know what it stands for, it has to be able to answer the following critical questions;[14]

- How do customers see us?
- What must we excel at?
- Can we continue to improve and create value?
- How do we look to shareholders?

A guiding structure then has to be provided which will galvanise the organisation to achieve a long-term competitive advantage. When this is in place and the principles by which it will be achieved are identified and agreed, the more detailed planning structure described earlier becomes truly meaningful.

The process of creating a long-term vision for the organisation is, nevertheless, difficult to achieve. In part, this is because the process relies less on analysis and logic and more on emotion and intuition. It is a lot easier to set a financial objective than it is to talk about guiding values and vision. Consequently, as with a personal vision, a vision which is meaningful cannot be developed overnight. As Bartlett and Ghoshal (1994) point out, new values cannot be instilled through a crash programme. Not only does the senior team need to share their collective maps and assumptions about the future and how their vision is to be achieved, they need to canvass others in the organisation for support. A guiding philosophy cannot guide if a large proportion of staff do not understand it or disagree with it.

THE EXPERTISE CAPABILITY

Functional knowledge

The executive's functional expertise influences what the executive focuses on, the structures they create for themselves and others and, often, is very much tied up with the individual's personal identity. Most executives are likely to have been brought up within a particular functional area and will have developed a high degree of expertise in their chosen discipline. Indeed, the executive's expertise is a vital contributor to effectiveness: it can also be a potential hindrance. Unless executives can see beyond their own discipline, the structures they create and the actions they take will be less than optimum.

Extreme specialisation in one area can dramatically impact the individual's overall effectiveness in personal and professional situations. It can affect an individual or group's ability to think, learn, solve problems and interact with others. For instance, individuals with specialised styles may have a blind spot in the ways they take in information, sort data and respond to situations. This can often lead to misunderstanding between individuals.

Withdrawing into or revelling in narrow functional specialisms at a senior level can be problematic. Although functional knowledge and expertise may give us satisfaction and make us feel comfortable, it can also narrow our focus and affect our capacity to prioritise. As a result, we may focus on areas which we know something about and feel competent dealing with, but which are neither Critical nor Constructive. Indeed, this problem can occur at the group or organisational level and cause communication breakdowns and cost to the organisation as a whole. For instance, Grindley (1991) has highlighted several problems when technical experts acquire board level positions. In some cases, IT directors have been appointed to the main board in order to close the so-called culture gap between IT staff and the rest of the company. However, instead of closing the gap the effect has been to widen it:

> The board often feels that it can relax, now that it has one of its own members looking after computers. The worry is that, faced with the culture gap and the insistence on showing artificial 'value for money' statements to back up their proposals, many IT directors are implementing the systems they believe are in the company's interests by means of hidden agendas.[15]

Thus, the executive needs to look beyond their initial area of expertise and be wary of others who cannot. However, given the range of expert knowledge that is possible, what should the executive concentrate on, where should they draw the line? Clearly, this depends to some extent on the business they are in. There is a growing body of research to suggest that functional background has implications for the industry and strategic situations faced by the executive. For instance, Hall (1976) found that firms in technologically sophisticated industries tended to have CEOs with technical backgrounds. CEOs in less technologically sophisticated industries had marketing and sales backgrounds. As pointed out previously, executives with expertise in production and cost control are more likely to be found in companies pursuing defensive strategies, while research and development expertise is more likely in 'prospector' firms.

Other approaches have attempted to highlight the areas of expertise top managers need in general. For instance, a large international survey found that CEOs ranked Strategy Formulation, Marketing/Sales, Human Resource Management and Negotiation/ Conflict Resolution as being the most important qualities needed up to the year 2000.[16] Although not neglected in this survey, financial expertise is also often emphasised. In the UK in recent years, the lack of financial expertise at board level has been the cause of particular concern.

Industry knowledge

As well as an understanding of additional technical areas of expertise, the executive also needs a solid industry knowledge. Kotter (1982) argues that successful general managers need to have detailed knowledge of the business they are managing. As Gabarro (1988) points out, lack of industry experience is likely to make it more difficult for executives to 'take charge' of their new positions and requires more learning and assimilation from them.

Many executives do, however, survive and prosper in new industries. John Sculley, ex-CEO of Apple, moved into the computer industry from Pepsi, the soft drink manufacturer. Bob Mansfield, originally at McDonalds, was appointed CEO of Optus communications in Australia. In 1992 the Optus board debated at some length which was more important – functional or generalist skills. However, while Mansfield knew little about telecommunications he was not lacking in several areas of expertise. A closer inspection of his background reveals a broad diversity of experience – including experience of managing start-up businesses, making acquisitions and being a high energy, motivating manager.[17] Once appointed, technical expertise was provided by the technocrats surrounding Mansfield (who average about 25 years in the industry) with Ian Boatman (ex-Mercury/UK) as Optus' Chief Operating Officer. What may be important is that the top team has the required expertise – rather than one person.

Overall, Mansfield's appointment highlighted that it is a combination of qualities which is important. What form these take will vary. Those with a lack of industry knowledge will usually bring a broader range of skills to a position which may, in the longer term, be just as valuable. Therefore, functional and industry expertise, whilst important, must be seen within a broader range of Capabilities.

SUMMARY

The Actioning/Structuring Capability is one of the most vital qualities needed at a senior level. It translates the executive's knowledge and skills (discussed in the previous chapters) into effective action. It is this Capability which helps executives maintain a high degree of energy in a very demanding role and provides a structure and direction for themselves and others.

The Expertise Capability has also been discussed. It is concerned with the functional knowledge of the executive and can be a vital contributor to effectiveness. It can also be a hindrance, however, if the executive is unable to see beyond his or her own particular discipline.

The majority of the chapter has been devoted to the Actioning/ Structuring Capability. Executives need to understand what motivates them so that they can maintain their energy. It is important that they understand how they mentally map out the world. This includes understanding what values they hold, their goals, agendas, priorities, areas of expertise and beliefs about what is important. They also need to think about the external structures and plans they create which act as a framework within which they and others can operate. Finally, these must be consistent with the overall purpose and vision of the individual and organisation.

Creating a vision at both a personal and corporate level can be exacting. However, without some tangible end-picture, the executive's capacity to choose between conflicting priorities, allocate resources and assess individual and corporate success, will be prone to doubt and uncertainty. As discussed in the final chapter, this end-picture is central to the executive role and the development of strategic leadership.

NOTES

1. Comments by Phil Lader (Bond University, Australia) who worked for Al Dunlap, MD of Consolidated Press Holdings, in the mid-80s. See *The Weekend Australian*, 6–7 June 1992.
2. Example quoted in Alex Taylor's article, 'GM's $11,000,000,000 Turnaround', *Fortune*, vol. 130, no. 8, 17 October 1994, 38–54.
3. Stratford Sherman, 'Is He Too Cautious to Save IBM?', *Fortune*, vol. 130, no. 7, 3 October 1994, 46–55.
4. Haire *et al.* (1966).
5. Hall and Donnell (1979).
6. Mills (1985).
7. Cox and Cooper (1988).

8. Alex Taylor III, 'Can GM Remodel Itself?', *Fortune*, vol. 125, no. 1, 13 January 1992, 20–6.

9. See John McCarthy and Jill Morrell's (1993) account of their ordeal, *Some Other Rainbow*, London: Bantam Press.

10. Gary Hamel and C. K. Prahalad, 'Seeing the Future First', *Fortune*, 5 September 1994, 72–6. This article is taken from their book *Competing for the Future*, Harvard Business School Press, Boston, 1994.

11. Study by McKinsey, 'Leveraging CEO Time' cited in Alan Deutschman's article, 'The CEO's Secret of Managing Time', *Fortune*, vol. 125, no. 13, 29 June 1992, 79–84.

12. See Mintzberg (1973) and Kotter (1982).

13. See Stephanie Winston's books, *Getting Organized* (1978) and *The Organized Executive* (1983).

14. See Jane Bird, 'Senior Service', *Management Today*, May 1994, 84–8.

15. *The Australian*, Tuesday, 17 March 1992.

16. *Reinventing the CEO: A Joint Study* by Korn/Ferry International and Columbia University Graduate School of Business, New York, 1988.

17. *The Australian*, Wednesday, 3 June 1992.

11   Strategic Leadership

INTRODUCTION

Senior managers are struggling to adapt themselves and their organisations to the 21st century business world that is rapidly approaching. Some argue we are not so much entering a new century – but a new era. It is one which will be characterised by the spread of market economies, the acceleration of technological progress and the freer flow of information, funds and skills throughout the world economy.

In order to thrive in this environment – rather than simply survive – companies are having to find ways to compete on a global basis. Many are trying to create further economies of scale, to find ways of selling better quality products at lower cost worldwide, or offer customised services in dozens of countries adapted to local needs. Across industries, organisations are forging networks of alliances with a range of players – including competitors, suppliers and customers. They are also experimenting with new tools, techniques and structures in an effort to make their organisations more responsive and adaptive to market needs.

Against this backdrop of change, the executive's capacity to discern a strategy for the organisation – and display the leadership skills needed to implement it – is critical. Often referred to under the heading of 'strategic leadership', this is seen by many practitioners and academics as the crucial managerial challenge confronting business organisations today.[1] Strategic leadership involves the ability to combine strategic thought with strategic action, and translate these into strategic direction and strategic change. This potential to combine strategic thought with action distinguishes the senior executive position from other levels in the organisation.

The processes needed to create and sustain new strategic directions require a range of behavioural and cognitive qualities. However, as Nutt and Backoff (1993) argue, the relationships (and indeed the conflicts) posed by a process meant to create and implement strategy have not been widely discussed. In this chapter, we argue that the Capabilities identified in our research can be used to illustrate the kinds of qualities needed by executives in order to provide strategic leadership. First, however, we start by examining the notions of strategy and leadership, how these have typically been understood and how they contribute to understanding strategic leadership.

STRATEGY AND LEADERSHIP

Bartlett and Ghoshal (1994) believe that the capacity of top managers to provide effective strategic leadership has been eroded over the past decade. The results of their study of 20 major US, European and Japanese institutions highlights some of the difficulties top managers face. For example, executives experienced problems reconciling strategies produced at different levels in the organisation. They had difficulty developing vision statements which would communicate and motivate. Moreover, senior managers found it increasingly difficult to stay in touch with developments of potential strategic importance.

However, while there is a clear need for effective strategic leadership within organisations, it is an illusive concept. Hambrick (1989) sees strategic leadership as focusing '. . . on the people who have overall responsibility for an organisation – their characteristics, what they do and how they do it'. It is concerned with the external and internal spheres of the organisation, dealing with ambiguity, complexity and the management of others. However, he also admits that strategic leadership is 'relatively diffuse and unchartered' and in fact there are several different interpretations of the term.

One reason for this may be due to the ways the core concepts of strategy and leadership are portrayed. Below, we highlight those aspects which are typically emphasised in each of these areas. The tendency to downplay some aspects at the expense of others, may in turn have restricted the focus on what it takes to provide strategic leadership at senior levels.

Strategy

Strategy is positioned at one end of the spectrum presented in Figure 11.1. Strategy is a term fraught with problems. Pearson (1990) argues that 'strategy, if such a thing exists, . . . is confused and incomplete', that strategy can be about anything and strategy theory seems muddled and its 'practice is often a mess'. However, he also

Fig. 11.1 *Strategic leadership in context*

argues that strategy is about the 'most important of management responsibilities, capable of the most profound impacts on corporate development and success'.

The most common view of strategy is that it is a plan, or set of guidelines intended to influence behaviour in the future. Chandler (1962) describes it as '. . . the determination of the basic long term goals and objectives of an enterprise, and the adoption of courses of action and the allocation of resources necessary for carrying out these goals'. Johnson and Scholes (1993) see strategy similarly as '. . . the direction and scope of an organisation over the long term: ideally, which matches its resources to its changing environment and in particular its markets, customers or clients so as to meet stakeholder expectations'.

As well as a set of intentions expressed through a plan, strategy can also be seen in terms of what people do, the decisions which are actually taken and whether there is any pattern to this process. Mintzberg and Waters (1983) point out that the press infers the US president's strategy by finding a pattern in his behaviour. Competitors do the same thing, as do subordinates to try to understand the strategies of senior executives in a company.

The outcome is that strategy can be both intended and unintended. Despite the certainty often implied by the strategic planning process, in reality strategy is a much more fluid process which depends as much on the executive looking for and grasping opportunities as it does on attempts to identify and detail strengths, weaknesses, opportunities and threats. As Bliss (1992) notes intentions are only half of the strategy-creation process.

Johnson and Scholes (1993) offer a more complete view, high-lighting three main elements in the strategic management process:

(1) Strategic Analysis – understanding the strategic position of the organisation
(2) Strategic Choice – formulating, evaluating and choosing between possible courses of action
(3) Strategy Implementation – planning how the choice of strategy can be put into effect and managing the changes required

Seen in this light strategic theory and concepts are a powerful way to help the executive view their business and the future. Nevertheless – and while this is not true of all commentators – the typical emphasis in most strategic writing has been on strategy formulation, under-standing trends in the environment and developing a strategic direction for the company. For example, Davies (1991) argues that strategic management is firmly based in strategic planning. Faulkner and Johnson (1992) admit that strategy is often taught as though it were basically conceptual in nature. For their part, Nutt and Backoff (1993) point out that strategic management still seems to stress 'idea development'.

The point is not that the implementation process is ignored completely: rather, that the emphasis has predominantly been more on strategy formulation than exploring the associated issues of internal development and change (that is, towards the left of the spectrum depicted in Figure 11.1).

Leadership

Clearly, the development of a strategic direction is only part of the story. At the other end of the spectrum, and often the more challenging task for the executive, is to bring about change within the organisation in line with strategic intentions. This focus is typically found in the writings on leadership which emphasise the interpersonal skills needed to communicate, and engender support for, organisational goals.

In Chapter 1, we defined Leadership as the capacity to help others overcome hurdles to achieve a common goal. This involves a range of interpersonal and communication skills which help the executive energise or motivate staff to follow a particular path. It also involves providing the resources and context which will facilitate this process.

Leadership is intrinsically tied up with communicating a vision or end state. If this vision is to be an effective guide for others in the organisation, it must clearly take into account changes in the external environment. Some writers – particularly those concerned with 'visionary leadership' – tend to emphasise *both* the interpersonal and more strategic issues such as these. However, the vast majority, while acknowledging the importance of vision, view leadership as a process primarily involved with internal transformation. Thus, leadership is more often associated with strategy implementation and change than with strategy formulation and direction (that is, the right-hand side of Figure 11.1).

STRATEGIC LEADERSHIP – THE FOCUS FOR SENIOR EXECUTIVES

In practice, however, the executive cannot afford to be at either end of the spectrum. Increasingly, executives must have the capacity to think through new strategic initiatives and have the wherewithal to put these into practice. They need to tackle issues with a mindset which goes beyond the emphases traditionally found in approaches to strategy and leadership. They have to think and act more in terms of strategic leadership, a synthesis between creating strategic direction and managing strategic change (that is, the centre position in Figure 11.1).

In Chapter 1, we argued that senior executives are concerned with Establishing the current position of the organisation as well as its future direction. They also Enable themselves and others to follow that direction by ensuring the necessary organisational infrastructures are in place. They Enact – that is, take actions and make decisions – which are critical to maintain and progress the organisation. Thus, an ability to combine strategy formulation and bring about organisational change is essentially what the senior role is about. Clearly, there will be different strategic imperatives for executives at different levels of the organisation and many will formulate strategy within a broader, corporate context. As we discuss later, however, an overall strategic purpose at corporate level should not blind executives at the business unit level to the need to provide strategic leadership.

Despite their importance, the qualities needed for strategic leadership are not, according to Nahavandi and Malekzadeh (1993), well researched. Nevertheless, some understanding of what is required can be gained from looking at the Capabilities and linking these to different elements of strategic leadership (see Figure 11.2). Let us begin by looking at the Capabilities needed for strategic thinking.

Strategic thinking

The cognitive capacity, thought processes and mindset of the executive underlie everything the strategic leader does (see Figure 11.2). However, there is some doubt over the quality of thought that is expended on strategic issues. One CEO comments, 'Highly skilled, visionary, innovative, strategic thinkers are now a highly valued breed of manager and they are rare'.[2] Nadler (1994) argues that in many organisations 'there's too much strategic planning and not enough strategic thinking'. In his experience, 'too much time is spent on analysis that ultimately influences very little behaviour, and too little time is spent on the creative process of thinking about forming, acting on, and learning about strategy.'

Strategic thinking is affected by many things. For instance, the way the planning process is structured can either help or hinder strategic thinking in an organisation. Planning may not involve the right people, it may be too rigid in design and inhibit discussion and the surfacing of new ideas. It may also fail to surface the assumptions senior people have about their organisation, its capabilities and the future direction of the industry.

Similarly, there will be a number of other factors influencing the individual's capacity to think in a strategic way. As Ibrahim and Kelly (1986) note, strategy involves a decision, a choice made by a leader. Like any decision making process, this will be filtered by our perception, personalities, motivation and expectations. Thus, to understand strategy one also needs to understand the decision maker, the strategist, his/her personality, values and motivation (see Chapter 2).

Most critically, executives have to learn to think outside the boundaries of what has made them successful in the past. For

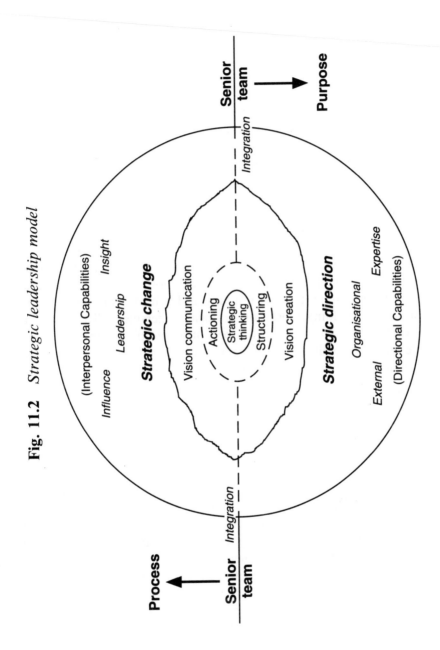

Fig. 11.2 *Strategic leadership model*

individuals, this may involve becoming less reliant on their core functional expertise. For executive teams, this may mean looking beyond their long held assumptions about the competition and ways of competing. Within the organisation as a whole, it may mean accepting that success is often fleeting and that the resources and qualities which built the organisation in the past, may not sustain it in the future.

If these mental traps are to be avoided, executives need to be prepared to challenge their assumptions as well as how they think. Developing strategy may not simply involve adopting different ideas, it may mean reframing the mental models one holds about a whole host of factors such as the strength of the competition, the limits of technology and the speed of one's competitive response. Unless attempts to reframe the way we think and behave are made, no radical strategic alternatives are likely to emerge or be implemented.

Pattern reframing is not easy, and is a process where conflict is most likely to occur, both within ourselves and between others (see Chapter 3). Nevertheless, it is the focal point of likely strategic success. Changing patterns of thinking and behaving are possibly the most critical building blocks of strategic leadership. All the data in the world, the best analysis, the best strategic plans, and the most noble intentions will never see the light of day unless executives have the capacity to change the way they think about these data and plans.

DEVELOPING STRATEGIC DIRECTION

Vision and the action/structuring capability

Another central element for the executive is the capacity to create a direction or vision for the organisation. Indeed, Nadler and Tushman (1988b) argue, perhaps the most critical demand on the executive is to develop a vision of his or her organisation's strategic position within a competitive industry environment.

Vision is an aspect of the executive's Action/Structuring Capability and is the vital link between strategy creation and organisation change (see Figure 11.2). Vision involves the creation of some kind of framework which will be sufficiently compelling to help motivate the individual executive and others in the organisation to move forward. For example, for over 20 years Komatsu's vision was to 'catch up and surpass Caterpillar'.[3] At first, few believed this could be done –

including Japan's influential trade organisation, MITI. However, each year, Komatsu's President, Kawai, would set a specific goal (such as improving product quality or reducing costs) using its arch competitor, Caterpillar, as the benchmark to outperform. Detailed operating plans were then developed and implemented using a system created by Kawai called PDCA (plan, do, check, act). By the early 1980s Komatsu had become Caterpillar's most serious competitor in the construction equipment market.

Thus, Kawai was able to establish a vision which helped motivate and focus people on the strategy of the organisation and then translate this into short-term operating targets. Interestingly, in the late 1980s the market changed and the goal of beating Caterpillar proved too narrow a focus. Again, however, vision, structure and planning were used by Kawai's successor to help redefine the organisation's strategic direction. A new banner of 'Growth, Global, Groupwide' was used to encourage managers to find new growth opportunities through market expansion using the organisation's core competencies.

Although, Komatsu succeeded in getting itself back on track, one cannot underestimate the difficulties faced by senior executives in similar positions. It is often exceedingly difficult to make sense of the chaos around us. And yet, it is the capacity to create structure from chaos and translate this into a long-term goal, as well as shorter-term deliverables, that is central to strategic leadership.

Directional capabilities

In order to develop a structure and a vision, the executive needs to have well-developed Directional Capabilities (that is, the Expertise, External and Organisational Capabilities shown in the bottom half of Figure 11.2). They must have the expertise to understand and manage the critical technical business issues both now and in the future. They must also have a strategic grasp of the external environment as well as the capacity to shape their organisation to respond.

One of the critical ways to achieve this is to identify and develop organisational core competencies. Organisational competencies are factors, such as quality, speed, flexibility, manufacturing expertise, around which the organisation builds a sustainable competitive advantage. Examples include R&D at Merck, marketing and promotion at Philip Morris and 3M's capacity to develop and innovate. As Hitt and Keats (1992) note, the ability to develop and utilise competencies across separate businesses, markets and locations may be distinctive and highly difficult to imitate by competitors, thereby creating a sustained competitive advantage.

Hamel argues that core competencies should be described in terms of benefits.[4] However, not all organisations use their resources, for instance, their staff's commitment, their technology, their information capital, in ways which benefit the organisation strategically. For example, despite the turnaround at Xerox during the 1980s, and its subsequent return to profitability, it was also the birthplace of the lap-top computer, icons, the mouse, laser printing and networks. It lost the opportunity to leverage these competencies because it saw its core strength in the photocopying business.

Competency building is a deliberate process. It is of little use, however, if the executive cannot spot market opportunities where competencies can be exploited. As Nadler and Tushman (1988b) argue, without an understanding of the industrial/environmental context it is not possible to recognise the situations in which strategic choice is required. Moreover, this process is dynamic. Core competencies evolve and adapt over time: the executive must be able to recognise when change is required.

Thus, in summary, the critical qualities needed to help the executive develop a strategic direction for the firm are to:

- Think strategically – challenge assumptions, change patterns of thinking
- Create a longer-term vision for the organisation
- Understand the external competitive environment
- Identify and enhance the core competencies of the organisation

CREATING STRATEGIC CHANGE – THE INTERPERSONAL CAPABILITIES

A number of Capabilities help the executive create strategic change. As we discussed in Chapter 10 (and earlier in this chapter), the Actioning/Structuring Capability helps executives create structures and frameworks which give focus and purpose to their actions. As the name implies, this Capability is also concerned with taking action which brings about strategic change.

Actions which bring about strategic change are based on the Interpersonal Capabilities (that is, Leadership, Insight, Integration and Influence). These play a critical role in helping the executive communicate the vision, develop and craft the organisation, in terms of its structure, systems, tasks and culture and move it towards its end goals (see the top half of Figure 11.2).

This is where the traditional notion of leadership comes to the fore. It is where, as Nutt and Backoff (1993) argue, effective guidance is provided and where the effective leader must mobilise, inspire and commit others to a course of action. In Chapter 5, we explored how the Leadership Capability can help executives inspire and mobilise others through a process of 'energising'. However, we also pointed out that leaders have to go beyond this and also 'empower' others, not just with great words, but by providing them with the tools to do the job and the environment, culture and structure in which to do it.

While all these elements are important, strategic leadership requires something more. It also requires an acceptance and ability to manage the realities of organisational life. To bring about change, particularly when dealing with entrenched and powerful stakeholders, the strategic leader needs to employ a range of skills, including a capacity to influence laterally within the organisation and externally.

Nutt and Backoff's (1993) research into public organisations highlights the necessity for an influence capability in bringing about strategic change. Most public organisations have stakeholders who may not support a long-term vision involving transformational change. A strategic leader can attempt to 'win over' these stakeholders and get them to become active supporters. However, for example, civil servants know they can often wait out leaders whom they distrust or disagree with. Indeed, in any organisation that has people with divided loyalties, leaders with short tenure and pervasive but subtle control being exercised from many quarters, bringing about strategic change can be a formidable challenge.

Teams and strategic leadership

This need to influence a range of players and the dependence of executives on support from others when carrying out strategic change, highlights the necessity for another critical, executive capability. The Integration Capability is concerned with building the senior executive team and integrating other important individuals and groups within the organisation as a whole. It is placed outside the main circle in Figure 11.2 to emphasise that executives have to bring others into their thinking and intentions, if they are to lead the organisation successfully.

One of the key groups the executive needs to work with is the executive team. In Chapter 6, we argued that in changing environments, where there is some synergy to be gained between functional or business units, the senior team is a vital resource. A senior team can provide a greater variety of perspectives on what is happening in the competitive environment. It can also contribute towards and reinforce the vision of the organisation.

It takes a particular skill, however, to focus the executive team on the longer-term purpose of the organisation, as opposed to short-term, operational issues. It is even more difficult to harness the collective knowledge and insights of those on the executive team for this involves such skills as the capacity to listen and the ability to deal with and manage conflict.

As we discussed in Chapter 6, the team can only do this if members are used to discussing and managing how the work gets done (that is, Team Process). If the processes are not right, the ramifications on others can be quite severe. It only takes a few powerful executives on the top team to stop a strategy being implemented. The importance of the senior team and its development in the strategic leadership process, therefore, cannot be emphasised enough.

The implication of this is that strategic leadership is not confined to one person. Indeed, as Gupta (1986) notes, the key decision makers in any succession event should at least consider the relationship between the dominant coalition and the strategic context, as much as how well an individual general manager might manage in different strategic scenarios.

STRATEGIC LEADERSHIP AS A MATCHING PROCESS

So far, strategic leadership has been defined as the ability to create a strategic direction for the organisation and bring about organisational change. This definition is not uncommon – indeed, the premise on which strategy is taught on many general management courses is that developing strategic direction and bringing about organisational change should be viewed together.

By contrast, the practice in many companies is to match individual leaders to particular strategic contexts, where the strategy has already been formulated. Nahavandi and Malekzadeh (1993) note the field of strategy has largely adopted a contingency approach, matching leaders' characteristics to particular situations to produce the most effective performance. Gupta (1986) also notes that the dominant view for achieving successful strategy implementation stresses that the choice of SBU general managers (or corporate CEOs) should be contingent on the type of strategy being implemented. The central assumption is that strategies are set prior to executive selection, with the focus on the role the leader plays in the implementation process rather than in the formulation of strategy.

Gupta (1986) points out that many organisations appoint executives based on this assumption. For example, Chase Manhattan Bank, Texas Instruments, Corning Glass and General Electric link executive selection to their strategic requirements.

Matching leaders to organisational life cycles

This practice can be beneficial both to the organisation and the individual executive. In theory at least, the executive should be more effective when they are well matched to the strategic circumstances. Matching managers to strategic contexts, usually takes one of two forms. The first of these was highlighted by Ansoff (1965) 30 years ago when he suggested that 'general management capability' should be modified to match different stages in the organisation life cycle. Rothschild (1993) also argues there is 'no one leader for all seasons' and instead argues that businesses should be led by one of four types of leader: Risktakers (such as the highly successful entrepreneur, Bill Gates of Microsoft); Caretakers (whose role is to nurture and build an organisation during the growth phase); Surgeons (for example, who make the necessary cuts in a mature business – such as Lee Iaccoca of Chrysler); and Undertakers (who redeploy or wind down operations).

Although there are other examples of this approach of matching managers to the life cycle of a business (for example, Ibrahim and Kelly, 1986), the categorisations are usually more sophisticated. Gerstein and Reisman (1983), for instance, highlight seven strategic situations: startup, turnaround, exact profit/rationalise, dynamic growth/existing business, deployment in effort in business, liquidation/divestiture, and new acquisition. They see these different strategic situations as shaping the core requirements for success in the job, and which in turn indicate the requirements of ideal candidates.

Boam and Sparrow (1992) point out that the practice of matching managers to different business life-cycle situations has been evident in the competency area. McBeath (1990) has described how BAT industries built an assessment of the different business scenarios and associated competency profiles based on the views of their top 200 managers. Boam and Sparrow (1992) outline a number of generic competencies that should be considered in different business scenarios (Table 11.1).[5] These can also help individual executives understand what kind of qualities are most appropriate in these situations.

Matching leaders to general industry strategies

The second approach is to relate individual qualities to general strategic approaches. As we highlighted in Chapter 5, two classifications in particular have been commonly used; that of Miles and Snow (1978) who uses the concepts of defender/analyser/prospector, and that of Porter (1980) who relies on the concepts of cost leadership and differentiation.

The 'defender' and 'cost leadership' approaches are low-risk strategies that are production and efficiency orientated and focus on well-defined markets and domains. Both strategies require centralised control and autocratic decision making and mechanistic structures in order to succeed. Gupta (1986) argues that a low-cost strategy depends on an ability to maximise internal throughput efficiency through tight operational and financial controls. Nahavandi and Malekzadeh (1993) argue that low challenge seekers are likely to select cost leadership strategies which focus on tried and true methods and mechanisms.

In contrast, 'prospector' and 'differentiation' strategies are high risk, innovative and R&D oriented and focus on growth and marketing opportunities. These strategies require decentralised control, participative decision making and organic structures. Gupta (1986) argues that for a differentiation strategy to succeed, industry knowledge, marketing and product R&D skills, and the ability to foster creativity are critical. High challenge seekers are likely to

Table 11.1 Business scenarios and associated management characteristics

Scenarios	Start up	Turnaround	Dynamic growth	Extracting profit	Redeploying efforts
Management characteristics	• Vision of finished business • Hands-on orientation • In-depth knowledge in critical technical areas • Organising ability • Staffing skills • Team-building capabilities • High energy level/stamina • Personal magnetism/charisma • Broad knowledge of all key functions • Creating vision of business • Establishing core technical and marketing expertise • Building management team	• 'Take charge' orientation • Strong leader • Strong analytical and diagnostic skills, especially financial • Excellent business strategist • High energy level • Risk-taker • Handles pressure well • Good crisis management skills • Good negotiator • Rapid accurate problem diagnosis • Fixing short-term and ultimately long-term problems	• Excellent strategic and financial planning skills • Clear vision of the future • Ability to balance priorities • Organisational and team-building skills • Good crisis-management skills • Moderately high risk-taker • Excellent staffing skills • Increasing market share in key sectors • Managing rapid change • Ability to build towards clear vision of the future	• Technically knowledgeable • Knows the business • Sensitive to changes • Ear to the ground • Anticipates problems • Strong administrative skills • Orientated to systems • Strong relationship orientation • Recognizes need for management succession • Stresses efficiency • Work towards stability • Senses signs of change	• Good politician/master of change • Highly persuasive – high interpersonal influence • Moderate risk-taker • Highly supportive, sensitive to people • Excellent 'system thinker' • Good organising and executive staffing skills • Established effectiveness in managing change • Supporting the dispossessed

Source: Boam and Sparrow (1992). See also note 5.

engage in high-risk strategies and therefore are likely to select differentiation strategies according to Nahavandi and Malekzadeh (1993).

The process of strategic selection

Matching executives to strategic situations is usually based on a process which involves identifying the strategic situation, developing specific job requirements and then itemising the individual qualities needed for the job. The Capabilities can be used as a basis for doing this. First, the strategic situation is identified and the more detailed job requirements are itemised for each Capability. Based on the items in Table 11.1 and our own factors, Table 11.2 suggests which qualities within the Capabilities are needed for different strategic scenarios. The table illustrates how the Capabilities can be applied rather than presenting a complete list. Nevertheless, it does provide a starting point for reviewing which aspects of the Capabilities are most necessary in different strategic contexts.[6] (The Development capability has not been included as the implication of the whole diagram is one of development and change for the executive.)

This approach to leadership has some merit. The assumption, as Gupta (1986) notes, is that strategies differ across organisations and over time. Consequently, different managerial skills will be more useful in some contexts than others. Moreover, as managers differ in the skills and orientations they bring to their position it follows that a systematic matching of managers to strategies will yield superior performance. This has benefits for the corporation in terms of getting the most able person for that strategic context. It also has benefits for the executive who only needs to concentrate on one strategic context. The more he or she can understand that context and has the appropriate Capabilities for it, in theory, the more successful this individual will be in that role. Moreover, the principles involved in this process are useful even outside the formal selection process. They give the executive some idea of the different kinds of characteristics that are more critical in different situations.

In essence, however, such approaches are about selecting different types of leader to match different strategic scenarios. Executives are picked to lead in a particular strategic context – or existing executives are asked to change their style to suit the strategy. Either way, this is

Table 11.2 Capabilities and different strategic scenarios

Capabilities	Start up	Turnaround	Dynamic growth	Extracting profit	Redeploying efforts
			Scenarios		
Cognitive	Analyses new situations and spots opportunities	Rapid accurate problem diagnosis	Sound decision making under pressure	Anticipates problems	Understands complex systems
Maturity	Extremely high risk-taker	Handles pressure well Risk-taker	Moderately high risk-taker	Ability to maintain momentum	Moderate risk-taker
Leadership	Personal magnetism/ charisma Hands-on orientation	Strong leader 'Take charge' orientation	Ability to maintain focus and keep others on track	Strong relationship orientation Works towards stability	Ability to take tough actions Supporting the dispossessed
Insight	Understands concerns of a range of influential actors	Ability to see areas of resistance and hidden agendas	Can see how to reward for effort and risk taking	Sensitive to changes Ear to the ground	Sensitive to people's skills, abilities & motives
Integration	Overall team building skills	Brings diverse parts of the business together and achieves focus	Capacity to focus the team and maintain team processes	Establish strong teams and well integrated departments	Ability to reform teams and reintegrate
Influence	Can convince a broad base of people to commit to the future	Negotiates well with a range of stakeholders	Can understand and manage shifting power bases	Maintain good relationships	Break up old power bases and reform alliances

Table 11.2 cont.

External	Understands core customers and major external players	Ability to evaluate true business position	Understand market share opportunities in key sectors	Establish strong relationships with customers and suppliers	Can see longer-term market opportunities
Organisational	Staffing skills Establishes core organisational systems	Restructuring ability Changing culture	Managing rapid change Excellent staffing skills	Orientated to systems Stresses efficiency Recognises need for management succession	Capacity to re-engineer systems and structures
Expertise	In depth knowledge of critical technical areas Broad knowledge of all key functions	Sound financial skills	Research & development Product technology	Technically knowledgeable Knows the business	Strong financial and system skills
Actioning/ structuring	High energy level Organising ability Creates vision of business	High energy level Good crisis management skills Fixes short and long-term problems	Clear future vision Excellent strategic and financial planning skills Good crisis management Ability to balance priorities	Strong administrative skills	Ability to set medium term priorities and follow through

what we would term 'executive leadership' rather than strategic leadership.

Indeed, there may be problems with such an approach. As Gupta (1986) points out, it may be demotivational if the manager is typecast and consistently matched to one type of strategic situation. It can also restrict the development of the executive and what is needed at a senior level. The higher one goes in the organisation the more SBUs there may be to manage. This gives rise to an increase in the diversity of strategic contexts across these SBUs. If the executive has been confined to one particular type of strategic context, for example creating new businesses or maximising short-term cash flow, there is a high probability that those SBUs whose strategies are foreign to the executive's experience will be either neglected or mismanaged. Consequently, in most corporations, exposure to, and experience of, managing different kinds of strategies and businesses needs to be viewed as an essential component of management development.

STRATEGIC LEADERSHIP AND EXECUTIVE LEVEL

The last point highlights that strategic leadership is likely to be more critical in some situations than others. Much will depend on the strategic requirements of the executive's role. As mentioned earlier, there are different levels of strategy which require different responses. Johnson and Scholes (1993) identify three major levels of strategy. The first of these is corporate strategy which is concerned with the overall scope of the organisation. It looks at how the organisation should be run in structural and financial terms and how resources are to be allocated to the various operations. The second level is business strategy which is more likely to be related to a business unit within the overall organisation. Here, strategy is concerned with how to compete in a given market and which products or services to develop. The third level is operational strategy which is concerned with how the different functions of the enterprise, marketing, finance and so forth, contribute to other levels of strategy.

Corporate strategy does not need to be completely in the hands of those at the very top. In an article describing the changing role of top management, Bartlett and Ghoshal (1994) challenge one of the long-standing assumptions 'that the CEO should be the corporation's chief strategist, assuming full control of setting the company's objectives and determining its priorities'. In practice, a number of other senior executives will be involved.

However, if a matching process is to occur, it would seem to be more appropriate at the lower levels of the executive hierarchy where a manager is likely to be responsible for only one SBU, rather than at higher levels where the management of several SBUs requires a much broader range of strategic ability. Nevertheless, even matching at the single SBU level has its downsides. As Gupta (1986) notes, even those executives who deal with one particular strategic context need to be able to respond outside of the life-cycle constraints of growth or decline and so on.

At all levels, therefore, senior executives are faced with a need for flexibility and responsiveness. This is particularly necessary under conditions of great uncertainty and rapid change. Moreover, product life cycles are getting shorter. The shorter the cycle and the more unpredictable the transition from one stage to another, the more important it is to have strategic flexibility and strategic leadership in the sense defined in this chapter.

Thus, there is a case for both executive leadership – which relies on matching executives to strategic contexts – and strategic leadership where executives both formulate and implement strategy. We believe the emphasis, however, should be on finding ways to develop strategic leaders given the increasingly complex and turbulent environments executives must contend with.

Changing capabilities

Here, we have argued that strategic leadership requires the full range of Capabilities. However, what is emphasised within each capability and its degree of importance will change depending on circumstances (see Chapter 1). Quinn (1988) points out that what constitutes effective performance will inevitably be dynamic and changing. As an organisation experiences different business scenarios, or itself matures, then the relevance of any one factor is bound to change.

Boam and Sparrow (1992) help to explain the possible dynamic and strategic nature of the Capabilities by putting forward their notion of competency life cycles. They suggest four different types of competency – emerging, maturing, transitional and core. Emerging competencies are currently less relevant, but will receive greater emphasis in the future. Maturing competencies will become increasingly less relevant in the future, although they may have been important in the past. Transitional competencies are necessary for a short period of time, often in unique circumstances. Finally, core competencies will always be important and remain vital to effectiveness whatever the changing strategic requirements.

We view the Capabilities as core elements. Leadership, influence, cognitive capacity, an ability to understand the external and organisational environments and so on, will always be necessary skills at senior levels. However, as we have argued throughout, these need to be customised depending on individual circumstances and changes in the strategic context. Thus, although the generic framework will remain, there will be different emphases and priorities within it. In Boam and Sparrow's terms, the various capabilities may be emerging, maturing or transitional.

As Vicere (1992) points out, if the strategic context changes this does not necessarily mean that the leader needs to be replaced. However, it does mean that the strategic leader needs to recognise these external changes and how these may impact on the Capabilities needed to do the job. If the emphasis does indeed change, they need to be able to adapt personally as a result.

SUMMARY

Strategic leadership is regarded as the crucial managerial challenge confronting business organisations today. Executives must discern a strategy for the organisation and display the leadership skills required to implement it.

This chapter has examined how the Capabilities relate to strategic leadership. It has described the pivotal nature of strategic thinking and vision and highlights those Capabilities which help the executive develop a strategic direction for the organisation. It has also focused on the 'softer', interpersonal skills executives need to embark on strategic change. Executives need skills to help them build and lead senior teams as well as insight and influence to realign other powerful stakeholders both within, and outside, the organisation. We also distinguish between the leadership skills needed to guide, inspire and empower others, and the full range of Capabilities required to provide strategic leadership.

Finally, the various approaches organisations use to select individual executives to manage different strategic contexts have been examined. Strategy is developed at several levels in the organisation and often, executives are matched to different strategic contexts. Whilst this may be expedient, in future we believe the real challenge is to develop flexible, dynamic and capable executives who can respond to a range of strategic circumstances, rather than simply be typecast to manage one particular strategic situation.

NOTES

1. See Liam Fahey and Samuel Felton, 'The New Strategic Leadership', *Planning Review*, vol. 21, no. 5, September/October, 1994.
2. Quoted in Harper (1992).
3. Cited in Bartlett and Ghoshal (1994).
4. Cited in Bernard Reimann's conference report, 'Gary Hamel: How to Compete for the Future', *Planning Review*, September/October, 1994, 39–43.
5. This table is based on the work of Child (1984) and Whetten and Cameron (1984), but also draws heavily on Gerstein and Reisman (1983).
6. For similar approaches see Nadler and Gerstein (1992b) and Gerstein and Reisman (1983).

Appendix   Senior Executive Capabilities Research

INTRODUCTION

The purpose of this book has been to explore what is known about senior executives and the qualities they need to operate effectively in senior management positions. In so doing, we have incorporated the views of a range of writers and researchers spanning the disciplines of managerial and organisational behaviour, psychology and strategy. We have used our own research findings as a platform to review this material and structure our discussion. For those who are interested, therefore, we have outlined below the research methods used to identify the Capabilities and highlight our principal findings. (A more detailed research paper is available from the authors.)

RESEARCH STAGES

The research was carried out in two stages in the UK and Australia. The first stage was concerned with exploring what is meant by senior executive effectiveness using qualitative methods. Data were gathered by various mechanisms including repertory-grid technique and in-depth interviews. The second stage was concerned with developing and testing our ideas. This was largely based on quantitative methods, using questionnaires and 360 degree evaluations of executives by peers, senior managers and staff.

First stage – exploratory research

The research was conducted over an eight-year period, starting in 1986. The early developmental research was concerned with identifying the characteristics that senior executives found to be important in effectively pursuing their work.[1] This involved using repertory grid technique and in-depth interviews of up to three hours duration, with 60 senior executives from seven major companies in the electronic, engineering and chemical industries. The repertory-grid technique provided a set of constructs from each manager which described their mental map of critical executive characteristics.

Over 500 different constructs were derived. Analysis, categorisation by external assessors and the removal of duplicating concepts reduced the constructs down to 40 different items or characteristics. These were then used as the basis for a 40-item questionnaire. This was administered to a further 30 executives in three separate companies who were asked to rate both themselves and their colleagues on each item in the questionnaire, on a five-point Likert scale.

Factor analysis of this data, produced three major groupings. This identified the Personal, Interpersonal and Directional Capability categories described in Chapter One.

Second stage – refinement and testing

The next stage involved defining, refining and developing these categorisations of senior executive behaviour and methods of testing them. Our aim was to produce a comprehensive framework which not only built on the main outcomes of the exploratory research, but also included critical behavioural factors highlighted by other researchers and writers on senior executives.

Additional in-depth interviews and a questionnaire were the main vehicles used to further the research. The questionnaire underwent four major revisions over a 12-month period and involved 153 executives. The questions were revised or replaced depending on their clarity and validity. The outcome was a reliable and valid self-questionnaire comprising 73 items which covered a comprehensive range of characteristics potentially related to executive effectiveness.

Our experience and reviews of the literature suggested that there were problems associated with investigating executive behaviour based on self-report data. For example, many researchers have reported the tendency for individuals to overrate their performance. Hence, we believed a more accurate picture could be obtained by getting an assessment of the executive's behaviour from several of their colleagues. Thus, in addition to the self-questionnaire, a similar 'others' questionnaire was developed which allowed higher level managers, peers and subordinates to assess the executive in relation to the items on the self-questionnaire.

In addition, a measure of effectiveness was also required. Again, the literature suggests that the use of self-assessments alone is unreliable. However, 'hard measures' such as financial targets, output, or increasing market share, while desirable, are also problematic. Such outcomes may not be directly attributable to the behaviour of the executive, particularly at senior levels where outcomes may be a result of a whole range of diverse factors. Moreover, such measures do not give comparability between executives in different companies and industries. As a result, we incorporated several items into the questionnaire which allowed colleagues to assess the executive's effectiveness and also to make comparisons between executives. The major basis of the effectiveness items was Tsui's (1984)[2] 'reputational effectiveness' scale, which she developed using a range of independent assessments including 'superior' ratings and performance outcomes.

Questionnaire reliability and validity

The questionnaire was administered to 20 senior executives and re-administered three weeks later. Test–retest reliability averaged .93. Internal reliability tests show strong Cronbach alphas ranging between .64 and .88.

Validity was assessed by asking a sample of 30 managers to evaluate the extent to which their own composite scores of the 11 Capabilities reflected their assessment of their strengths and weaknesses. The average ratings on a scale of 1 to 5 (1 . . . not a true reflection, 5 . . . very true) ranged from 4.3 to 4.7.

The same group of managers was asked to rate the 11 Capabilities in terms of how important each category was for effectiveness in their managerial job. The average scores ranged from between 4.0 to 4.6 for each of the Capabilities (that is, the ratings were between, 4 . . . very important and 5 . . . critical to their job).

RESULTS

A factor analysis and regression analysis was conducted on the data. The entire sample on which the factor analysis is based consists of

1065 executives and their staff and colleagues. The regression analysis is based on 700 individuals from this sample, that is, the colleagues of 140 senior executives covering a wide cross section of industries in the UK and Australian public and private sectors. Each of the 140 executives completed the 'self' questionnaire and a minimum of five colleagues completed the 'others' questionnaire on each executive.

Analysis

A factor analysis of the entire sample using principle factoring with iteration and oblimin rotation produced 12 factors with eigenvalues equal or greater than 1. This accounts for 60 per cent of the variance. Of these 12 factors, 11 factors were significant. Table 12.1 presents the 11 factors and the items which loaded significantly on each factor.

A regression analysis of the 11 factors was then performed. The 11 factors were entered as the independent variables and the effectiveness measure entered as the dependent variable. The results (Table 12.2) show a highly significant regression equation ($F = 154.4$ $p < .0001$). These factors, or Capabilities, explain over 70 per cent of the total variance.

All except one of the independent variables are statistically significant. The most significant variable is the Actioning/Structuring Capability (β .284). Also highly significant are the Leadership (β .238) and Influence (β .150) Capabilities. The Insight Capability did not add significantly to the result. It is, however, only marginally outside the significance level of $p > .05$. This last point, and the fact that several writers have highlighted the importance of insight in the literature, encouraged us to keep this variable as part of the model.

One variable is significantly correlated with effectiveness, but in a negative direction. This is the Expertise Capability (G). Examination of the items which make up this variable show that they are concerned with the executive's general expertise rather than specific functional or technical ability. The negative relationship suggests there may be a limit to how much of a generalist the executive needs to be. As we discuss in the book, the degree of expertise an executive should have is controversial, although this result indicates that specific technical expertise, rather than a completely generalist orientation, is necessary at senior levels.

Table 12.1 Significant factors

Factor A (Integration Capability)
7   They have team development skills
22 They provide an environment where others can perform at their best
49 They encourage others to develop effective teamwork in their own environments
35 They generally work to reach mutually beneficial outcomes
45 They allow others to have control over important issues where necessary
21 They frequently involve others in making decisions
63 They are able to get different groups and departments working together effectively

Factor B (Leadership Capability)
47 They build a good rapport with most people
33 They treat people with respect
36 They frequently help others find ways of overcoming their work problems
50 During periods of change people look to them for guidance
64 They can motivate others to attain higher levels of performance than they would normally achieve
8   People do things for them because they want to rather than because they have to
60 They understand what their staff need in order to develop in their jobs

Factor C (External Capability)
53 They have a good understanding of competitors and their intentions
67 They are aware of the implications of market changes for the business
11 They understand their customers' needs
25 They are aware of how changes in technology impact on the business
34 They have a strong network of contacts

Factor D (Cognitive Capability)
58 They are good at thinking through problems and finding a solution
30 They are good at analysing data and large amounts of information
10 They understand the technical issues necessary to fulfil their role
44 They seem to be able to understand complex issues without difficulty

Factor E (Development Capability)
43 They tend to experiment with new ideas and approaches
2   In general they are more willing to consider creative solutions to problems than other people
15 They are able to take on board feedback from others about their performance or ability
29 They welcome new situations and challenges
23 They try to find ways around hurdles they are faced with
3   They do not lose heart and give up when solutions to problems cannot be found readily

Factor F (Influence Capability)
6   Colleagues take notice of their views

20 They influence people outside their organisation successfully
48 They are able to influence superiors in order to achieve their goals
61 They communicate their views effectively to others
62 They have good negotiation skills
46 They show awareness of organisational politics
39 They are aware of the agendas of the major external stakeholders with regard to the business

Factor G (Expertise Capability)
24 They are regarded as a generalist rather than a technical specialist
38 They are not thrown by other people's technical input
66 They are able to stand back from the technical detail needed to do their job
69 They do not get caught up in the detail of their work at the expense of thinking about broader issues

Factor H (Actioning/Structuring Capability)
65 They can be depended on to get things done
37 They act on problems quickly
51 They ensure the important issues are followed through
27 They are able to prioritise things which are important
13 They have a long-term vision of the future for their department/business
9 They put a lot of energy into their job

Factor I (Organisational Capability)
68 They understand the impact that different communication methods can have on the organisation
26 They understand what needs to be done to improve the efficiency of the organisation as a whole
55 They show they have a good idea of the steps needed to achieve the goals of the organisation
12 They understand how their department/business should be organised to make it as effective as possible
40 They are capable of effectively implementing change in the organisation
54 They know what reward structures are necessary to improve the effectiveness of the organisation

Factor J (Maturity Capability)
16 They are willing to consider the different approaches of other people
31 They can cope with ambiguous situations
17 On issues important to them, they often take a stand even against strong opposition
59 They seem to be able to cope with the emotional strains of work

Factor K (Insight Capability)
18 They are able to understand the views of others
70 They understand what resources are needed by others to do their job
41 They understand the wider implications of their decisions
57 They seem to have thought deeply about their management strengths and weaknesses

Table 12.2 Regression analysis

Independent variables	β	F	Significance
A Integration Capability	.098	5.34	.0211
B Leadership Capability	.238	28.25	.0000
C External Capability	.058	3.89	.0487
D Cognitive Capability	.079	7.62	.0059
E Development Capability	.103	11.29	.0008
F Influence Capability	.150	18.16	.0000
G Expertise Capability	−.099	14.17	.0002
H Actioning/structuring Capability	.284	76.83	.0000
I Organisational Capability	.142	14.78	.0001
J Maturity Capability	.062	4.20	.0406
K Insight Capability	.056	3.81	.0511

Overall $F = 154.47$ Significance $= 0001$ adjusted $R^2 = 705$

Overall, the research shows that it is not any one factor (for example, the leadership or cognitive capacity) that is important, but a range of Capabilities. In our view, therefore, the challenge now is how to continue to refine and develop these in order to help executives improve their performance and the effectiveness of their organisation.

NOTES

1. Part of the early work was conducted with Andrew Kakabadse, Professor of Management Development at Cranfield School of Management.
2. Tsui A.S. (1984) 'A Role-Set Analysis of Managerial Reputation', *Organizational Behaviour and Human Performance*, 34, 64–96.

Bibliography

Adams, J., Hayes, J. and Hopson, B. (1976) *Transition: Understanding and Managing Personal Change* (London: Martin Robertson).

Agor, W. H. (1986a) 'The Logic of Intuition: How Top Executives Make Important Decisions', *Organizational Dynamics*, vol. 14, no. 3, Winter, 5–18.

—— (1986b) *The Logic of Intuitive Decision Making: A Research-Based Approach for Top Management* (New York: Quorum Books).

Aguilar, F. J. (1988) *General Managers in Action* (New York: Oxford University Press).

Alexander, L. D. (1989) 'Successfully Implementing Strategic Decisions', in D. Asch and C. Bowman (eds) *Readings in Strategic Management* (London: Macmillan).

Allison, G. T. (1971) *Essence of Decisions* (Boston: Little, Brown and Co).

Ancona, D. G. and Nadler, D. A. (1989) 'Top Hats and Executive Tales: Designing the Senior Team', *Sloan Management Review*, vol. 31, no. 1, Fall, 19–28.

Anderson, J. V. (1993) 'Mind Mapping: A Tool for Creative Thinking', *Business Horizons*, vol. 36, no. 1, 41–6.

Ansoff, I. H. (1965) *Corporate Strategy: An Analytical Approach to Business Policy for Growth and Expansion* (New York: McGraw-Hill).

Anthony, W. P., Bennett III, R. H. Maddox, E. N. and Wheatley, W. J. (1993) 'Picturing the Future: Using Mental Imagery to Enrich Strategic Environmental Assessment', *The Academy of Management Executive*, vol. 7, no. 2, 43–56.

Argyris, C. (1991) 'Teaching Smart People How to Learn', *Harvard Business Review*, vol. 69, no. 3, May/June, 99–109.

—— (1983) 'Productive and Counterproductive Reasoning Processes', in S. Srivastva and Assoc. (ed.) *The Executive Mind* (San Francisco: Jossey Bass).

—— (1977) 'Organizational Learning and Management Information Systems', *Accounting, Organizations and Society*, vol. 2, no. 2.

—— and Schon, D. A. (1978) *Organizational Learning: A Theory of Action Perspective* (Reading, Mass: Addison-Wesley).

Baddeley, S. and James, K. (1987) 'Owl, Fox, Donkey or Sheep: Political Skills for Managers', *Management Education and Development*, vol. 18, pt. 1, 3–19.

Baker, B. (1991) 'MCI Management Competences and APL: The Way Forward for Management Education and Development?', *Journal of European Industrial Training*, vol. 15, no. 9, 17–26.

Bantel, K. A. and Jackson, S. E. (1989) 'Top Management and Innovations in Banking: Does the Composition of the Top Team Make a Difference?', *Strategic Management Journal*, vol. 10, Summer, 107–24.

Barczak, G., Smith, C. and Wilemon, D. (1987) 'Managing Large-Scale Organizational Change', *Organizational Dynamics*, vol. 16, no. 2, Autumn, 23–35.

Barham, K. and Oates, D. (1991) *The International Manager* (London: The Economist Books).

Bartlett, C. A. and Ghoshal, S. (1994) 'Changing the Role of Top Management: Beyond Strategy to Purpose', *Harvard Business Review*, vol. 72, no. 6, November/December, 79–88.

—— and Ghoshal, S. (1989) *Managing Across Borders: The Transnational Solution* (Boston, Mass: Harvard Business School Press).

Bass, B. M. (1990) *Bass and Stogdill's Handbook of Leadership: Theory, Research and Managerial Applications*, 3rd edition (New York: Free Press).

—— (1985) *Leadership and Performance Beyond Expectations* (New York: Free Press).

—— (1983) *Organizational Decision Making* (Homewood, Ill: Irwin).

Beckhard, R. and Harris, R. T. (1977) *Organizational Transitions: Managing Complex Change* (Reading, Mass: Addison-Wesley).

Beer, M., Eisenstat, R. A. and Spector, B. (1990) 'Why Change Programs Don't Produce Change', *Harvard Business Review*, vol. 68, no. 6, November/December, 158–66.

Behling, O. and Neckel, N. L. (1991) 'Making Sense Out of Intuition', *Academy of Management Executive*, vol. 5, no. 1, February, 46–54.

Belbin, R. M. (1981) *Management Teams: Why they Succeed or Fail* (London: Heinemann).

Bennis, W. G. (1993) *An Invented Life: Reflections on Leadership and Change* (Reading, Mass: Addison-Wesley).

—— (1989) *On Becoming a Leader* (Reading, Mass: Addison-Wesley).

—— and Nanus, B. (1985) *Leaders: The Strategies for Taking Charge* (New York: Harper & Row).

Bentz, V. J. (1987) 'Explorations of Scope and Scale: The Critical Determinant of High-Level Executive Effectiveness', *Technical Report No. 31* (Greensboro, North Carolina: Center for Creative Leadership), September.

Bettenhausen, K. L. (1991) 'Five Years of Group Research: What We've Learned and What Needs to be Addressed', *Journal of Management*, vol. 17, no. 2, June, 345–81.

Bleeke, J. and Ernst, D. (1995) 'Is Your Strategic Alliance Really a Sale?', *Harvard Business Review*, vol. 73, no. 1, January/February, 97–105.

—— and Ernst, D. (1993) *Collaborating to Compete: Using Strategic Alliances and Acquisitions in the Global Marketplace* (New York: John Wiley).

Bliss, D. R. (1992) 'Strategic Choice: Engaging the Executive Team in Collaborative Strategy Planning', in D. A. Nadler, M. S. Gerstein and R. B. Shaw and Assoc. *Organizational Architecture* (San Francisco: Jossey-Bass).

Boam, R. and Sparrow, P. (1992) *Designing and Achieving Competency: A Competency-Based Approach to Developing People and Organizations* (London: McGraw-Hill).

Bolt, J. E. (1993) 'Achieving the CEOs Agenda: Education for Executives', *Management Review*, May, 44–8.

Bonoma, T. V. and Lawler, J. C. (1989) 'Chutes and Ladders: Growing the General Manager', *Sloan Management Review*, vol. 30, no. 3, Spring, 27–37.

Bowen, K. H., Clark, K. B., Holloway, C. A., Leonard-Barton, D. and Wheelwright, S. C. (1994) 'Regaining the Lead in Manufacturing', *Harvard Business Review*, vol. 72, no. 5, September/October, 108–30.

Bowman, C. (1992) 'Charting Competitive Strategy', in D. Faulkner and G. Johnson (eds) *The Challenge of Strategic Management*, Cranfield Management Research Series (London: Kogan Page).

—— and Johnson, G. (1991) 'Surfacing Managerial Patterns of Competitive Strategy: Interventions in Strategy Debates', paper presented to the American Academy of Management Conference, Florida.

Boyatzis, R. E. (1982) *The Competent Manager: A Model for Effective Performance* (New York: John Wiley.

Braddick, W. A. G. (1988) 'How Top Managers Really Learn', *The Journal of Management Development*, vol. 7, no. 4, 55–62.

Brass, D. J. (1985) 'Men's and Women's Networks: A Study of Interaction Patterns and Influence in an Organization', *Academy of Management Journal*, vol. 28, no. 2, 327–43.

Bray, D. W., Campbell, R. J. and Grant, D. L. (1974) *Formative Years in Business: A Long Term AT&T Study of Managerial Lives* (New York: John Wiley).

Brunsson, N. (1985) *The Irrational Organisation* (Chichester: John Wiley).

Burns, J. M. (1978) *Leadership* (New York: Harper & Row).

Burns, T. and Stalker, G. M. (1961) *The Management of Innovation* (London: Tavistock).

Burrell, G. and Morgan, G. (1979) *Sociological Paradigms and Organisational Analysis: Elements of the Sociology of Corporate Life* (London: Heinemann).

Byrum-Robinson, B. and Womeldorff, J. D. (1990) 'Networking Skills Inventory', *The 1990 Annual: Developing Human Resources* University Associates (Erlander, Kentucky: Pfeffer & Co).

Buzan, T. and Buzan, B. (1993) *The Mind Map Book* (New York: Dutton).

Canning, R. (1990) 'The Quest for Competence', *Industrial and Commercial Training*, vol. 22, no. 5, 12–16.

Carroll, S. J. and Gillen, D. J. (1987) 'Are the Classical Management Functions Useful in Describing Managerial Work?', *Academy of Management Review*, vol. 12. no. 1, 38–51.

Casey, D. (1985) 'When is a Team Not a Team?' *Personnel Management*, January, 26–30.

Chandler, A. D. (1962) *Strategy and Structure: Chapters in the History of American Industrial Enterprise* (Cambridge, Mass: MIT Press).

Child, J. (1984) *Organisations: A Guide to Problems and Practice* (London: Harper & Row).

Cohen, A. R. and Bradford, D. L. (1990) *Influence Without Authority* (New York: John Wiley).

Conger, J. A. (1993) 'The Brave New World of Leadership Training', *Organizational Dynamics*, vol. 21, no. 3, Winter, 46–58.

—— (1990) 'The Dark Side of Leadership', *Organizational Dynamics*, vol. 19, no. 2, Autumn, 44–55.

—— (1989) *The Charismatic Leader: Behind the Mystique of Exceptional Leadership* (San Francisco: Jossey-Bass).

——, Kanungo, R. N. and Associates (1988) *Charismatic Leadership* (San Francisco: Jossey-Bass).

Covey, S. R. (1989) *The Seven Habits of Highly Effective People: Restoring the Character Ethic* (New York: Simon & Schuster).

Cox, C. and Cooper, C. L. (1988) *High Flyers: An Anatomy of Managerial Success* (Oxford: Blackwell).

Crabb, S. (1991) 'Certified Competent', *Personnel Management*, vol. 23, no. 5, May, 57–8.

Dainty, P. H. and Kakabadse, A. (1992) 'Brittle, Blocked, Blended or Blind: Top Team Characteristics That Lead to Business Success or Failure', *Journal of Managerial Psychology,* vol. 7, no. 2, 4–17.

Davies, A. H. T. (1991) *Strategic Leadership: Making Corporate Plans Work* (Cambridge, UK: Woodhead-Faulkner).

Deal, T. E. and Kennedy, A. A. (1982) *Corporate Cultures* (Reading, Mass: Addison-Wesley).

Drucker, P. F. (1973) *Management: Tasks, Responsibilities and Practices* (New York: Harper & Row).

—— (1955) *The Practice of Management* (London: Heinemann).

Dulewicz, V. (1989) 'Assessment Centres as the Route to Competence', *Personnel Management*, vol. 21, no. 11, 56–9.

Duncan, R. (1979) 'What is the Right Organization Structure? Decision Tree Analysis Provides the Answer', *Organizational Dynamics*, Winter, 59–80.

Dunford, R. W. (1992) *Organisational Behaviour: An Organisational Analysis Perspective* (Sydney: Addison-Wesley).

Dunphy, D. and Stace, D. (1992) *Under New Management: Australian Organizations in Transition* (Sydney: McGraw-Hill).

Eisenhardt, K. M. and Bourgeois III, L. J. (1988) 'Politics of Strategic Decision Making in High-Velocity Environments: Toward a Midrange Theory', *Academy of Management Journal*, vol. 31, no. 4, 737–70.

Evans, P. (1992) 'Developing Leaders and Managing Development', *European Management Journal*, vol 10, no. 1, March, 1–9.

Faulkner, D. and Johnson, G. (1992) *The Challenge of Strategic Management*, Cranfield Management Research Series (London: Kogan Page).

Ferris, G. R. and Kacmar, K. M. (1992) 'Perceptions of Organizational Politics', *Journal of Management*, vol. 18, no. 1, 93–116.

Finkelstein, S. (1992) 'Power in Top Management Teams: Dimensions, Measurement and Validation', *Academy of Management Journal*, vol. 35, no. 3, 505–38.

Fiol, C. M., and Huff, A. S. (1992) 'Maps For Managers: Where Are We? Where Do We Go From Here?' *Journal of Management Studies*, vol. 29, no. 3, May, 267–85.

Ford, C. H. (1977) 'The "Elite" Decision Makers: What Makes Them Tick', *Human Resource Management*, vol. 16, no. 4, Winter, 14–20.

French, J. R. P. and Raven, B. H. (1959) 'The Bases of Social Power', in D. Cartwright (ed.) *Studies in Social Power* (Ann Arbor: University of Michigan).

French, W. and Bell, C. (1983) *Organization Development* (Englewood Cliffs, N.J.: Prentice-Hall).

Friedlander, F. (1983) 'Patterns of Individual and Organizational Learning', in S. Srivastva and Assoc. (eds), *The Executive Mind* (San Francisco: Jossey-Bass).

Furnham, A. (1990) 'A Question of Competency', *Personnel Management*, vol. 27, no. 8, 37.

Gabarro, J. J. (1988) 'Executive Leadership and Succession: The Process of Taking Charge', in Hambrick, D. C. (ed.) *The Executive Effect: Concepts and Methods for Studying Top Managers* (Greenwich, Conn.: JAI Press).

—— (1987) *The Dynamics of Taking Charge* (Boston: Harvard Business School Press).

—— (1978) 'The Development of Trust, Influence and Expectations', in A. G. Athos and J. J. Gabarro (eds) *Interpersonal Behaviour: Communication and Understanding in Relationships* (Englewood Cliffs, N.J: Prentice-Hall).

Gandz, J. and Murray, V. V. (1980) 'The Experience of Workplace Politics', *Academy of Management Journal*, vol. 23, no. 2, 237–51.

Garfield, C. A. (1986) *Peak Performers: The New Heroes of American Business* (New York: W. Morrow).

Gerstein, M. and Reisman, H. (1983) 'Strategic Selection: Matching Executives to Business Conditions', *Sloan Management Review*, vol. 24, no. 2, Winter, 33–49.

Gibson, J. L., Ivancevich, J. M. and Donnelly, J. H. (1994) *Organizations: Behaviour, Structure, Processes* (Burr Ridge, Ill: Irwin).

Gilbert, N. (1991) 'New Hero on the Block: The CFO', *Across the Board*, vol. 28, no. 9, September, 36–9.

Gimpl, M. L. and Dakin, S. R. (1984) 'Management and Magic', *California Management Review*, vol. 27, no. 1, 125–36.

Goodstein, L. D. and Burke, W. W. (1991) 'Creating Successful Organization Change', *Organizational Dynamics*, vol. 19, no. 4, Spring, 5–17.

Goold, M. (1991) 'Strategic Control in the Decentralized Firm', *Sloan Management Review*, vol. 32, no. 2, Winter, 69–81.

—— and Campbell, A. (1988) 'Managing the Diversified Corporation: The Tensions Facing the Chief Executive', *Long Range Planning*, vol. 21, no. 4, 12–24.

——, Campbell, A. and Alexander, M. (1994) *Corporate-Level Strategy: Creating Value in the Multibusiness Company* (New York: John Wiley).

Gregory, M. (1994) *Dirty Tricks* (London: Little, Brown).

Greiner, L. E. (1986) 'Top Management Politics and Organizational Change' in S. Srivastva and Assoc. (eds) *Executive Power* (San Francisco: Jossey-Bass).

Grindley, K. (1991) *Managing IT at Board Level: The Hidden Agenda Exposed* (London: Pitman).

Gupta, A. K. (1988) 'Contingency Perspectives on Strategic Leadership: ·Current Knowledge and Future Research Directions' in D. C. Hambrick (ed.) *The Executive Effect: Concepts and Methods for Studying Top Managers* (Greenwich, Conn: JAI Press).

—— (1986) 'Matching Managers to Strategies: Point and Counterpoint', *Human Resource Management*, vol. 25, no. 2, Summer, 215–34.

Haire, M., Ghiselli, E. E. and Porter, L. W. (1966) *Managerial Thinking: An International Study* (New York: John Wiley).

Hall, D. T. (1986) 'Dilemmas in Linking Succession Planning to Individual Executive Learning', *Human Resource Management*, vol. 25, no. 2, 235–65.

—— and Foulkes, F. K. (1991) 'Senior Executive Development as a Competitive Advantage', *Advances in Applied Business Strategy*, vol. 2, 183–203.

Hall, J. and Donnell, S. M. (1979) 'Managerial Achievement: The Personal Side of Behavioural Theory', *Human Relations*, vol. 32, no. 1, 77–101.

Hall, J. L. (1976) 'Organizational Technology and Executive Succession', *California Management Review*, vol. 19, no. 1, 35–9.

Hambrick, D. C. (1989) 'Putting Top Managers Back in the Strategy Picture', *Strategic Management Journal*, vol. 10, Special Issue, Summer.

—— (1988) (ed.) *The Executive Effect: Concepts and Methods for Studying Top Managers* (Greenwich, Conn.: JAI Press).

—— (1987) 'The Top Management Team: Key to Strategic Success', *California Management Review*, vol. 30, no. 1, Fall, 88–108.

—— and Fukutomi, G. D. S. (1991) 'The Seasons of a CEO's Tenure', *Academy of Management Review*, vol. 16, no. 4, 719–42.

—— and Mason, P. A. (1984) 'Upper Echelons: The Organization as a Reflection of its Top Managers', *Academy of Management Review*, vol. 9, no. 2, 193–206.

Hamel, G. and Prahalad, C. K. (1994) *Competing for the Future* (Boston, Mass.: Harvard Business School Press).

—— and Prahalad, C. K. (1989) 'Strategic Intent', *Harvard Business Review*, vol. 67, no. 3, May/June, 63–76.

Hammer, M. and Champy, J. (1993) *Reengineering the Corporation: A Manifesto for Business Revolution* (London: Nicholas Brealey Publishing).

Handy, C. (1992) 'Balancing Corporate Power: A New Federalist Paper', *Harvard Business Review*, vol. 70, no. 6, November/December, 59–72.

Harper, S. C. (1992) 'The Challenge Facing CEOs: Past, Present and Future', *Academy of Management Executive*, vol. 6. no. 3, August, 7–25.

Harvey-Jones, J. (1988) *Making it Happen: Reflections on Leadership* (London: William Collins & Co.).

Hersey, P. and Blanchard, K. H. (1982) *Management of Organizational Behaviour: Utilising Human Resources*, 4th edn (London: Prentice-Hall International).

——, Blanchard, K. H. and Natemeyer, W. E. (1979) *Situational Leadership, Perception and the Impact of Power* (Escondido, CA: Leadership Studies).

Herzberg, F., Mausner, B. and Snyderman, B. (1959) *The Motivation to Work* (New York: John Wiley).

Hickson, D. J., Butler, R. J., Cray D., Mallory, G. R. and Wilson, D. C. (1986) *Top Decisions: Strategic Decision Making in Organisations* (Oxford: Blackwell).

Hitt, M. A. and Keats, B. W. (1992) 'Strategic Leadership and Restructuring: A Reciprocal Interdependence', in R. L. Phillips and J. G. Hunt, *Strategic Leadership: A Multiorganizational-Level Perspective* (Westport, Conn.: Quorum Books).

Hodgson, T. (1988) 'Stimulating Self-Development', in M. Pedler, J. Burgoyne. and T. Boydell (eds) *Applying Self-Development in Organizations* (New York: Prentice-Hall).

Hollenbeck, G. P. (1991) 'What Did You Learn in School? Studies of a University Executive Program', *Human Resource Planning*, vol. 14, no. 4, 247–60.

Hooijberg, R. and Quinn, R. E. (1992) 'Behavioural Complexity and the Development of Effective Managers', in R. L. Phillips and J. G. Hunt (eds) *Strategic Leadership: a Multiorganizational-Level Perspective* (Westport, Conn.: Quorum Books).

Honey, P. and Mumford, A. (1986) *Manual of Learning Styles* (London: Honey).

Horton, T. R. (1986) *What Works for Me. 16 CEOs Talk About their Careers and Commitments* (New York: Random House).

Hughes, G. D. and Singler, C. H. (1985) *Strategic Sales Management* (Reading, MA: Addison-Wesley).

Iaccoca, L. and Novak, W. (1984) *Iaccoca, An Autobiography* (New York: Bantam Books).

Ibrahim, A. B. and Kelly, J. (1986) 'Leadership Style at the Policy Level', *Journal of General Management*, vol. 11, no. 3, Spring, 37–46.

Iles, P. A. (1992) 'Centres of Excellence? Assessment and Development Centres, Managerial Competence and Human Resource Strategies', *British Journal of Management*, vol. 3, no. 2, 79–90.

Isabella, L. A. (1992) 'Managing the Challenges of Trigger Events: The Mindsets Governing the Adaptation to Change', *Business Horizons*, vol. 35, no. 5, Sept–Oct., 59–66.

Isenberg, D. J. (1984) 'How Senior Managers Think', *Harvard Business Review*, vol. 62, no. 6, November/December, 80–90.

Jacobs, R. (1989) 'Getting the Measure of Management Competence', *Personnel Management*, vol. 22, no. 6, June, 32–7.

Jacobs, T. O. and Jaques, E. (1987) 'Leadership in Complex Systems', in J. A. Zeide (ed.) *Human Productivity Enhancement Organisations and Personnel* (vol. 11) (New York: Praeger).

Jahoda, M. (1958) *Current Concepts of Mental Health: A Report to the Staff Director, Jack R. Ewalt* (New York: Basic Books).

Janis, I. L. and Mann, L. (1977) *Decision Making: a Psychological Analysis of Conflict, Choice and Commitment* (New York: Free Press).

Jaques, E., and Clement, S. D. (1991) *Executive Leadership: A Practical Guide to Managing Complexity* (Oxford: Basil Blackwell).

Javidan, M. (1991) 'Leading a High-Commitment, High-Performance Organization', *Long Range Planning*, vol. 24, no. 2, 28–36.

Johnson, G. and Scholes, K. (1993) *Exploring Corporate Strategy: Text and Cases*, 3rd edn (New York: Prentice-Hall).

Kakabadse, A. (1991) *The Wealth Creators: Top People, Top Teams and Executive Performance* (London: Kogan Page).

—— (1984) *The Politics of Management* (Aldershot: Gower).

——, Ludlow, R. and Vinnicombe, S. (1987) *Working in Organisations* (Aldershot: Gower).

Kanter, R. M. (1994) 'Collaborative Advantage: The Art of Alliances', *Harvard Business Review*, vol. 72, no. 4, July/August, 96–108.

—— (1992) 'From the Editor, Six Certainties for CEOs', *Harvard Business Review*, vol. 70, no. 2, March/April, 7–8.

—— (1988) 'Change Masters: Playing a New Game', *Executive Excellence*, vol. 5, no. 1, January, 8–9.

—— (1983) *The Change Masters: Innovation and Entrepreneurship in the American Corporation* (New York: Simon & Schuster).

—— (1979) 'Power Failure in Management Circuits', *Harvard Business Review*, vol. 57, no. 4, July/August, 65–75.

—— (1977) *Men and Women of the Corporation* (New York: Basic Books).

Kanungo, R. N. and Misra, S. (1992) 'Managerial Resourcefulness: A Reconceptualization of Management Skills', *Human Relations*, vol. 45, no. 12, December, 1311–32.

Kaplan, R. E. (1992) 'Character Shifts: When Behavioural Change Alone does not Improve Executive Performance', *Issues and Observations Newsletter* (Greensboro, North Carolina: Center for Creative Leadership), vol. 12, no. 2.

——, Drath, W. H. and Kofodimos, J. R. (1991) *Beyond Ambition: How Driven Managers Can Lead Better and Live Better* (San Francisco: Jossey-Bass).

——, Drath, W. H. and Kofodimos, J. R. (1985) 'High Hurdles: The Challenges of Executive Self-Development', *Technical Report No. 25* (Greensboro, North Carolina: Center for Creative Leadership).

Katz, D. and Kahn, R. L. (1978) *The Social Psychology of Organizations*, 2nd edn (New York: John Wiley).

Katz, R. L. (1974) 'Skills of an Effective Administrator', *Harvard Business Review*, vol. 52, no. 5, September/October, 90–102.

Katzenbach, J. R. and Smith, D. K. (1994) 'Teams at the Top', *McKinsey Quarterly*, no. 1, 71–9.

——, Smith, D. K (1993a) 'The Discipline of Teams', *Harvard Business Review*, vol. 71, no. 2, March/April, 111–20.

——, Smith, D. K (1993b) *The Wisdom of Teams: Creating the High- Performance Organization* (Boston, Mass: Harvard Business School Press).

Kearns, D. T. and Nadler, D. A. (1992) *Prophets in the Dark: How Xerox Reinvented Itself and Beat Back the Japanese* (New York: Harper Business).

Kelly, D. and Amburgey, T. L. (1991) 'Organizational Inertia and Momentum: A Dynamic Model of Strategic Change', *Academy of Management Journal*, vol. 34, no. 3, 591–612.

Kelly, J. (1993) 'Executive Behaviour: Classical and Existential', *Business Horizons*, January/February, 16–21.

Kelso, G. and Robinson, C. (1992) 'Competency Based Assessment. A Competency-based Approach to Identifying and Developing Top Performers' (Boston, Mass.: Hay/McBer).

Kets de Vries, M. F. R. (1989) *Prisoners of Leadership* (New York: John Wiley).

Kipnis, D., Schmidt, S. M., Swaffin-Smith, C. and Wilkinson, I. (1984) 'Patterns of Managerial Influence: Shotgun Managers, Tacticians and Bystanders', *Organizational Dynamics*, vol. 12, no. 3, Winter, 58–67.

——, Schmidt, S. M. and Wilkinson, I. (1980) 'Intraorganizational Influence Tactics: Explorations in Getting One's Way', *Journal of Applied Psychology*, vol. 65, no. 4, August, 440–52.

Kirk, P. and MacDonald, I. (1989) 'The Role of Feedback in Management Learning', *Management Education and Development*, vol. 20, pt 1, 9–19.

Klemp, G. O. and McClelland, D. C. (1986) 'What Characterizes Intelligent Functioning Among Senior Managers', in R. J. Sternberg and and R. K. Wagner (eds), *Practical Intelligence: Nature and Origins of Competence in the Everyday World* (Cambridge: Cambridge University Press).

Kobasa, S. C. (1988) 'Conceptualisation and Measurement of Personality in Job Stress Research', in J. J. Hurrell, L. R. Murry, S. L. Sauter and C. L. Cooper. (eds) *Occupational Stress: Issues and Developments in Research* (New York: Taylor & Francis).

—— (1982) 'The Hardy Personality: Towards a Social Psychology of Stress and Health' in J. Suls and G. Sanders (eds) *The Social Psychology of Health and Illness* (Hillsdale: Erlbaum).

Kofodimos, J. R. (1991) 'Teamwork at the Top: The Need for Self-Development', *Issues and Observations*, vol. 11, no. 1 (Greensboro, North Carolina: Center for Creative Leadership).

Kolb, D. A. (1984) *Experiential Learning: Experience as the Source of Learning and Development* (Englewood Cliffs, N.J.: Prentice-Hall).

Kotler, P. (1988) *Marketing Management: Analysis, Planning, Implementation and Control*, Prentice-Hall Series in Marketing, 6th edn (Englewood Cliffs, N.J: Prentice-Hall).

Kotter, J. P. (1990) *A Force for Change: How Leadership Differs from Management* (New York: Free Press).

—— (1986) 'Why Power and Influence Issues are at the Very Core of Executive Work', in S. Srivastva and Assoc. (ed.) *Executive Power* (San Francisco: Jossey-Bass).

—— (1982), *The General Managers* (New York: Free Press).

—— (1977) 'Power, Dependence and Effective Management', *Harvard Business Review*, vol. 55, no. 4, July/August, 125–36.

—— and Heskett, J. L. (1992) *Corporate Culture and Performance* (New York: Free Press).

—— and Schlesinger L. A. (1979) 'Choosing Strategies for Change', *Harvard Business Review*, vol. 57, no. 2, March/April, 106–14.

——, Schlesinger, L. A. and Sathe, V. (1979) *Organization: Text, Cases, and Readings on the Management of Organizational Design and Change*, The Irwin Series in Management and the Behavioural Sciences (Homewood, Ill.: Irwin).

Kouzes, J. M. and Posner, B. Z. (1987) *The Leadership Challenge: How to Get Extraordinary Things Done in Organizations* (San Francisco: Jossey-Bass).

Kuhn, T. S. (1962) *The Structure of Scientific Revolutions* (Chicago: University of Chicago Press).

Kubler-Ross E. (1969) *On Death and Dying* (New York: Macmillan).

Latting, J. E. (1985) 'A Creative Problem-Solving Technique', *Developing Human Resources*, University Associates (Erlanger, Kentucky: Pfeffer & Co.).

Leavitt, H. J. (1986) *Corporate Pathfinders: Building Vision and Values into Organizations* (Homewood, Ill.: Dow Jones-Irwin).

—— (1964) 'Applied Organizational Change in Industry: Structural, Technical and Human Approaches' in W. W. Cooper, H. J. Leavitt and M. W. Shelley (eds) *New Perspectives in Organization Research* (New York: John Wiley).

Lessum R. (1993) *Business as a Learning Community* (London: McGraw-Hill).

Lefton, R. E. and Buzzotta, V. B. (1987) 'Teams and Teamwork: A Study of Executive Level Teams', *National Productivity Review*, vol. 7, no. 1, Winter, 7–19.

Levy, A. and Merry, U. (1986) *Organizational Transformation: Approaches, Strategies, Theories* (New York: Praeger).

Lewin, K. (1947) 'Frontiers in Group Dynamics', *Human Relations*, vol. 1, no. 1, 16–40

Lewis, P. and Jacobs, T. O. (1992) 'Individual Differences in Strategic Leadership Capacity: A Constructive/Developmental View', in R. L. Phillips and J. G. Hunt (eds) *Strategic Leadership: A Multiorganizational-level Perspective* (Westport, Conn.: Quorum Books)

Limerick, D. C. (1990) 'Managers of Meaning: From Bob Geldof's Band Aid To Australian CEOs', *Organizational Dynamics*, vol. 18, no. 4, Spring, 22–33.

—— and Cunnington, B. (1993) *Managing the New Organization* (Chatswood, NSW: Business and Professional Publishing).

Lindblom, C. E. (1959) 'The Science of 'Muddling Through', *Public Administration Review*, vol. 19, no. 2, 79–88.

Lombardo, M. M. and McCauley, C. D. (1988) 'The Dynamics of Management Derailment', *Technical Report No. 34* (Greensboro, North Carolina: Center for Creative Leadership).

Longenecker, C. O. and Gioia, D. A. (1992) 'The Executive Appraisal Paradox', *Academy of Management Executive*, vol. 6, no. 2, May, 18–28.

Longenecker, C. O. and Gioia, D. A. (1988) 'Neglected at the Top-Executives Talk about Executive Appraisal', *Sloan Management Review*, vol. 29, no. 2, Winter, 41–7.

Lorsch, J. W. and MacIver, E. (1989) *Pawns or Potentates: The Reality of America's Corporate Boards* (Boston, Mass.: Harvard Business School Press).

MacCrimmon, K. R. and Wehrung, D. A. (1990) 'Characteristics of Risk Taking Executives', *Management Science*, vol. 36, no. 4, April, 422–35.

Mahler, W. R. and Drotter, S. J. (1986) *The Succession Planning Handbook for the CEO* (Midland Park, New Jersey: Mahler Publishing).

Mahoney, T. A., Jerdee, T. H. and Carroll, S. J. (1963) *Development of Managerial Performance: A Research Approach* (Cincinnati: South Western).

Mainiero, L. A. (1994) 'On Breaking the Glass Ceiling: The Political Seasoning of Powerful Women Executives', *Organizational Dynamics*, vol. 22, no. 4, Spring, 5–20.

Mangham, I. L. (1979) *The Politics of Organizational Change* (London: Associated Business Press).

Mann, R. W. and Staudenmier, J. M. (1991) 'Strategic Shifts in Executive Development', *Training and Development*, vol. 45, no. 7, July, 37–40.

March, J. G. (1982) 'Theories of Choice and Making Decisions', *Society*, 20, November/December.

Margerison, C. J. and Kakabadse, A. P. (1984) *How American Chief Executives Succeed: Implications for Developing High Potential Employees*, American Management Association Survey Report.

Margerison, C. J. and McCann, D. J. (1984) *The Margerison–McCann Team Management Index* (Bradford: MCB University Press).

Maslow, A. H. (1954) *Motivation and Personality* (New York: Harper & Row).

Mazneviski, M. L., Rush, J. C. and White, R. E. (1993) 'Drawing Meaning From Vision', in J. Hendry, G. Johnson and J. Newton (eds) *Strategic Thinking, Leadership and the Management of Change* (Chichester: John Wiley).

McBeath, G. (1990) *A Competency Based Approach to Improve Individual and Corporate Performance: A Business Strategy*, Conference – Identifying and Applying Competencies Within Your Organisation (London: Resource Ltd).

McCall, M. W. (1992) 'Executive Development as a Business Strategy', *Journal of Business Strategy*, vol. 13, no. 1, Jan/Feb, 25–31.

—— and Lombardo, M. M. (1983) 'Off The Track: Why and How Successful Executives Get Derailed', *Technical Report No. 21* (Greensboro, North Carolina: Center for Creative Leadership,

——, Spreitzer, G. M. and Mahoney, J. (1994) 'Identifying Leadership Potential in Future International Executives', paper presented to the International Consortium for Executive Development Research, Boston, October.

McClelland, D. C. and Burnham, D. H. (1976) 'Power is the Great Motivator', *Harvard Business Review*, vol. 54, no. 2, March/April, 100–10.

McDonald, A. (1972) 'Conflict at the Summit: A Deadly Game', *Harvard Business Review*, 50, 21, 59–68.

Miles, R. E. and Snow, C. C. (1978) *Organizational Strategy, Structure and Process* (New York: McGraw-Hill).

Miles, R. H. (1980) *Macro Organizational Behaviour* (Santa Monica, CA: Goodyear Publishing).

Miller, D. (1990) *The Icarus Paradox* (New York: Harper Business).

Mills, D. Q. (1985) *The New Competitors* (New York: John Wiley).

Mintzberg, H. (1994) *The Rise and Fall of Strategic Planning* (New York: Prentice-Hall).

—— (1976) *Planning on the Left Side and Managing on the Right*, Harvard Business Review, vol. 54, no. 4, July/August, 49–58.

—— (1973) *The Nature of Managerial Work* (New York: Harper & Row).

—— and Waters, J. A. (1985) 'Of Strategies Deliberate and Emergent', *Strategic Management Journal*, vol. 6, no. 3, July/September, 257–72.

Morgan, G. (1988) *Riding the Waves of Change: Developing Managerial Competencies for a Turbulent World* (San Francisco: Jossey-Bass).

Moulton, H. W. and Fickel, A. A., (1993) *Executive Development: Preparing for the 21st Century* (New York: Oxford University Press).

Mumford, A. (1988a) 'Developing Managers for the Board', *Journal of Management Development*, vol. 17, no. 1, 13–23.

—— (1988b) *Developing Top Managers* (Aldershot: Gower).

——, Robinson, G. and Stradling, D. (1987) *Developing Directors: The Learning Process* (Sheffield: Manpower Services Commission).

Nadler, D. A. (1994) 'Collaborative Strategic Thinking', *Planning Review*, vol. 22, no. 5, September/October, 30–1.

—— and Gerstein, M. S. (1992) 'Strategic Selection: Staffing the Executive Team', in D. A. Nadler, M. S. Gerstein and R. B. Shaw and Assoc., *Organizational Architecture* (San Francisco: Jossey-Bass).

—— and Tushman, M. L. (1990) 'Beyond the Charismatic Leader: Leadership and Organizational Change', *California Management Review*, vol. 32, no. 2, Winter, 77–97.

—— and Tushman, M. L. (1988a) 'Organizational Frame Bending: Principles for Managing Reorientation', *Academy of Management Executive*, vol. 3, no. 3, August, 194–204.

—— and Tushman, M. L. (1988b) *Strategic Organization Design: Concepts, Tools and Processes* (Glenview, Ill.: Scott, Foresman).

Nahavandi, A. and Malekzadeh, A. R. (1993) 'Leader Style in Strategy and Organizational Performance: An Integrative Framework', *Journal of Management Studies*, vol. 30, no. 3, May, 405–25.

Noon, J. (1985) *'A' Time: The Busy Manager's Action Plan for Effective Self-Management* (Wokingham: Van Nostrand Reinhold).

Norburn, D. and Birley, S. (1988) 'The Top Management Team and Corporate Performance', *Strategic Management Journal*, vol. 9, no. 3, 225–37.

Nutt, P. C. (1990) 'Strategic Decisions Made by Top Executives and Middle Managers with Data and Process Dominant Styles', *Journal of Management Studies*, vol. 27, no. 2, March, 173–94.

—— (1989) 'Selecting Tactics to Implement Strategic Plans', *Strategic Management Journal*, vol. 10, no. 2, Mar/April, 145–61.

—— and Backoff, R. W. (1993) 'Transforming Public Organizations with Strategic Management and Strategic Leadership', *Journal of Management*, vol. 19, no. 2, Summer, 299–347.

Ohmae, K. (1982) *The Mind of the Strategist: The Art of Japanese Business* (New York: McGraw-Hill).

Organ, D. W. and Bateman, T. (1986) *Organizational Behaviour: An Applied Psychological Approach* (Plano, Texas: Business Publications).

O'Reilly, C. A. (1983) 'The Use of Information in Organizational Decision Making: A Model and Some Propositions', in B. M. Staw and L. I. Cummings (eds) *Research in Organizational Behaviour*, vol. 5 (Greenwich: JAI Press).

O'Toole, J. and Bennis, W. (1992) 'Our Federalist Future: The Leadership Imperative', *California Management Review*, vol. 34, no. 4, Summer, 73–90.

Ouchi, W. (1981) *Theory Z* (Reading, Mass: Addison-Wesley).

Parker C. and Lewis R. (1981) 'Beyond the Peter Principle-Managing Successful Transitions', *Journal of European Industrial Training*, vol. 5, no. 6.

Parker, G. M. (1990) *Team Players and Teamwork: The New Competitive Business Strategy* (San Francisco: Jossey-Bass).

Pascale, R. T. and Athos, A. G. (1981) *The Art of Japanese Management: Applications for American Executives* (New York: Simon & Schuster).

Payne, A. and Lumsden, C. (1987) 'Strategy Consulting – A Shooting Star?', *Long Range PLanning*, vol. 20, no. 3, 53–64.

Pearson, G. J. (1990) *Strategic Thinking* (New York: Prentice-Hall).

Pedler, M. and Boydell, T. (1985) *Managing Yourself* (London: Fontana/Collins).

Peters, T. J. and Waterman, R. H. (1982) *In Search of Excellence: Lessons from America's Best-Run Companies* (New York: Harper & Row).

Pettigrew, A. M. (1992) 'On Studying Managerial Elites', *Strategic Management Journal*, vol. 13, Winter, 163–82.

—— (1986) 'Some Limits of Executive Power in Creating Strategic Change', in S. Srivastva and Assoc. (ed.) *Executive Power* (San Francisco: Jossey-Bass).

—— (1973) *The Politics of Organizational Decision Making* (London: Tavistock).

—— and Whipp, R. (1991) *Managing Change for Competitive Success* (Oxford: Blackwell).

Pfeffer, J. (1992) *Managing with Power: Politics and Influence in Organizations* (Boston, Mass.: Harvard Business School Press).

—— (1981) *Power in Organizations* (Marshfield, Mass.: Pitman).

Porac, J. F., Thomas, H. and Emme, B. (1987) 'Knowing the Competition: The Mental Models of Retailing Strategists', in G. Johnson (ed.) *Business Strategy and Retailing* (New York: John Wiley).

Porter, M. E. (1985) *Competitive Advantage* (New York: Free Press).

—— (1980) *Competitive Strategy: Techniques for Analyzing Industries and Competitors* (New York: Free Press).

Quick, J. C., Nelson, D. L. and Quick J. D. (1990) *Stress and Challenge at the Top: the Paradox of the Successful Executive* (New York: John Wiley).

Quinn, R. E. (1988) *Beyond Rational Management: Mastering the Paradoxes and Competing Demands of High Performance* (San Francisco: Jossey-Bass).

Raskas, D. F. and Hambrick, D. C. (1992) 'Multifunctional Managerial Development: A Framework for Evaluating the Options', *Organizational Dynamics*, vol. 21, no. 2, Autumn, 5–17.

Ready, D. A. (1994) *Champions of Change: A Global Report on Leading Business Transformation*, published jointly by the International Consortium for Executive Development Research and Gemini Consulting.

——, Vicere, A. A. and White, A. F. (1993) 'Executive Education: Can Universities Deliver?', *Human Resource Planning*, vol. 16, no. 4, 1–12.

Revans, R. W. (1982) *The Origins and Growth of Action Learning* (Lund, Studentlitteratur, Bromley: Chartwell-Bratt).

Roddick, A. (1992) *Body and Soul* (London: Vermilion).

Rothschild, W. E. (1993) *Risktaker, Caretaker, Surgeon, Undertaker: The Four Faces of Strategic Leadership* (New York: John Wiley).

Ryan, M. (1989) 'Political Behaviour and Management Development', *Management Education and Development*, vol. 20, part 3, 238–53.

Sashkin, M. (1992) 'Strategic Leadership Competencies', in R.L. Phillips and J.G. Hunt (eds) *Strategic Leadership: A Multiorganizational-Level Perspective* (Westport, Conn.: Quorum Books).

Sashkin, M. and Burke, W. W. (1987) 'Organization Development in the 1980s', *Journal of Management*, vol. 13, no. 2, 393–417.

Schein, E. H. (1986) *Organizational Culture and Leadership, Jossey-Bass Management Series* (San Francisco: Jossey-Bass).

—— (1984) 'Coming to a New Awareness of Organizational Culture', *Sloan Management Review*, vol. 25, no. 2, Winter, 3–16.

Schroder, H. M., Driver, M. J. and Streufert, S. (1967) *Human Information Processing: Individuals and Groups Functioning in Complex Situations* (New York: Holt, Rinehart & Winston).

Sculley, J. and Byrne, J. A. (1987) *Odyssey: Pepsi to Apple* (New York: Harper & Row).

Senge, P. M. (1990a) *The Fifth Discipline: The Art and Practice of the Learning Organization* (New York: Doubleday/Currency).

—— (1990b) 'The Leader's New Work: Building Learning Organizations', *Sloan Management Review*, vol. 32, no. 1, Fall, 7–23.

Shashkin, M. and Burke, W. W. (1990) 'Understanding and Assessing Organizational Leadership', in K. E. Clark and M. B. Clark (eds) *Measures of Leadership* (New Jersey: Leadership Library of America).

Shaw, R. B. and Nadler, D. A. (1991) 'Capacity to Act', *Human Resource Planning*, vol. 14, no. 4, 289–308.

Shea, G. P. and Guzzo, R. A. (1987) 'Group Effectiveness: What Really Matters?', *Sloan Management Review*, vol. 28, no. 3, Spring, 25–31.

Shrivastava, P. and Mitroff, I. I. (1984) 'Enhancing Organizational Research Utilization: The Role of Decision Makers' Assumptions', *Academy of Management Review*, January, vol. 9, no. 1, January, 18–26.

Simon, H. A. (1977) *The New Science of Management Decision*, revd edn (Engelwood Cliffs, NJ: Prentice-Hall).

Sinclair, A. (1994) *Trials at the Top: Chief Executives Talk About Men, Women and the Australian Executive Culture* (Melbourne: University of Melbourne).

—— (1992) 'The Tyranny of a Team Ideology', *Organization Studies*, vol. 13, no. 4, 611–26.

Sinclair, J. and Collins, D. (1991) 'The Skills Time Bomb Part 3: Developing a New Skills Mix.' *Leadership and Organisation Development Journal*, vol. 12, no. 5, 17–20.

Spekman, R. E., Isabella, L. A., MacAvoy, T. and Forbes, T. (1994) *Strategic Alliances: A Normative Approach to Strategic and Managerial Fit*, ICEDR Research Project 94-02, October.

Srivastva, S. and Cooperrider, D. L. (1986) 'Ways of Understanding Executive Power', in S. Srivastva and Assoc. (ed.) *Executive Power* (San Francisco: Jossey-Bass).

Stagner, R. (1969) 'Corporate Decision Making', *Journal of Applied Psychology*, 53, 1–13.

Staw, B. M. (1981) 'The Escalation of Commitment to a Course of Action', *Academy of Management Review*, vol. 6, no. 4, 577–587.

Steele, F. (1983) 'The Ecology of Executive Teams: A New View of the Top', *Organizational Dynamics*, Spring, 65–78.

Stewart, R. (1993) *The Reality of Organisations*, 3rd edn (London: Macmillan).

—— (1982) *Choices for the Manager* (Englewood Cliffs, NJ: Prentice-Hall).

Sutton, H. (1989) 'Keeping Tabs on the Competition', *Marketing Communications*, vol. 14, no. 1, January, 42–5.

Tichy, N. M. and Devanna, M. A (1986). *The Transformational Leader* (New York: John Wiley).

—— and Sherman S. (1993) *Control Your Destiny or Someone Else Will: How Jack Welch is Making General Electric the World's Most Competitive Corporation* (New York: Doubleday).

Thach, L. and Woodman, R. W. (1994) 'Organizational Change and Information Technology: Managing on the Edge of Cyberspace', *Organizational Dynamics*, vol. 23, no. 1, Summer, 30–46.

Thorpe, R. (1990) 'Alternative Theory of Management Education', *Journal of European Industrial Training*, vol. 14, no. 2, 3–15.

Torrington, D., Waite, D. and Weightman, J. (1992) 'A Continuous Development Approach to Training Health Service Personnel Specialists', *Journal of European Industrial Training*, vol. 16, no. 3, 3–12

Tsui, A. S. (1984) 'A Role-Set Analysis of Managerial Reputation', *Organizational Behaviour and Human Performance*, 34, 64–96.

Tuckman, B. W. (1965) 'Developmental Sequences in Small Groups', *Psychology Bulletin*, 63, 384–399.

Ulrich, D. and Lake, D. (1990) *Organizational Capability* (New York: John Wiley).

Vandermerwe, S. and Vandermerwe, A. (1991) 'Making Strategic Change Happen', *European Management Journal*, vol. 9, no. 2, June, 174–181.

Vicere, A. A. (1992) 'The Strategic Leadership Imperative for Executive Development', *Human Resource Planning*, vol. 15, no. 1, 15–31.

Watkins, K. E. and Marsick, V. J. (1993) *Sculpting the Learning Organization: Lessons in the Art and Science of Systemic Change* (San Francisco: Jossey-Bass).

Watzlawick, P., Weakland, J. H. and Fisch, R. (1974) *Change: Principles of Problem Formation and Problem Resolution* (New York: Norton).

Weber, M. (1947) *The Theory of Social and Economic Organisation*, trans. A. M. Henderson and T. Parsons (New York: Free Press).

Westley, F. and Mintzberg, H. (1989) 'Visionary Leadership and Strategic Management', *Strategic Management Journal*, vol. 10, Summer, 17–32.

Whetten, D. A. and Cameron, K. S. (1984) *Developing Management Skills*, the Scott Foresman Series in Management and Organizations (Glenview Ill.: Scott, Foresman).

Whipp, R. and Pettigrew, A. M. (1993) 'Leading Change and the Management of Competition', in J. Hendry, G. Johnson and J. Newton (eds) *Strategic Thinking, Leadership and the Management of Change* (New York: John Wiley).

Wiersema, M. F. and Bantel, K. A. (1992) 'Top Management Team Demography and Corporate Strategic Change', *Academy of Management Journal*, vol. 35, no. 1, March, 91–121.

Wilson, M. G. and Page, C. (1993) 'New Zealand Management Competencies: Concepts, Comparisons and Concerns', paper presented to the Australian and New Zealand Academy of Management, December.

Yukl, G. A. and Falbe, C. M. (1990) 'Influence Tactics and Objectives in Upward, Downward and Lateral Influence Attempts', *Journal of Applied Psychology*, vol. 75, no. 2, April, 132–40.

Yukl, G. A. (1994) *Leadership in Organizations*, 3rd edition (Englewood Cliffs, NJ: Prentice-Hall).

Zahra, S. A. and Chaples, S. S. (1993) 'Blind Spots in Competitive Analysis', *Academy of Management Executive*, vol. 7, no. 2, May, 7–28.

Index of Names

Agor, W. H., 49, 50, 52, 56
Aguilar, F. J., 155
Alexander, L. D., 271
Alexander, M., 245
Allison, G. T., 115
Amburgey, T. L., 260
Ancona, D. G., 28, 158, 169, 174, 186, 293
Ansoff, I. H., 214, 221, 327
Anthony, W. P., 306, 308
Argyris, C., 50, 51, 52, 67, 69, 233, 260

Backoff, R. W., 315, 318, 325
Baddeley, S., 125
Baker, B., 12
Bantel, K. A., 175, 187
Barczak, G., 288
Barham, D., 74
Bartlett, C. A., 309, 310, 316, 333, 336
Bass, B. M., 33, 126, 132
Bateman, T., 41, 65, 237, 241, 268, 274
Beckhard, R., 261, 265, 272
Beer, M., 268, 270
Behling, O., 65
Belbin, R. M., 176
Bell, C., 278
Bennett III, R. H., 306, 308
Bennis, W. G., 14, 128, 131, 142, 145, 155, 245
Bentz, V. J., 3
Bettenhausen, K. L., 177
Birley, S., 176
Blanchard, K. H., 125, 147, 148, 156
Bleeke, J., 224, 225, 228
Bliss, D. R., 318
Boam, R., 28, 328, 334
Bolt, J. E., 76, 88, 91
Bourgeois III, L. J., 113, 114
Bowen, K. H., 260
Bowman, C., 66, 217, 218, 219
Boyatzis, R. E., 13, 15, 28
Boydell, T., 69
Braddick, W. A. G., 81, 92, 231
Bradford, D. L., 107, 108–10, 111, 115
Brass, D. J., 128
Bray, D. W., 29
Brunnson, N., 60
Burke, W. W., 155, 274, 277, 285, 288

Burnham, D. H., 293
Burns, J. M., 155
Burns, T., 246
Burrell, G., 65
Butler, R. J., 42, 64
Buzan, T., 66
Buzzotta, V. B., 186
Byrum-Robinson, B., 101

Campbell, A., 242, 244, 245
Campbell, R. J., 29
Canning, R., 28
Carroll, S. J., 14, 28
Casey, D., 167, 168, 187
Champy, J., 261
Chandler, A. D., 317
Chaples, S. S., 44, 45, 66, 194, 201, 205, 211, 227
Child, J., 336
Clark, K. B., 260
Clement, S. D., 36
Cohen, A. R., 107, 108, 109, 110, 111, 115
Collins, D., 28
Conger, J. A., 73, 84, 86, 88, 92, 133, 134, 140, 142, 156
Cooper, C. L., 14, 29, 113, 291, 292, 294, 313
Cooperrider, D. L., 125
Covey, S. R., 294, 308
Cox, C., 14, 29, 113, 291, 292, 294, 313
Crabb, S., 29
Cray, D., 42, 64
Cunnington, B., 254

Dainty, P. H., 186
Dakin, S. R., 52
Davies, A. H. T., 187, 306, 318
Deal, T. E., 257
Donnell, S. M., 313
Donnelly, J. H., 133, 155, 156
Drath, W. H., 76, 77, 79
Driver, M. J., 64
Drotter, S. J., 3, 4
Drucker, P. F., 184, 291
Dulewicz, V., 15
Duncan, R., 261
Dunford, R. W., 39, 261
Dunphy, D., 276, 279, 280

Eisenhardt, K. M., 113, 114
Eisenstat, R. A., 268, 270
Ernst, D., 224, 225, 228
Evans, P., 73, 83, 91, 92

Falbe, C. M., 95, 108
Faulkner, D., 318
Fayol, H., 28
Ferris, G. R., 125
Fickel, A. A., 85, 87
Finkelstein, S., 187
Fiol, C. M., 57
Fisch, R., 65
Forbes, T., 225
Ford, C. H., 40, 53, 54
Foulkes, F. K., 74, 92
French, J. R. P., 99
French, W., 278
Friedlander, F., 92
Fukutomi, G. D. S., 82
Furnham, A., 28

Gabarro, J. J., 8, 9, 29, 82, 102, 111, 297, 312
Gandz, J., 99
Garfield, C. A., 308
Gerstein, M. S., 22, 327, 336
Ghiselli, E. E., 313
Ghoshal, S., 309, 310, 316, 333, 336
Gibson, J. L., 133, 155, 156
Gilbert, N., 291
Gillen, D. J., 14, 28
Gimpl, M. L., 52
Gioia, D. A., 79
Goodstein, L. D., 274, 285, 288
Goold, M., 241, 242, 244, 245
Grant, D. L., 29
Gregory, M., 156
Greiner, L. E., 99, 113, 174
Grindley, K., 311
Gupta, A. K., 28, 84, 326, 327, 328, 330, 333, 334
Guzzo, R. A., 186

Haire, M., 313
Hall, D. T., 74, 92
Hall, J., 313
Hall, J. L., 311, 313
Hambrick, D. C., 82, 84, 158, 163, 164, 176, 186, 187, 289, 316
Hamel, G., 199, 200, 206, 212, 214, 219, 224, 232, 265, 300, 309
Hammer, M., 261
Handy, C., 245

Harper, S. C., 67, 73, 80, 336
Harris, R. T., 261, 265, 272
Hersey, P., 125, 147, 148, 156
Herzberg, F., 293
Heskett, J. L., 259
Hickson, D. J., 42, 64
Hitt, M. A., 324
Hodgson, T., 69
Hollenbeck, G. P., 92
Holloway, C. A., 260
Honey, P., 69
Horton, T. R., 156
Huff, A. S., 57

Iaccoca, L., 156
Ibrahim, A. B., 320, 327
Iles, P. A., 29. 80
Isabella, R. A., 225
Isenberg, D. J., 5, 20, 37, 40, 49, 56, 62, 111
Ivancevich, J. M., 133, 155, 156

Jackson, S. E., 187
Jacobs, R., 28
Jacobs, T. O., 3, 29, 40, 64, 85
Jahoda, M., 92
Jaques, E., 3, 29, 36, 64
James, K., 125
Janis, I. L., 39, 66
Javidan, M., 134, 135, 143
Johnson, G., 66, 199, 200–6, 210, 211, 213, 216, 228, 256, 261, 317, 318, 333

Kacmar, K. M., 125
Kahn, R. L., 268
Kakabadse, A., 48, 92, 125, 186
Kanter, R. M., 95, 101, 105, 108, 112, 144, 226, 258, 287
Kanungo, R. N., 11, 29, 133
Kaplan, R. E., 76, 77, 79, 89
Katz, D., 268
Katz, R. L., 145
Katzenbach, J. R., 158, 162, 165, 179, 186
Kearns, D. T., 1, 28, 37, 43, 51, 64, 65, 66, 113, 131, 144, 155, 156, 227, 228, 288
Keats, B. W., 324
Kelly, D., 260
Kelly, J., 65, 320, 327
Kennedy, A. A., 257
Kets De Vries, M. F. R., 140
Kipnis, D., 108, 115
Klemp, G. O., 21

Kobasa, S. C., 53
Kofodimos, J. R., 76, 77, 79, 171
Kolb, D. A., 68, 70
Kotler, P., 223
Kotter, J., 2, 3, 6, 8, 10, 14, 15, 20, 29, 40, 65, 75, 76, 77, 83, 84, 85, 91, 92, 98, 101, 103, 105, 125, 128, 135, 156, 259, 272, 273, 297, 307, 312, 314
Kouzes, J. M., 14, 19, 21, 131, 133, 134, 136, 137, 142, 155, 156
Kubler-Ross, E., 92, 289
Kuhn, T. S., 65

Lake, D., 234, 236, 239, 248, 249, 252, 260, 261
Latting, J. E., 56
Leonard-Barton, D., 260
Leavitt, H. J., 8, 11, 288
Lefton, R. E., 186
Lessum, R., 234
Levy, A., 269
Lewin, K., 156, 274, 275
Lewis, P., 40, 85
Lewis, R., 282, 288, 289
Limerick, D. C., 14, 20, 254
Lindblom, C. E., 42
Lombardo, M. M., 77
Longenecker, C. O., 79
Lorsch, J. W., 173, 184, 187
Lumsden, C., 288

MacAvoy, T., 225
MacCrimmon, K. R., 54
MacGregor Burns, J. M., 155
MacIver, E., 173, 184, 187
Maddox, E. N., 306, 308
Mahler, W. R., 3, 4
Mahoney, J., 15, 19, 28, 29, 74, 91, 92
Mainiero, L. A., 125
Malekzadeh, A. R., 130, 320, 327, 328, 330
Mallory, G. R., 42, 64
Mangham, I. L., 125
Mann, L., 39, 66
Mann, R. W., 88, 91, 92
March, J. G., 42
Margerison, C. J., 92, 176
Marsick, V. J., 233
Maslow, A. H., 293
Mason, P. A., 163, 186, 187
Mausner, B., 293
Mazneviski, M. L., 58, 59, 65, 66
McBeath, G., 328

McCall, M. W., 15, 19, 28, 29, 74, 77, 83, 91, 92
McCann, D. J., 176
McCarthy, J., 298, 314
McCauley, C. D., 77
McClelland, D. C., 21, 293
McDonald, A., 99, 125
Merry, U., 269
Miles, R. E., 130, 163, 328
Miles, R. H., 237
Miller, D., 129
Mills, D. Q., 293, 313
Mintzberg, H., 2, 5, 6, 33, 40, 49, 55, 63, 65, 155, 314, 317
Misra, S., 11, 29
Mitroff, I. I., 43
Morgan, G., 29, 65, 262
Moulton, H. W., 85, 87
Mumford, A., 67, 68, 69, 76, 80, 83, 85, 92, 292
Murray, V. V., 99

Nadler, D. A., 1, 22, 28, 64, 65, 66, 113, 141, 155, 156, 158, 169, 174, 186, 227, 228, 237, 269, 277, 279, 288, 293, 304, 308, 309, 322, 324, 336
Nahavandi, A., 130, 320, 327, 328, 330
Nanus, B., 14, 155
Natemeyer, W. E., 125
Neckel, N. L., 65
Nelson, D. L., 19, 53, 54
Noon, J., 305
Norburn, D., 176
Novak, W., 156
Nutt, P. C., 65, 176, 272, 315, 318, 325

Oates, D., 74
Ohmae, K., 61, 224
O'Reilly, C. A., 41
Organ, D. W., 41, 65, 237, 241, 268, 274
O'Toole, J., 245

Page, C., 13, 29
Parker, C., 282, 288, 289
Parker, G. M., 172
Payne, A., 288
Pearson, G. J., 198, 203, 211, 212, 213, 228, 316
Pedler, M., 69
Peters, T. J., 22, 29, 46, 49, 145, 156, 241
Pettigrew, A. M., 28, 117, 127, 281
Pfeffer, J., 19, 96, 104, 107, 111, 113, 120, 125
Porter, L. W., 313

Porter, M. E., 130, 198, 199–206, 214–17, 328
Posner, B. Z., 14, 19, 21, 131, 133, 134, 136, 137, 142, 155, 156
Prahalad, C. K., 199, 200, 206, 212, 214, 219, 224, 232, 265, 300, 309

Quick, J. C., 19, 53, 54
Quick, J. D., 19, 53, 54
Quinn, R. E., 20, 92, 334

Raskas, D. F., 84
Raven, B. H., 99
Ready, D., 12, 28, 91
Reisman, H., 327, 336
Revans, R. W., 86
Robinson, G., 292
Roddick, A., 65
Rothschild, W. E., 129, 130, 147, 151, 327
Rush, J. C., 58, 59, 65, 66
Ryan, M., 120, 125

Sashkin, M., 28, 155, 277
Schein, E. H., 257
Schlesinger, L. A., 272, 273
Schmidt, S. M., 108
Scholes, K., 199, 200–6, 210, 211, 213, 216, 228, 256, 261, 317, 318, 333
Schon, D. A., 233, 260
Schroder, H. M., 64
Sculley, J., 102, 156
Senge, P. M., 40, 51, 56, 91, 135, 233
Shaw, R. B., 304, 308, 309
Shea, G. P., 186
Sherman, S., 155, 156
Shrivastava, P., 43
Simon, H. A., 33
Sinclair, A., 125, 162
Sinclair, J., 28
Smith, C., 288
Smith, D. K., 158, 162, 165, 179, 186
Snow, C. C., 130, 163, 328
Snyderman, B., 293
Sparrow, P., 28, 328, 334
Spector, B., 268, 270
Spekman, R. E., 225
Spreitzer, G. M., 15, 19, 28, 29, 74, 91, 92
Srivastva, S., 125
Stace, D., 276, 279, 280
Stalker, G. M., 246
Staudenmier, J. M., 88, 91, 92

Staw, B. M., 66
Steele, F., 173
Stewart, R., 8, 98, 114, 297
Stradling, D., 292
Streufert, S., 64
Sutton, H., 195
Swaffin-Smith, C., 108

Thach, L, 261
Thorpe, R., 28
Tichy, N. M., 155, 156
Torrington, D., 28
Tsui, A. S., 339, 343
Tuckman, B. W., 169, 170
Tushman, M. L., 141, 237, 269, 277, 279, 288, 322, 324

Ulrich, D., 234, 236, 239, 248, 249, 252, 260, 261

Vandermerwe, A., 62, 275, 288
Vandermerwe, S., 62, 275, 288
Vicere, A. A., 335

Waite, D., 28
Waterman, R. H., 22, 29, 46, 49, 145, 156, 241
Waters, J. A., 63, 317
Watkins, K. E., 233
Watzlawick, P., 65
Weakland, J. H., 65
Weber, M., 139
Wehrung, D. A., 54
Weightman, J., 28
Westley, F., 155
Wheatley, W. J., 306, 308
Wheelwright, S. C., 260
Whipp, R, 127, 281
White, R. E., 58, 59, 65, 66
Wiersema, M. F., 175
Wilemon, D., 288
Wilkinson, I., 108
Wilson, D. C., 42, 64
Wilson, M. G., 13, 29
Winston, S., 314
Womeldorff, J. D., 101
Woodman, R. W., 261

Yukl, G. A., 95, 108, 149, 155

Zahra, S. A., 44, 45, 66, 194, 201, 205, 211, 227

Index of Subjects

Action learning, 86, 90
Actioning/Structuring Capability, 22, 290, 296, 313, 322
Agenda setting, 6, 8, 307
Ambiguity, 4, 78, 97, 167
Analysis of business environment
  economic and technology issues, 197–8
  social and political issues, 196–7
Assertiveness, 108

Benchmarking, 89, 266
Blind spots, 194–5, 227
Boston matrix, *see* market positioning
Boundaries, *see* organisational structure
Breadth and focus
  importance of, 37–9, 40–1
  link with mindset, 60
  see also prioritising

Capabilities
  applying the, 22–7
  customising the, 24, 26, 335
  definition and outline description, 15–17
  developing, 73–5
  research basis for, 337–43
  required for strategic leadership, 320–7, 331–2
Centralisation, 114, 236, 244–5, 252
Charisma, 106–7, 127, 132, 139–41
Credibility, 137
Cognitive Capability, 16, 17, 18–19, 74
Cognitive maps, 57–8, 296, 297
Cognitive power, 101–2, 106
Commitment, 129, 133
Communication skills, 106–7, 132
Competency
  life cycles and changing business scenarios, 328, 334–5
  models and their application, 12–15
Competitors, 205–6
  see also industry; strategy
Complexity, 3, 4, 15, 36, 43, 316
Conflict, 107, 115, 117, 171
Contingency theories, 147
Control, 114, 131, 255–6, 300

Corporate governance, 184
Cost leadership, *see* strategy
Creativity
  and intuition, 50, 55–6
  and right-brain thinking, 47–50
  stifling of, 146
Currencies, *see* influence

Decentralisation, 131, 236, 241–4, 252
Decision making, 37, 100, 115, 303
  see also problem solving
Derailment, *see* transition into senior management
Development
  as distinct from learning, 69, 90
  of interpersonal skills, 73, 88
  of self, 74, 89, 90, 285–6
Development Capability, 16, 17, 18, 19, 74
Differentiation, *see* strategy
Divisional structures, *see* organisational structure

Effective performance, 2, 14–16, 22, 95, 297, 310, 327, 334
Emotions
  and the capacity to cope, 52–3 (*see also* mental resilience)
  influence on decision making, 52
  and reactions to change, 272
  and self-development, 74, 81
Empowerment
  and issues of control, 253, 258
  processes, 142–4
  and transformational leadership, 134
  value of, 266
Enabling, 9–10, 24, 152, 299, 301
Enacting, 10–11, 24, 299, 301
Energy, 107, 137, 138, 154
  see also actioning
Establishing, 8–9, 24, 298
Executive development
  inhibitors to, 77–9
  link with strategy, 75–6, 84, 86
  process, 70–2
  trends in, 80, 85–9
Executive drive, 291–2

Executive selection, 1, 327–30
Executive thinking
  and development of strategy, 303
  difficulties with, 50–2
  influences upon, 39, 41–2
  problem solving at senior levels, 34–6
  and rational analysis, 33, 35–7
  see also creativity, perception,
    strategic thinking
Expert power, 102
Expertise, 73, 77, 101, 310–12
Expertise Capability, 21, 291, 310
External Capability, 21, 73, 192–3

Federalism, *see* organisational structure
Feedback
  and appraisal processes, 79–80
  and development, 74
  from others, 16, 80, 338–9
  to others, 138, 284
Flexibility, 107, 109, 144, 154, 226
Functional knowledge, 106, 310
  see also expertise
Functional structures, *see*
    organisational structure

Globalisation, 33, 73, 87, 212, 239, 246

Hidden agendas, 173

Industry analysis, 198–205
Industry knowledge, 312
Information power, 102
Influence
  Capability, 19–20
  comparison with leadership, 96
  definition, 96
  as an 'exchange' process, 109–12
  and insight, 98, 116
  strategic, 117–20, 124–5
  techniques, 108
Insight Capability, 17, 18, 20–1, 111–12
Inspirational leadership, 100, 126, 141
Instrumental leadership, 141, 154
Integration Capability, 20, 158
  see also senior teams
Interpersonal processes, 111, 169
Intuition, *see* creativity

Learning
  from experience, 74, 83–5
  and failure to do so, 77, 83
  organisations, 233, 266

see also transitions curve
Leadership
  and change, 128, 131–4, 150
  at senior levels, 127–9
  and strategic context, 129, 149, 150,
    154 (*see also* strategic
    leadership)
  styles, 153
  and vision, 128, 133–5 (*see also*
    motivation, resources)
Leadership Capability, 20, 74, 88

Market
  attractiveness, 210–12
  environment, 193
  positioning, 208–10
  segmentation, 206–8
Matrix structures, *see* organisational
    structure
Maturity Capability, 16, 17, 18, 19, 34, 74
Mental resilience, 53–4, 141
  see also emotions
Mentoring, 85, 143
Mindset
  and global orientation, 73
  and organisational change, 265,
    274–5, 281
  and organisational design, 231–2
  and strategic leadership, 319
  types of, 44, 60–3
Motivation
  and executives' needs, 293–5
  and others' commitment, 128
  and persistence, 292
  and vision, 134–5, 138–42

Negotiation skills, 107
Network building, 9, 105, 142, 303–4
Network organisations, 246
Network power, 100–1
Networks, 42, 118, 119, 135, 247
  see also enabling

Organisational Capability, 22, 230, 263
Organisational change
  and change goals, 265–7
  depth and scale of, 268–71
  impediments to, 271
  top management support for, 262,
    270, 272–3
  see also resistance to change,
    organisational change
    frameworks *and* management

Organisational change frameworks, 263–4, 274–5
Organisational change management
issues to consider, 276–7
maintaining, 286–7
methods of, 277–81
problems with implementation, 275–6, 281
Organisational components, 230–1, 267–8
Organisational core competencies, 323–4
Organisational culture
and change, 234–6, 259
key components of, 257–9
Organisational design, 236, 251–3
Organisational power, 99–100, 104
Organisational structure
and boundaries, 246–7
definition of, 237
different types of, 238–46, 248–50
Organisational systems
control, 255
putting in place, 303
rewards, 9, 256, 257, 268

Perception, 43–5, 306, 320
Persistence, 292
Personal power, 102–3, 106
Personality, 47, 100, 102
Planning
and the senior executive role, 5–6
personal, 305
short- and long-term, 307
strategic, 305–7
Politics
and decision making, 42
definition, 96
protection from, 145
at senior levels, 96–8, 112–17, 236
within senior teams, 159, 173
Power
acquiring and maintaining, 103–4
bases, 4, 99, 124
definition, 96
importance at senior levels, 98, 270, 293
Prioritising, 302–4, 305
Problem identification, 304–5
Problem solving
at senior levels, 34–6
within senior teams, 167–8
traditional models, 36–7
Process re-engineering, 250–1, 267

Reorganisations, 104, 229, 235
Resistance to change, 147, 152, 154, 272–3
Resources, 100, 128, 144–5, 255
Restructuring, *see* reorganisations
Rewards, *see* organisational systems
Risk-taking, 54–5, 78, 133, 145–6, 285

Self-awareness, 16, 74, 76–9, 81
Self-concept, 74, 294
see also values
Senior executives
compared with lower level managers, 4–5, 315
definition of, 1–4
nature of the role, 5–6, 303, 319
principal requirements of, 6–11
Senior teams
at board level, 161, 173–4, 184–5
distinguishing characteristics, 159
factors affecting performance, 162–5, 175 (*see also* team purpose, process)
and strategy, 158–9, 163–4, 310
and strategic leadership, 325–6
Sensitivity, 107
Setting direction, 212–14, 232–3
see also establishing, vision,
Situational leadership, 147–9
Stakeholders, 4, 10, 98, 136, 149, 185, 272, 276, 279, 325
Strategic alliances, 224–6, 237
Strategic change, 315, 324–5
see also organisational change
Strategic control, 245
Strategic direction, 212–14, 322–4
Strategic influence, 9
Strategic intent, 212–14, 219, 265
Strategic leadership
definition and explanation of, 315–19
at different executive levels, 333–4
vs executive leadership, 330–3, 334
model of, 317
see also strategic thinking, strategic change
Strategic management, 49, 318
Strategic planning, *see* planning
Strategic thinking, 320–2
see also executive thinking
Strategy
attempts to define, 316–18
generic options, 214–20

Strategy (*cont.*)
  market options, 220–4
  see also strategic alliances
Strength of character, 103
Stress, 52–4, 81, 138, 264
Succession
  issues and senior teams, 174–5
  planning, 1, 2, 16
Symbols, 137, 159

Team design
  definition, 165
  operating structure, 178–9
  personnel structure, 175–7
  rewards for teamwork, 177–9
Team development
  difficulties associated with, 162
  model of, 179–83
  stages of, 169–71
Team process
  definition, 165
  skills required, 169
Team purpose
  definition, 165
  problems with, 166–8
Technology
  impact on industry structure, 197–8
  impact on organisations, 231, 247–8
Time
  available to implement
    change, 275–6
  pressures, 291–2, 295

private, 304
for reflection on personal
  limitations, 77
spent on external *vs* internal
  issues, 300–1
Top management teams, 160–2
  see also senior teams
Traits, 127
Transformational leadership, 132–4, 148
Transition into senior management
  building relationships, 9
  and enhancing one's power base, 104
  and the need to change, 77
  reliance on prior experience, 102, 312
Transitions curve, 281–6
Transnational teams, 177
Trust, 111,112, 133, 137, 226

Values
  importance of, 45–6
  of senior teams, 176
  and organisational culture, 257–8
  understanding, 39
  and vision, 134, 136
Vision
  communicating, 136–8
  of the corporation, 309
  creating, 134–5, 310
  endorsing, 143–4
  of the individual, 308–9
  link with intuition, 49
  see also leadership